Sticks & Stones

Sticks & Stones

LIVING WITH UNCERTAIN WARS

Edited by

Padraig O'Malley, Paul L. Atwood,
and Patricia Peterson

University of Massachusetts Press · Amherst and Boston

Published in association with

John W. McCormack Graduate School of Policy Studies,
University of Massachusetts Boston

LC 2006017930
ISBN 1-55849-534-7 (library cloth ed.); 535-5 (paper)

Designed by Jack Harrison
Set in Adobe Garamond and ITC Stones Sans by dix!
Printed and bound by The Maple-Vail Book Manufacturing Group

Library of Congress Cataloging-in-Publication Data

Sticks and stones : living with uncertain wars / edited by Padraig O'Malley, Paul L. Atwood, and
Patricia Pererson.
    p.   cm.
Includes bibliographical references.
ISBN 1-55849-535-5 (pbk. : alk. paper) — ISBN 1-55849-534-7 (library cloth : alk. paper)
    1. World politics—20th century.   2. Military history, Modern—20th century.
3. War.   4. Terrorism.   5. War—Moral and ethical aspects.   6. War and society.
I. O'Malley, Padraig.   II. Atwood, Paul L.   III. Peterson, Patricia.
    D445.S77   2006
    303.6'6—dc22   2006017930

British Library Cataloguing in Publication data are available.

no ✗   *(Contents file)*

Contents

X / Ronan 6

X / Acknowledgments

The genesis of *Sticks and Stones: Living with Uncertain Wars* was the two volumes of the *New England Journal of Public Policy* (vol.19, no.1 [Summer 2004] and vol.19, no. 2 [Winter 2005]) on the subject of war published by the John W. McCormack Graduate School of Policy Studies.

I would like to thank all those who made these two issues possible: Patricia Peterson, whose persistence, professionalism, and enthusiasm ensured that we could not fail; Jamie Ennis, who helped with the preparation of the text; Sandy Blanchette, assistant dean of the McCormack Graduate School, who kept us in the budget "loop"; and Edmund Beard, dean of the McCormack Graduate School, for being there. Paul Atwood, coeditor of those issues and of this book gave unstintingly of himself, pursued contributors and would-be contributors tenaciously, and provided a vision for the issue that was rooted in his personal experience of war. To him and to Kevin Bowen, director of the Joiner Center for the Study of War and Social Consequences at University of Massachusetts Boston, our thanks.

Our thanks also to the Institute on Global Leadership at Tufts University. Its stellar EPIIC symposia (Education for Public Inquiry and International Citizenship) addressed the topics "Dilemmas of Empire and Nationbuilding" in February 2004 and "Sovereignty and Intervention" in February 2003, and from that initial encounter came several of the chapters in this volume. To the inspirational director of these efforts, Sherman Teichman, and his associates Heather Barry, Ben Mann, Erica Levine, and their students we are grateful, for it is certainly through their long-term acquaintance and friendship with many of our authors that we were able to proceed.

From the University of Massachusetts Press, our thanks to Paul Wright, editor, for his diligence in pursuing this project, and to Bruce Wilcox, director, for turning it into a reality with such quiet and persistent standards.

But one final word, and the word is *indispensable*. Sometimes a person is indispensable to something happening, in the very real sense that if the person were not there something wouldn't happen. So, I want to acknowledge Patricia Peterson's indispensability to those first issues and her Herculean labors as coeditor of *Sticks and Stones*. Without her we would have become a casualty of other wars.

Padraig O'Malley

X / Introduction

PADRAIG O'MALLEY

The twenty-first century had hardly put its fledgling year behind it when the promise of its possibilities, so endlessly recapitulated at the millennium's turn, was shattered. The television images of two huge Boeing jets lumbering at low altitude across the skyline of a bright Manhattan morning—bellies full of baleful fuel, and ripping into the twin towers of the World Trade Center, symbols of New York's global stature, and the towers collapsing in the inferno of a towering rage— were replayed endlessly across our planet, imprinting indelible memories of random mayhem and sudden death, as the once unthinkable became an instant reality.

September 11 redefined the new century's connection with the twentieth century just as the madness of World War I redefined that century's connection with the nineteenth.

It did more than destroy the twin towers and rupture America's belief in its invulnerability to attack; it instilled a sense of the dread of an invisible enemy that could strike without warning, directing its wrath at people, not armies, and not at the state but at its ordinary citizens living ordinary lives.

That morning dumped memories of the twentieth century into their own ground zero. With its new obsessive preoccupation with the threats of imminent dangers—color codes indicating levels of terror alert, a president who announced that America arrogated to itself the right to take preemptive action against any country that *appeared* to pose a threat to its national security, a U.S.–led invasion of Iraq on grounds that later proved to be baseless, the harping on regime change as a policy instrument and the U.S. administration's fixation on the so-called axis of evil—the twentieth century in the United States was swallowed by the immediacy of the present. "Imminent threat" became the parlance of choice, although those who assiduously cultivated the threat of imminence increasingly found difficulty identifying where the threat was coming from and just how imminent something was that could not be detected. But the logic of the newly created insecurity argued that the less definable the threat the greater the danger it posed.

In the early 1990s, Europeans watched nightly reports of ethnic cleansing and hidden concentration camps in Bosnia, heard repeated accounts of the rape of Muslim women by Serbian militias, and yet stood idly by, allowed the indescribable to happen before their eyes and then calmly ate their suppers. Ethnic cleansing, certainly not a new phenomenon, was "dusted off" and refashioned as a weapon of war that could be used to great strategic effect. Now when you take control of a piece of territory you insure your permanent presence by murdering those who might pose a threat to your hegemony in the future—the ultimate, perverse form of conflict resolution. By getting rid of potential majority/minority dichotomies, you eliminate one source of intrastate conflict.

The inexorable flood of information impels us to dismiss everything except the instantaneous flow of the instantaneous. Our full memories erase the past to make room for the present. In our rush for immediate interpretations of events as they unfold, we reduce complicated trajectories of history to simple stories: right and wrong, good and bad. The task of untangling the complicated threads is brushed aside.

A Century of Slaughter

The twentieth century will be remembered for many things—breakthroughs in physics, medicine, biology, genetics, and communications that were unthinkable mere decades before. The impact of discovery in these fields transformed the way we live and think and communicate. Each discovery had an exponential impact on the next, each accelerated the next; the obsolete became the commonplace.

But with every innovation that improved the quality of life, we managed to find new and improved ways of killing ourselves. Our ultimate accomplishment: weapons of mass destruction that will, if used, annihilate every living being and deplete the planet of Man.

At the century's turn, the arsenal of our extinctive dreams amounted to twenty-one hundred strategic nuclear weapons in the possession of five countries and between twenty-three thousand and thirty-two thousand tactical nuclear missiles in the possession of the same five plus another three. Other countries—thirty at one count—are eagerly biting at the nuclear cherry. Despite all the safeguards that have been put in place to preclude illicit transfers of illicit technology, they take place with seamless ease.

Countries with nuclear aspirations pursue them using the clandestine underground arms networks. The nuclear black market is extensive. It operates with startling impunity and thoroughness to supply raw uranium, machines for enriching it, or blueprints for turning nuclear fuel into atomic bombs.

No country has a monopoly on the technology of mass destruction; technology crosses borders as easily as illicit drugs because all borders are porous. What exists will some day be used. Knowledge, as easily transferable as money from one account to another in a small bank, cannot be destroyed. Attempts to develop anti-nuclear shields mistakenly will make the countries that develop them believe they have an "edge," subconsciously implanting another belief—that they have the capacity to launch a "first strike," without having to worry about retaliation. Non-proliferation treaties are meaningless pieces of paper (Russia now claims to have developed a new strategic missile system that can evade the latest U.S. antimissile defense program. "Not a single country in the world has such a weapons system at the moment," the Russian president Vladimir Putin boasted when he announced that his country possessed this "powerful means of warfare").[5]

According to the Stockholm International Peace Research Institute (SIPRI),[6] world military spending, fuelled by the United States' war on terrorism, rose on average by 6 percent annually over the three-year period from 2002 to 2004 and exceeded one trillion dollars in 2004. The United States accounted for 47 percent of the total, more than the combined total of the next thirty-two most powerful nations, its expenditures exceeding the combined gross domestic products of the sixty-two countries on the lower rung of the United Nations developmental scale.

The five permanent members of the UN Security Council are the world's five top suppliers of conventional arms to developing countries. The market is insatiable; countries that cannot feed their people gorge themselves with arms.

One result of the massive sums of money the United States allocates to military expenditure is that the it now increasingly relies on might rather than diplomacy to address conflict issues. Some argue that this proclivity for might is germane only to the Bush administrations, but no matter how you analyze the question, one conclusion is indisputable: The United States is a military empire.

The Pentagon has divided the planet into five area commands: NORTHCOM, SOUTHCOM, EUCOM, CENTCOM, and PACOM. No part of the earth is unaccounted for. "At the turn of the century the United States had bases and base rights in fifty-nine countries and troops on deployment from Greenland to Nigeria, and from Norway to Singapore," writes Robert Kaplan in *Imperial Grunts: The American Military on the Ground.*[7] And "even before the terrorist attack . . . on September 11, 2001, the U.S. Army's Special Operations Command was conducting operations in 170 countries per year."[8]

The century's toll just in terms of the number of human beings killed? At the lower boundary for the number of dead we have estimates that range from 167 million to 175 million, the upper bounds from 188 million to 258 million.[9]

At the beginning of the twentieth century, the ratio of combatants to civilians killed in war was 8:1—eight combatants for every civilian; at the end of the century the figures were reversed, the ratio was 1:8—eight civilians were killed for every combatant. In the space of one hundred years, the nature of war itself had been redefined: people with weapons of war kill unarmed civilians, not each other. In war you are now safer being a soldier in one of the competing armies than being a civilian.

The percentage of civilian casualties among all casualties in wars in which the United States was involved escalates from as low as 5 percent of total casualties in

World War I, to 54 percent in World War II, to 71 percent in the Vietnam War, and to perhaps as high as 78 percent in the Iraq War.[10] The dead become "collateral damage" and so are robbed of their humanity.

Suicide bombers add a new weapon to the arsenals of death—the personal "acts of war" of ordinary people can provoke consequences across the political spectrum and derail attempts to negotiate across barriers of distrust.

The suicide bomber needs no technology to carry out his acts, putting at a disadvantage societies that rely on advanced technology to secure their safety. Terrorist groups, equipped with modern technology, can communicate among cells located within several sovereign states. They are not only extraordinarily elusive, they are recombinant.

There is no antidote to a determined suicide bomber. Rather than aberrant fanatics eagerly courting martyrdom in order to luxuriate in the hereafter in the embrace of heaven knows how many virgins—as much of the West would wish to believe—suicide bombers are now more numerous than ever, are driven by deeply held convictions, and are increasingly ordinary people.[11]

The purpose of war is no longer to defeat an "enemy" but simply to kill. What we refer to as the "new" war—the war on terrorism—is the incremental extrapolation of what we subconsciously came to accept as "normal" ways to eliminate ourselves. September 11 simply raised the threshold, elevated the level of sophistication, set a record to be beaten. And it will be beaten.

The 1990s was the world's first post–Cold War decade. But the promise the demise of the Cold War portended did not materialize; rather we face greater instability, not less. New freedoms became a catalyst for a resurgence of long-repressed ethnic and nationalist rivalries. Eastern Europe and the former Soviet Union were not a network of nations but a patchwork of ethnic groups and nationalist rivalries. These rivalries played themselves out in the former Yugoslavia, each group—Muslim, Christian, Serb, Kosovar—asserting old claims on the past.

Should We Have Learned?

A convincing case can be made that the slaughter of the wars and conflicts of the twentieth century emanated from societies that were nondemocratic, failed states, states teetering on the brink of failure, states where historical majority/minority cleavages erupted, legacies of colonialism in both the nineteenth and twentieth centuries and the unfinished business of two world wars. Slaughter was brought to a halt where democracies prevailed, sustainable democratic governance successfully embedded, power-sharing governance acceptable to majority/minority dichotomies was implemented, or one tyranny overcame another.

The importance democracy plays in conflict prevention is twofold. Not only is there no recorded case of democracies embarking on war with each other but, as important, no democracy has ever embarked on the slaughter of its own citizens. Democratization is an antidote to conflict. But democracy and human rights are inextricably interlinked. The promise of the UN's Universal Declaration of Human Rights remains woefully unfilled. Nations pay lip service to the declaration; but what are rights in one value system are not in another, creating tensions where principles of interventionism and sovereignty clash.

National sovereignty—the right to national determination—was one of the great mantras of the twentieth century. But with decolonization, either the result of violence as indigenous populations organized themselves in armed opposition to their western colonizers or withdrawal and disengagement on the part of the colonizers, frequently brought more violence as struggles for self-determination were replaced by struggles for power.

Multilateralism works. The Allies' cooperation in World War II overcame Nazism, proving that when countries work together to achieve defined ends and subordinate some of their national interests in the name of a larger purpose they can prevail. Post–World War II, the emergence of the European Common Market, which evolved into the European Union from the core six nations and subsequent enlargement into a twenty-five-nation economic giant, showed that a century of enmity could be successfully addressed when the key combatants, France and Germany, developed institutional and governance arrangements with each other to ensure that their wars of the past could never be repeated.

In Africa, colonization created artificial countries. Decolonization left new states with these same artificial boundaries. In most, one-party states emerged, often after violent conflict. During the 1990s, however, democratization began to find its footing and in twenty-five countries variants of multiparty democracies replaced one-party states, although the ruling party invariably remained the dominant party. The institutional infrastructure to establish sustainable democracy, however, remains weak; all countries are mired in poverty and disease. HIV/AIDS has inflicted an exacting toll—with 10 percent of the world's population, Africa accounts for 70 percent of the world's HIV/AIDS cases. Few have created the basis for sustainable development. In the Great Lakes region, the biggest war since World War II straddled two centuries (1998–2001); with three million civilian casualties and perhaps an equal number of displaced people, the war in the Democratic Republic of the Congo was dubbed Africa's "First World War" but evoked little attention in the West. At century's end, Africa remained a failed continent.

Globalization, the outcome of revolutions in communications, transportation, production, and consumption, with concomitant increasing economic and social interdependence among nation-states, has put new constraints on the limits of national sovereignty, redefining rights and obligations, what is intranational, and what is supranational. Globalization increases vulnerability at every level of the interdependence chain. Hence, a global preoccupation with security is increasing. Human rights and security are often antithetical.

The advent of nuclear weaponry has changed the nature of warfare forever. With its potential to erase the human species, its awesome lethality poses a threat that has increased since the end of the Cold War. Weapons of mass destruction pose "a real and imminent threat," yet global expenditure on armaments, especially by the United States, continues to spiral out of proportion to any threat imminent or otherwise.

The revolutions in digitalization and miniaturization now make it feasible to manufacture and transport lethal nuclear devices in small containers. "Even an assembled device, like a 'suitcase' nuclear weapon (0.1 of kiloton), could be sent in a Federal Express package, shipped in a cargo container, or checked as airline luggage."[12] With an estimated two million sources of radioactive materials in the United States alone,[13] the UN International Atomic Energy Agency has warned of the increasing likelihood of the detonation of a "dirty" bomb, which can be assembled by attaching radioactive materials to ordinary chemical explosives.[14]

Technological advance and scientific innovation in the twentieth century transformed the way we live and work and communicate in such fundamental ways as to arguably outweigh in scope and magnitude the aggregated advances of previous centuries. But most important, it vastly improved the ways we kill. Change is exponential, outstripping our capacity to reorient social and economic systems. One result is perceptions of relative deprivation are increasing, both within nations and among nations, especially between the rich North and the developing South. Another is the rise of the quasi state, nonstate actors who use technological and communications assets to become global actors in their own right.

At century's end, the United States was unchallenged as the global military superpower; Islamic extremism was not among the West's priority preoccupations as the looming threat to its security and millennium goals were set to halve world poverty by 2015.

Sticks and Stones

The collection of essays that comprises *Sticks and Stones: Living with Uncertain Wars* is divided into four clusters. "Understanding the World as We Have Known It" identifies key sources of war and conflict in the twentieth century; "Global Uncertainties" examines aspects of the war on terror; "Whose Values? Whose Justice?" juxtaposes the use of unjust means to achieve just ends; and "Shaping a New World" assesses the global instruments in place to preclude a repetition of the slaughter of the last century.

There are two subtexts: the experiences of the twentieth century and the lessons we might draw from them and how we should interpret the challenges of the opening decades of the twenty-first century in the light of these lessons.

There are four subthemes. The first challenges U.S. behavior in a unipolar world, especially with regard to the war in Iraq. The second is dismissive of the belief that Western models of democracy can be "imposed" on countries with no culture or tradition of democracy and value systems that are different from ours. The third identifies inherent contradictions in current U.S. foreign policy as obstacles to achieving the intended policy objectives—its support of authoritarian regimes who support its war on terror; the use of nondemocratic means to promote democratization, its advocacy of a culture of human rights while engaging in covert operations that violate the human rights of others, and its propensity to set itself above international protocols.

The authors in this collection raise questions we face in the coming decades: If terrorism persists and becomes even more sophisticated and random, a crisis will emerge between the protection of rights and what people demand in the way of the protection of security, posing a crisis for democracy. Does a people's right to protection from random acts of terrorism supersede other rights guaranteed by democratic constitutional dispensations? Is the use of extreme torture ever justifiable if there is a reasonable probability that the information elicited will prevent a catastrophic loss of live? When, if ever, is the use of unjust means for a just end permissible? How do we balance the rights of sovereign states in a global world that recognizes the international primacy of human rights? When does oppression reach a point where intervention on humanitarian grounds should give way to forceful intervention?

To judge from the course of wars and conflict in the opening years of this century, we are forced to conclude that we have not learned very much, that a collective amnesia informs. George Santayana's much repeated aphorism, "Those who do not remember the past are condemned to repeat its mistakes" is true only *if* we fail to act on what knowledge of the past teaches us.[15] Knowledge itself is no guarantee that we will be able to adjust our behavior. And that, perhaps, is a more accurate description of the state of where we stand: The world order cannot adapt quickly enough to deal with present crises, despite having knowledge of the catastrophes that will inevitably follow as a consequence of the failure to act.

The conclusions reached by contributors to *Sticks and Stones* help us define the parameters of the global order that must emerge in the post–George Bush world if we are to use the knowledge we have to avert conflict and create mechanisms to promote global collaboration and cooperation.

They stress three major concerns: the relative impotence of the UN in matters of conflict prevention and intervention; the relative inability of the United States to impose democracy in formerly nondemocratic countries; and the way U.S. unilateralism marginalizes the UN.

Reform of the UN and a United States that has repositioned itself in the global community are intrinsically linked. The corollary is that given the enormous economic power of the United States and the breadth of its military engagements, successful interventions, too, are dependent on U.S collaboration. Without the democratization of the Security Council, UN reform will be cosmetic and remain fragmented. The UN cannot advance an agenda encouraging democratization among member states if its highest organ itself resists democratization.

"Democratization" is offered as the panacea for conflict. But the penchant for rushing headlong into elections and then using free and fair elections as a yardstick for democratization is misguided. The authors here emphasize the rule of law, protection of individual human rights, and the need to establish the conditions that will encourage civil society to grow and flourish, among them freedom of expression, a media free from state control, and nongovernmental organizations (NGOs) that are representative as the sine qua non for democratization. Elections without sufficient institutional infrastructure in place are likely to produce contested outcomes where no agreed mediating mechanism can adjudicate differences, thus stoking the embers of violence or perhaps the emergence of one dominant party—a recipe for the centralization of power in the executive and a truncated democracy. This concentration of power at the center as often as not impedes the growth of the other necessary components of democracy. Elections are a necessary ingredient of democracy but not a sufficient one.

The authors do not buy the idea that democracy can somehow be imposed, that despotic regimes have simply to be removed and the innate propensity of free men and women will exercise itself in spontaneously formed political organizations committed to Western-type governance, a full set of checks and balances, and written constitution with full protections for individual human rights. Democracy, unlike other systems through which societies are governed, is a bottom-up not a top-down process. It cannot be "delivered" to a country from a boilerplate. It is not something that can be ordered and assembled by NGOs according to an instruction book. Attempts to plant on barren ground will yield little.

Considerations of a not dissimilar kind also apply to attempts to "win" the war on terror by increasing policing powers—holding suspected terrorists without charge for long periods, limiting their access to legal advice, passing laws that provide for indiscriminate surveillance of individuals such as telephone wiretapping or search warrants on broad and ill-specified grounds. Laws that allow the state to infringe on human rights will invariably be used for purposes for which they were not intended.

Given the very real likelihood of more—and more deadly—terrorist attacks on urban centers in the West and on infant democracies, and given the public demands for more security that are to be expected and anticipated, governments will want to be seen as taking tough measures to restore public confidence and reduce

f | *9*

fear. But terrorism wins once it undermines the values that are the bedrock of our societies, and we do not want to find ourselves redefining (and diminishing) our "human rights," just as we have redefined the criteria for a just war. The real problem in this regard will emerge if a dirty bomb or dirty nuclear bomb results in large-scale loss of life, social disorder, and economic panic.

A more immediate problem relating to the potential diminution of democratic values is explored in this volume in relation to the United States. The clandestine wars that the United States engaged in during the latter part of the last century, the detention policies at Guantánamo Bay, the use of interrogation practices highly suggestive of torture, Abu Ghraib and the "export" of detainees to clandestine U. S. Central Intelligence Agency prisons in Eastern Europe so that the United States cannot be held legally accountable for their treatment—all these are policies that were designed and continued to be used in the name of protecting freedom. The gross abuse of the human rights of some in the name of protecting the human rights of the many degrades the human rights of all. Moreover, these policies have alienated much of the moderate Muslim world and fertilize the breeding grounds of Islamic extremism in Muslim countries and within the nations of the West itself.

Essays in all four clusters articulate a historical undercurrent: the role of perceived and stored historical grievances and remembered but unaddressed loss as a source of conflict. Many of the conflicts of the twentieth century had their origins in the early decades of the century. Some, outgrowths of the collapse of successive empires ranging from the Ottoman Empire after World War I, the British Empire after World War II, and the Soviet Empire after the Cold War, are still either unresolved or dormant and include the Middle East, ethnic minority/majority cleavages in the Balkans, Central Russia, and parts of Africa. The paradox of globalization is the contradictory pull of integration and the push for fragmentation, of the erosion of national sovereignty and concomitant demands for self-determination.

Most convincingly, authors make the case for the need of clear and unambiguous criteria to guide the international community in making humanitarian interventions. Lacking an agreed definition of what constitutes a just intervention, the international community hesitates and fails to act decisively when egregious violations of human rights are committed by member states. Here the international community has not lived up to the moral standards it has set itself; indeed, cannot do so until intervention is "depoliticized" and sufficient resources allocated so that interventions can reconcile realpolitik and long-term commitment. Darfur may not be Rwanda, but the chest-thumping mea culpae on the part of the UN and some member states for the egregious abdication of its responsibilities in the face of overwhelming evidence of genocide rings hollow as the UN fine tunes definitions of mass murder while watching the slow slide of Darfur into another genocide. Romeo Dalliare's voice haunts us, but it has not moved us to action.

Terrorism is an ever-present concern that weaves its way through the chapters. But our authors caution against lumping all acts of terrorism together. Islamic extremism has a deep ideological underpinning. In the end it will be "defeated" only if moderate Muslim countries assume the primary responsibility of confronting it. The role of the West is to assist in this task, to play coach, not captain. As long as the "war against terrorism" is seen by most of the Islamic world as America's war, there will be no shortage of jihadists. But the West should not fall into the trap of believing that democratization is an antidote to terrorists. There is no convincing evidence to suggest that it is.[16]

The continuing U.S. military presence in Iraq ensures continuing conflict, which many analysts already categorize as having reached the point of incipient civil war. The Catch 22, however, is that without an American presence the country might just as easily slip into civil war. There are no good options, especially for the people of Iraq, who were freed from one tyranny only to find themselves the random victims of another. As the war became more and more unpopular in the United States, the Bush administration increased its determination to "stay the course," although with disaffection with the war hardening and deepening among Americans, the administration is preparing the way for a partial withdrawal before congressional elections in November 2006 on the grounds that Iraqi security forces will be trained well enough to handle an increasing level of the security burden. In short, the administration is adopting a variant of what Vermont senator George Aiken suggested at the height of the Vietnam War: Declare victory and bring the troops home.[17] And those damning television cameras will follow.[18]

It is sometimes argued that Al Qaeda is reminiscent of the anarchists at the end of the nineteenth century who were much feared but ultimately a passing phenomenon. The differences, of course, far outweigh the similarities—globalization, the communications revolution, the capacity of one individual to wreak enormous destruction in life and property. In Bali, bombings in 2002 and again in 2005 and other major terrorist attacks since either linked to or claimed by Al Qaeda include Casablanca, Morocco, May 2003; Riyadh, Saudi Arabia, 2003; Istanbul, Turkey, November 2003; Madrid, Spain, March 2004; London, England, July 2005; Annan, Jordan, November 2005. Determined terrorists can strike at soft targets no matter what security precautions are in place. For the "free" world, the issue becomes the balance of the tradeoff: To what degree are people prepared to trade individual rights for the illusion of more security?

As some authors reiterate: The objective of terrorism is not to hijack airplanes to plow them into buildings but to create uncertainty; the markets will do the rest. Thus we have become already the hostages of the technologies we have created. Risk, we can assess and prepare for; uncertainty, however, morphs into fear.

One suicide bomber in the right place can cause more international havoc than twenty tank divisions with precision computer-guided systems. U.S. military power is multilinear, with horizontal and vertical organizational structures and lines of command, but the might that falls under the umbrella of the new terrorism is amoebic, with every adversity it mutates, replicates in a slightly different form, has no command structure, and takes off in a different direction. In the end, it may exist only as a frame of mind.

We fear it because we fight it without fully understanding it. We are "embedded" in old paradigms but have not found new ones.

Only lack of ingenuity and imagination hinder the quasi state, whether group or individual, from elevating levels of terrorism to science-fiction proportions. The imagery of destruction or its aftermath, captured by the ubiquitous camera and replayed across the globe until every still is imprinted permanently on the psyche changes the nature of the terrorist act.

Delivering a BBC Reith lecture in 2004, Wole Soyinka, the Nigerian Nobel Laureate in Literature observed:

> This quasi state instills the greatest fear and to complicate matters even more, often boasts a liberating manifesto of seductive ideals. Choice remains the bedrock of the democratic process, and if a people have made a choice that eliminates all further necessity for the ritual rounds of choosing, well . . . that argument appears to have reached its terminal point. History has been fulfilled.
>
> The perennial problem with that proposition of course is that this denies the dynamic nature of human society, and preaches that the purely fortuitous can substitute, at any time, for the eternal and immutable. Such a position opens the way for the triumph of a social order that is based on the concept of The Chosen—a mockery of the principle of choice—and totally eliminates the impulse to change, or even experimentation, as a factor of human development. On the political field, it entrusts power in the hands of a clique of rulers, whose qualification could rightly range from membership of a military class to that of a Masonic order, a labor or clerical union. Revelation replaces enquiry, dictation dismisses debate.[19]

Einstein averred that he didn't know what weapons would be used in the third world war, but the fourth would surely be fought with sticks and stones. Einstein would have ringingly endorsed Soyinka's sentiments.

NOTES

1. Available at http://www.wand.org (accessed November 15, 2005).
2. Available at http://www.isis.org (accessed October 17, 2005).
3. In 2004 the "father" of Pakistan's nuclear weapons program, Abdul Qadeer Khan, "tearfully" admitted to sharing nuclear technology with a number of countries—Iran, North Korea, and Libya. The Pakistan president General Pervez Musharraf pardoned Khan. The U.S. reaction? Silence. In its war against terror the United States desperately needs Pakistan. Only Pakistan Special Forces can comb the cavernous enclaves deep in the unforgiv-

ing mountains—which have defied penetration for centuries—that straddle the border between Pakistan and Afghanistan, to track down and push Taliban and Qaeda fighters across the border into Afghanistan, where the American forces will be waiting for them. *New York Times,* February 23, 2004. Cooperation has a price. Thus a little nuclear hanky panky can go unrebuked, when the culprit's continued utility is thought to outweigh the magnitude of a past transgression.

4. *New York Times,* February 15, 2004.

5. *Boston Globe,* February 19, 2004.

6. SIRPI Yearbook 2005, "Armaments, Disarmaments and International Security" (Stockholm: SIRPI, 2006).

7. Robert Kaplan, *Imperial Grunts: The American Military on the Ground* (New York: Random House, 2005).

8. Ibid.

9. In *Out of Control: Global Turmoil on the Eve of the Twenty-first Century"* (New York: Collier, 1994), Zbigniew Brzezinski, former national security adviser to President Jimmy Carter, provides the following calculations: "Lives deliberately extinguished by politically motivated carnage": 167 million to 175 million. These figures include war dead: 87 million—military dead account for 33 million, civilians for 54 million. Add to that not-war dead of 80 million and Communist oppression of 60 million. Stéphane Courtois in *The Black Book of Communism* (trans. Jonathan Murphy and Mark Kramer [Cambridge: Harvard University Press, 1999]), puts the carnage of Communism at 85 million. Milton Leitenberg uses different categories of classification: "politically caused deaths" in the twentieth century range between 214 million and 226 million; "deaths in wars and conflicts, including civilians," between 130 million and 142 million; and "political deaths" between 1945 and 2000 at approximately 50 million. In short, more people were killed by political violence after World War II than in both world wars put together. In *Death by Government* (New Brunswick, N.J.: Transactions, 1994), Rudolph J. Rummel, ascribes 169 million deaths between 1900 and 1987 to "Democides"—that is, "government inflicted deaths," of which "Communist Oppression" accounts for 110 million. The number killed in war according to his calculations comes to 34 million and "Non-Democidal Famine" deaths to 49 million in China (1900–87) and in Russia approximately 6 million (1921–47). This brings his total body count to 258 million for all categories. Matthew White, *Historical Atlas of the Twentieth Century* (http://users.erols.com/mwhite28/20centry.htm) uses yet another set of classifications, "Deaths Genocide and Tyranny," 83 million; "Military Deaths in War," 42 million; "Civilian Deaths in War," 19 million; "Man-made Famine," 44 million. In all 188 million.

10. The statistics regarding civilian casualties as a percentage of all war casualties come from the following sources: WWI, Simon Chesterman, ed., *Civilians in War* (Boulder, Colo.: Lynne Rienner, 2001), quoted in Charles Tilly, "Violence, Terror, and Politics as Usual," *Boston Review* (summer 2002), available online at http://www.bostonreview.net/BR27.3/tilly.html; WWII, www.historylearningsite.co.uk/civilian_casualties_of_wrld_war.htm; Vietnam War, www.vhfcn.org/stat.htm and www.rjsmith.com/kia_tbl.html; Iraq War, http://news.bbc.co.uk/1/hi/world/middle_east/4525412.stm.

11. See Robert A. Pape, *Dying to Win: The Strategic Logic of Suicide Terrorism* (New York: Random House, 2005); Farhad Khosrokhaver, *Suicide Bombers: Allah's New Martyrs,* trans. from the French by David Macey (London: Pluto Press, 2005); Terry McDermott, *Perfect Soldiers: The Hijackers; Who They Were and Why They Did It* (New York: HarperCollins, 2005).

12. Graham Allison, *Nuclear Terrorism* (New York: Time Books, 2004).

13. Ibid.

14. *New Scientist,* June 2, 2004.

15. *The Times* of London on Iraq in September 1919: "[Many people] think that the local inhabitants will welcome us because we have saved them, and that the country only needs developing to repay our expenditure, but this is clearly wrong, since we are asking the Arab to exchange his pride and independence for a little Western civilization." Also on Iraq: "In Iraq we have been led "into a trap from which it will be hard to escape with dignity and honor. . . . Things have been far worse than we have been told, our administration more bloody and inefficient than the public knows. . . . We are today not far from a disaster." T. E. Lawrence in August 1920.

16. Gregory Gause, "Can Democracy Stop Terrorism?" *Foreign Affairs,* September/October 2005.

17. Scott Shane, "Bush Speech on Iraq Echoes Voice of Analyst," *New York Times,* December 4, 2005.

18. Duke University professor Peter Feaver, who joined the National Security Council in June 2005, conducted an analysis of polls on the Iraq war conducted during 2003–4. He found that Americans would support a war with mounting casualties on only one condition: if they were sure of ultimate success. Hence the genesis of the administration's "National Strategy for Victory in Iraq" (www.whitehouse.gov). In his speech to the Naval Academy on November 30, 2005, announcing the strategy, President Bush mentioned the word *victory* fifteen times. The administration is increasingly stressing the improvements in Iraqi security forces, their readiness to take over, and gave the first indication in December 2005 that a small number of troops could be withdrawn in 2006—with Iraq's new parliament in place.

19. Wole Soyinka, "The Climate of Fear," BBC Reith Lecture, 2004.

x/13

UNDERSTANDING THE WORLD
AS WE HAVE KNOWN IT

x/14 is blank

The first cluster reviews what we learned from the wars of the past century and establishes some benchmarks for gauging whether knowledge translates into changes in the behavior of our political cultures. In "What Have We Learned from the Wars of the Twentieth Century" Winston Langley suggests that those wars are best understood in two contexts: relative deprivation (RD)—the perceived incongruity between what a nation-state believes it is entitled to and what it actually has—and "othering"—the propensity for human beings to divide themselves along the lines of "them" and "us"—to exclude from our group those whom we deem to be different and less vulnerable.

The three great ideologies of the twentieth century, nationalism, liberalism, and Marxism, Langley argues, all competed against each other and in so doing contributed in profound ways to the perception of individuals and groups that they were deprived. He advocates the Universal Declaration of Human Rights as an instrument that promises to lessen the conditions that marginalize people and cause war, even while acknowledging that more people have died in wars and conflicts in the second half of the twentieth century (after the creation of the United Nations) than in the first half. Without the authoritative tools to make of its provisions something more than noble aspirations, the Declaration of Human Rights remains an idealistic proclamation in a very untidy world.

The degree of inequality between North (roughly what we think of as the developed world) and South (the less developed world) is increasing. The ratio of incomes of the richest 20 percent of people living in the world in the richest countries to those of the 20 percent of people living in the poorest countries increased from 30:1 in 1960 to 74:1 in 1997.[1] Such disparity augurs for resentment, anger, and a desire to strike back on the part of developing countries. The young are enticed by the allures of consumer goods they cannot access, which are more pronounced because of the global dominance of Western consumer culture and its accoutrements, and they protest. Some go further.

Relative deprivation and resource deprivation affect social cohesion both within developing countries, among developing countries, and within developed countries, fostering alienation, exploitation, and dependency—a recipe for violence. The riots that engulfed France in November 2005 when the accidental death of two Muslim teenagers fleeing police triggered a wave of riots, first in the poor Arab-Muslim suburbs of Paris, then in copy-cat attacks across the country, are but the latest harbinger of what the future may hold for countries where social and economic grievances, pervasive discrimination, and exclusion go unaddressed.

15

Global television feeds the envy and resentment that disparities in income generate. Violent conflicts are most likely to occur within countries with weak social cohesion, that is, in countries where the informal sectors of the economy are most pervasive, where surviving and protecting one's meager assets requires guile, alliances with gangs. In poor and extremely poor countries where informal sectors of society are expanding, adherence to the rule of law is mostly an abstraction because there is no rule of law, only excessive consumption by the elites and the petty corruption that survival in the informal world necessitates.

The link between poverty and terrorism is not easy to demonstrate. Poverty expands the political appeal of terrorist causes and provides fertile grounds for nurturing recruits. Yet, the countries most in need of aid for development rarely receive it. The limited resources that developed countries are prepared to allocate to development aid is sent to countries where the infrastructure exists that offers the prospect for a high return on the aid they receive, that is, countries already some significant way up the developmental ladder. Those countries at the lowest rungs lack the basic capacity to utilize aid or aid ends up in the coffers of corrupt officials. Such countries are too difficult to aid and too often are simply written off.

The failure of the United States to construct a security policy that is not entirely reliant on military and intelligence sectors is addressed by Brian Atwood. In "The Link between Poverty and Violent Conflict," Atwood calls for "a new 'culture of prevention' that will reorder resources and create institutions capable of taking cooperative, preemptive steps rather than waiting for crises to develop." If we are to reduce violent conflict, assuage its potential, alleviate threats and acts of terrorism, and address the causes that drive individuals and groups to engage in such acts, we must not neglect the lessons of the twentieth century—the relationship between poverty and violent conflict, between terrorism and poverty, and the interrelationship.

The developed world has heard the figures repeated ad nauseam, yet remains disconnected from their far-reaching implications: half of the world's 6 billion people live under the poverty line of $2 a day, 1.2 billion live on less than $1 a day; a child dies every five seconds. By 2020 the world population will increase by a further 2 billion people, most of them in developing-world countries of poverty and extreme poverty. An aging North faces an explosion of young people facing lifetimes of poverty and little prospect for better lives. Marginalization incubates itself. Globalization that leaves billions of people in perpetual free-fall is a prescription for violent conflicts, out of which will emerge new terrorist groups with agendas of hate and access to the technologies—and weapons—to give lethal expression to that hate. As a first step, Atwood proposes a cabinet-level position in the U.S. government—a Department of International Development Cooperation. Unless national security analysts include in their security calculus the link between poverty and violent conflict and how poverty creates conditions that are breeding grounds for terrorist groups, their analyses of possible terrorist threats will be incomplete and possibly wrong. Military power will not "defeat" terrorism; developmental power may. But that calls for a re-ordering of our thinking. Allowing the populations of the West to believe that their countries can somehow hoard the wealth of the earth without consequence in the face of increasing abject poverty among the majority of the world's population is an invitation to fiddle with apocalypse.

Writing in the *New York Times Sunday Book Review* in February 2004, Serge Schmemann reluctantly concluded that what he would have considered even a decade earlier as a frivolous proposition had now to be taken seriously. "Though I have lived abroad for many years and regard myself as hardened to anti-Americanism, I confess I was taken aback to have my country depicted, page after page, book after book, as a dangerous empire in its last throes, as a failure of democracy, as militaristic, violent, hegemonic, evil, callous, arrogant, imperial and cruel." [2] With each passing year, however, these sentiments have deepened, become more fixed in the collective consciousness of much of the world.

Alfred McCoy's chapter, "The Costs of Covert Warfare: Airpower, Drugs, and Warlords in the Conduct of U.S. Foreign Policy," is a searing indictment of the American use of military power to advance and protect its national interests regardless of the cost—not in terms of American lives, but the lives of other people. McCoy raises disturbing questions about the conduct of American foreign policy in Asia during the past forty years. The United States carried on covert wars waged by the Central Intelligence Agency (CIA). These wars had the unintended outcome of strengthening and facilitating the drug trade and they have empowered drug mafias, nonstate actors who plough their profits into the illegal arms market and thereby fuel the ethnic conflicts that have spread west from Pakistan. (In Kosovo, NATO troops faced Kosovar militias financed by illicit drug activities that could be traced to CIA-backed drug warlords in Afghanistan.)

McCoy tells us that after CIA intervention in the 1950s, Burma's opium production rose from eighteen tons in 1958 to six hundred tons in 1970. During the CIA's covert war of the 1980s, Afghanistan's harvest increased from an estimated one hundred tons in 1971 to two thousand tons in 1991and then kept rising to forty-six hundred tons in the war's aftermath. A decade after the end of the Cold War, the CIA's three covert battlegrounds along the five-thousand-mile span of the Asian opium zone— Afghanistan, Burma, and Laos—were, in that order, the world's three largest producers of opium. In 2004, opium accounted for approximately two-thirds of Afghanistan's GDP—a "narcomocracy."

These were also wars in which America began to rely increasingly on "proxies,"— local militias to do the fighting on the ground backed with the full might of American airpower. But policy sometimes backfires when local militias have their own political agendas. The United States armed fifty thousand Islamic *mujahideen* to fight the Soviet regime in Afghanistan and in another lifetime the *mujahideen* transmogrified itself into the Taliban.

It leaves us with questions. Does even democracy inevitability impose its own oppressions? Can perceptions of marginalization and the resentment it breeds ever be adequately understood without conflict? Have we created an irreversible basis for civilians being the targets of the armies of nations and the new "armies" of the quasi state? The twenty-first century has started with a new othering—the Judeo-Christian West "othering" Muslims for a religion it identifies with justifying terrorism; jihadists othering the Westerners as infidels.

Padraig O'Malley

NOTES

1. Joseph Nye Jr., *The Paradox of American Power* (Oxford: Oxford University Press, 2002).

2. Serge Schmemann, "The Coalition of the Unbelieving," *New York Times Sunday Book Review,* February 25, 2004. The books reviewed were Ivo H. Daalder and James M. Lindsay, *America Unbound: The Bush Revolution in Foreign Policy* (Washington, DC: Brookings Institution Press); Chalmers Johnson, *The Sorrows of Empire: Militarism, Secrecy, and the End of the Republic* (New York: Metropolitan Books/Henry Holt & Company); George Soros, *The Bubble of American Supremacy: Correcting the Misuse of American Power* (New York: Public Affairs); Tariq Ali, *Bush in Babylon: The Recolonisation of Iraq* (New York: Verso); Robert Jay Lifton, *Superpower Syndrome: America's Apocalyptic Confrontation with the World* (New York: Thunder's Mouth Press/Nation Books); Michael O'Hanlon and Mike Mochizuki, *Crisis on the Korean Peninsula: How to Deal with a Nuclear North Korea* (New York: A Brookings Institution Book/McGraw-Hill); Emmanuel Todd, *After the Empire: The Breakdown of the American Order* (New York: Columbia University Press).

What Have We Learned from the Wars of the Twentieth Century?

WINSTON LANGLEY

With the dawn of a new millennium, few areas of human enquiry and re-flection can rival, in moral and social importance, the lessons we have learned from the social scourge we call war. My focus here has a central theme (with sub-themes) that has been examined before, but that theme has frequently been largely confined in its application to intranational conflicts and has even more often been burdened with a limiting definition.

The theme or concept is that of relative deprivation, soon to be defined and dis-cussed. My thesis is that the wars of the twentieth century, both the civil and the international kind, have been caused by relative deprivation and its associated twin, the "othering" of human groupings. We will seek to advance proof for this claim by defining relative deprivation and the context within which that definition is being used; by examining the relationship between the concept and the idea of "extinction"—an idea that has not generally been explored; by discussing what we mean by "othering"; and by reviewing a few wars that have defined the twentieth century. Following all these discussions, we will touch on another lesson that, though not brought to us by the wars we will have discussed, has been partly informed by them in shaping the prominent place that lesson has begun to occupy in our lives.

Relative deprivation I understand to mean the actual or presumed existence of a discrepancy between one's "life conditions," including the goods and other val-ues that define one, and the value expectations one has, including that to which one feels entitled, by virtue of one's self-assessed or other-ascribed capabilities. In other words, there is a felt contradiction or incongruity between what one believes one is entitled to and what one actually has.[1] Two elements, the first expressed, the other implied, must be immediately dealt with, if we are to progress in an orderly manner with our definition.

The term *one,* as used above, refers to all self-conscious human groupings—ethnic, national, racial, social, and religious, among others. But in our discussions, we will emphasize the nation-state, giving due weight to its ethnic, religious, ra-cial, social, and other components. The implied element encompasses the phe-nomenon of change—a sociological phenomenon not frequently discussed in this context. Were it not for this notion of change (and to an extent the idea of "prog-ress" that modernism has associated with it), the meaning and significance of rela-tive deprivation might not have become so clear in its operation.

19

Change, among other things, means that one's position and condition in life need not last forever; that one's status, cause, or direction can be altered; and that such alteration might even include a radical transformation of or substitution for that which pre-existed. Since a change in status, direction, or cause can affect the self that interacts with the change, it means that even the self (or one's sense of self) might be transformed. In some societies (be they familial, tribal, national, or international), changes take place with a minimum of politically organized violence; in other societies, violence is pervasive. For us here the focus is primarily on international society.

Any discussion of international society, however, must properly begin with the ideological outlook (nationalism) out of which the nation-state has arisen. That ideology, perhaps the most powerful humans have ever experienced, originated in the West and has expanded throughout the world. In its description of and justification for the nation-state, it has claimed that humanity is *naturally* divided into psycho-cultural entities called nations; that people constituting a nation should enjoy the right to national self-determination; that this right is best expressed through the attainment of sovereign status (becoming a nation-state); and that the nation-state, in interstate relations, is the ideal, when compared with other models of the state such as the city-state and the empire-state. The latter claim is usually made in light of the "fact" that the nation is said to offer security not only in the military sense but also in the social and psychological sense that people gain a sense of wider belonging among people who, by reason of their shared character and affiliation, will help if one needs help.[2] Also, by virtue of its sovereign status as a nation-state, its members—whether called nationals or citizens—collectively gain equality with all like peoples or nations; and members, the ideology holds, owe their highest loyalty to their respective nations.

While the existence of the nation helps its people, who had traditionally had their identities based on clans, towns, or cities, to gain a sense of new identity as well as wider belonging, that existence has also carried on a tradition of claimed distinctiveness (by virtue of certain actual or supposed shared markers) between and among people constituting "different" human groupings. In doing so, the nation as well as the *idea* of the nation came to be associated with very important expressions of exclusiveness. But what do we mean by the term *nation* and how does this meaning bear on relative deprivation?

I understand nation to be a group of people with an actual or attributed common past, and, based on that common past, they aspire to have a common future together. This common past is generally linked to certain shared markers (often with accompanying symbols) that help to define the group and, concomitantly, differentiate it from other groups. These markers include race and ethnicity (two areas further differentiated into physical characteristics such as skin color, bone structure, height, and build, among others), religion, language, traditions, and history. This history, which may be based on common suffering or triumphs, might, for instance, be further encoded in institutions such as a basic law, constitution, or ritual celebrations, above and beyond the more general or collective memory it might shape. And this memory, in turn, produces a psychological capacity in each member of the group to participate in the ideas, fears, hopes, or general feeling of other members. We call this capacity "empathy."

Nationalism and the idea of nation emerged following the Treaty of Westphalia of 1648 that ended a century of religious wars by setting the principle that each ruler determined the religion of his region and subjects. This concept of sovereignty developed and gained widespread support alongside the growth and expansion of multinational and empire-states, during the eighteenth century. But the sociopolitical and psychological dynamics, which both the idea and reality of the nation threw into the system of interstate relations, did not become fully evident until the nineteenth century, and did not gain full, affirming international recognition until the beginning of the twentieth century.[3] Among the dynamics has been the view that the "best" state is one whose physical borders are co-extensive with the cultural and psychological group we call the nation—a view that clashed with multinational states, whose borders extend over at least two nations. It also clashed with the notion of the empire-state, which has always operated on the principle of the political domination of several nations by a state, while the *idea* of the nation speaks of a largely voluntary association or community. Third, the principle of national self-determination threatened both the multinational state and the empire-state, because, apart from introducing ideas of the equality of citizens/nationals, of loyalty, and of cultural differences, neither of these other two types of states could be certain what the granting of sovereign independence to a national group within its border would mean. Would doing so, for example, invite clamors for independence from other like groups? And would the granting of such independence reduce its power in relationship to other states?

All of what has just been said should be understood in the context of the international system itself, and the manner in which nationalism, in practice—as distinct from its theoretical definition—operates. It should also be understood in the context of the fact that few countries, despite the power of nationalism, are actually nation-states. Let us review them, in reverse order.

Because nationalism became such a powerful idea—even an ideal—most states sought to designate themselves as nations or as nation-states; and, in doing so, sought to elevate what is called the "national interest" to the level of the highest moral good to which anyone—leader or led—could aspire. This patriotism (love of one's nation and its supposed interest) came to be equated with collective support of that interest and individual or "subnational" subordination to that interest. Far from having their physical borders correspond to a single cultural grouping, most sovereign countries have been either multinational states or empire-states, with certain ethnic or social collectivities dominating the rest of citizens within the borders of the country.

Nationalism, as practiced, reflected the intrastate ethnic, racial, social, religious, linguistic, and other cultural dynamics just mentioned in relationship to the empire-state and the multinational state, as well as to the nature of the "international system itself." In the case of that system, it has no central authority, so each state is left to insure its security and socioeconomic well-being. And since the interest of a state is said, under nationalism, to be protectable only if that state has power (not the goodwill of other states, including allies) to offer such protection, the international system is not only anarchic but competitive, with each state competing to marshal most of the sources of power.

Among the resources of power—apart from money, status, industrial might, and the capacity to engage in exchange, especially trade—is national unity. So not only have states emphasized unity and treated internal criticism as evidence of disloyalty but each (without exception) has bought internal unity by emphasizing not so much its claimed common experience as the supposed extent to which that experience and its preached distinctiveness made the state and its people different from others. In other words, unity and identity were purchased at the price of depicting other people as "unlike" and as untrustworthy. One can trust only one's own. Further, while states, for purposes of international relations, have preached national unity, internally, they have had differences based on social classes, race, and ethnicity, and even nationality, in the case of multinational states. And while these differences invited—and often resulted in—the prohibited interference in the internal affairs of countries (usually for the sought advantage of the interfering party or parties), the privileged social elites within the borders of states would often employ the principle of noninterference in the internal affairs of states, the supposed differences between people inside and people outside the state's borders, and the need for national unity to justify the preservation of their own privileged positions (and, by extension, the unfavorable positions of others). In short, the internal sociopolitical system of states has generally cleaved along national borders. And this brings us back to relative deprivation (RD).

We had earlier said that RD has an ascribed twin, called "othering"—the act or practice by which an individual or social entity employs some actual or imputed difference to deny attributes or characteristics generally shared by human beings, in order to suggest that one person or group of persons is wholly unlike, is other than oneself, is of another kind, is in fact "another." This "another" is seen to be at odds, inharmonious, discrepant, incompatible, and not the same. Nationalism, in its attempt to construct the identity of nationhood and insure the successful mobilization of power, has consistently engaged in the practice of "othering." So, too, have social elites within and between countries, as they have sought to maintain their positions of privilege.

A fuller appreciation of how the concept of RD can help to illuminate what we have learned from the wars of the past century requires that we also bring into our discussion the two other dominant ideologies of the time: liberalism and Marxism. The former, which dominated the West during the time in question and which, through the influence of the West, had gained important footholds elsewhere in the world, was then (as it is now) closely associated with capitalism. Indeed, liberalism generally accepted the idea of the nation-state and espoused a number of positions about the "true" nature of such a state. Included in those positions has been the claim that liberty is and should be the most important social value. Further, it has contended that the circumstances of social life are not the offsprings of mysticism or miracle but the results of causes that are explainable; and that those causes (laws) are capable of being understood by individual human beings. It promised that human beings would find that their possibilities are virtually unlimited, if liberty were respected and the free expression of one's rational faculties were allowed and encouraged. The state under liberalism (the liberal state) should therefore guarantee liberty and the free exercise of people's rational faculties, with a minimum of interference in the lives of citizens.

In espousing the above positions, liberalism became the "perfect host" for capitalism, which preached that economic activities (production and distribution of goods and services) should be organized by the market. That is, the elements of production, such as goods, services, land, labor, and money, should be made available for exchange (sale) on the market and be permitted to find their own price, without any government intervention. Liberalism therefore came to espouse something called the self-regulating or the free market—one that allows economic activities to operate, with the exception of having the state guarantee legal protection of private property and private contract, free of any government intervention.

Marxism, which furnishes a critical appraisal of capitalism, does not accept either the state of the nationalist or that of the liberal as legitimate, because—contrary to the claims of their respective advocates—neither acts in the interest of the broad masses of people. Why? Because societies, and the states that serve them, are expressions of history, which is dialectical—that is, history not only is defined by change and is conflict-laden but is inherently conflictual, disclosing its meaning only to those who understand its essential movement and grasp its defining contradictions. Further, Marxism claims that the conflicts throughout history are based on the material circumstances of people—principally in the mode of production and exchange of goods and services. It is the sum total of relations that people enter into, in order to effect the production and exchange just mentioned, that determines the social and political structure of societies.

Marxism claims that people find themselves, throughout history, in varying relations to the mode of production, giving rise to social and intellectual differentiation. That differentiation manifests itself most significantly in the form of social classes, with the dominant class in every historical era gaining its status from its control of the means of production (land, money, skills, technology, plants, and the like) and using that status to originate, develop, and mold the sociopolitical institutions and belief systems to promote and secure its interests. Within liberal-capitalist societies, Marxists saw the dominant economic class amassing more and more wealth, while the laboring classes became not only poorer and poorer but increasingly subject to destitution and social abandonment. In exchange for such class-governed domination—and its associated "social and moral othering"— Marxism promised the poor, the lowly, and industrial workers, in particular, relative material equality, social solidarity (within the context of communal sharing), and freedom from social abandonment.

Nationalism, liberalism, and Marxism—the three great ideologies of the twentieth century—competed against each other and, to a large degree, formed part of the context for our understanding of the relative deprivation of the time. All three may be said to have contributed, in profound ways, to the perception on the part of individuals and groups that they were being relatively deprived. As such, the ideologies themselves might be said to have contributed to the wars we are attempting to analyze and explain. For example, those nations that lived under the political domination within multinational states or empire-states felt relatively deprived, in the face of the discrepancy between their condition and the right to liberty and national self-determination, which, respectively, liberalism and nationalism espoused. The right of workers to the wealth they are said by Marxism to have created certainly invited a sense of being relatively deprived. And the presence of RD in both instances is linked to "othering." But how does the perception of RD lead to actual warfare? After all, every society has had certain mechanisms to help deal with social dissatisfaction on the part of groups within its borders.

The answer to the question lies in the "fear of extinction"—a fear on the part of individuals and groups that they will cease to be. That is, a fear that the "self," which is linked to the positions or status they hold, will be extinguished, if the positions or status were to be radically altered or were to cease to be. And the fear of "ceasing to be" is linked to the type of change that would have to take place if RD were to be corrected or remedied. This idea of extinction can be refined and better grasped if we include in our discussion certain variables: economic participation, political access (power), and cultural identity.[5]

Economic participation I understand to mean the degree to which a group shares in the economic activities of a society and finds, from that degree of participation, returns that are comparatively satisfactory. Political access refers to the extent that groups are seen to be represented in the institutions that make decisions concerning the norms and processes by which society is governed and values allocated. Finally, cultural identity refers to those areas of human collective being and

behavior that emphasize a group's sense of self, of belonging, and of a future together as a group.

In relative deprivation, all three variables might be present in a given context,
although one or two may be dominant. Changes may be seen as possible in the
case of one variable because they do not threaten feared extinction, but not in another variable because fear of extinction might be present. Very important, also, in
the fear of extinction, is a sort of zero-sum psychological dynamic in which one
party's gain is seen as an absolute loss for the other party. Let us try to apply the
concept.

Two wars should be helpful in defining the twentieth century, in the sense that
they exercised a controlling influence over that century. They are what I term the
latter-day Thirty Years' War of 1914 to 1945, and the Cold War, from 1945 to
1985. In the case of the former, which many varyingly see as having been caused
or continued by the assassination of Archduke Franz Ferdinand of the Austro-
Hungarian Empire, the tense military alliances that existed in 1914, the severe
economic sanctions imposed on postwar Germany, and the political rise of Adolph
Hitler. But one should ask: why the assassination, the alliances, the severity, and
the rise? The answer lies in RD.

The beginning of the twentieth century found Britain occupying a dominant
political position in the world, by virtue of its navy, its financial power (London
was the financial capital of the world and the pound was the key currency for international transactions), its industrial output, and its empire. Britain was not
only conscious of its position but felt that it had achieved that position by reason
of the claimed superiority of its political and social culture. According to one of its
most eminent historians, the late Arnold Toynbee, by the beginning of the twentieth century, Britain felt it wombed within its culture the consummation of human
evolution and possibilities. It had led humankind to the end of history. Others
should emulate Britain.[6]

Lending plausibility to the self-proclaimed end of history was the fact that this
small island state had succeeded in building and controlling the largest empire in
the history of the world—one on which, as the British then boasted, "The sun
never sets." This empire, from which immense wealth was derived, served in significant measure as an outlet for the huge amounts of capital that had accumulated
in Britain in the form of profits from industrial enterprises. And because by then
Britain produced but 30 percent of the food it consumed and even a smaller portion of its industrial raw materials, London became dependent on its Asian, Pacific, African, and (to an extent) Caribbean possessions to supply it with foodstuffs
and industrial raw materials. In short, the status and identity that Britain had at
the beginning of the twentieth century were linked to its empire.

That empire (along with the status and the identity it offered)—the governing
class in Britain understood—could be preserved only if London had unchallenged

naval power and could preserve its string of strategically located outposts that supported unobstructed communication with all areas of the empire. Hence one finds
the same anxiety to secure Gibraltar, Cyprus, and the Suez Canal in the Mediterranean; Aden (now Yemen) and Somalia on the opposite shore of the Red Sea; and
Kenya, India, Burma, Malaya, Singapore, and Hong Kong—all securing London's
Asian, Pacific, and East African possessions. Britain used its navy and its economic
and industrial power to prevent Russia (which felt relatively deprived of warm-
water ports) and the Ottoman Empire from challenging its position. The Anglo-
Russian tensions and wars, during the nineteenth century, all had to do with
preventing Russia from gaining foothold ports in the Mediterranean, in the Per-
sian Gulf, or in the Indian Ocean (through Persia or Afghanistan).

By 1912, Germany, as a result of its economic dynamism, had caught up with
and had surpassed Britain as "the most productive economic power in Europe."
But the future of its dynamism was threatened by the absence of markets outside
Europe, to which Berlin could, like Britain, sell some of its industrial products,
invest some of its capital, and secure foodstuffs and industrial raw materials. "The
markets of the world were being penetrated, dominated, and increasingly mo-
nopolized by three great powers": the United States in Latin America; Britain in
East and South Africa, South Asia, and the Pacific; and France in West Africa, the
Balkans, and Russia.[7] In view of its own self-assessed capabilities, Germany perceived that it was relatively deprived and felt that it, too, should have a "place in
the sun." It wanted an overseas empire that would enable it to enjoy a status com-
parable to that of the country whose industrial standing it had outdistanced. As
early as 1906, it had sought to gain primacy in Morocco and that course of conduct had brought it into conflict with France. Britain, fearing the rising power of
a relatively deprived Germany, had thrown its support to France, and Germany
had to back down. But now Germany wanted a navy that would enable it to support an empire, to engage in greater international economic participation, and,
in so engaging, to gain access to greater political power. Britain saw any such
economic and political gain by Germany as threatening its status as the world
leader, and Britain formed alignments with France and Russia to thwart Germany's
ambitions.

Austro-Hungary also should be brought into this part of our discussion. It
sought, with the support of Germany, to fill "the void in the Balkans" caused by
the withdrawal of the Ottoman Empire from the area during the latter part of the
nineteenth century. In doing so, however, it found the same type of relative deprivation among the formerly subject peoples that the Ottoman Empire had faced.
These peoples of the Balkans—the Serbs, for example—wanted to enjoy the right
to national self-determination. But political leaders in Vienna were fearful that
their multinational state and empire would crumble (following what they envisioned as one nation after another demanding independence) and become but a

"worm-eaten museum piece," if Serbia were allowed independence.[8] Following the assassination of Archduke Ferdinand, the emperor and his officials imposed terms of settlement on the "othered" Serbs that they knew the Serbs could not accept. And those harsh terms, in part, led to World War I because of the complex system of diplomatic military alliances. In short, the fear of extinction on the part of the governing class in Vienna induced the attempted quashing of Serbia's search for political access (independence, which would confer on it all the rights of a state).

France, of course, had a major role in the coming of the war. After it had lost the 1871 war to Germany (and its, until then, dominant place in continental Europe), it sought psychological compensation abroad, by expanding its empire and by seeking economic ties with the people of the Balkans and with Russia. It, too, felt that its standing was being challenged by Germany when it sought greater economic participation outside of Europe. So Paris used its influence in the Balkans and in Russia, with the collaboration of Britain, to frustrate Germany's ambitions. But in doing so, France invited a fear, on the part of Germany, that it was being "encircled" (France and Britain in the west, Russia in the east, and the Balkans in the southeast). That fear—a fear of having its status as the most powerful country in continental Europe extinguished—induced Germany's military leaders to develop a strategy for a two-front war, a strategy that required an undelayed, preemptive execution of specific military orders, once specified contingencies arose. Coupled with all these expressions of RD was the othering of the opponent.

In World War II, the second phase of the Thirty Years' War, RD continued. Italy, for example, felt that it had been denied access to certain deliberations of the Paris Peace Conference and economic participation and control of certain areas of the Adriatic, while Britain and France had enriched themselves with the fruits of victory. So Italy sought to (and it later did under the leadership of Benito Mussolini) revise the international order during the 1920s and 1930s. Russia, too, felt relatively deprived, having lost more people and territory (Finland, Estonia, Latvia, Lithuania, and Romania, among other areas) than even the defeated Germany. And Japan, which could not even secure a statement on racial equality at the conference, left embittered. For Germany, claims about national self-determination and equality of nations made it feel even more RD, when it noted that it alone had been deemed guilty of causing the war, that Britain and France had given up none of their colonies, that it was again being "encircled" by French diplomacy in Eastern Europe (Paris was afraid that it would again lose its status as Europe's strongest continental power, if Germany were to regain its power), and that Britain had retained its "empire first" strategy—that of controlling the sea communication between the British Isles and the British Empire, maintaining its status/identity, and, thus, retaining the capability to frustrate Germany's search for a change in its own socioeconomic conditions and its identity. Germany also saw the harsh terms visited on it as an effort to insure its long-term inferior status in Europe, a fact that led to the social and economic crises that sponsored the rise of Hitler.

Italy, Japan, Russia (to an extent France), and certainly Germany felt that RD induced them to act in a manner calculated to change the established international order and, in doing so, defied those who benefited from and sought to preserve it. That deprivation, linked to a sense of a self that was denied esteem and denied "being like," largely induced Germany and Russia to enter into secret military deals and impelled Japan to act "like the Europeans" to secure greater economic participation and, thereby, gain access to political equality.[9] It was RD also that brought the "othering" of potential enemies or victims (inhuman, subhuman, less human, animals, brutes, superhuman) to unprecedented public exchange and justified a brutalization of humans in Europe and the Pacific that even today is hard to comprehend.[10] World War II was particularly brutal, because loyalty to nation and race were combined, transmuting individual selfishness into national/racial egoism—a form of supposed and taught altruism. And when that felt altruism, faced with the need for staving off feared extinction by "animals" was allowed the freedom and power to act, it invited actions that are without moral restraints. The Cold War also gives us some insights into RD.

I understand the Cold War to mean the intense diplomatic and military confrontation that took place between the West, led by the United States, and the East, led by the former Soviet Union, from 1945 to 1985—a confrontation that, though not having resulted in actual warfare between the leaders, had never ceased to threaten one. This war, however, properly seen and contextualized, is perhaps the greatest historical expression of RD, because it involved the world at large.

To understand it fully, we must disregard the use of the terms *West* and *East* in the preceding definition and substitute in their stead liberal-capitalism and Marxist-Leninist communism. The former dominated the West and western-influenced societies elsewhere in the world, espoused a market economy that was defined by private property, economic inequality, and even social abandonment, if the market required it. Further, liberal-capitalism spoke for political equality and personal freedom, within the context of social order. Marxist-Leninist communism, in contrast, contended that private property is a form of theft, in that all wealth is something that is socially produced; that the disparities in the ownership and distribution of wealth—which is produced by workers—is the result of the expropriation of workers, the socially deprived; and that since economic resources are those that determine social and political equality, there can be no political equality if there is economic inequality. Further, while liberal-capitalists preached social harmony (social order), Marxist-Leninists argued that societies are products of historical change, and that history itself is inherently conflictual. In short, Marxist-Leninist communism sought to identify socioeconomic contradictions, sharpen people's consciousness of them, and use the sense of RD to urge a systematic overthrow (extinction) of those who controlled the liberal-capitalist societies. If workers were to gain the increased economic participation that Marxists espoused (plus the associated political access that economic equality would bring), were unburdened by the fear of social abandonment, and were allowed a change of identity (from that of nationals/citizens of states that would disintegrate to that of comrades who were not loyal to or even recognized national borders), then there would indeed be an extinction of the capitalist class. On one hand, this fear of extinction induced the worldwide focus on the "rolling back" or the "containment" of communism; also, the use of relative deprivation felt by many groups (women, racial and ethnic minorities, religious believing, and colonized people, among others) gave Marxist-Leninist prospects for the future a fearsome countenance and sent shock waves into the minds of the socially privileged. On the other hand, liberal-capitalism, especially its Anglo-American model, regrouped itself, offered some limited expressions of improvement in people's social conditions, contended that its modes of social order had more to offer humans, and exposed a relative deprivation found in Marxist-Leninist communism: that of political access and personal freedom. So the variables of economic participation, political access, and cultural identity confronted each other throughout the world, including in Vietnam.

The war that ravished that country and caused so much social and psychological dislocation in the United States and elsewhere could have been avoided, but for the fear of the extinction of British standing in India and, more generally, British standing in the world. In the words of President Franklin Roosevelt, who was troubled by the fact that France had had control of Vietnam "for nearly one hundred years, and the people were worse off than they were at the beginning":

> I have been terribly worried about Indochina. . . . I suggested . . . to Chiang, that Indochina be set up under a trusteeship—have a Frenchman, one or two Indochinese, and a Chinese and a Russian, because they were on their coast, and maybe a Filipino and an American, to educate them for self-government. . . . Stalin liked the idea, China liked the idea. The British didn't like it. It might bust up their empire, because if the Indochinese were to work together and eventually get their independence, the Burmese might do the same thing.[11]

In other words, the Vietnamese, whom, in the words of President Roosevelt, France had "milked . . . for one hundred years"[12] and who on the basis of relative deprivation were seeking greater economic participation and political access through their clamors for national self-determination, should be denied what they sought. If they were to succeed, they would be a bad example for Burma and other areas of the British Empire in Asia. Such areas might demand the same and extinguish the British position in the world. What happened to Vietnam was repeated again and again in other areas of the Global South. And that denial has been a source of unending conflicts.

What is said above with respect to international relations is, in fact, true of intrastate relations. One has but to look at Northern Ireland and Sri Lanka to discover the truth of the assertion. In Sri Lanka, the substitution of direct elections for communal rule—which had given the Tamils a guaranteed level of political representation—and of Sinhala (official language) for a number of languages, including English (which had formerly given those who mastered it special privileges to university education, government service, and private sector profession)—altered the sociopolitical and cultural life of the country. The Tamils who, though a numerical minority, had used their proficiency in English and their guaranteed political access to insure their economic and social ascendancy and the relative deprivation of the Sinhalese, now found themselves in reversed circumstances, in the face of a change in language emphasis (allowing greater economic participation to the majority) and emphasis on direct election (which gave equal political access to all). Their former status and identity were threatened with extinction, so they sought to fight; and the formerly RD Sinhalese, who now stand to benefit, are also fighting to defend their potential gain. In Northern Ireland, despite some increased economic benefits to the Catholic community there, the Protestant majority is afraid to concede political access to Catholics, because they (the Protestants) fear extinction of their political and social status.[13] This fear is why the 1998 Good Friday Agreement in power sharing has been suspended and is currently being reviewed.

The "othering" of people—which has fueled RD through the use of religious, ethnic, social, socioeconomic, and national cleavages to define the conflicts we earlier mentioned—has also been successfully pursued throughout human history by the use of race. During the second half of the twentieth-century Thirty Years' War, the "othering" use to which race was put—drawing on a long history of socialization—produced human slaughter of a scale hitherto unknown. After the war, the UN's Economic and Social Council (ECOSOC) and its Educational, Scientific, and Cultural Organization (UNESCO) were created, in recognition of the degree to which RD and "othering" had led to that war, and in acknowledgment of the need to provide a new international system that would radically move human beings away from RD.

The creation of ECOSOC expressed the feeling that the UN would have to help remove the social and economic privations that many people felt, if wars were going to be contained. ECOSOC was to help in that containment by promoting higher standards of living, full employment, and conditions of economic and social progress and development. With respect to UNESCO—the objective of which was to remove the cultural stereotypes (false markers) that people held about others and to help to create global moral solidarity—its functions were seen as critical to the evolution of a peaceful world. No area of sought change or reform, however, was as far-reaching in its ambition to deal with the causes of war (RD) than that of human rights.

Designed to eliminate othering, develop empathy, afford economic and political access, and create a common moral and human identity, the human rights regime that was inaugurated in 1948 accepts that each human being is a member of a single *human* family, recognizes the "inherent dignity and the equal and inalienable rights of all members," and contends that both that acceptance and recognition are "the foundation of freedom, justice and peace in the world." The first article of the Universal Declaration of Human Rights proclaims, "All human beings are born free and equal in dignity and rights." And this very article goes on to require that we "should act towards one another in the spirit of [sisterhood] brotherhood."

The human rights regime therefore rejects the exclusivity of nationalism, the socioeconomic inequality of liberal capitalism, and the class preference of Marxism. Most important, it seeks to eliminate the claimed distinctiveness, which, for each of these ideologies, serves as the marker that breeds RD. Indeed, while recognizing and celebrating human cultural and other differences, it makes the centrality of one's humanity the cornerstone of the social and political order. For instance, it recognizes one's right to work, to a fair trial, to social security, to freedom of thought and conscience and religion, to medical care, to assemble, to food, to freedom of speech, to education, to housing, to freedom of movement, to participation in the cultural life of the community, and to freedom from torture and degrading treatment. Further, one is entitled to a social and international order—a life-sustaining environment and peace—within which the rights recognized can be fully realized. And the Declaration of Human Rights goes on to state that *everyone* is entitled to *all* the rights and freedoms provided *"without distinction* [my emphasis] of any kind, such as race, color, sex, language, religion, political and other opinion, national or social origin, property, birth or other status." In other words, the old markers that thwarted political access, undermined fair economic allocations, and threatened cultural identity, are potentially removed. And *human* security and identity, not national, social, racial, or other ones, were to preside in the world.

The possibility that the twentieth century provided for the elimination of RD, through the human rights regime, brought with it the dangers of war, also. First, the recognition of those rights inspired new and emboldened demands for social equality and political access. Second, those demands threatened to extinguish the remaining privileges and identities that social groups and states claimed. And third, the movement the regime elicited (the human rights movement) became so powerful that it created new divisions (the global North-South axis, for instance), invited fears that concessions on issues such as the creation of a "new international economic order" or the establishment of an International Criminal Court would only excite new demands, and weakened the very institution (the UN) through which peaceful resolution of differences was envisioned. The end of the Cold War, which had exposed certain hidden forms of RD, far from creating a "peace dividend," increased the sense of RD among groups and invited new or aggravated old anxieties throughout the world. As I write, a more sharpened cleavage in the international system seems to be emerging, as Arabs and Muslims are being othered, and the United States, with the help of its allies, seeks to maintain its threatened, "sole superpower" status. Like Britain facing similar challenges during the nineteenth century, the United States feels that its status and identity as a superpower would be diminished, demeaned, and undermined, if it were not to "fight and teach the enemy" a lesson.

What all the wars of the twentieth century have taught us is that only the marginalization of the conditions that marginalize people—and breed RD—will enable us to find peace. The human rights regime has been an attempt to put that lesson into practice, but those who fear extinction and the impatience of those who seek change have prevented that practice from coming into being. Until we institute that practice, there will be no peace in the world, and military engagement, no matter how apparently promising, will only undermine prospects for peace.

NOTES

1. I am aware of the pioneering work of Robert T. Gurr in this field, but I have some differences with Gurr's definition and application of the concept. See Gurr's "A Causal Model of Civil Strife: A Comparative Analysis Using New Indices," *American Political Science Review* 62 (December 1968): 1104–24. See also, Robert T. Gurr and Barbara Harff, *Ethnic Conflict in World Politics* (Boulder, Colo.: Westview Press, 1994).

2. See Hermann Wellenmann, "Nation-Building and Personality Structure," in Karl Deutch and William Foltz, eds., *Nation-Building*, 33–35 (New York: Atherton Press, 1966).

3. This recognition came about because both Woodrow Wilson of the United States and V. I. Lenin of the former Soviet Union supported the idea of nation. Wilson, in his Fourteen Points, gave particularly strong diplomatic and legal support to the idea.

4. One should note the use of the term *international*, not *interstate*, system. Nation is the ideal.

5. The idea of extinction and the three variables, joined together, were brought to my attention by Landon E. Hancock, in his "The Pattern of Ethnic Conflict" (paper presented at the Conflict Studies Conference, sponsored by the Graduate Programs in Dispute Resolution, University of Massachusetts–Boston, October 23–24, 1998).

6. Arnold Toynbee, *Civilization on Trial* (New York: Oxford University Press, 1948), 16–19.

7. See William R. Keylor, *The Twentieth-Century World* (New York: Oxford University Press, 1996), 46.

8. John G. Stoessinger, *Why Nations Go To War* (New York: St. Martin's Press, 1993), 6–7.

9. See John Dower, *War without Mercy* (New York: Pantheon Books, 1948).

10. Along with Dower, see Sven Lindqvist, *"Exterminate the Brutes"* (New York: New Press, 1996).

11. Arthur M. Schlesinger Jr., *The Bitter Heritage: Vietnam and American Democracy, 1941–1966* (New York: Houghton Mifflin, 1966), 23.

12. Ibid., 22.

13. See Raymond C. Taras and Rajat Ganguly, *Understanding Ethnic Conflict* (New York: Longman, 1998).

The Link between Poverty and Violent Conflict

J. BRIAN ATWOOD

"Blessed are the [poor] for they shall inherit the earth."[1] This biblical aphorism is being realized at an alarming pace. Almost half the world's six billion people live under the poverty line of two dollars a day: 1.2 billion people earn less than one dollar a day and are in the extreme poverty category.[2] By 2020, the globe likely will add two billion more people, 95 percent of whom will reside in the developing world.[3] Absent any dramatic shift in policy priorities, the poor may indeed inherit the earth in the lifetimes of most of us.

The implications of these demographic realities for the earth's well-being have many dimensions. They include the loss of forest cover and biodiversity as well as the spread of infectious disease and food insecurity, to name but a few. This predictable population growth will create huge mega-cities as urbanization growth trends in the developing world continue unabated. It will also create an explosion of young people in the developing world at a time when the populations of Western nations will be aging dramatically.

Does all of this mean that more violent conflict is inevitable? Some scholars hold that there is no empirical evidence to support the hypothesis that conditions of poverty cause conflict.[4] Pervasive poverty alone is not a sufficient condition to create a major conflict, or even to cause an individual to commit an act of violence. Yet, many studies show that there is a strong correlation between the absence of material well-being and the prospects for violence, from crime in inner-city neighborhoods[5] to instability in poor nations.[6]

Sampson, Raudenbush, and Earls, in their 1997 study of neighborhoods and violent crime, examined race and class segregation in poor Chicago neighborhoods and its impact on "collective efficacy," or social cohesion among neighbors. They found that "alienation, exploitation, and dependency wrought by resource deprivation acts as a centrifugal force that stymies collective efficacy." The greater the effect of this resource deprivation—a phenomenon the authors call the "concentrated disadvantage" factor—the stronger the correlation to the level of violence.[7]

The study by Sampson, Raudenbush, and Earls focuses on race and class issues within American society, which, because of its egalitarian ethos, may intensify individual feelings of alienation and exploitation. This focus may limit the study's value in examining the effects of poverty in developing nations. But "alienation,

33

exploitation, and dependency" are highly relevant factors there as well. They cause social and political stress both within poor nations and between poor and rich regions, especially in an information age when social and economic discrepancies are more obvious.

Governments in the developing world and donor agencies supporting their development agendas are facing much the same "centrifugal force" referred to in the Sampson study. The report of the Commission on Global Governance entitled Our Global Neighborhood alludes to Sampson's "concentrated disadvantage" factor when it states, "Absolute poverty provides scant basis either for the maintenance of traditional society or for any further development of participation in civic life and governance. . . . Unfair in themselves, poverty and extreme disparities of income fuel both guilt and envy when made more visible by global television."[8]

That awareness of "extreme disparities of income" should cause both guilt and envy should not be surprising. How this relates to the need for "social cohesion" and the political integration necessary for a state to function and to prevent outbreaks of violence are crucial to this discussion. The World Bank report entitled Breaking the Conflict Trap argues that an unequal distribution of wealth exacerbates societal tensions and "increases the perception of relative deprivation." This, in turn, the report states, leads to "perceived grievances and potential strife."[9] While this refers specifically to the distribution of wealth within a nation-state, the widening gap between income in the developed world and the developing world also increases the perception of relative deprivation and has real implications for global governance.

The report on state failure, prepared under the auspices of the University of Maryland by several scholars on behalf of the U.S. intelligence community, examines the correlation between several development factors and the failure of state institutions.[10] Such failure correlates strongest with three factors: infant mortality rates, fragile democratic institutions, and dependency on imports. Each of these factors contributes to the "centrifugal force that stymies collective efficacy," to use the language of the Sampson study.[11] Certainly, parents feel deprived when their children are dying of diseases that they know can be treated in the developed world. Fragile democracies that provide universal suffrage but do not have the institutional capacity to manage social stress, are clearly vulnerable to collapse. Economies that cannot produce sufficient goods and services internally and service only their elite with imports are bound to have severe distribution of wealth issues. The report concludes: "Empirically the most striking pattern is that civil war is heavily concentrated in the poorest countries. . . . The key root cause of conflict is the failure of economic development."[12]

The condition of poverty may not be sufficient in itself to cause widespread conflict, but these studies clearly show that poverty, more than any other factor, contributes to feelings of "alienation, exploitation, and dependency" and these feelings in turn contribute to a breakdown of social cohesion and to violent conflict. The nations that are most vulnerable to this phenomenon possess an inadequate level of social cohesion in the first instance. Many have top-heavy bureaucratic structures and weak legal systems. Their poorest citizens are often forced to live and work outside the legal framework of their society. As Hernando DeSoto has demonstrated in his research, surviving and protecting one's meager assets in this illegal state (the so-called informal sector), requires considerable guile, alliances with criminal elements, and, frequently, a resort to violence.[13] This need to exist within an unprotected illegal environment coupled with other forms of deprivation, such as food insecurity, environmental degradation, unsustainable urban population growth, and infectious disease, produces antisocial behavior, anger, and desperation.

The Poverty-Terrorism Link

The link between poverty and terrorism is more difficult to demonstrate than the link between poverty and conflict. Terrorist networks that have operated over the past twenty years have been led by educated people of means. Groups such as the Irish Republican Army, the Basque group ETA, Al Qaeda, and Hamas have been motivated by serious political grievances or extreme religious beliefs, or some combination of both. But scholars who have studied the modus operandi of these groups have observed that they invariably have exploited the conditions of poverty to expand the political appeal of their cause and recruit their foot soldiers.[14] In addition, extremely poor nations have been unable or unwilling to reject these well-endowed organizations and thus have become safe harbors for them.

The U.S. government endorsed this view of the terrorism threat in its controversial National Security Strategy (which also creates a justification for preemptive military strikes). In a letter accompanying this new doctrine, President Bush addressed the threats posed by states weakened by failing institutions and poverty: "The events of September 11, 2001, taught us that weak states, like Afghanistan, can pose as great a danger to our national interests as strong states. Poverty does not make poor people into terrorists and murderers. Yet poverty, weak institutions, and corruption can make weak states vulnerable to terrorist networks and drug cartels within their borders."

The effort to defeat or marginalize terrorist organizations must integrate all of the elements of a nation's national security establishment. Military power is necessary, although, as we have seen, it has its limitations. Indeed, misuse of military power can reduce the effectiveness of other instruments. Diplomacy is essential to gain the cooperation of other nations and to enhance the effectiveness of international legal and enforcement mechanisms. Accurate intelligence information and precise analysis of local situations are also crucial. All of these tools are enhanced when governments are cooperating widely to attack poverty, a significant cause of alienation and anger.[15] Can this be done more effectively under a new paradigm of international development cooperation?

Development for Security

If we are to take effective action against the conditions of poverty that contribute most to violent conflict, it is first necessary to recognize the constraints we face within governments and internationally. These are quite severe and will require a dramatic change in outlook.

First, there are limited resources available for development. The most recent Development Assistance Committee (OECD) "volume" report reflects an official development assistance level of $78 billion. This worldwide sum seems a healthy amount, but it pales next to the $478 billion the United States spends on its military budget.[16] In addition, most of this amount is directed at developing nations that are already committed to reform and thus make good partners. Two types of nation are generally excluded as recipients of assistance: emerging economies with large pockets of poor citizens and heavily skewed distributions of wealth, and weak, poorly performing nations.

Second, while donor nations have targeted extreme poverty—the 2000 Millennium Challenge Goals of the UN vow to reduce by one-half the approximately 1.2 billion who earn less than a dollar a day—most of these people are beyond the reach of traditional programs in that they are not part of the formal economy. Traditional development programs are normally implemented through governments, which are reluctant to acknowledge the existence of the informal sector or to change the status quo.[17]

Third, governments tend to place more emphasis on mainstream national security objectives than on development strategies. For example, Western governments are more interested in preserving their industrial base by conserving their access to oil or expanding international trade and investment opportunities.[18] While developing new markets may be a long-range goal, it is difficult for governments that operate on annual budgets to see beyond the horizon.

Fourth, because development objectives are not only secondary to mainstream national security objectives but also are long-term and preventive, there is little incentive to adopt more coherent approaches to the challenge of eradicating poverty. Thus, while limited resources are devoted to development projects, much larger amounts are expended, for example, to subsidize agricultural exports. In addition, international financial decisions taken though the International Mone-

tary Fund tend to emphasize macro-economic stability often at the expense of development or growth strategies.[19]

A New Paradigm

Overcoming these significant constraints will require an acceptance of the real
threat constituted by growing poverty. Currently, the desire to pursue a comprehensive effort that would include development cooperation is absent from the effort to defeat terrorism. Part of the challenge is proper analysis of the threat. The
other is a failure to see beyond the current crisis. What is needed is a new "culture
of prevention" that will re-order resource priorities and create institutions capable
of taking cooperative, preemptive steps rather than waiting for crises to develop.[20]

On the analytical side, what is missing in the current assessments is a development perspective. A study by the Canadian Bernard Wood for the Emergency
Response Division of the UN Development Programme advocates improved
analyses of the areas of underdevelopment in nations vulnerable to crises. In other
words, areas that are most likely to create social tension and conflict are largely ignored. Development experts are more likely to consider these issues carefully than
are traditional intelligence analysts.[21] Early warning systems that incorporate a
development perspective could in turn transform decision making and enable
governments to intervene more quickly with assistance in a timely manner.

What types of intervention are most conducive to preventing a state from losing social cohesion and spinning into violent conflict? The world's bilateral and
multilateral donor agencies and the UN system have undertaken a number of
studies in recent years on how best to support global efforts to combat terrorism
and to prevent violent conflict. A recent report by the Development Assistance
Committee (DAC) of the OECD entitled "A Development Co-Operation Lens
on Terrorism Prevention" offers several possibilities.[22] It builds on a 2001 DAC
report entitled "Helping Prevent Violent Conflict." That these helpful reports
have received so little attention is a reflection of the limited mindset that characterizes today's national security establishments.

The premise of the DAC report is that "terrorism is a form of violent conflict
and conflict prevention is an integral part of the quest to reduce poverty." The report points out that development cooperation cannot directly address "all the
'root causes' of terrorism," but it does have an important role to play. "Many conditions that allow terrorists to be politically successful, build and expand constitu-
encies, find recruits, establish and finance terrorist organizations, and secure
safe-havens fall within the realm and primary concerns of development co-operation," according to the DAC report.[23]

The specific interventions recommended by the DAC report are revealing in
that they attempt to ameliorate the conditions of "concentrated disadvantage"

that the Sampson study suggests contribute most to the unraveling of "social co-hesion."[24] Among the interventions designed to "dissuade disaffected groups from embracing terrorism and other forms of violent conflict" were the following:

- Support community-driven development to build the capacity of communities to resist extreme religious and political ideologies based on violence. Encourage intra- and inter-faith exchanges
- Help build effective and responsible media and public information strategies as powerful tools to prevent violence
- Give greater attention in donor programming to young people's job opportunities and education to prevent the emergence of fragile, disenfranchised youth
- Support democratization and modernization from within local value systems to reconfirm and build the beliefs of societies
- Stay engaged and work in fragile, conflict-prone societies *no matter how difficult the partnership may become* [my emphasis]
- Strive to make globalization an inclusive process, which will help reduce support for terrorism. *This requires an increased aid effort as well as greater policy coherence* [my emphasis].[25]

This and other reports by development professionals have been largely ignored by governments that are otherwise seized with concern that violent conflict and terrorism are threatening the international system. These governments, most prominent among them being the United States, have responded to terrorist threats by increasing defense spending and by attempting to build elaborate homeland security systems.

The United States government, which takes the lead in the war against terrorism, is very poorly organized to employ development assistance as a preventive tool. Its Agency for International Development (USAID) possesses the core of knowledge and experience, but it is not at the cabinet level and often is not able to influence policy decisions. Furthermore, many U.S. government departments and agencies expend resources on development, but they pursue their domestic mission, have no overseas presence, and implement programs with great difficulty and little effect.

As has been mentioned, there is also little coherence in the approach of the United States, and often its policies on trade and finance run directly counter to its development objectives. There is a clear need for a new cabinet-level Department for International Development Cooperation that would be built on the foundation of USAID's professional staff and would coordinate all U.S. development activities including oversight of the UN voluntary agencies and the World Bank. The secretary for this new department would also have a stronger voice on development policy vis-à-vis the Treasury and Commerce Departments and thus contribute to a more coherent approach to the development agenda.

The international community cannot wait long for enlightened American leadership in this crucial area. It is becoming overwhelmed with crises of varying degrees of seriousness. What does this mean for the next two decades when the population of the world's poor will grow exponentially?

The international architecture created after World War II has served the world for over fifty years. The institutions and legal regime are already overtaxed. There are now four times as many nation-states as there were in 1945 and numerous radical groups who pursue their objectives without regard for sovereignty, international law, or institutional frameworks of any kind. The global community is suffering the loss of "collective efficacy." This situation can only grow worse as the number of the world's poor increases.

It is long past time to acknowledge the link between poverty and conflict and to act on it. Accepting that poverty contributes to violent conflict will lead to an inevitable choice: to target development strategies to prevent the disintegration of social structures and trade and finance policies that promote development. If we cannot muster the political will to address the poverty-conflict connection, we will condemn future generations to global class warfare, as an ever-contracting Western world confronts an expanding and increasingly violent developing world.

NOTES

1. Matt. 5:5 (King James Version), with original meek replaced by poor.

2. World Bank Group, Global Poverty Monitoring home page: http://www.worldbank.org/ (this data base, while improved, is still dependent on imperfect country-generated information).

3. J. F. Richard, *High Noon* (New York: Basic Books, 2002).

4. K. Von Hippel, "The Roots of Terrorism: Probing the Myths," *Political Quarterly* 73 (August 2002): 25–39.

5. R. J. Sampson, S. W. Raudenbush, and F. Earls, "Neighborhoods and Violent Crime," *Science* 277 (1997): 918–24.

6. J. A. Goldstone, T. R. Gurr, B. Harff, et al., State Failure Task Force Report, Phase III Findings (MacLean, Va..: Science Applications International Corporation, September 2000), available at http://www.cidcm.umd.edu/paper.asp?id=9.

7. Sampson, Raudenbush, and Earls, "Neighborhoods."

8. Commission on Global Governance, *Our Global Neighborhood: Report of the Commission on Global Governance* (Oxford: Oxford University Press, 1999), 22.

9. Breaking the Conflict Trap: Civil War and Development Policy (World Bank Policy Research Report no. 26121), available at http://www.worldbank.org/.

10. Goldstone et al. "State Failure."

11. Sampson, Raudenbush, and Earls, "Neighborhoods."

12. Goldstone et al., "State Failure."

13. Hernando DeSoto, *The Other Path* (New York: Basic Books, 1989), 131–87.

14. Von Hippel, "Roots of Terrorism."

15. J. B. Atwood, "Foreign Assistance: The Fourth Dimension in the War against Terrorism" (lecture presented at the Kennedy School of Government, October 23, 2001).

16. "Fiscal 2004 DOD Budget Release," Defense LINK, home page, http://www.defenselink.mil/comptroller/defbudget/fy2004 (accessed February 23, 2006). (The DOD appropriation for FY04 was $391 billion; the $478 billion amount includes the $87 billion supplemental for Iraq.)

17. DeSoto, Other Path, 131–87.

18. Michael T. Klare, *Resource Wars: The New Landscape of Global Conflict* (New York: Metropolitan Books, 2001).

19. Joseph E. Stiglitz, *Globalization and Its Discontents* (New York: Norton, 2002), 214–52.

20. J. B. Atwood, "The Development Imperative: Creating the Preconditions for Peace," *Journal of International Affairs* 55, no. 2 (Spring 2002): 333–49.

21. Bernard Wood, *Development Dimensions of Conflict-Prevention and Peace Building* (Ottawa: Wood, 2001).

22. "A Development Co-Operation Lens on Terrorism Prevention" (OECD/DAC report), http://www.oecd.org/dataoecd/17/4/16085708.pdf (accessed October 16, 2003).

23. Ibid.

24. Sampson, Raudenbush, and Earls, "Neighborhoods."

25. "Development Co-Operation Lens."

The Costs of Covert Warfare
Airpower, Drugs, and Warlords in the Conduct of U.S. Foreign Policy

ALFRED W. MCCOY

In his address to Congress after the events of September 11, 2001, President George W. Bush told the nation that America's current war against terrorism would be like no other our nation had ever fought. On this point Mr. Bush seemed ill-advised. Our ongoing war in Afghanistan is the logical outcome of a succession of covert wars that the United States has fought along the mountain rim of Asia since the end of World War II.

Looking back on the long history of American intervention in highland Asia, there are two particularly troubling aspects: first, the rise of a problematic doctrine of covert warfare; and, second, a contradictory relationship to the global drug trade. Through four secret wars fought over the span of fifty years, the United States has developed a covert-warfare doctrine that combines special-operations forces with airpower. In the thirty years since the end of the Vietnam War, this use of airpower as a substitute for infantry has placed the United States at increasing variance with international law in a way that one day risks outright violation. More broadly, the conduct of foreign policy through covert operations removes these secret wars from both congressional oversight and conventional diplomacy, leaving their battlegrounds black holes of political instability—with profound regional and global ramifications.

In highland Asia, opium has proven the most sensitive index of such instability. While these covert wars are being fought, Central Intelligence Agency (CIA) protection transforms tribal warlords into powerful drug lords linked to international markets. In the wasteland that is the aftermath of such wars, only opium seems to flower, creating regions and whole nations with a lasting dependence on the international drug traffic.

Laos in the 1960s

Under its Cold War doctrine of containing communism, the United States, through its CIA, fought a succession of secret wars in highland Asia. In the late 1940s, the Iron Curtain came crashing down across the Asian landmass. To contain Soviet and Chinese expansion, the United States mounted covert operations along communism's soft underbelly—a highland rim that stretched for five thousand miles across Asia from Turkey to Thailand.

Along this strategic frontier, geopolitics has produced recurring eruptions at two flash points—Burma and Laos in the east and Afghanistan in the west. For forty years, the CIA fought a succession of covert wars at these two points—at Burma during the 1950s, Laos in the 1960s, and Afghanistan in the 1980s. In one of history's accidents, moreover, the Iron Curtain had fallen along Asia's historic opium zone, drawing the CIA into ambiguous alliances with the region's highland warlords.

In Laos from 1960 to 1974, the United States fought the longest and largest of these covert wars, discovering new military doctrines that have since become central to its foreign policy. Since this war was classified then and is, even now, little studied, most Americans are unaware of the lessons we learned in Laos and their lasting influence on the later conduct of U.S. foreign policy.

The CIA's secret war in Laos was an unplanned byproduct of America's bipartisan foreign policy during the Cold War. At the start of U.S. intervention in Indochina in 1955, the Eisenhower administration, mindful of the region's geopolitical imperatives, had made Laos its primary bastion against communist infiltration into Southeast Asia. Unwilling to continue Eisenhower's Cold War confrontation over Laos, President John Kennedy pulled back by signing a treaty with Moscow in 1962 to neutralize Laos and relied instead on counterinsurgency inside South Vietnam to contain communism. In effect, Kennedy withdrew conventional forces from Laos in favor of his new special warfare doctrine of using American advisers to train the South Vietnamese in counterinsurgency. In retrospect, Kennedy's withdrawal from Laos was a strategic miscalculation.[1] When the Vietnam War started two years later, in 1964, there was no longer any restraint on North Vietnamese infiltration through Laos into South Vietnam. Washington was treaty-bound to respect Laos's neutrality and thus found itself in an ambiguous, even contradictory, position—forced to intervene in a country where it could no longer intervene.[2]

Ambiguity forced improvisation, leading the United States to develop a new military doctrine that substituted tribal mercenaries and massive airpower for the conventional ground forces the United States was now barred from deploying inside Laos. For more than a decade, the CIA led a secret army of thirty thousand Hmong mercenaries in covert war against communist guerrillas in the rugged mountains of northern Laos—a formative lesson for the agency in the use of tribal warriors.[3]

Simultaneously, the U.S. Air Force fought the largest air war in military history over Laos, dropping 2.1 million tons of bombs on this tiny, impoverished nation—an amount equivalent to that dropped on Germany and Japan by the Allied powers in all of World War II. Although the bulk of this tonnage was dropped on the Ho Chi Minh trail in the jungles of southern Laos, the U.S. Air Force still blocked the annual communist offensives on the capital Vientiane by dropping 500,000 tons on populated areas surrounding the strategic Plain of Jars in northern Laos.[4]

This massive bombardment of bamboo villages in northern Laos—blasted by three times the intensity of the conventional tonnage dropped on industrial Japan during World War II—made a wasteland of this narrow, forty-mile plain and its fifty thousand peasants, bamboo villages, market towns, and medieval Buddhist temples. "By 1968 the intensity of the bombings was such that no organized life was possible in the villages," wrote the UN adviser George Chapelier, who interviewed refugees from this air war. "The villages moved . . . deeper and deeper into the forest as the bombing reached its peak in 1969 when jet planes came daily and destroyed all stationery structures. Nothing was left standing. The villagers lived in trenches and holes or in caves. They farmed only at night. All of the informants, without any exception, had his village completely destroyed."[5]

In 1971, an American development volunteer working in Laos, Fred Branfman, interviewed refugees from this air war on the Plain of Jars who expressed a deep sense of suffering, sadness, and displacement. A thirty-three-year-old woman spoke with emotion of her experience of peasant life under this secret air war:

> I saw this in the village of my birth, as every day and every night the planes came to drop bombs on us. We lived in holes to protect our lives. . . . I saw my cousin die in the field of death. My heart was most disturbed and my voice called out loudly as I ran to the houses. Thus, I saw life and death for the people on account of the war of many airplanes in the region of Xieng Khouang. Until there were no houses at all. And the cows and the buffalo were dead. Until everything was leveled and you could see only the red, red ground. I think of this time and still I am afraid.[6]

While the bombs still rained, some American intellectuals criticized this air war, branding it a "war crime." After flying over the Plain of Jars in early 1972, a correspondent for the *Far Eastern Economic Review,* T. D. Allman, termed the bombing there "an operation that lies well down the spectrum between a military scandal and a provable war crime." A group of Cornell University scientists, led by the physics professor Raphael Littauer and the astronomer Carl Sagan, reported that U.S. bombing violated the principle under international law "that a reasonable proportionality exist between the damage caused and the military gain sought."[7] In his preface to this report, the Pulitzer Prize–winning *New York Times* reporter Neil Sheehan concluded: "The air war may constitute a massive war crime by the American government and its leaders."[8]

At the time, these voices were ignored. Today they have largely been forgotten. In the real world of the 1970s, there was no international body with the authority, much less the will, to call the United States to account for these crimes.

By fighting what became history's largest air war, the Pentagon made an important discovery. Through this massive bombing, the U.S. Air Force overturned the military dictum that only infantry can take and hold ground. Freed from the usual restraints, the air force was able to conduct an ad hoc experiment in aerial bombardment. "When the situation got close to desperate in June [1969] in Laos," Major General Robert L. Petit, deputy commander of the 7/13 Air Force, based in Udorn, Thailand, told the U.S. Congress: "Certain restrictions were removed and we were allowed to use air power in a little freer manner. We also had available at this time what might be termed a sufficient quantity of air power."[9] In effect, to compensate for the absence of ground forces, this new strategy required an aerial bombardment of unprecedented intensity, producing indiscriminate destruction that defied international law with regard to proportionality between damage and objective.

Significantly, this air-war strategy gained an additional advantage in the post-Vietnam era—minimization of American casualties as a military goal. In the decades since the end of the Vietnam War with its heavy, senseless U.S. casualties, the American people have become strongly adverse to even moderate troop losses, making a new force-projection strategy a domestic political imperative. In this air war over Laos, the United States had discovered a strategy for intervention without infantry and their inevitable casualties that has since become central to U.S. foreign policy in Iraq, Bosnia, Kosovo, and, most recently, Afghanistan.

In the quarter century since the Vietnam War, this strategy has placed the United States at variance with international law that, under Protocol I of the Geneva Convention, banned indiscriminate military force against a civilian society. U.S. representatives signed Protocol I to the Geneva Convention in 1977, but a decade later, President Ronald Reagan, under pressure from the Pentagon, recommended that the Senate reject this treaty.[10] In the thirty years since the United States bombed civilian villages in Laos, Washington has become wedded to an air-war strategy that weakens its leadership in the campaign for an international rule of law.

Of equal importance, in fighting this secret war in Laos from 1960 to 1974, the CIA supplemented its airpower with the secret army of thirty thousand Hmong—tough highlanders whose only cash crop was opium. Through its reliance on an ethnic warlord to mobilize these mercenaries, the agency became implicated in an opium trade that sustained the household economy of its tribal allies.

With only one U.S. adviser for every thousand tribal fighters in the mountains of northern Laos, the agency lacked the manpower for direct command and instead relied on a single warlord, a minor officer named Major Vang Pao, to mobilize the Hmong villagers for this bloody secret war.[11] To prosecute a war that offered the ordinary Hmong soldier little more than rice and death, the CIA gave its chosen warlord control over all air transport into the tribal villages scattered across the mountain tops of northern Laos—both the shipment of rice, the tribe's main subsistence commodity, into the villages and the transport of opium, the tribe's only cash crop, out to markets in Vientiane and beyond. With a chokehold over the two economic essentials of every Hmong household after 1965, General Vang Pao, now commanding both the CIA's Armée Clandestine and the Royal Lao Army's Military Region II, was soon transformed into a powerful warlord. With such control, the CIA's Armée Clandestine could impose a central command over this disparate tribe and extract boy soldiers from remote villages for slaughter in a secret war that was, for the Hmong, not only endless but hopeless.[12]

Since opium thus reinforced the authority of tribal leaders, pragmatism dictated that the CIA should tolerate the drug traffic. When Hmong officers loaded opium on the CIA's helicopters and the commander-in-chief of the Royal Lao Army, the genial General Ouane Rattikone, opened the world's largest heroin laboratory, the agency was silent. In a secret internal report compiled in 1972, the CIA's inspector general expressed "some concern" that "local officials with whom we are in contact . . . have been or may be still involved in one way or another in the drug business. . . . What to do about these people is a particularly troublesome problem, in view of its implications for some of our operations, particularly in Laos." The inspector identified some problematic military allies whose activities may explain the reasons for the agency's silence: "The past involvement of many of these officers in drugs is well known, yet their goodwill . . . considerably facilitates the military activities of Agency-supported irregulars."[13]

Instead of trying to restrain drug trafficking by its Laotian assets, the agency engaged in concealment and cover-up. When I went to Laos to investigate the drug trade in 1971, the Lao army's commander, General Ouane, cordially opened his opium accounts for examination, but the U.S. Embassy insisted that this same general had never been involved in the drug trade. When I was in a remote highland village investigating Hmong opium shipments on the agency's helicopters, CIA mercenaries ambushed my research team. Several days later, a CIA operative threatened to murder my Lao interpreter unless I abandoned my investigation. When my manuscript was in press, Cord Meyer Jr., the CIA's director of plans (a synonym for covert operations), visited my publisher's offices and insisted, unsuccessfully, that my book be suppressed.[14]

The consequences of such complicity detracted from the overall U.S. war effort in Vietnam. Heroin from these Laotian laboratories was smuggled into South Vietnam where, according to a White House survey, 34 percent of U.S. troops were addicted by 1971.[15] If we accept this figure, then there were some eighty thousand American heroin addicts in South Vietnam, far more than the estimated sixty-eight thousand addicts back in the United States—and all supplied by America's covert warfare allies.[16] After U.S. combat forces left Vietnam, Southeast

Asian syndicates followed the troops home and were, by 1974, supplying a quarter of U.S. demand with Golden Triangle heroin.

In Laos, we can see most clearly the problems involved in the CIA's use of war-lords to mobilize tribal armies. Leaders like General Ouane Rattikone exploited the CIA alliance to become drug lords, expanding opium production and export-ing refined heroin to international markets. Since ruthless drug lords made effec-tive anticommunist allies and heroin profits amplified their power, CIA agents did not tamper with the requisites of success in such delicate covert operations.

When the United States withdrew from Laos in 1974, it left behind a covert-warfare wasteland of the kind that we would see a decade later in Afghani stan. While the United States ended its conventional war in South Vietnam with a formal treaty that allowed for resolution of key issues such as POWs, Wash-ington quietly retreated from its covert battleground in Laos without any formal negotiations—whether for the return of any American POWs or for postwar re-construction. Statistics can only begin to describe the traumatic impact of this massive covert war on an impoverished Laotian society—over two tons of bombs dropped per inhabitant, an estimated 200,000 dead, some 3,500 villages destroyed inside the former communist zone, and refugee displacement of some 750,000 people, a quarter of the population. After a decade of bombing, northern Laos was covered with untold numbers of antipersonnel bomblets that still, even today, kill and maim hundreds every year.[17]

This weakened, traumatized society was captured by a harsh communist regime that still holds power. Hill farmers continued to grow opium under socialism, and, during the 1990s, Laos would become the world's third largest producer.[18] But contained between stable states—China, Vietnam, and Thailand—Laos's trauma, in striking contrast to Afghanistan's a decade later, did not ramify beyond its borders.

Afghanistan in the 1980s

The CIA's third covert war along the Asian rim began in 1979, when the Soviet Union invaded Afghanistan to save its client regime in Kabul. Seeing an opportu-nity to wound its enemy, Washington worked with Pakistan in a ten-year war to drive the Soviets out of Afghanistan. Instead of fighting this war directly as it had in Laos, the United States subcontracted much of its covert operations to Pakistan's Inter-Services Intelligence, or ISI, which would grow, through this operation, into an enormously powerful and problematic force in the region.

When the ISI proposed its Afghan client, Gulbuddin Hekmatyar, as over-all leader of the anti-Soviet resistance at its start in 1979, Washington—with few alternatives and less intelligence—agreed. Over the next ten years, the CIA supplied some $2 billion to Afghanistan's *mujahideen* through ISI, giving half to

Hekmatyar—a violent fundamentalist warlord who threw acid in the faces of unveiled Afghan women, murdered rival leaders, and dominated Afghanistan's heroin trade.[19] Once again, the CIA was mounting a major covert war in the remote highlands of the Asian opium zone. And, as it had done in Laos, the CIA fought this Afghan war through a single local commander, making its success synonymous with his power. Under such circumstances, the CIA had little leverage when its ally decided to exploit a covert operation to become a drug lord.

Within two years, ISI's covert supply system for delivering CIA arms to Afghan rebels had been inverted to move opium from Afghanistan's guerrilla zones, through heroin laboratories in Pakistan's North West Frontier Province, and then into international markets. As the *mujahideen* captured prime agricultural areas inside Afghanistan during the early 1980s, they pressed their peasant supporters to grow poppies as a revolutionary tax—raising production tenfold from 250 tons in 1981 to 2,000 tons in 1990.[20] Once the *mujahideen* brought the opium across the border, they sold it to Pakistani heroin refiners who operated under the protection of ISI's General Fazle Huq, governor of Pakistan's North West Frontier Province. By 1988, there were an estimated one hundred to two hundred heroin refineries in the province's Khyber district alone.[21]

Although this region had zero heroin production in the mid 1970s, by 1981 Pakistan had become the world's largest heroin producer. Reporting from Tehran in the mid 1970s, U.S. Ambassador Richard Helms, the former CIA director, insisted that there was no heroin production in this region—only a localized opium trade.[22] In 1981, by contrast, the U.S. Attorney General, William French Smith, announced that Pakistan was the source of 60 percent of the illicit American supply. Across Europe, Afghan-Pakistani heroin captured an even larger share of local markets.[23] In Pakistan itself the number of heroin addicts rose from near zero in 1979 to 5,000 in 1980, 70,000 in 1983 and then, in the words of Pakistan's own Narcotics Control Board, went "completely out of hand" to over 1.3 million addicts in 1985.[24]

At the outset of this operation in 1983, Washington's implicit choice to sacrifice the Drug War in order to fight the Cold War was articulated clearly during congressional hearings over the Reagan administration's request for $583 million in aid for Pakistan. In his testimony, Dominick DiCarlo, assistant secretary of state for narcotics, stated that General Fazle Haq, ISI's warlord of the North West Frontier, was pursuing opium eradication and warned that pressing our ally further on the issue would "be disastrous."[25]

With seventeen agents and a budget of $20 million between 1985 and 1988, the U.S. Drug Enforcement Administration (DEA) unit in Islamabad did not mount any serious investigations or participate in any major arrests while the CIA was operating in the North West Frontier—making the Afghanistan-Pakistan border, in effect, an enforcement-free zone. Indeed, in 1988, the U.S. Government Accounting Office reported that "not a single significant international Pakistani trafficker is known to have been imprisoned prior to 1984," and those jailed after that date "were quietly released after serving a few months."[26] In May 1990, as the CIA operation was ending, the *Washington Post* broke the media silence on this sensitive subject by publishing a page-one article, charging that the CIA's Afghan ally, Hekmatyar, was operating heroin laboratories in Pakistan under the protection of ISI.[27]

The former CIA director of the Afghan operation, Charles Cogan, has since admitted that his agency had sacrificed the Drug War to fight the Cold War. "Our main mission was to do as much damage as possible to the Soviets," Cogan told Australian television in 1995. "We didn't really have the resources or the time to devote to an investigation of the drug trade. I don't think that we need to apologize for this. Every situation has its fallout. . . . There was fallout in terms of drugs, yes. But the main objective was accomplished. The Soviets left Afghanistan."[28]

Since the United States had fought this war in Afghanistan covertly through the CIA, all the normal diplomatic processes of postwar reconstruction were aborted and the country was simply abandoned. After investing $2 billion in Afghanistan's destruction, Washington refused to invest any diplomatic or financial capital in its reconstruction. In effect, Washington just walked away, leaving Afghanistan deeply destabilized, with over a million dead, 4 million more driven into neighboring nations as refugees, 10 million land mines that killed and wounded 800,000 people, and well-armed tribal warlords primed to fight for land and power.[29]

Through this covert war, Pakistan was also destabilized by narco-politics that corrupted the already weak democratic forces; an intelligence service, the ISI, that had gained, through its alliance with the CIA and control over the heroin trade, unprecedented power inside the military; and radical Islamic parties that were working with the ISI to fight Pakistan's continuing covert wars in Afghanistan and Kashmir. After the United States withdrew, Pakistan continued to pursue its long-term goal inside Afghanistan of installing a Pushtun-dominated client regime in Kabul.

Afghanistan in the 1990s

During the 1990s, the aftermath of this covert war in Afghanistan and the simultaneous breakup of the Soviet Union combined to produce a decade of dramatic changes in Central Asia's drug traffic. As Afghanistan's opium production climbed relentlessly toward a record harvest of forty-six hundred tons in 1999, this war-ravaged land became history's first opium monocrop—that is, the first monocultural nation with much of its land, capital, water, and labor dedicated to the production of opium. Although the country was ravaged by war, its concentration of surviving resources in poppy cultivation was so intense that Afghanistan was soon producing 75 percent of the world's heroin.[30]

These rising heroin exports also financed a bloody civil war inside Afghanistan and fueled an eruption of ethnic insurgency across a three-thousand-mile swath from Central Asia to the Balkans—in Uzbekistan, North Ossetia, Chechnya, Georgia, Kosovo, and Bosnia. When the United States intervened in Afghanistan again at the end of this decade, it would find that its long-term goal of rebuilding stability was greatly complicated by the fallout from its last covert war of the 1980s.

During the 1990s, Afghanistan's soaring opium harvest fueled an international smuggling trade that knitted Central Asia, Russia, and Europe into a vast illicit market of arms, drugs, and money laundering—with drugs moving west toward Europe, while guns, money, and precursor chemicals headed east across Central Asia. In this three-thousand-mile journey to Europe by truck, camel, air, and sea, narcotics swept westward with stunning speed across a dozen boundaries, almost immune to interdiction or interference.

In 1998, the UN estimated that 42 percent of Afghanistan's harvest fed European and other distant markets, but the balance, 58 percent, sustained addicts within the region—three million in Iran, another two million in Pakistan, and lesser numbers in Tajikistan, Kyrgyzstan, and Kazakhstan.[31] Between 1990 and 1997, Iran's opium seizures along its Afghan border surged from 21 to 162 metric tons, forcing Tehran to close the border in 1998.[32]

After Iran and Pakistan absorbed the bulk of Afghanistan's opium harvest, the balance joined the traffic of some two hundred trucks moving northward daily from Jalalabad and Kabul toward the Tajikistan frontier—the first stage in a complex traffic that provided 90 percent of Europe's heroin supply during the 1990s.[33] Once across the Caspian Sea, Central Asia's diffuse routes merged as they entered the Caucasus with its volatile mix of contested boundaries, ethnic insurgency, local mafias, and criminal clans. From the Caucasus, drug shipments moved around and across the Black Sea into Turkey; and from there, now as refined heroin, into the Balkans, where rival ethnic militias used drug profits to purchase arms and pay troops.

During the mid 1990s, within Serbia and its satellite states, the notorious "Arkan" (Zeljko Raznatovic), one of several narco-nationalists backed by Belgrade's state security, used drugs, contraband, and counterfeiting to finance his "Scorpion" gang that terrorized Kosovo and murdered rival Kosovar drug dealers.[34]

From Skopje, Pristina, and Tirana, a Kosovar criminal diaspora smuggled heroin across the Adriatic into Western Europe, where Albanian exiles have, since the early 1990s, used drug profits to purchase Czech and Swiss arms for shipment back to Kosovo for the separatist guerrillas of the Kosovo Liberation Army (KLA). Even after the Kumanovo agreement of June 1999 settled the Kosovo conflict, the former commanders of the KLA, both local clans and aspiring national leaders, continued to dominate the narcotics traffic through the Balkans to Europe. In Switzerland and the Czech Republic, Kosovars controlled the local heroin trade, producing notorious criminals like Prince Dobroshi, one of Europe's leading traffickers, who used his heroin profits to purchase arms for the KLA until his capture in March 1999.[35]

Across these vast distances, ad hoc alliances within ethnic diasporas provided the criminal linkages to move drugs, guns, and cash—Kosovars scattered from Geneva to Macedonia, Turks from Berlin to Kazakhstan, Armenians from Moscow to Lebanon, Azerbaijanis from Sumgait to Kyrgyzstan, and Chechens from Baku to Kazakhstan. In the cities that served as trading posts in this traffic—Osh, Tashkent, Samarkand, Baku, Tbilisi, Skopje, Pristina, and Tirana—extraordinary profits from drugs and guns have produced mafia gangs, criminal diasporas, tribal warlords, and rebel armies.

Wherever this traffic touched ground, the illicit enterprise quickly ramified through drug production, official corruption, mass addiction, and HIV infection. The northern routes toward Russia touch ground in Kyrgyzstan, where they have fostered a lethal mix of intravenous injection and HIV infection, with 32 to 49 percent of all addicts in Osh sero-positive by October 2000.[36] In releasing the UN's annual AIDS review in November 2001, its program director, Dr. Peter Piot, highlighted an "explosion" of HIV from Eastern Europe to Central Asia with 250,000 new infections, largely from injected drugs, raising the total of those who are HIV-positive to over a million.[37]

During the 1980s, this flood of drug money had transformed Pakistan into a "narco-state"—corroding already weak democratic institutions and contributing to the later collapse of the governments under Benazir Bhutto (1988–90) and Nawaz Sharif (1990–93). Both were funded by drug lords whose unprecedented power came from a black-market commerce that accounted for some 30 to 50 percent of Pakistan's economy. With profits from its role as the CIA's intermediary and a continuing income from the Afghan-Pakistani heroin traffic, Pakistan's ISI won increased influence within the military, allowing it the autonomy to continue covert wars inside Afghanistan and Kashmir in alliance with militant Muslim parties.[38]

Following the withdrawal of the United States and Soviet Union from Afghanistan in 1992, Afghan rebels, armed with opium profits, plunged into a devastating civil war that ravaged an already weakened society. When the independent Northern Alliance forces took Kabul in 1992, Pakistan first backed its client Hekmatyar in two years of shelling and rocketing Kabul that left the capital ruined and some fifty thousand dead.[39] During this period of intensive civil war from 1992 to 1994, ruthless local warlords emerged to combine arms and opium in a brutal struggle for local power—almost as if the soil had been sown with dragons' teeth.

When Hekmatyar failed to take power, Pakistan's ISI armed a new force, the Taliban, which captured Kabul in September 1996 and then battled the Northern Alliance, with Pakistan's support, for control of the valleys beyond. During this protracted civil war, rival factions used opium to finance the fighting.[40]

After growing tenfold during the covert war of the 1980s, Afghanistan's opium harvest then doubled again during the civil war of the 1990s, reaching a record forty-six hundred tons in 1999.[41] During these two decades of warfare, Afghanistan was transformed from a diverse agricultural system—with herding, orchards, and sixty-two field crops—into an opium monocrop. With much of its arable land, labor, water, and capital devoted to opium, the drug trade became the dominant economic force shaping this nation's destiny. These twenty years of fighting, in effect, devastated Afghanistan's society and ecology. By 1992, fourteen years of covert and civil warfare had left behind—in a population of some 23 million—about 1.5 million dead, 4.5 million refugees, a full third of the total population displaced, and rural subsistence economies "deliberately destroyed."[42]

Lying at the northern extremity of the monsoon where the rain clouds are squeezed dry, Afghanistan is an arid land with a delicate human ecology that could not recover, unaided, from such unprecedented devastation. When the covert war started in 1979, the country's fragile ecosystem was already straining to carry a heavy population through a delicate balance of annual field crops, orchards, and herding. In these dry mountains where irrigation relies on snowmelt and droughts are regular, Afghan societies had long favored tree crops—walnut, pistachio, and mulberry—since they root deep, resist drought, and serve as famine relief in the periodic dry years. In the northern Nuristan Valley, for example, one walnut tree could sustain an adult for a full year.[43] In the early 1970s, a survey of 410 villages on the Shamali Plain near Kabul found that 91 percent grew wheat and 72 percent tended mulberry trees.[44] During these two decades of war, however, modern firepower ravaged the herds and destroyed orchards that would have survived the traditional warfare of centuries past, crippling this fragile ecology's capacity for recovery. Moreover, the Taliban, with an unerring instinct for their society's economic jugular, violated the unwritten rules of traditional warfare by destroying the orchards. In 1999, for example, the Taliban attacked the Northern Alliance's mass base by cutting down mulberry and walnut trees across a swath of ethnic-Tajik areas on the Shamali Plain, destroying life in once-prosperous villages and creating one hundred thousand refugees.[45]

As the strands of postwar devastation wove themselves into a Gordian knot of social, economic, and ecological suffering, opium became the Alexandrine solution. Without any aid to rebuild their ravaged herds and orchards after the covert war of the 1980s, farmers, including some three million returning refugees, now turned to opium, a reliable annual crop whose cultivation was already a part of traditional Afghan agriculture. Since opium required nine times more labor per hectare than the country's traditional staple, wheat, poppy cultivation created jobs at a time of high postwar unemployment. In 1999, opium offered seasonal employment for over a million Afghans—about a quarter of the potential labor force and possibly half of those actually employed.[46]

In this devastated economy, Afghan opium merchants could accumulate capital rapidly, which they used to provide poor farmers with crop advances equivalent to over half their annual income—credit critical to the survival of many poor villagers.[47] Finally in an arid ecosystem with chronic water shortage and periodic drought, opium had the advantage of needing far less water than food crops such as wheat.[48]

After the Taliban took power in 1996, its policies provided stimulus, both direct and indirect, for a nationwide expansion of opium cultivation, doubling production to forty-six hundred tons in 1999 and protecting complementary heroin processing. By eliminating bandits and capricious warlords who preyed upon the opium trade, the Taliban brought an order that allowed farmers and traders to work in a relatively stable regulatory environment.

During their first year in power, the Taliban began collecting a 20 percent tax from the nation's opium harvest, including both opium farmers and heroin refiners, earning revenues estimated variously at $20 million to $100 million. Farmers saw the regime's agricultural tax as implicit support for the opium trade and felt encouraged to expand cultivation.[49] As their commanders occupied the countryside, the Taliban soon controlled 97 percent of Afghanistan's opium. In some prime agricultural districts, particularly in Nangarhar Province, farmers began planting up to 60 percent of their arable land to opium.[50]

In retrospect, however, the Taliban's most important contribution to the illicit traffic was its support for the introduction of large-scale heroin refining. As Pakistan responded to American pressure by eradicating poppy cultivation and closing heroin refineries during the mid 1990s, heroin production moved westward across the border from Peshawar, Pakistan, to Jalalabad, capital of Afghanistan's opium-rich Nangarhar Province. There the Taliban protected hundreds of heroin labs clustered around the city in exchange for a modest production tax of seventy dollars per kilogram of heroin.[51]

Through their field surveys, UN researchers found that the Taliban presided over regional opium markets and a well-ordered drug export industry. Lying at the heart of the Helmand irrigation district, source of half of Afghanistan's opium harvest, Sangin's "free market" bazaar had some two hundred traders who specialized in the export of smoking-opium west across the desert into Iran. At the Ghani Kel bazaar in eastern Nangarhar Province, producer of a quarter of the country's opium, the trade was centralized under forty merchants who worked through Pushtun tribal connections to export heroin and morphine eastward into Pakistan.[52]

Significantly, the Taliban regime's ban on the employment and education of women created a vast pool of low-cost labor to sustain this accelerated expansion of opium production. In northern and eastern Afghanistan, women of all ages played, the UN found, "a fundamental role in the cultivation of the opium poppy"—planting, weeding, harvesting, cooking for laborers, and processing by-products such as oil.[53]

During the Taliban's first years in power, its leader, Mullah Omar, made periodic offers to both the UN and the United States to swap an opium ban for international recognition—overtures that gave the UN Drug Control Program access to Afghanistan for a failed attempt at opium eradication.[54] Although the Taliban promised a one-third reduction in cultivation, donors, including the United States, were unconvinced and provided only half the $16.4 million that the UN had requested.[55] In May 1999, Kabul's Anti-Narcotics Department finally announced a modest eradication effort in three districts of Kandahar, destroying only 325 hectares in a region with 5,602 hectares planted to poppy.[56] In sum, during the late 1990s, the Taliban's theocracy introduced policies that, by design and default, lent state support to the transformation of the country into an opium monocrop.

Afghanistan after 9/11

In July 2000, as drought brought mass starvation to Afghanistan, the Taliban suddenly ordered a total ban on all opium cultivation in a desperate bid for international recognition and support. With the drought reducing yields, the recently completed harvest was already down sharply to 3,276 tons of opium from the 1999 peak of 4,600 tons. But Afghan farmers usually hoard up to 60 percent of their harvest, so the country still had massive stockpiles to cushion the blow.[57]

Three months later, in an apparent bid for the Afghan seat in the General Assembly, the Taliban sent a delegation to UN headquarters in New York, where its Deputy Foreign Minister Abdur Rahman Zahid denounced the Northern Alliance government as a "band of thugs" who controlled the country's heroin traffic.[58] Though the UN ignored the Taliban delegation, crop surveys confirmed that the regime had indeed eradicated 99 percent of the opium in its territories. The CIA reported that Afghanistan's opium production had dropped from 4,042 tons in 2000 to 82 tons in 2001.[59]

A UN survey of 10,030 villages found that the Taliban, by enforcing its ban with mass arrests, had cut Afghanistan's opium harvest to only 185 metric tons in 2001—a 94 percent reduction that virtually eliminated opium in two of the country's three main opium districts. In the Taliban's two main opium districts, Helmand and Nangarhar, the reduction was over 99 percent. But in Northern Alliance areas, poppy planting more than doubled, making this opposition coalition the country's top drug lords with over 80 percent of Afghanistan's opium production and much of its heroin smuggling.[60]

In eradicating opium, the Taliban had destroyed the country's only surviving industry. By the time the Taliban banned opium in July 2000, Afghanistan had, by design and default, become dependent on poppy production for most of its taxes, all export income, and much of its employment. In this context, the Taliban's edict was an act of economic suicide that brought an already weakened society to the brink of collapse.

When the massive U.S. bombing campaign began in October 2001, a year after the opium ban, the Taliban regime collapsed with a speed that R. W. Apple of the *New York Times* called "so sudden and so unexpected that government officials and commentators on strategy . . . are finding it hard to explain."[61] Though the U.S. bombing did enormous damage, its role may have been catalytic, not causal—accelerating an ongoing internal collapse that might have eventually swept the Taliban from power without any foreign intervention. I would argue that the Taliban's economic evisceration left their theocracy a hollow shell of military force that shattered with the first American bombs.

The start of war with the United States in September 2001 ended the Taliban's opium ban. At the start of fall planting in early September, the Taliban announced an end to the opium prohibition over its Voice of Shariat radio, and UN observers soon saw peasants preparing poppy fields in Nangarhar and Kandahar provinces, the regime's heartland. Only days after the United States started military operations, local traders dumped their stockpiles on the market, sending opium prices down by 500 percent and filling gaps in global supply.[62]

As the Taliban collapsed in mid November, this dragons' teeth soil suddenly raised a new crop of warlords who used their drug money to arm fighters and seize territory. Using the covert-warfare doctrine first seen in Laos, Washington had deployed massive airpower and Special Forces as advisers to Afghan warlords—providing arms and money that reinvigorated local commanders after four tough years under the Taliban.

Across the country, the brutal warlords, eclipsed by the Taliban victory in 1996, re-emerged to fight for territory, seize food shipments, and smuggle drugs. Along the country's northern tier, the CIA delivered bundles of unmarked U.S. bills to mobilize Northern Alliance warlords, long active in the local drug trade, for attacks on Kabul and other key cities. In the southeast, the agency delivered money to Pushtun warlords, who dominated drug smuggling on the Pakistan border, to drive the Taliban out of their spiritual heartland. By the time the Taliban forces were in full flight, the CIA had distributed, through its agents and Special Operations forces, $70 million in "direct cash outlays on the ground in Afghanistan," an expense that President George W. Bush called one of history's biggest "bargains." But this was a bargain with a high hidden cost. After Taliban rule collapsed suddenly in November 2001, these same "corrupt and brutal" warlords quickly filled the political void by moving into towns and cities with thousands of militia armed from their arsenals, creating conditions ideal for the resumption of heroin trafficking.[63] In the northeast, the Northern Alliance's local commanders, who had long dominated drug smuggling into Tajikistan, expanded their territorial control. In the Pushtun-dominated southeast, former warlords, long active in the heroin trade with Pakistan, suddenly reappeared to seize local power.

Under the interim Eastern Shura government at Jalalabad, for example, the Pushtun warlord Hazarat Ali, notorious for opium smuggling when he ran the airport in the early 1990s, used his wealth to arm six thousand militia and capture the city, a center for heroin refining. In this same region, the overall warlord, Abdul Qadir, took control of Nangarhar Province where, in the early 1990s, he had once supervised over a rapid growth in opium production. Within weeks, the Eastern Shura's senior drug control official reported a burst of poppy planting in the heroin-heartland of Nangarhar Province.[64]

Further south in Kandahar, Gul Agha Shirzai, the pre-Taliban governor of the province, returned to power at the head of three thousand fighters after seven years on the Pakistan border engaged in what the *New York Times* called, with wry wit, "getting rich through commerce of a sometimes murky nature."[65] Thus, only weeks after the Taliban's fall, all of Afghanistan's key opium-producing regions—Helmand, Nangarhar, and Badakhshan—were again under the control of powerful drug lords.

Only days before the international donors conference at Tokyo in January 2002, interim prime minister Karzai issued a pro-forma ban on opium growing and heroin processing without any means to enforce it against the power of local warlords.[66] Indeed, in October the UN reported, from its field surveys, that the country's 2002 opium harvest had surged from 185 tons the year before to 3,400 tons—again the world's highest and the same level that it had been before the Taliban's poppy ban. Significantly, the UN estimated the value of this opium harvest, most of it under the control of local warlords, at $1.2 billion—an amount greater than foreign aid actually delivered to the Karzai regime in Kabul and an economic imbalance that helps explain both the political survival of these brutal commanders and the weakness of the central government.[67] In 2003, this pattern was, according to the UN, repeated with opium production rising to 3,600 tons and illicit drugs providing some $2.3 billion for Afghanistan, more than double foreign aid and nearly half the country's economic activity.[68] Once again, Afghanistan was in the grip of the warlords and its land given over to opium, arms, and warfare.

Conclusion

Looking back on these covert wars, I would argue that their unseen costs, once recognized and calculated, might be considered unacceptably high. During the Cold War, CIA agents allied with Asian warlords to wage covert wars that were catalysts for the region's opium traffic at several critical points in its postwar history.

In mountain ranges along the southern rim of Asia—whether in Afghanistan, Burma, or Laos—opium was a key element in the apparatus of local power. Once allied with the CIA, these warlords used the agency's protection to expand local opium production and become powerful drug lords. Focused on their covert mission, the CIA operatives usually ignored drug dealing by their assets. Once the CIA allied itself with one of these opium warlords, it could not afford to compromise an important covert-action asset with drug charges.

Respecting the national security imperatives of these covert operations, the DEA kept its distance from agency assets, whether in Afghanistan or Laos. Such implicit tolerance allowed covert-war battlefields to become enforcement-free areas where the opium trafficking could expand without restraint.

From a narrow Cold War perspective, such informal tolerance of drug dealing often amplified the CIA's operational effectiveness. As tribal societies mobilized to fight the CIA's secret wars, they diverted critical manpower from subsistence agriculture to combat. In effect, this diversion of labor from subsistence crops was covered by a rapid increase in cash-crop drug sales. From the CIA's viewpoint, narcotics income thus spared the agency the prohibitive cost of providing welfare for tribes with dependents numbering in the hundreds of thousands. Of equal importance, control over this cash crop allowed the CIA's chosen warlords to command tribes, clans, and villages in bloody campaigns that ground on for a decade or more. In sum, through its tolerance of the opium trade, the CIA's expenses declined and its operational effectiveness increased.

Looking back on these CIA covert campaigns, one sees a striking contrast between their short-term military gains and their long-term diplomatic costs. During each operation and its aftermath, there is a sharp rise in both opium production and heroin exports to international markets, including Europe and the United States.

Once the operation is over, both the market linkages and warlord power remain to make these regions major drug suppliers for decades to come. Of equal importance, the peculiar character of covert warfare denies its battlegrounds the elements of postwar reconstruction that often follows conventional combat. Since these secret wars are fought outside the normal diplomatic channels, their postwar rehabilitation remains beyond the realm of conventional international intercourse.

Even when covert warfare is followed by foreign aid, as it has been in Afghanistan since 2002, the costs of CIA covert warfare are still high. During the fighting, the combination of U.S. airpower and CIA alliances with Afghan warlords was, in a sense, the ultimate test of the new warfare doctrine developed in Laos thirty years before. In the short term, this strategic doctrine proved surprisingly successful in defeating the Taliban regime with just a few Special Operations forces and almost no American casualties. But this manipulation of Afghan society to advance the warlords, a tactic central to this covert warfare doctrine, left these corrupt commanders in control of the countryside once the fighting was over, creating a lasting source of conflict for both Afghanistan and Central Asia. Once again, CIA covert warfare, so successful in the short term, has left behind an ambiguous political legacy that may, yet again, make Afghanistan a source of regional and international instability.

In the absence of international aid, these highland societies often expand their opiate production as an ad hoc form of postwar reconstruction. Over time, narcotics not only sustain a traumatized society during its postwar recovery but also reinforce its isolation from legitimate resources of the international community. After CIA intervention in the 1950s, Burma's opium production rose from eighteen tons in 1958 to six hundred tons in 1970. During the CIA's covert war of the 1980s, Afghanistan's harvest increased from an estimated one hundred tons in 1971 to two thousand tons in 1991 and then kept rising to forty-six hundred tons in the war's aftermath.[69] A decade after the Cold War's end, the CIA's three covert battlegrounds along the five-thousand-mile span of the Asian opium zone—Afghanistan, Burma, and Laos—were, in that order, the world's three leading opium producers. Though small and remote, these covert-war wastelands can become significant sources of international instability—veritable wounds on the international body politic.

This history of covert warfare also raises some important questions about the CIA's future role in U.S. foreign policy. At the broadest level, this review of covert operations indicates some of the hidden political costs of investing an executive agency with extraordinary powers—a problem that American society has refused to address, in the aftermath of the Cold War, in a serious, sustained manner.

As the winner of the Cold War, the United States has been spared any painful self-examination, any need to question the methods used or price paid for victory. Alone among the major covert agencies that fought the Cold War, only the CIA survives unreformed, its files still sealed, its failings unexamined. Not only has the CIA survived, but it has parlayed its claims of victory over communism, and now terrorism, to win massive budget increases that make it one of the most powerful of federal agencies.

On its fiftieth anniversary in November 1997, the CIA looked into a future without communism and proclaimed its new missions as the fight against terrorism and international crime, particularly drug trafficking. As President Bill Clinton put it, the agency would be charged with "protecting American citizens from new transnational threats such as drug traffickers, terrorists, organized criminals, and weapons of mass destruction."[70]

As an intelligence, espionage, and covert-action agency, the CIA has developed an ingrained institutional culture of operating outside the law. Unless we are to adopt President Richard Nixon's option of wholesale assassination of drug lords, the CIA is ill-equipped for the fight against crime.[71] Unlike the FBI or DEA, the CIA simply does not have the experience to collect evidence within the law in ways that will allow successful criminal prosecutions.

The time may have come to put aside the comfortable self-assurance from our victories in the Cold War and the War on Terror and begin asking some hard questions about the CIA's future. Now that the Cold War is over, do we really need a CIA armed with the extraordinary powers that place it beyond the law? If so, do we want the CIA to fight the Drug War and the War on Terror with the same covert-action arsenal it used in the Cold War? Do we want the CIA to preserve its Cold War powers to conduct covert operations exempt from both legal restraint and legislative oversight?

As we saw in the 1980s and are seeing again in Afghanistan, the CIA's alliances with warlords cum drug lords were not just an aberration, not just an expedient born of the Cold War. To mount complex covert operations in remote foreign territories, CIA agents often seem to require the services of criminal assets skilled in what the CIA agent Lucien Conein once called "the clandestine arts"—that unique capacity, shared by spies and criminals, to conduct vast enterprises and major operations outside the bounds of civil society.[72]

Simply put, the CIA's liaisons with warlords, drug lords, and criminals are an integral part of its covert operational capacity. Now, more than a decade after the end of the Cold War, it seems that we are faced with some choices. We can either deny the U.S. executive the authority to conduct these extra-legal covert operations, or we can accept that these missions may well involve the CIA in criminal alliances and leave behind covert-warfare wastelands of the kind we have seen in Laos and Afghanistan.

Arguably, every nation needs an intelligence service to warn of future dangers. But should this nation have the right, under U.S. or international law, to conduct its foreign policy through clandestine operations involving bribes, black propaganda, murder, torture, criminal alliances, and covert warfare? The time may have come to put aside the complacency from our victories in the Cold War and the War on Terror and ask some hard questions about both the long-term costs of covert warfare and the future conduct of U.S. foreign policy.

NOTES

1. Arthur J. Dommen, *Conflict in Laos: The Politics of Neutralization* (New York: Praeger, 1971), 97–111, 200–222.

2. Hugh Toye, *Laos: Buffer State or Battleground* (London: Oxford University Press, 1968), 187–95.

3. Fred Branfman, "Presidential War in Laos, 1964–1970," in Nina S. Adams and Alfred W. McCoy, eds., *Laos: War and Revolution*, 242–50 (New York: Harper & Row, 1970).

4. Raphael Littauer and Norman Uphoff, eds., *The Air War in Indochina* (Boston: Beacon Press, 1972), 11, 199, 204.

5. Fred Branfman, *Voices from the Plain of Jars: Life Under an Air War* (New York: Harper & Row, 1972), 3–29; Arthur J Dommen, "Plain of Jars," in Spencer C. Tucker, ed., *Encyclopedia of the Vietnam War: A Political, Social, and Military History* (New York: Oxford University Press, 2000), 331; Walt Haney, "The Pentagon Papers and United States Involvement in Laos," in Noam Chomsky and Howard Zinn, eds., *The Pentagon Papers*, vol. 5 (Boston: Beacon Press, 1972), 275–79; Littauer and Uphoff, *Air War in Indochina*, 76–86, 204.

6. Branfman, *Voices from the Plain of Jars*, 127.

7. Littauer and Uphoff, *Air War in Indochina*, 82, 126–29.

8. Ibid., ix.

9. Ibid., 81.

10. U.S. Senate, 100th Cong., 1st sess., *Protocol II Additional to the 1949 Geneva Conventions, and Relating to the Protection of Victims of Noninternational Armed Conflicts* (Washington, D.C.: U.S. Government Printing Office, 1987), in *Senate Treaty Documents Nos. 1–10: United States Congressional Serial Set* (Washington, D.C.: U.S. Government Printing Office, 1989), iii–15; Hans-Peter Gasser, "An Appeal for Ratification by the United States," *American Journal of International Law* 81 (October 1987): 912–25; Barbara Crossette, "Parsing Degrees of Atrocity within the Logic of Law," *New York Times*, July 8, 2000, A15, 17; Adam Roberts and Richard Guelff, *Documents on the Laws of War* (Oxford: Clarendon Press, 1989), 273, 456.

11. *The Pentagon Papers: The Defense Department History of United States Decisionmaking on Vietnam*, Senator Mike Gravel edition, vol. 2 (Boston: Beacon Press, 1972), 646–47. For a discussion of Vang Pao's background and efforts to raise his social status among the Hmong, see Alfred W. McCoy, "The Politics of the Poppy in Indochina: A Comparative Study of Patron-Client Relations under French and American Administrations," in Luiz R. S. Simmons and Abdul S. Said, eds., *Drugs Politics and Diplomacy: The International Connection* (Beverly Hills, Calif.: Sage, 1974), 122–29.

12. Alfred W. McCoy, *The Politics of Heroin: CIA Complicity in the Global Drug Trade* (New York: Lawrence Hill Books, 2003), 305–31.

13. U.S. Senate, Select Committee to Study Governmental Operations with Respect to Intelligence Activities, 94th Cong., 2d sess., *Foreign and Military Intelligence, Book I: Final Report*, Report No. 97–775 (Washington, D.C.: U.S. Government Printing Office, 1976), 228–32.

14. For the details of the CIA's attempt to suppress my book, see, Alfred W. McCoy, "A Correspondence with the CIA," *New York Review of Books* 19, no. 4 (September 21, 1972).

15. U.S. Executive Office of the President, Special Action Office for Drug Abuse Prevention, *The Vietnam Drug User Returns: Final Report* (Washington, D.C.: U.S. Government Printing Office, 1974), 29, 57.

16. Edward Jay Epstein, *Agency of Fear: Opiates and Political Power in America* (New York: G. P. Putnam's Sons, 1977), 173–77.

17. Martin Stuart-Fox, *A History of Laos* (Cambridge: Cambridge University Press, 1997), 143–45.

18. U.S. Department of State, Bureau for International Narcotics and Law Enforcement Affairs, *International Narcotics Control Strategy Report* (Washington, D.C.: U.S. Department of State, March 2000, 53, 55; United Nations, United Nations Office for Drug Control and Crime Prevention, *Lao PDR: Extent, Patterns, and Trends in Illicit Drugs* (May 1999), 12, 22, http://www.odccp.org:80/laopdr/lao_pdr_country_profile.pdf (accessed October 31, 2001).

19. John F. Burns, "Afghans: Now They Blame America," *New York Times Sunday Magazine*, February 4, 1990, 37; Lawrence Lifschultz, "Dangerous Liaison: The CIA-ISI Connection," *Newsline* (Karachi), November 1989, 52–53.

20. U.S. Central Intelligence Agency, "Memorandum, Subject: Iran: An Opium Cornucopia," September 27, 1979; U.S. Department of State, Bureau of International Narcotics Matters, *International Narcotics Control Strategy Report* (Washington, D.C.: U.S. Department of State, February 1984), 4; U.S. Department of State, Bureau for International Narcotics and Law Enforcement Affairs, *International Narcotics Control Strategy Report* (Washington, D.C.: U.S. Department of State, March 1998), 23; *Geopolitical Drug Dispatch*, "Afghanistan: Aiming to be the Leading Opium Producer," no. 3 (January 1992), 1, 3.

21. Kathy Evans, "The Tribal Trail," *Newsline* (Karachi), December 1989, 26.

22. Richard Helms, From: U.S. Embassy Tehran, To: Department of State, Subject: "Revised Narcotics Action Plan," Date: March 4, 1974, Airgram, Department of State, in Eric Hooglund, ed., *Iran: The Making of U.S. Policy, 1977–1980* (Washington, D.C.: National Security Archives and Chadwyck-Healey, 1992), item no. 00849.

23. William French Smith, "Drug Traffic Today: Challenge and Response," *Drug Enforcement,* Summer 1982, 2–3.

24. Pakistan Narcotics Control Board, *National Survey on Drug Abuse in Pakistan* (Islamabad: Narcotics Control Board, 1986), iii, ix, 23, 308.

25. U.S. House of Representatives, Committee of Foreign Affairs, 98th Cong., 1st sess., *Foreign Assistance Legislation for Fiscal Years 1984–85,* 229, 234–35, 312–13, 324–25, 326–27, 500–504, 513, 528–29, 544–45, 548–50.

26. U.S. General Accounting Office (GAO), *Drug Control: U.S. Supported Efforts in Burma, Pakistan, and Thailand,* Report to Congress, GAO/NSIAD 88–94 (Washington, D.C.: GAO, February 1988), 25–34; Lawrence Lifschultz, "Inside the Kingdom of Heroin," *Nation* November 14, 1988, 495–96; Ahmed Rashid, *Taliban: Militant Islam, Oil and Fundamentalism in Central Asia* (New Haven: Yale University Press, 2000), 121.

27. *Washington Post,* May 13, 1990.

28. *Dealing with the Demon: Part II,* produced by Chris Hilton (Sydney: Aspire Films, 1994).

29. Virtual Information Center (VIC), *Afghanistan Primer,* September 25, 2001 (sent via e-mail from cschuster @vic-info.org); Rashid, *Taliban* vii, 126–27; Nigel J. R. Allan, "Impact of Afghan Refugees on the Vegetation Resources of Pakistan's Hindukush-Himalaya," *Mountain Research and Development* 7, no. 3 (1987): 200–202; *New York Times,* December 18, 2001.

30. U.S. Department of State, *International Narcotics Control Strategy Report* (March 2000), 56; United Nations, United Nations International Drug Control Programme (UNDCP), *Afghanistan: Annual Survey 2000* (Islamabad: UNDCP, 2000), 15.

31. Rashid, *Taliban,* 122; VIC, *Afghanistan Primer;* Alain Labrousse and Laurent Laniel, "The World Geopolitics of Drugs, 1998/1999," *Crime, Law, and Social Change* 36, nos. 1–2 (2001): 53.

32. Rashid, *Taliban,* 122, 124; United Nations, United Nations Office for Drug Control and Crime Prevention, Pakistan Regional Office, *Strategic Study #2: The Dynamics of the Farmgate Opium Trade and the Coping Strategies of Opium Traders,* http://www.odccp.org:80/pakistan/report_1998 (accessed October 11, 2001); Labrousse and Laniel, "World Geopolitics of Drugs, 1998/1999," 65.

33. Rashid, Taliban, 122, 124; United Nations, *Strategic Study #2;* Labrousse and Laniel, "World Geopolitics of Drugs, 1998/1999," 65.

34. *Geopolitical Drug Dispatch,* "Turkey: Routes Shift Still Further East," no. 61 (November 1996): 1, 3–4; *Geopolitical Drug Dispatch,* "Azerbaijan: Mafia Groups Settle Scores in Government," no. 44 (June 1995): 1, 3; *Geopolitical Drug Dispatch,* "Yugoslavia: Balkan Route Fuels War," no. 1 (November 1991): 1, 3.

35. Philippe Chassagne and Kole Gjeloshaj, "L'émergence de la criminalité albanophone," *Cahiers d'études sur la Méditerranée orientale et le monde turco-iranien* 32 (July–December 2001): 169, 182–86; Association d'Études Geopolitiques des Drogues, "Macedonia Serbia: Dangerous Liaisons," *Geopolitical Drug Newsletter,* October 2001, 2–4; Labrousse and Laniel, "World Geopolitics of Drugs, 1998/1999," 30, 150.

36. *New York Times,* April 2, 2002.

37. Ibid., November 29, 2001.

38. Miriam Abou Zahab, "Pakistan: d'un narco-Etat a une 'success story' dans la guerre contre la drogue?" *Cahiers d'études sur la Méditerranée orientale et le monde turco-iranien* 32 (July–December 2001): 147–53; Rashid, *Taliban,* 121–22; M. Emdad-ul Haq, *Drugs in South Asia: From the Opium Trade to the Present Day* (New York: St. Martin's Press, 2000), 213. Syed Saleem Shahzad, "US Turns to Drug Baron to Rally Support," *Online Asia Times,* December 4, 2001, http://www.atimes.com/ind-pak/CLO4Df01.html (accessed December 11, 2001.

39. *New York Times,* November 14, 2001, April 4, 2002.

40. Jason Burke, " The New 'Great Game,' " *Observer* (London), November 4, 2001; Emdad-ul Haq, *Drugs in South Asia,* 213; Michael Griffin, *Reaping the Whirlwind: The Taliban Movement in Afghanistan* (London: Pluto Press, 2001), 149; Abou Zahab, "Pakistan," 149–53; *New York Times,* December 8, 2001, May 29, 2002.

41. U.S. Department of State, *International Narcotics Control Strategy Report* (March 2000), 56; United Nations, *Afghanistan: Annual Survey 2000,* 15.

42. VIC, *Afghanistan Primer;* Rashid *Taliban,* vii, 126–27; Allan, "Afghan Refugees," 200–202; *New York Times,* December 18, 2001; Jonathan Goodhand, "From Holy War to Opium War? A Case Study of the Opium Economy of North Eastern Afghanistan," *Central Asian Survey* 19, no. 2 (2000): 266.

43. Nigel J. R. Allan, "Modernization of Rural Afghanistan: A Case Study," in Louis Dupree and Linette Albert, eds., *Afghanistan in the 1970s* (New York: Praeger, 1974), 117–18; Nigel J. R. Allan, "Human Geo-ecological Interactions in Kuh Daman, a South Asian Mountain Valley," *Applied Geography* 5, no. 1 (1985): 17.

44. Nigel John Roger Allan, "Men and Crops in the Central Hindukush" (Ph.D. diss., Syracuse University, 1978), 63–65, 92–94, 222.

45. *New York Times,* November 26, 2001.

46. United Nations, United Nations International Drug Control Programme (UNDCP), *Strategic Study #4: Access to Labour: The Role of Opium in the Livelihood Strategies of Itinerant Harvesters Working in Helmand Province, Afghanistan* (Islamabad: UNDCP, 1999), 2; *New York Times,* May 24, 2001, December 4, 2001; United Nations, *Afghanistan: Annual Survey* 2000, 23.

47. United Nations, United Nations Office for Drug Control and Crime Prevention, Pakistan Regional Office, *Strategic Study #3: The Role of Opium as a Source of Informal Credit,* http://www.odccp.org:80/pakistan/report_ 1999 (accessed October 30, 2001).

48. *New York Times,* November 26, 2001, March 12, 2002.

49. Rashid, *Taliban,* 119; Labrousse and Laniel, "World Geopolitics of Drugs, 1998/1999," 63–64; Association d'Études Geopolitiques des Drogues, "Afghanistan: Drugs and the Taliban," *Geopolitical Drug Newsletter,* October 2001, 1.

50. United Nations, United Nations International Drug Control Programme, *World Drug Report* (Oxford: Oxford University Press, 1997), ii; United Nations, International Narcotics Control Board, *Report of the International Narcotics Control Board for 1999* (New York: United Nations, 2000), para. 370–71, 49; U.S. Department of State, Bureau for International Narcotics and Law Enforcement Affairs, *International Narcotics Control Strategy Report* (Washington, D.C.: U.S. Department of State, March 1999); Labrousse and Laniel, "World Geopolitics of Drugs, 1998/1999," 62.

51. Rashid, *Taliban,* 119, 123–24; Labrousse and Laniel, "World Geopolitics of Drugs, 1998/1999," 63–64; Association d'Études, "Afghanistan,"1; *New York Times,* October 22, 2001; *Geopolitical Drug Dispatch,* "Afghanistan: Deceptive 'Destruction' of Laboratories," no. 90 (April 1999): 5–6.

52. United Nations, *Strategic Study #2.*

53. United Nations, United Nations Office for Drug Control and Crime Prevention, *Strategic Study #6: The Role of Women in Opium Poppy Cultivation in Afghanistan. June 2000,* http://www.odccp.org:alternative_development_studies (accessed October 31, 2001.

54. Griffin, *Reaping the* Whirlwind, 155.

55. *New York Times,* October 22, 2001; Rashid, *Taliban,* 123–24; *Geopolitical Drug Dispatch,* "Afghanistan: Deceptive 'Destruction,' " 5–6.

56. *Geopolitical Drug Dispatch,* "Afghanistan: Deceptive 'Destruction,' " 5–6; *Geopolitical Drug Dispatch,* "Afghanistan: Money Talks to the Taliban," no. 93 (September 1999), 7–8; United Nations, *Report of the International Narcotics Control Board for 1999,* para. 370–71, 49.

57. United Nations, *Afghanistan: Annual Survey 2000,* iii, 14; *New York Times,* December 16, 2001.

58. *New York Times,* September 21, 2000.

59. Ibid., October 22, 2001.

60. United Nations, *Afghanistan: Annual Survey 2000,* iii, 11, 15–17; *New York Times,* November 23, 2001.

61. *New York Times,* November 30, 2001.

62. Luke Harding, "Taliban to Lift Ban on Farmers Growing Opium if US Attacks," *Guardian* (Manchester), September 25, 2001; Kamal Ahmed, "Troops Will Target Drugs Stockpile," *Observer* (London), September 30, 2001; *New York Times,* October 22, 2001; *New York Daily News,* December 10, 2001.

63. *New York Times,* January 15, 2002; Bob Woodward, *Bush at War* (New York: Simon & Schuster, 2002), 35, 139–43, 194, 253, 298–99, 317.

64. *New York Times,* April 1, 2002, October 24, 2001, November 15, 2001, December 28, 2001, December 1, 2001, December 29, 2001; Luke Harding, "Taliban to Lift Ban"; Paul Harris, "Victorious Warlords Set to Open the Opium Floodgates," *Observer* (London), November 25, 2001; Syed Saleem Shahzad, "US Turns to Drug Baron to Rally Support."

65. *New York Times,* December 17, 2001, December 1, 2001; Peter Maass, "Gul Agha Gets His Province Back," *New York Times Sunday Magazine,* January 6, 2002, 34–37.

66. U.S. Department of State, Bureau for International Narcotics and Law Enforcement Affairs, *International Narcotics Control Strategy Report:2001* (Washington, D.C.: U.S. Department of State, March 2002), http://www.state.gov/g/inl/rls/nrcrpt/2001/rpt/8483.htm (accessed March 28, 2002), Southwest Asia; *New York Times,* January 17, 2002, April 5, 2002.

67. *Washington Post,* October 26, 2002.

68. "Opium 'Threatens' Afghan Future," BBC, October 20, 2003; "Opium Crop Clouds Afghan Recovery," BBC, September 22, 2003; Ian Traynor, "Afghanistan— At the Mercy of Narco-Terrorists," *The Guardian,* October 30, 2003; "Afghan Poppy Crop Leaping," Reuters News Service, November 28, 2003.

69. Chao Tzang Yawnghwe, *The Shan of Burma: Memoirs of a Shan Exile* (Singapore: Institute of Southeast Asian Studies, 1987), 57; U.S. Cabinet Committee on International Narcotics Control (CCINC), *World Opium Survey 1972* (Washington, D.C.: CCINC, July 1972), 10–11, 47; U.S. Department of State, Bureau of Interna-

tional Narcotics Matters, *International Narcotics Control Strategy Report* (Washington, D.C.: U.S. State Department, April 1994), 4; *Geopolitical Drug Dispatch*, "Afghanistan: Aiming to be the Leading Opium Producer," no. 3 (January 1992), 1, 3.

70. Alexander Cockburn and Jeffrey St. Clair, *White Out: The CIA, Drugs and the Press* (New York: Verso, 1998), 385–92.

71. Interviews with Tom Tripodi, special agent U.S. Drug Enforcement Administration, New Haven, Conn., March–April 1972.

72. Interview with Lieutenant Colonel Lucien Conein, McLean, Virginia, June 18, 1971.

GLOBAL UNCERTAINTIES

x/ p. 64 is blank

X/65

The second cluster examines dimensions of the war on terror and begins with the answers participants in the 2004 Tufts symposium gave to the question, "What do we know about the war on terror?"

Gwyn Prinz starts by defining terrorism. He distinguishes between "traditional" terrorists, such as the IRA, who have political demands that can be satisfied, and "unconditional terrorists," such as Al Qaeda, who have no such specific demands. He believes that the Islamic fundamentalists, who divide the world into themselves and infidels, have hijacked what he calls the Islamic revolution. Containment is no longer possible. For the West, he believes, preemption is a necessity "because it is a fight to a finish."

Stanley Heginbotham, who distinguishes between a "global war on terror" and the war on Al Qaeda (a largely invisible decentralized structure), observes that the war in Iraq has strengthened Al Qaeda and expanded the boundaries of its activities. The war rhetoric itself discourages analytic approaches to the extent that suggesting that modifying the cultural, social, and political conditions can moderate the threat of terrorism is "easily seen as bordering on disloyal." The war in Iraq, say John Cooley and Stephen Van Evera, was a mistake. It has broadened the base of support for Islamic fundamentalism, created problems for secular Muslim states, made democratization more problematic, and otherwise had unforeseen consequences that may radically alter the relationship between Western Europe and the Muslim world.

Indeed, this is a *political* insurgency, a war of propaganda, not of military victories. Insurgencies organized as guerilla warfare are fought over decades, not weeks or months. They ebb and flow. They are wars of will, not wars of numbers. Wars of what Antonio Gramsci, the Italian political theorist and activist, called maneuverability of position not on the field of battle but in the terrain of the mind.

Jonathan Schell calls the "war on terror" a subterfuge for the Bush administration's real agenda: establishing the United States as the global hegemon. The administration, he asserts, subsumed the issue of weapons of mass destruction with which the world has coexisted for more than fifty years, under the rubric of the war on terror. American foreign policy, he maintains, has undergone a fundamental and largely unchallenged change in focus: containment and deterrence, which sufficed during the Cold War, have been abandoned for preemption. In his view, the policy underwriting this change in direction, as set out in the administration's national security document, *The National Security Strategy of the United States,* represents nothing less than an assertion of "an absolute, permanent, global dominance." Imperial rule: endless imperial wars disguised as endless wars on terror.

Drawing extensively on the research findings of Arab scholars, Chris Patten argues

65

that the Arab world is not angry at Americans but at American policies, that Arab countries aspire to values similar to those close to American hearts, albeit often much discarded in the policies American governments pursue. This contradiction between what the United States purports to stand for and how it behaves is cause for the damning reactions it invokes in large parts of the Muslim world and much of the non-Muslim world. Sam Huntington's "clash of civilizations" thesis, he concludes, is at best a special case scenario of relations between the Muslim world and the Judeo/Christian West, an eventuality that depends on the triumph of the extremes.

The Islamic world, Patten points out, embraces both Islamic fundamentalism and political Islam. The Judeo/Christian world embraces both Christian fundamentalism and political Christianity. An ascendant West, however, tends to analyze cleavages in the Muslim world in western terms and thus both misunderstands the nature of the cleavages and prescribes "solutions" that insult the Muslim and aggravate differences between the West and Islam.

Patten sees a stand-off between Christianity and Islam emerging. Islam is the fastest growing religion in the world. In the latter part of the last century, the Pentecostal-Charismatic movement spread across the West, Africa, and Asia to over half a billion, making it the second largest expression of faith, second only to the Catholic Church. The statistical mean follower of Christianity today is under twenty, lives in Asia, and has a per capita income of less than six hundred dollars a year.

The Muslim world is dispersed, not a monolith poised to launch a jihad against the advance of Western civilization. While pockets of Islamic extremism exist here and there as epitomized by the quasi state, he cautions against extrapolating a particularized phenomenon into a coordinated global strategy subscribed to by Muslims in general.

Muslims should be part of Europe, not segregated but assimilated. Turkey should be part of the European Union. Christian and Muslim worlds will be joined in political wedlock, the bridging of East and West. Working with Arab scholars, the United Nations Development Program (UNDP) has drawn up a blueprint for laying the groundwork for democratization—not democratization in the narrow western sense but in the broader constructs of respect for the rule of law, institution building, and managing the interwoven complexities of modernization and tradition.

Greg Mills agrees with Patten's contention that "the clash of civilizations" postulate is a special-case scenario, but one, nevertheless, that has to be taken seriously unless the West, especially the United States, is seen by the Muslim world to be assisting in addressing its grievances, whether in Palestine, Kashmir, or Chechnya—tasks that almost certainly lie beyond America's capacity to dictate action. Of particular importance, he writes, is how Muslim states themselves contain radicalism, of which terrorism, as defined by the mostly non-West-aligned Muslim regimes, is but a particular manifestation.

How Muslim states themselves contain radicalism is increasingly important. The contradictory policies of the United States—the drive to export democracy to non-democratic countries, arguing that the values it embodies are the best antidote to the incubation of terrorism, coupled with its support for clearly authoritarian regimes that support its war on terror—encourage them to move slowly, if at all, and then only in response to what they perceive as internal threats to their own political hegemony.

At present, Pakistan is the coal face of the war on terror; the Pakistani military have penetrated the inaccessible corridors in the mountains of the northwest, straddling Pakistan and Afghanistan. Supposedly weeding out Bin Laden and Al Qaeda, agents of the Pakistani intelligence, the Inter-Services Intelligence of Pakistan, have penetrated terrorist networks. No one questions what methods the Pakistani military uses as it stalks the remnants of the Taliban. Respect for the rule of law does not get in the way of the tactics used to squeeze information out of not-so-cooperating Pathans. But to which rule of law should we refer adherance: *ours* or the Sharia law to which the local population subscribes?

Musharraf tries to simultaneously balance Islamic radicalization, poverty, corruption, and poor regional relations while civilizing his government, what Greg Mills calls the fine line between "keeping onside with the United States and maintaining legitimacy at home."

Calls on Musharraf to restore democracy capture the essence of our propensity to entrap ourselves in our own ideology. Mills suggests that dealing with the post-9/11 brand of Islamic terrorism will take at least a generation. "In Pakistan, attempts to confront Islamic militants through military clampdowns are complicated by the self-governing system outside of Islamabad's control in the North West Frontier Province." There is also "considerable local sympathy for Al Qaeda and other far-right religious groups in these tribal frontiers known as the *ilaqa ghair*—lawless country—to local Pathans."

Because radicalization has a social dimension, analysis should not discount both the extent of religious ideological content and the organization behind it—what regional conflict specialists describe as "spiritual poverty."

The International Institute for Strategic Studies published a report in October 2004 that offers a sobering assessment of Iraq. In the Muslim world the invasion and occupation of Iraq by the United States is seen as an attempt to change political systems in the Arab world to advance U.S. strategic and political interests. It has "enhanced jihadist recruitment and intensified Al Qaeda's motivation to encourage and assist terrorist operations." Hence, impetus for the attacks in Saudi Arabia, Morocco, and Turkey, the train attacks in Madrid, and the gathering of foreign fighters against the U.S.-led coalition. Al Qaeda is present in more than sixty countries. With an estimated eighteen thousand such "warriors" trained in Al Qaeda camps, the fighters in Iraq represented only "a minute fraction of its strength"; radical Islam is increasing in Western Europe where Muslims are feeling increasingly marginalized; the Iraq coalition lacks cohesion.[1]

The Pentagon's assessment of the strength of the insurgency indicated that that the United States had severely underestimated the number of fighters, the indigenous nature of the insurgency, and the access to financial resources. When foreign fighters and the network of the Jordanian militant Abu Musab al-Zarqawi were counted with home-grown insurgents, estimates put the hard-core resistance numbers between eight thousand and twelve thousand people, a tally that swelled to more than twenty thousand when active sympathizers or covert accomplices were included. The core of the Iraqi insurgency, it concluded, now consists of as many as fifty militant cells that draw on "unlimited money" from an underground financial network run by former Baath Party leaders and Saddam Hussein's relatives. Their financing is supplemented in great part by wealthy Saudi donors and Islamic charities that funnel large sums of cash through Syria. Only half the estimated $1 billion the Hussein government put in Syrian banks before the war has been recovered.[2]

In September 2005, the Saudi foreign minister, Prince Saud, came to Washington, D.C., to warn the Bush administration that Iraq was heading to disintegration, a development, he said, that could drag the region into war: "There is no dynamic now pulling the nation together. All the dynamics are pulling the country apart." The worry of Iraq's neighboring countries—Jordan, Syria, Turkey, Iran, and Kuwait, as well as Saudi Arabia—is that the potential disintegration of Iraq into Sunni, Shiite, and Kurdish states would "bring other countries in the region into the conflict." Turkey has long threatened to send troops into northern Iraq if the Kurds there declare independence. Iran is sending money and weapons into the Shiite-controlled south of Iraq and, according to Saud, would probably step up its relationship, should the south become independent. Saudi Arabia is wary of Iran's influence in the region, given that it is a Shiite theocracy. (Appearing before the U.S. Senate Armed Service Committee on September 29, 2005, General George Casey, the U.S. commander in Iraq, said that the Iraqi military had only one battalion—about six hundred soldiers—capable of fighting on its own and that insurgents had infiltrated both the Iraqi police and military.)

Exponentially increasing levels of globalization mean that any unilateral actions on the part of any state have multilateral consequences that are not always within its competence to control. Accordingly, whenever the United States acts unilaterally it exposes itself to unpredictable fallouts that may often severely compromise the intended purpose of its actions. These unintended consequences may alter the nature of the intended outcome itself.

One can provide no better example than Iraq. Since parliamentary elections in December 2005, Iraq has been enveloped by either creeping or outright civil war, depending on one's definition, savaged by violence, increasing sectarianism, and the blurring of lines between religious paramilitaries and the state's nascent security forces. It is high1ly doubtful whether the national unity government, cobbled together under Prime Minister Nuri al-Maliki after months of horse trading among Iraq's ethno-religious nationalisms, can douse the fire of insurgency and prevent the slide into sectarian chaos. The free-floating hope that the trophy head of Abu Musab al-Zarqawi might somehow defuse the insurgency is premised on the false assumption that the insurgency has a center. In the ultimate ironic twist to unintended consequence, Nuri al-Maliki, within weeks of taking office in May 2006, accused the U.S. military of engaging in killing sprees against civilians as a "regular phenomenon."

The French riots should be a wake-up call for Europe. With 4 million Muslims in France, 2.5 million in Germany, and 1.75 million in the United Kingdom, "othering" is pervasive. Compounding the problem for policymakers is the fact that Muslim communities, even second generation, have chosen to live outside the mainstream and have not been assimilated; nor have they sought in any obvious way to be assimilated into national identities that are in many respects founded on value systems (liberal and secular) that are antithetical to the value systems Islam espouses.

For many Muslim communities Islam is the basis of identity. Polls in Islamic and Arab countries show that people take their primary identity from being Muslim, and only then identify themselves as Moroccans or Saudi Arabians.[4] The French writer Amin Maalouf coined the expression "wounded identity" to refer to people's propensity to see themselves in terms of whichever of their multiple allegiances is most under attack.[5] For centuries Islam was a vibrant and innovative civilization. The change came only when the balance of power politics tilted to the west and the West supported tyrannical regimes primarily in the interests of cheap oil and the containment of Soviet expansionism in the region, thus subverting indigenous nationalisms and creating the political space for Islamic extremism to flourish.

In Russia, the Islamic "threat" is perceived in terms of its capacity to undo the country itself. Chechnya separatism has taken on an Islamic character. The Russian crackdown in Chechnya (91 percent Muslim) is having spillover effects in other republics with large Muslim populations—Bashkortostan, 63 percent; Tatarstan, 54–68 percent; Dagestan, 85 percent; Ingusheta, 63 percent; Kabardino-Balkariya, 78 percent; Karachayevsk-Cherkessia, 92 percent. The Muslim Spiritual Department appoints Islamic leaders and Muslims who practice their religion outside of state-sanctioned mosques are routinely harassed and detained.[6]

The essence of Bin Laden's grievance, some suggest, is that "the West has placed its business interests over popular sovereignty in the Middle East for 80 years. Middle Eastern oil will be important for another 80 years. With 1 billion followers of Islam in the world, listening to the other side has never been more important."[7]

In the United Kingdom, after the suicide subway bombings on July 7, 2005, that killed fifty-four people, the British were as traumatized by the fact that the bombers were British citizens, born and raised there, not immigrants. They spoke with British accents, lived ordinary lives in middle-class communities; two had wives and children; one, Mohammad Sidique Khan, was a highly respected teaching assistant and community activist. These were not foreigners; they were *themselves*. They were not poor and underprivileged, uneducated, unemployed. So what drew them to Islamic extremism? Making trips to Pakistan and attending a *madaris*? Spiritual poverty? In a prerecorded video released by Al Qaeda some weeks after the bombings, Khan explained their motives: The Americans and British had rained bombs on their Muslim brothers and sisters, indiscriminately killing. When the British people reelected Tony Blair and the Labour Party in May 2005, they had given their approval to his government's actions and thus, they, too, were legitimate targets of death. The individual with the homemade bomb is as powerful as the Stealth bomber. And we are more afraid of him.

Padraig O'Malley

NOTES

1. International Institute of Strategic Studies, London, October 2004.
2. *New York Times,* October 20, 2004.
3. Ibid., September 23, 2005.
4. David Gardner, "The Politics of Wounded Identity," *Financial Times,* July 29, 2005.
5. Amin Maalouf, *On Identity* (London: Harvill Press, 2000).
6. *Sunday Times* (South Africa), December 11, 2005.
7. David Warsh, *Boston Globe,* October 14, 2001.

X/ # The War on Terror * Source

GWYN PRINS   Terrorism is very strange, very frightening, and appears amorphous, so I want to try to bound the problem. We need to know what it is that we are talking about. Just before 9/11, I chaired a study for the U.K. Ministry of Defense that gave us the opportunity to review what everybody was saying at that time in the open and in some of the not-open literature. In the open literature, without any question, the best study on terrorism that was published before September 11, 2001, was by the Norwegian Defense Search Agency. It pointed out that we were moving into a world in which the security threat to industrial countries from terrorism was most likely to come from what they called "low-probability high-impact events," precisely the sort that happened on that September morning.

What we did in the study, however, was to define quite closely what we mean by terrorism and what we do not mean by terrorism. So the first part of the proposition is that a terrorist act is, by definition, an act by a nonstate actor. That means that the loose talk about state terrorism is strictly nonsense; it cannot happen. States cannot be terrorists. States do something much worse; they commit Terror with a capital T: the Committee on Public Safety in the French Revolution, Stalin, Mao. Terror has killed in history far more people than terrorism, and today there is no change from the trends of the 1990s, which is that terrorism as a secular phenomenon in the world is in decline in terms of absolute numbers of attacks and numbers of people killed also.

Second, terrorist acts are acts that are aimed deliberately at randomly chosen victims. These are not targeted assassinations. The very point of the terrorist act is that everyone should know that he or she is a potential target because, third, the acts are committed with the intention of compelling involuntary political change; people being made to do things that they would not otherwise want to do. And I suggest that those three are actually rather useful bounding parameters for the concept.

Terrorism, in the narrower sense that I have defined it, comes in two variants: conditional and unconditional. Conditional terrorism occurs when a terrorist has a political demand that can be satisfied; that was the position with the FLN in Algeria—they wanted the French out, they wanted an independent Algeria. It was the position with the IRA in Northern Ireland—they wanted the British out; they wanted a united Ireland. It is the position with the Tamil Tigers, and so on.

From the EPIIC Symposium at Tufts University, "Dilemmas of Empire and Nationbuilding," February 2004

Conditional terrorists are quite different from unconditional terrorists in the way in which they behave and the way in which they have to be handled, because unconditional terrorists are people who have no specific demand of you and me because we are infidels and we deserve to die. As the convicted leader of the Aum Shinri Kyo cult in Japan pointed out at the beginning of his trial, the only thing that they were trying to do was to kill very large numbers of people. They did not succeed, fortunately, but that was what they were trying to do.

Now what tactics are available? Clearly type-A, conditional terrorism can be addressed in a number of ways because if you are the British government and you are confronted with the IRA you could capitulate. There are many people who think that that is exactly what Tony Blair did with the so-called Good Friday Agreement, that he effectively gave the IRA what they were asking for and therefore they stopped doing further nasty things. Another interpretation of the Good Friday Agreement is that you can bribe a conditional terrorist, you can offer that person something to desist; it may be political, it may be other. If you do not want to deal with the person at all, you can contain that sort of terrorist; you just throw a cordon of some sort such that they cannot get out and they cannot hurt others. Possibly, you can deter such a terrorist. I say "possibly" because I think it is much less clear that deterrence is an open course of action. And, of course, you can get to them before they get to you. You can take preemptive action, which will often, for terrorists, mean assassination. Those are the options that you have for dealing with conditional terrorists.

When you turn to type-B, unconditional, terrorists, the ones that we are now mostly worried about, your options are much more limited. You can possibly contain, you can make sure that Mr. bin Laden does not get out of the hill country of northern Pakistan and southern Afghanistan. But the surest way of dealing with unconditional terrorists, and clearly the tactic of choice, is preemption, because with these people there is no compromise possible. It is a fight to the death.

Our concern here is very much in the second, B, category. So I want to offer some thought, briefly, to what has made Islamic unconditional terrorism the sort that preoccupies so many in the West now. We live in strange times, and one characteristic of the present is that we have five continuing unfinished revolutionary processes going on in the world: unfinished revolutions in Eastern Europe (by my count, the third revolution since the end of communism in Russia); the European revolutions surrounding the end of the European Union; two sorts of revolution in Asia, some to do with China, some with the Asian Tigers; and Islamic revolution, the unfinished questions about whether Islam can find a way to live viably with modernity.

But this is happening in a world that has changed in fundamental ways. Ours is a world with new actors and new factors. The actors are well enough known. We have large-scale multinational corporations, and we have empowered individual actors who are new in the political order, and what makes both of them possible is information. Empowering individuals, making possible the leverage that people get from the control and access to information, makes possible two very important processes: systematic synergisms bringing together things that otherwise might not, and risk cascades.

On September 11, Islamic revolutions were able to come together with systemic synergisms to produce a risk cascade. In military terms the will, which was implacable, was able to be linked to means, and the means—and the technical military brilliance of the attack of September 11 lay in the use of the means—was such that the terrorists themselves had to do virtually nothing. The timing of the operation was produced by the ABC airline guide; the skills were provided by flying schools in the United States. The timing of the attacks was clearly intended to produce the picture that you all saw, many of you, I am sure, in real time as it happened, and, of course, you will recollect that just before that airplane hit the tower the pilot pulled it up; he was going at maximum speed in the dive and then he pulled it up about twelve stories. I was advising ITN [International Television Network] at the time. We quickly called in a structural engineer and said, "What would you do if you wanted to knock down that tower?" And the answer is that you would hit it at exactly the point where the airplane hit it. Why? Because you have to melt the metal, and then with enough weight above, you produce an effect that will drive down the tower. Osama bin Laden was trained as a structural engineer. His company, his family's companies, are very large in Saudi Arabia.

Subsequently, we have had from Al Qaeda the bombs in Bali and Saudi Arabia, the UN bomb in Iraq that killed the future Secretary-General of the UN, the Red Cross bomb that drove the Red Cross out of Iraq, and two sets of Turkish suicide bombs. What these do, I suggest, is that they underline the common threat to the West and its friends.

Now, there are the other consequences of the Islamic revolution as interpreted by Islamic fundamentalists who render it as a very simple black-and-white question. The world for them is divided into Dar al-Islam and the world of war in which we, the infidels, live; and we, as infidels, deserve only one thing, which is death. The only circumstance under which we will be spared is if we consent to the status of the infidel whose life is spared by the caliph, who, in his mercy, allows that person to live as a slave in a condition of complete and abject political subordination. That is effectively the choice that is put to those of us in the West by this group, which is why it is a fight to the finish.

The final point that I would make is something very important about the nature of the political dynamic that terrorists attacks face. There is a piece of mathematical topography called a cusp catastrophe. The upper surface is safe to walk along—it goes up and down a little, but it is not dangerous. Whereas, if you walk along the lower surface, there is a serious risk that you will, at a certain unpredictable point, fall over the edge. So you start out and you do not know that you are walking into danger, but if you continue, you go over the cliff. That is what happened with September 11. If you take a course of action that leads you back to the safe slope, then you will find that you have not put yourself into danger.

The key question for all strategic analysts, all intelligence departments in the world today, is where are we in that circle? Where are we now, and where are we going? Those are the questions we have to answer with regard to terror and terrorists—two different phenomena. In particular, with regard to the question of unconditional terrorism, we have to decide whether we have any options other than the two that I have mentioned: containment and preemption.

STANLEY HEGINBOTHAM We are not in a global war on terror. In reality, we are at war with a largely identifiable enemy, Al Qaeda and its associated organizations and institutions. This enemy has attacked the United States primarily because of what it sees as American cultural, economic, and military imperialism in the Arab Moslem world. The command structure of the enemy is physically located in the mountainous, remote, and historically ungoverned—and many would say ungovernable—North West Frontier province of Pakistan and adjacent areas in Afghanistan. That command structure is highly decentralized. It has institutionalized mature organizational patterns because many of its elements evolved in the insurgency against the Soviets in Afghanistan and in subsequent insurgencies.

We are told that we are in a "global war on terror" because this is a rhetorical device that serves the Bush administration's narrowly conceived national security and political goals. One can argue, "OK, Bush is president; he wants to lead; he wants a slogan that's catchy and is going to get our attention. Is there anything wrong with that?"

Yes there is. It is damaging, dangerous, and misleading to simply repeat, "We're in a global war on terror." We need to be specific about what we are fighting because it is a very important enemy and it deserves careful and focused attention.

The success of the Bush administration's "global war on terror" rhetoric in diverting our attention from our real enemy has had three identifiable negative consequences for U.S. national security. First, that rhetoric provided the justification for initiating the war on Iraq. Iraq was defined in the president's national security statement as a rogue state that not only was hostile to all aspects of American society but also sought weapons of mass destruction to distribute to terrorist organizations. This was not an empirical finding on the part of the administration; it was an assertion, a statement of belief. But the war on Iraq had nothing to do with the war on the terrorist organizations that are the core of the American enemy. And more important, the war on Iraq diverts both public attention and enormous amounts of national security resources away from the legitimate war we should be giving priority: the war on Al Qaeda and associated terror organizations.

This displacement of the war on Al Qaeda onto the war on Iraq was a calculated strategy. Bob Woodward, in his book *Bush at War,* reproduces something close to a transcript of the early National Security Council meetings right after 9/11. It contains arguments made by Condoleezza Rice and Donald Rumsfeld to the effect that we are in trouble because there are no reasonable targets in Afghanistan and it is going to be very hard to identify solid targets in that country. Rice, a Soviet military expert, certainly knew that U.S. troops—like the Soviet Army before it—were likely to get bogged down in Afghanistan. She and Rumsfeld agreed that we needed a diversion. It is important to remember that we went into Afghanistan not to fight the Taliban but to destroy Al Qaeda. Taliban was an impediment to reaching Al Qaeda. We have failed to win the war against Al Qaeda, in large measure because the war against Iraq has diverted national resources away from that war. We do not have the resources to do both Iraq and Al Qaeda, and we have chosen to fight the wrong war.

Second, the war on Iraq has, in two identifiable ways, increased the threat of anti-American terrorism. We have solved for Al Qaeda a central challenge faced by terrorist organizations: How do we reach meaningful targets? We have delivered right to the Iraqi doorstep of Al Qaeda and its associated organizations the extraordinary gift of a whole range of American targets and institutions as well as a set of Iraqi institutions that are seen as complicit with the American occupation. And we have effectively strengthened the terrorist attacks by dramatically enhancing the recruitment pool for Islamic terrorists in general and for Al Qaeda specifically. Our invasion and occupation of an Arab country has encouraged anti-American elements to support, protect, and join Al Qaeda and its extremist allies.

The third negative consequence of the administration's global war on terror rhetoric is that it has created an intellectual and policy climate that discourages open analytic approaches to terrorism and terrorists. When one is "at war" with global terrorists, policy advocates are under great pressure to reify the enemy: Terrorists are evil, they are unremittingly hostile to all aspects of American culture and society, they need to be fought and destroyed. To suggest—as is patently true—that terrorists or terrorist organizations are products of cultural, social, and political conditions and that modifying those conditions can moderate the threat of terrorism is easily seen as bordering on disloyal.

At the risk of being accused of being disloyal, then, let me conclude with four points about terrorists and terrorism that provide guidance for how we should be fighting our real enemy. First, the resort to terrorism is an act of political despair. It is a form of acting out against political powers that are seen as repressive and unassailable by political or conventional military means. It is the ultimate asymmetric tactic of the weak and of those who perceive themselves as intolerably weak. Humiliation is often a central component of those who are pushed to the extreme of becoming terrorists. I cannot overemphasize the enormous sense of humiliation and weakness that is felt by elements of the Arab world that I have been familiar with since I lived in Israel in the early 1950s. Organizational and military weakness and ineffectualness in dealing with the West are sources of enormous frustration, humiliation, and rage among many Arabs. Militant extremism and terror often seem the only plausible instruments for expressing this rage.

Second, terrorism is rooted not only in constructed identities but also in constructed ideologies. Islam has provided an important source of historical and religious doctrine that emphasizes past deprivations and the legitimacy of extremism as a means of punishing the West and demonstrating Arab effectiveness.

Third, the ideological and religious worlds of the terrorist may or may not bear much relationship to the real world. Certainly, much of what Al Qaeda and the Islamists believe bears little relationship to the real world. Other aspects of their world views, however, are grounded in reality, and in some cases terrorists are pushing for satisfaction that is quite reasonable. This calls for us in the West to recognize that when Arab extremists use unacceptable means of pursuing legitimate goals, we need to seek out and accommodate Arabs who are using reasonable tactics for pursuing those goals.

Fourth, a central tactic of terrorists is to push to the extremes and to destroy moderates—on their own side as well as that of their nominal adversaries—who offer accommodation and compromise. The Tamil Tigers in Sri Lanka, for example, directed much of their terror against moderate Tamils because the Tigers wanted to eliminate the possibility of compromise solutions.

We have heard much about military and intelligence activities that are very important aspects of anti-terrorist strategies: activities such as protection of vulnerable targets, proactive attacks on the structures of terrorist institutions, and the strengthening of human intelligence that can penetrate terrorist organizations. But a balanced strategy requires that we also work to modify the context and the perceptions within which terrorists and potential terrorists operate. In the Middle East we want to avoid increasing the levels of humiliation of Arabs. Rather, we want to build a sense of confidence and autonomy among Arabs, and we want to promote and encourage indigenous alternatives to extremist ideologies.

JOHN COOLEY President George W Bush's war on terror has, since 9/11, become the main concern of his administration. In one of his rare, longer interviews, the one with *Meet the Press* on February 8, 2004, Tim Russert never asked the president about terrorism or what the word *terrorism* means. However, Mr. Bush used the word or its variants twenty-two times by my count in that interview. Well, very few American politicians or commentators that I have noticed have dared to question the conventional wisdom that terrorism, or as our Israeli allies often prefer to call it, simply "terror," is the greatest threat facing the world. There is no agreed definition of terrorism. The word is so subjective that it can mean all things to all men while at the same time it is, through excessive use and abuse, becoming devoid of any real inherent meaning. We use it and abuse it by applying it to whatever we dislike or hate. This can be useful in fighting terrorism defined as objectionable political violence. The danger comes when people—whether governments, politicians, or even law enforcement officers—use the word *terrorism* as a way of avoiding rational thought and discussion and sometimes excusing their own illegal and immoral behavior.

One classic literary case, paradigm if you like, of terrorism is Joseph Conrad's short novel, published around 1920, called *The Secret Agent.* A diplomat of an unnamed rogue state, perhaps belonging to a contemporary axis of evil, instigates a group of people to commit acts of "destructive ferocity so absurd as to be incomprehensible, inexplicable, almost unthinkable, in fact mad." The rogue states' purpose is to stir the British and other western governments to take extreme repressive measures. These measures would violate human rights to such an extent that the masses would embrace a widespread transnational revolutionary movement that will sweep simultaneously through Western society and overthrow the established order. Conrad's story ends with both a bang and a whimper. The first chosen target of these terrorists' weapons of mass destruction, a bomb, is to be that Victorian-era symbol of scientific progress, the Observatory at Greenwich outside London. The bomb kills the inadvertent suicide bomber before he can reach the observatory. This is the bang. The whimper is the dissolution of the little group of would-be terrorists, some of whom scramble for safety and lose their lives in the process.

Although 9/11, by its huge scale, the number of its victims, and its careful planning was certainly a first in these categories, it was not a first in American history. On September 16, 1920, at lunchtime in New York City a horse-drawn wagon pulled up outside J. P. Morgan and Company offices in Wall Street. About one hundred pounds of dynamite remotely detonated blew people and vehicles into the air and scattered half a ton of steel shards from steel window sashes in the wagon for blocks around. Forty people were killed and about three hundred maimed or wounded. It was a horse-and-buggy equivalent of Timothy McVeigh's Oklahoma City attack. The *St Louis Post Dispatch,* perhaps ignoring the possible targeting of J. P. Morgan, reported, "There was no objective except general terrorism." The bomb was directed against the public, anyone who happened to be near. The Wall Street attack stunned an American public already traumatized by a world war, a flu epidemic, and fear of labor riots, immigrants, Bolshevik infiltrators, and bomb-throwing anarchists. A red scare gripped the country. In some ways it resembled the anti-Arab and anti-Muslim hysteria that followed 9/11.

Terrorism whether in the United States or abroad is a label applied more and more frequently these days to three quite different, quite separate kinds of threats and actions. The first is simply the criminal act of psychopaths like the murderer Charles Manson and his so-called family in California a generation ago. To outsiders, at least, such crimes seem to be aimless, violence for the sake of violence.

The second kind is politically directed action with such generalized motives that uninitiated observers sometimes have difficulty understanding or responding. Here we are reminded of Conrad's cabal of London terrorists. Osama bin Laden's original Al Qaeda movement stemming from the anti-Soviet jihad in Afghanistan may fall in this second category. For all of his theocratic fatwas, communiqués, and tirades, bin Laden, to my knowledge, has never provided a really clear definition of exactly what he is for and what he is against, at least in terms that non-Arab minds and the minds of many Arabs and Muslims as well can readily understand.

The third category is specific in objectives, clear in motivation: anticolonial liberation and various other national movements, usually secular. My own first encounter with this kind of violence was when I lived as a young reporter in North Africa in the early fifties. Morocco was still under French colonial protectorate. I was living in Casablanca; the French settlers lobby in Morocco in 1953 had prevailed on the government in Paris to exile the popular king of Morocco, Mohammed V, who had been promised, apparently by Franklin D. Roosevelt at the wartime Casablanca conference in 1943, that Morocco, like other colonies, would win its freedom and independence. The National Democratic Party began to resort to violence; they blew up a café in my Casablanca days, killing several friends of mine. This was the prelude to years of covering much, much more violence in the eight-year Algerian war and afterward through three decades of Palestinian-Israeli conflict and several wars between Israel and the Arabs.

What can be done? First, the psychopaths. Any society contains marginal people who are or who can become violent with or without a cause. Some societies have tolerated or even venerated it. Think of the huge sums expended and the pleasure people derive from books, articles, films, and videos about warriors and gunslingers such as, to name just one recent example, the Hollywood film of Martin Scorsese, *The Gangs of New York*.

In the second loose category of violence, unless we include bin Laden and Al Qaeda, which in some ways would seem to fit in all three categories, one main objective seems to be money. The Mafia and organized crime in general and the virulent Mafia clones in Russia and in overseas communities of ethnic Chinese, Latin Americans, and others seem to have this objective.

The second category spills over into the third one, that of politically directed terrorism. Even the toughest imaginable American city mayor could not conceive of bombing Harlem because it houses drug dealers or downtown Miami because Colombian drug merchants may operate there. However, the Bush administration could and did invade Afghanistan for harboring bin Laden and followers, once our trainees and allies, not in George W. Bush's war on terror, but rather in the war against what we then called "world communism." The same type of people, in some cases the same people or their sons or heirs who trained in CIA or Pakistani military camps to use terrorism against the Soviet occupiers of Afghanistan, are now to be found in a prison camp of unlawful combatants in Guantánamo Bay. The veterans of the CIA-managed jihad against the Russian invaders of Afghanistan became the extended family, which bin Laden and company gradually molded into Al Qaeda, now a very loosely linked band of brothers.

Afterward, Al Qaeda and its hangers-on rebelled against corruption and worldliness of the Saudi ruling family and its supporters inside and outside the kingdom. America became a target, primarily at the beginning, I think, because of its unconditional support for the Saudi royal family.

My final point, based on my own past experiences in places like Algeria, Iran, Lebanon, and Iraq, is that it is a fatal flaw in policy to ignore or artificially separate from the others the Palestine-Israel issue. This is the one Middle East issue that over a billion Muslims and many other people from Casablanca to Jakarta care about most and is most likely to breed violence and terrorism. Whether we like it or not, many millions overseas are ignoring or deprecating the most visible benefit of invading and occupying Iraq, the demise of Saddam Hussein. Unless better planning and rapid change truly do unify and democratize Iraq, both terrorists and nonviolent critics of U.S. policy will continue to equate the United States in the Middle East both with the European colonizers who were protectors of past decades and with the continued settler colonialism of the present time in Israel/Palestine.

STEPHEN W. VAN EVERA Al Qaeda poses a very serious threat to the United States. It lost important bases in Afghanistan after the United States ousted the Taliban in 2001, but it has since morphed into a decentralized organization that remains very dangerous. The possibility remains that Al Qaeda will buy or steal weapons of mass destruction and use them against the United States.

Yet the Bush administration is waging only a one-dimensional war on Al Qaeda. It fights what should be a four-front war on only one front. At the same time the administration is spreading itself too thin by pursuing diversions against secondary enemies. In short, we need a much stronger effort against Al Qaeda—a war fought on every relevant front—and a commitment to refrain from diversions until the Al Qaeda threat is defeated.

I agree with what Stanley Heginbotham said about the need to focus on Al Qaeda. The current struggle should never have been defined as a war on terror. Rather, it always should have been defined as a war on Al Qaeda.

I also agree that the war in Iraq was a mistake if for no other reason that when you are in a deadly serious war you focus on the worst threat first. You do not go after secondary threats. Saddam posed a secondary or tertiary threat; hence, we should have sidestepped him. We had him boxed in and could have left him there. We also should not define all the world's terrorist outfits as anti the United States. There are scores of them out there, most of them having no beef with the United States and posing no threat to it. The United States should focus on groups that do threaten the United States. It should not be our policy to go abroad seeking to make new enemies.

A successful war on Al Qaeda will require a large change in the U.S. national security establishment. We face a changed world that is as much changed since the Cold War as the world was after World War II. Then we had to re-orient from the German and Japanese threats to meet a quite different Soviet threat. A large change in the U.S. security establishment was required. Today even bigger changes are required. The U.S. military services should not even be the key instruments in the new war we face against Islamist terror. The main instruments in this war are, instead, entities that include the State Department's Office of Public Policy, the Cooperative Threat Reduction Agency (which locks down loose nuclear weapons and materials in Russia and elsewhere), the Centers for Disease Control, local law enforcement and other first responders, the Coast Guard, the Agency for International Development, and other outfits that are not usually considered the main spearhead of U.S. national security policy. But they should be spearheads in the struggle we now face.

Let me elaborate on the Al Qaeda threat. Al Qaeda is a new and different beast in the world of terror in its desire to accomplish mass killing. Until the early nineties the axiom among students of terrorism was that in the world of terror it was universally true that terrorists got a lot of people watching, not a lot of people dead, as Brian Jenkins once said. Terrorists did not aspire to mass killing. Now Al Qaeda's goal is to kill as many people as possible. The spokesman for Al Qaeda, Suleiman Abu Ghaith, has been quoted as saying he believes Al Qaeda has a right to kill four million Americans, including two million children. This is a remarkable and chilling claim. When was the last time a major world figure claimed an entitlement to mass murder children? Hitler did it but he did not claim a right to do it.

Al Qaeda also remains powerful. About two-thirds of their leaders are either dead or in custody. Nonetheless, their organization has merged into a more decentralized one, but still capable and dangerous. People should not take any comfort from the fact that there has not been another large attack on the United States

X/81

since 9/11/01. Unless we destroy it, Al Qaeda will be back. It is a patient organization with a long planning cycle. It learns from its mistakes. It will strike if and when by our folly we give it the opportunity.

Moreover, if Al Qaeda is clever, it may gain access at some point in the next few years to weapons of mass destruction. Our foolish, indeed bizarre, failure to move energetically to lock down nuclear materials and bio-weapons materials in Russia has substantially increased this danger. The possibility that extremists in Pakistan will transfer nuclear weapons or materials to Islamist terrorists poses another grave risk. And the progress and spread of weapons of mass destruction (WMD) technology increases the danger that Al Qaeda or related terrorists could fashion their own WMD. Bottom line: unless we act wisely, WMD terrorism could well be in our future.

I have not been a Jeremiah in the past, warning of threats around every corner. During the Cold War, I thought we usually inflated the Soviet threat. We surely inflated the threat posed by communism in the Third World and greatly overreacted to it, much to our own and others' misfortune. So I am sounding a different tone than I have in the past.

The war on Al Qaeda should be waged on four major fronts. You can think of five or six fronts if you want to, but to me it should be four big fronts. The first of these fronts is the offensive. It involves destroying regimes that give sanctuary to Al Qaeda, preventing anarchic conditions that allow Al Qaeda to find sanctuary in failed states, and rolling up the Al Qaeda organization around the world through intelligence cooperation with other governments. These efforts require destroying, deterring, or preventing the emergence of rogue states, preventing state failure, and preventing civil war, since all of these phenomena create conditions that help Al Qaeda to find a home. The Bush administration has put nearly all its energy into this front.

And even on the offensive front the Bush team has not handled the job well. They basically bungled the war in Afghanistan, allowing the Al Qaeda leadership to escape at Tora Bora and then bungling again in Operation Anaconda. The public thinks of the Bush team as very tough guys who fight a hard fight, but in these battles they lost their nerve and allowed the Al Qaeda leadership to escape because they would not put U.S. troops at risk. Then they failed to finish the job by putting in the resources needed to secure Afghanistan from a resurgent Taliban and Al Qaeda. Successful intervention requires a strong postwar political and economic policy to create stability and prosperity. Otherwise a failed state ensues. The Bush team did too little in Afghanistan, so conditions there are deteriorating.

The Bush team also made grave mistakes in its occupation of Iraq. As a result Iraq may lapse into a failed state. This will pose a serious security threat to the United States by giving Al Qaeda a new potential haven. All in all, then, even on its favorite front, the offensive, the Bush team has produced very mixed results.

The second front is the defense of the homeland, in the form of homeland se-curity. Spending for homeland security has increased but overall the Bush team's homeland security effort is half-hearted. Major U.S. infrastructure targets are still wide open for attack. The administration has been afraid to confront the nuclear industry and so has not required it to better protect nuclear facilities from attack. Ditto for the chemical industry. As a result we face the possibility of a very destruc-tive attack on a chemical plant that could kill tens of thousands or more. U.S. in-surance laws need to change to give an incentive for U.S. businesses to secure their buildings and other infrastructures against terrorist attack. So there is a whole range of ways in which homeland security is something that is still waiting to happen.

The third front is the locking down of loose nuclear and biological materials and scientists around the world. These materials and people pose an extremely grave risk, especially if they get loose in quantity. The problem in Russia is that the system for protecting these materials and people during the Soviet age was the police state that surrounded nuclear and biological facilities. The facilities them-selves were very soft, but the materials were secure because the KGB was making sure no one went anywhere in the USSR without permission. So when the KGB vanished, a huge nuclear and biological materials security problem suddenly emerged. And for reasons that totally mystify me—I cannot tell you why this is—the U.S. government, and most especially the current administration, have treated this grave security danger as a trivial concern, doing little about it. They are now spending only a billion dollars a year on the effort to lock these dangerous materi-als down, and they will not have the project finished for years.

The nuclear materials I am discussing are sufficient to make forty thousand Hiroshima-sized atomic bombs. If even a tiny fraction of these materials were to go missing, world history would be forever changed. The perennial possibility of sudden vast destruction would then hang over civilization. So this is a danger you do not want to play games with.

Yet the Bush administration has failed even to appoint a high-level official to carry out the lockdown project. The administration complains that the Russians will not cooperate with us on this project, but you do not know the cooperation you will get from the Russians until you send a major Washington mover-and-shaker—a James Baker–type—over there who can tell Putin he has the president's cell phone and cut a deal. Whoever is in charge of the project is so obscure that he surely cannot act effectively.

Most everyone who has studied the "loose nukes" problem cannot fathom why it is not treated as a national emergency. But it's not.

Finally, the fourth front is the war of ideas. We cannot defeat Al Qaeda without reaching a modus vivendi with the Arab and Islamic world. This will require a change of the terms of debate in the Islamic world that, in turn, will require some organized effort to effect the terms of debate. To me that breaks into two prob-lems: public diplomacy and peacemaking. The United States must use its instru-ments of persuasion—propaganda if you will—to affect the terms of debate in the Islamic world when and where it can. It also must use its peacemaking power to end conflicts that are inflaming the Arab and Islamic world against the United States. Most important, it must move to dampen or end the Israel-Palestinian conflict. It should also do what it can to dampen the Kashmir conflict.

Let me comment first on public diplomacy. The Islamic world is awash with false accusations against the United States that must be answered or they will be believed. For example, the charge circulates widely that the Israelis and, or the CIA knocked down the Twin Towers, as proven by the fact that three thousand Jews allegedly did not show up for work at the Twin Towers on 9/11/01. Such charges are clearly refutable and the U.S. government should refute them. But the State Department Office of Public Diplomacy remains underfunded and has not been well led. We have seen a musical chairs of directors, a situation suggesting that the Bush administration does not take public diplomacy seriously. This is a major blunder. The United States has large powers to persuade and it wastes a valuable asset by leaving these powers unused.

Second, with regard to the Arab-Israeli conflict, the United States should move energetically to get back on a peace track. The Bush administration has not been doing what everyone knows it must do to end that conflict: frame a final status settlement that the United States endorses, like the Clinton plan, and move the parties toward that final-status settlement by firmly applying carrots and sticks to both sides. Bush has chosen not to do this. Instead, he has stood content with a far weaker policy of occasional mediation and a little cajoling here and there.

A final point: The Iraq war is weakening our national security because it is di-verting intelligence, special forces, expertise, high-level management, other assets and skills away from the war on Al Qaeda into what will be a very long-term, very difficult problem in Iraq. This is a tar baby we never should have touched. In the future let us refrain from such diversions. Some in Washington now counsel mili-tary confrontations with Syria and Iran. This would be an immense folly.

JONATHAN SCHELL   There has been a very interesting and somewhat surpris-ing drift in the conversation here, which is that this supposedly endless war on terrorism is not being fought as hard or as effectively as it should be. I want to take that drift of thought a little further and provocatively state that I do not think that the war on terror can be endless, as suggested, because I do not think there is a war on terror. I think there was one, but now it is over. Let me explain what I mean.

Of course, one can speak of a war on anything—war on drugs, war on poverty—but that is metaphor. And, of course, in that same sense you can speak of a campaign against terror, which I do think exists and should exist, as a war on terror. There was an actual war on terror; it was the war in Afghanistan in which the Taliban was overthrown in the effort to get at Al Qaeda, but somehow we missed them, which is one of the complaints that we have heard about the unseriousness of our war on terror or our "campaign against terror," as I would call it. I think there is a danger of endless war here, and we have been hearing that perhaps we are not fighting this war on terror as effectively as we could. But I would like to suggest that the problem is not just that we are aiming at that target but somehow missing it. I suggest that another target has been put up for us to aim at, and I want to say a few things about what that is.

I will begin with a few comments about the origins of the Bush foreign policy post–September 11. A key element was to define the effort in prospect as a war on terror, not as, say, a campaign against Al Qaeda—a more limited and definite thing. By naming the campaign as a war, the president put the world on notice that the full, awesome military of the United States would be brought to bear, and, of course, by his naming the generic terrorist the target was not Al Qaeda. That suggested that there was no corner of the earth where this might not take place. I think there was an evolution here with several critical expansions: first, calling it war and calling it terror. The second expansion was in the idea that, as we were told by the president shortly after September 11, regimes were as responsible as the terrorists themselves. That introduced the famous idea of regime change, a very serious escalation, of course, and this was a very radical idea in terms of previous American policy.

But then came another expansion, which may have been the most important of them all. Having lumped together terrorists and the regimes that supported them—so-called rogue regimes—into one lump, the president went on to incorporate into this policy the gravest issue that any president of our era has had to face and still faces, and that is the danger from nuclear arms and other weapons of mass destruction. That step of expansion occurred in the president's Axis of Evil speech in which he named three countries that were in the gun sights of the United States: Iraq, Iran, and North Korea, and by implication they were cited as lessons for other countries that ought to watch their step. As the president put it, the United States of America will not permit the world's most dangerous regimes to threaten us with the world's most destructive weapons, thereby subsuming the question of weapons of mass destruction, which has existed for more than fifty years, under the rubric of this war on terror.

Once you have taken that step you cannot wait until someone has the weapons of mass destruction; you have to go out there and get at them preemptively, and that led, of course, to the idea—as famous as regime change—of preemptive war. And so the president said that containment and deterrence, which had sufficed during the Cold War, would no longer be enough. In the new era we had to move to the idea of tough preemption.

When you put all of this together (and the White House did so in its document *The National Security Strategy of the US,* which you can find on the White House Web site) it really amounted to an assertion—and this is not something that was hidden away between the lines; it is right there in the text of the document and of other speeches and documents of this administration. The United States was asserting an absolute, permanent, global dominance, including the right of preemptive war and of so-called regime change. The president did not call this plan an imperial one, but many of the supporters of the policy have done so, and this word has somehow gone from being a term of abuse to being, rather, a term of praise. I think that this is the policy that came to life in the war on Iraq, and to call this a war on terror is really to abuse language.

I think we miss the point if we try to understand the war on Iraq, or this entire policy, which really does have a danger of endless war attached to it, if we try to conceive it as a sort of botched or misbegotten war on terror. I think it is about something else altogether. I think it is about hegemony. I think it is about dominance, I think it is about supplanting a previous system of world order based more on cooperation with one based on military force with the United States in the lead. I do not think we should make any mistakes about it. I think that the United States has now embarked on an imperial enterprise, and I do not think this is subtle or indirect. It has actually begun the occupation of countries like the British and the Raj in previous generations.

Many of the features of imperial rule that we have seen in the past have made their appearance here, such as the awesome disparity in power between the conqueror and the conquered, which has been a feature of imperialism from its earliest days down to now. We see the scramble for loot, in this case oil. We also hear the high-sounding ideals about which the great turn-of-the-century writer on imperialists, Hobson, described perfectly when he said, "Imperialism has been floated on a sea of vague, shifty, well-sounding phrases, which are seldom tested by close contact with fact."

So in concluding, I would say that we should really rephrase our question and not ask if there is an endless war on terror, but whether there will be endless imperial wars.

X/Islam and the West

At the Crossroads

CHRIS PATTEN

If Samuel Huntington were a share, he would today be what market tip-sters call a strong buy. That is bad news, because the clash of civilizations, which he predicted in his essay for *Foreign Affairs* in 1993,[1] at the moment casts a gibbet's shadow over the prospects for liberal order around the world. Depressingly, wit-lessly, we have to a great extent shaped our own disaster-in-waiting.

Some of the global problems that we shall face in this century; for example, whether China can make an accommodation between economic license and po-litical authority, are matters for a circumscribed few, in this case a small cadre of bureaucratic politicians in Peking. Others, like "Day after Tomorrow" environ-mental disasters, have to some extent already been set in train by past greed and ecological pillage. But a clash between the world that likes to think of itself as being primarily made in the mold of the New Testament and the Islamic world of another Book is a catastrophe that we seem sedulously set on triggering through acts both of omission and commission. How can things have come to this?

Let me jog back for a moment to Huntington's thesis. Hot on the heels of liber-alism's triumph—the breaching of the Berlin Wall, the fall of Europe's last empire, the opening of markets by technology and international agreement—Huntington warned against the easy assumption that we could now relax, a cold war won with-out the use of any of those engines of death stockpiled in silos from Utah to the Ukraine. Conflict was not, after all, a subject for the history books. "The most important conflicts of the future," he wrote, "will occur along the cultural fault lines separating . . . civilizations from one another." The differences between civi-lizations were more fundamental than those between political ideologies, and the more the world was shrunk by technology, the more we became aware of them. Globalization weakened local and national identities, and the gap was filled by re-ligion with non-Western civilizations returning to their roots, re-Islamizing, for example, the Middle East. Moreover, cultural, or as he largely argues it, religious characteristics are less likely to change than those that are political or economic. "Conflict," he notes, "along the fault line between Western and Islamic civiliza-tions has been going on for 1,300 years" and "on both sides the interaction be-tween Islam and the West is seen as a clash of civilizations." Popular in academic

Speech given at the Oxford Centre for Islamic Studies, May 24, 2004.

X 87

circles in the West, his theories are also extensively quoted on jihadist Web sites in the Arab world.

There were other civilizational clashes as well to which Huntington drew attention. But his arguments never convinced me. I spent a good deal of time during my years in Hong Kong pointing out that there was not some cultural divide between the so-called Confucian world ("so-called" usually by those who have never read Confucius and tend to confuse him with Lee Kuan Yew) and the West, which strips Asians of civil liberties and denies them democracy. Sun Yat Sen had apparently never existed. Many of us argued that human rights were universally valid, and that democracy under the rule of law was the best system of government everywhere. And with the Asian financial crash and the discrediting of the Asian model of crony capitalism and authoritarian politics, the controversy seemed done and dusted. The clash of civilizations was the stuff of provocative academic seminars. Then the planes slammed in to the Twin Towers, and the world changed.

Well, of course, it was not quite that simple. The pretexts, the causes, the narrative of atrocity began much earlier than 2001. And we had scholarly guides to point us down the right exploratory tracks. Oh, to have been the publisher of Professor Bernard Lewis, sage of Princeton. I admit to a personal debt to his scholarship. I have enjoyed, and I hope, learned from a number of his books.

But I have started to worry as I read on from *What Went Wrong?* to *The Crisis of Islam* that I am being carefully pointed in a particular direction, lined up before the fingerprints, the cosh, the swag bag, and the rest of the evidence. "Most Muslims," he tells us in *The Crisis of Islam,* "are not fundamentalists, and most fundamentalists are not terrorists, but most present-day terrorists are Muslims and proudly identify themselves as such." [2] Well, yes, and it is a sentence that resonates in parts of the policymaking community in Washington. But what if I had tried a similar formulation on some of these same policy makers just after the IRA bombed Harrods in London: "Most Catholics are not extremist Irish republicans, and most extreme republicans are not terrorists, but most terrorists in Britain today are Catholic and proudly identify themselves as such." I suspect that it is not a sentence that would have increased my circle of admirers in America not because it is wrong but because it is so loaded with an agenda. Anyway, what we have been taught is that there is a rage in the Islamic world—in part the result of history and humiliation—that fuels hostility to America and to Europe too, home of past crusaders and present infidel feudatories of the Great Satan. Clash, go the civilizations.

There are many ways of coming at this issue, but I wish to be rather prosaic. I will not therefore deal with the religious arguments, leaving them to retired archbishops and other distinguished theologians, only noting in doing so that according to a *Sunday Times* survey in January, more Muslims attend a place of worship in the U.K. each week than Anglicans. Nor do I want to penetrate deep into the debate about whether Europe and its very secular Union represent Christian civilization, a rather up-market exclusive club, ties for dinner, that sort of thing. There is a past and present to this discussion. Having been brought up on the medieval scholarship of Richard Southern, who examined me when I came up to Oxford as a sixteen-year-old, perhaps I know a little more about the past, certainly enough to remember the doctor in Chaucer's *Canterbury Tales* who established his credentials by recalling the great names of medical science with which he was familiar: six were from Greece and Rome, three from the medieval Islamic world. And what of Thomas Aquinas? He read Latin versions of the Greek philosophers, courtesy of the scholars at the Muslim School of Translation in Toledo, to which we owe so much of our knowledge of the scientific, religious, and philosophical works of the ancient world.

As for the present religious, ethnic, or civilizational nature of our European club, there are probably about 12 million Muslims living in Western Europe, approaching 4 million in France, 2.5 million in Germany, 1.75 million here. Their religion is the fastest growing in the world. They practice it in Europe in a union of nation-states formed out of the bloody wreckage of the twentieth century. Our recent history of gas chambers and gulags, our Christian heritage of flagrant or more discreet anti-Semitism do not entitle us to address the Islamic world as though we dwelt on a higher plane, custodians of a superior set of moral values. Our prejudices may be rock solid, but our pulpits are made of straw.

What of this Islamic world that allegedly confronts our own civilization? It is sometimes forgotten that three-quarters of its 1.2 billion citizens live beyond the countries of the Arab League, in, for example, the democracies of Malaysia, Indonesia, and India. Asian Muslim societies have their share of problems, not least dealing with pockets of extremism, but it is ludicrous to generalize about an Islamic anger engulfing countries from the Atlantic seaboard to the Pacific shores.

If we focus on a narrower range of Arab countries—the Magreb, the Mashreq, the Gulf, the countries in the cockpit of current struggle and dissent, what do we find? In 2002, the Arab Thought Foundation commissioned a survey by Zogby International of attitudes in eight countries: Egypt, Israel, Jordan, Lebanon, Kuwait, Morocco, the United Arab Emirates, and Saudi Arabia. They questioned thirty-eight hundred people and their results confirmed other similar if not identical surveys; for example, by the Pew Research Center. What is pretty clear is that, like Americans or Europeans, Arabs are most concerned about matters of personal security, fulfilment, and satisfaction. Perhaps it is a surprise that they do not appear to hate our Western values, and their cultural emanations— democracy, freedom, education, movies, television. Sad to say their favorite TV program is *Who Wants to Be a Millionaire?* Other survey evidence underlines this point about the most significant values. The Second Arab Human Development

Report published in 2003—I shall return to its predecessor later—quotes from the World Values Survey, which shows that Arabs top the world in believing that democracy is the best form of government. They are way ahead of Europeans and Americans, and three times as likely to hold this view as East Asians.

There is not much sign of a clash of values here. The problem seems to be rather simpler. The Arab world does not mind American and European values, but it cannot stand American policies and by extension the same policies when embraced or tolerated by Europeans. So the Arab world holds very negative opinions of the United States and the United Kingdom (even while holding, according to the same survey, positive views about American freedom and democracy). Why is the U.K. in this pit of unpopularity? Partly, I suppose, because of what we are seen to do, and partly because of what we are silent about. I don't know how widely Saint Thomas More is read in Arab lands but *"qui tacet consentire videtur"* is true everywhere. Perhaps it cheers us to discover that France comes best out of these surveys, scoring very positive ratings, as do Japan, Germany, and Canada.

What sort of policies turns Arabs off? Today Iraq would certainly feature high on the list. But in 2002 the issue that stands out from the Zogby survey is, hardly surprisingly, the absence of peace in the Middle East. Let me quote what the survey's authors say: "After more than three generations of conflicts, and the betrayal and denial of Palestinian rights, this issue appears to have become a defining one of general Arab concern. It is not a foreign policy issue; . . . rather, . . . the situation of the Palestinians appears to have become a personal matter." As the recent work of, for example, Richard Perle and David Frum has shown, this apparently incontestable point is, for a particular school of American thought, a deliberate and alarming blind-spot.

The treatment of the Palestinians is one of four areas of policy where the approach we pursue in America and Europe could abate or exacerbate Arab hostility and build rather than burn bridges between the West and the whole of the Islamic world. The other three that I want to examine are how we engage in the debate on reform in the Arab world; where we go from here in the dreadful situation in Iraq; and how we handle Turkey's aspirations for European Union membership. But before I come to my main argument, let me take one short diversion to consider whether they could help us to overcome the terrorist threat that has given such a savage twist to these debates. To try to understand the reasons for terrorism, and, where possible and appropriate, to address them, is not to condone the wickedness of random murder for political ends.

Our history from Kenya to Israel to Ireland to South Africa is peppered with examples of terrorism that events have elided into politics. Terrorism sometimes has precise political causes and objectives: the Mau Mau, the Stern gang, the IRA, the ANC.

Sometimes it has had less focused aims; for example, Enrico Malatesta's "propaganda of the deed," which tried to draw attention to injustice and destroy the nerve of ruling elites by murdering presidents and princes, tsars and kings.

Today's terrorism by Islamic groups, able through the advance of technology to shatter civilized order through terrible acts of destruction, seems closer to the anarchists than to the gun-toting politicians, for example, the ones I myself know best who were notorious for their ability to carry both a ballot box and an Armalite. The ideas that sustain Osama bin Laden and those who think like him, not all of them the members of a spectacularly sophisticated network of evil, but nonetheless fellow believers in a loose confederation of dark prejudices, can hardly be dignified with the description of a sophisticated political manifesto. They do not travel far beyond the old graffiti "Yankee, Go Home." But they do represent a form of political, social, and cultural alienation, which we should seek to comprehend.

Joseph Conrad investigated these dark corners in *The Secret Agent*. Remember these lines:

> He was no man of action; he was not even an orator of torrential eloquence, sweeping the masses along in the rushing noise and foam of a great enthusiasm. With a more subtle intention, he took the part of an insolent and venomous evoker of sinister impulses which lurk in the blind envy and misery of poverty, in all the hopeful and noble illusions of righteous anger, pity and revolt. . . . The way of even the most justifiable revolutions is prepared by personal impulses disguised into creeds.

It is not normal for men and women to want to get up in the morning and strap bombs to themselves or to their children and set out to kill and maim. How does a sense of injustice, which so often inspires, surrender to religious simplicity, come to trigger evil? Why does our own notion of the spread of freedom, capitalism, and democracy look to others like licentiousness, greed, and a new colonialism? We should surely try to fathom the answer to these questions and understand that we can make them either more or less soluble. Is it really a surrender to organized evil to assert that there are some policies that would demobilize the recruiting sergeants of terrorism? I believe that all four of the hardly original issues I have raised fall into this category.

First, let me deal with some of the arguments aroused by the American proposal to launch a "Greater Middle East Initiative." *Time* magazine cited the UNDP's [United Nations Development Programme] Arab Human Development report as the most important publication of 2002. The report unleashed a tidal wave of debate across Arab countries about the reasons for the region's comparative backwardness and inadequate performance. Well over a million copies of the report were downloaded from the Internet, many in Arab countries. Why did a scholarly survey have such an impact?

The first reason is that its authorship caused surprise and endowed credibility.

It was written by Arab scholars and policy makers, not well-meaning outsiders. Second, its analysis was captivatingly honest and politically bold. How could it be that in terms of economic performance in the last quarter of the twentieth century, the only region that did worse than the Arab countries was sub-Saharan Africa? Why had personal incomes stagnated through these years?

Why had wealth per head in this region fallen from a fifth of the OECD [Organisation for Economic Co-operation and Development] level to a seventh? Why were productivity, investment efficiency, and foreign direct investment so low? How could the combined GDP of all Arab countries be lower than that of a single European country, Spain?

The answer came in the prescription summarized by the UNDP's Arab regional director. Arab countries needed to embark on rebuilding their societies on the basis of:

1. Full respect for human rights and human freedoms as the cornerstones of good governance, leading to human development
2. The complete empowerment of Arab women, taking advantage of all opportunities to build their capabilities and to enable them to exercise those capabilities to the full
3. The consolidation of knowledge acquisition and its effective utilization

Governance, gender, education—the Arab world's own formula for improvement and modernization, and a formula, too, that European partners on the other side of the Mediterranean have been trying gently—perhaps a little too gently—to promote through the Barcelona process for almost a decade. We have been attempting to establish a free trade area around our shared sea. The ambitious aim is to complete it by 2010, to encourage more trade between Arab countries, and to assist those (like Morocco and Jordan) who are themselves committed to modernization, democratic reform, and the nurturing of a more lively civil society.

There is in my view a strong link between better government and better economic performance, and between the accomplishment of both those objectives and greater stability. Authoritarian governments are less likely to be good economic managers; they shelter corruption and suppress the sorts of pluralism—a free press, for example—that bring transparency to economic governance. The result of authoritarianism is two-fold. First, lower economic growth fails to create the jobs that demographic pressures constantly demand in the Arab world. Young men without jobs, without the dignity of work and some money in their pockets, are easily attracted to other causes than the relatively innocent occupation of making money. Second, the denial of civil liberties itself causes resentment, driving debate off the street and out of the coffee shops into the cellars. Bad economic performance, especially when associated with large wealth and income differences, combines with the suppression of dissent to breed trouble.

How should the West, how should the Arab world's European neighbors support a process of modernization that is so greatly in our own interest, lowering the pressures from illegal immigration, opening new and expanding markets, exporting stability to our near neighborhood? I do not for a moment accept that it is none of our business, since successful and stable neighbors are very much in our own interest. Nor do I buy the argument that encouraging democracy in the Arab world only creates trouble, with the risk that we will replace more or less compliant authoritarian friends with rabid fundamentalist regimes, established on the basis of one man, one vote, once. I have never been convinced by the argument that free politics is inherently more unstable than command politics.

On the other hand, there do seem to me to be some ground rules that outside well-wishers should follow. We are talking about other people's lives and countries, not our own.

"Better" as T. E. Lawrence argued, "to let them do it imperfectly than to do it perfectly yourself, for it is their country, their way, and your time is short" (even if in other ways, he is not perhaps the perfect role model for the G8 as we approach these questions). It is imperative that the agenda of modernization—in education, in the rule of law, in participatory government, in opportunities for women, in nourishing civil society—should be owned by Arab countries themselves.

Recognition that this will all take time, and that you need to prepare for the long haul, is not code for procrastination. Developing democracy is not like making instant coffee. We also have to be careful not to preach or offer—as we have in such grotesque profusion—evidence of double standards. We should expect the same of everyone regardless of how pliable some authoritarian countries may be when passing strategic interests throw up new short-term imperatives. If democratic modernization looks like a Western tactic for securing our own interests, we risk discrediting the ideas in which we believe and turning our Arab friends who share the same ideas into seeming stooges. Above all, you cannot impose a free society through invasion and military might, spreading democracy through the region in the tracks, as it were, of Jeffersonian tanks.

All this and more was set out plainly in the follow-up Human Development Report in 2003, which made it less congenial reading in parts of Washington (whether we must now add "in parts of London" too, is a worrying after-thought). We could, however, do little better than follow much of the advice of the Arab scholars who wrote it, engaging the modernizers on their strategic agenda as well as on our own, listening to their views of where we get things wrong, and providing more assistance (not least financial) for modernization programs. I favor a much greater emphasis on positive conditionality in our generous development programs in the region—spending more money to assist those who are genuinely committed to reform.

I suppose all this leads naturally, if gloomily, to my second theme, to what Winston Churchill called "the thankless deserts of Mesopotamia." I cannot help recalling also what he wrote in *My Early Life:* "Never, never, never believe any war will be smooth and easy, or that anyone who embarks on the strange voyage can measure the tides and hurricanes he will encounter. The statesman who yields to war fever must realize that once the signal is given, he is no longer the master of policy but the slave of unforeseeable and uncontrollable events."[4]

So here we are today, having in the prophetic words of the secretary-general of the Arab League "opened the gates of hell," struggling to close them, or in some disreputable cases to run away from them and hope they will close themselves. On this matter, at least, I agree with our prime minister: for Britain and America, to "cut and run," before there is a functioning and democratic Iraqi government in place, is not an honorable option; it does not even secure our own short-term interests, let alone Iraq's; and we cannot salve our consciences by thinking we have dealt a blow for effective multilateralism by dumping Iraq in the lap of the UN before we bolt for home.

The aim is as difficult as it is clear. To secure it will naturally require the authority of the UN. But it will also require the combined efforts of the international community, led by the United States, which is only likely to be successful—an outcome in all our interests—if it recognizes explicitly that it is unwise of any big country, especially the world's only superpower, to behave as though it believed in Machiavelli's maxim, "It is better to be feared than loved."

In Iraq we have to endow local and autonomous governing institutions with as much political authority as possible, recognizing that until there have been elections, legitimacy and power will inevitably be limited. January 2005 looks a long way off, and the intervening months will test us with events difficult to control if not always to foresee.

Why do I say that? Because one eminently predictable development will be the attempt to discredit or murder the moderate leadership in each community—Kurd, Shia, and Sunni. This will be the great test. Moderate leaders of these communities need to be able to appeal convincingly to their followers not to drift to the extremes. If that happens, the whole of this not-so-carefully stitched together country could fly apart, with dangerous regional implications.

There are so many lessons to learn from this wretched adventure. But for the time being, we do not have the luxury of picking over all the "I told-you-so's." America and Europe have to work together to try to end the whole affair in tolerable order. We will all be damaged if we fail.

Third, I return to that issue, which as I said before, is not regarded as a matter of foreign policy by most Arabs—I guess even less so after the televising of the events in Rafah: Palestine and Israel, two communities locked into a downward spiral of death and destruction, each seemingly intent on causing pain to the other. In my experience, even the most studious attempts at neutrality and even-handedness bring down accusations of bias and prejudice on one's head. I simply say in passing—enough I am sure to attract waves of criticism—that there seem to me to be two legitimate howls of rage, two story lines not one. All I wish to do today against a background of continuing mayhem—the plotting of revenge and the exacting of terrible retribution against the last act of revenge—is to take a cue from the story of the small boy and his naked monarch.

We know that there are ways of ending the bloodshed. We came close at Camp David some years ago and at Taba. The Mitchell Commission showed us what would be involved. The Quartet's Road Map provided a political gazetteer. The Geneva initiative demonstrated that there were still some courageous men and women in Israel and Palestine who could find the path to peace. We know what that peace will require if two states are to live harmoniously side by side in what, with shame if not irony, we still call the Holy Land. How to get there?

The international community's policy in the last few years has been based on three propositions: first, that Mr. Sharon and his government believe in the creation of a viable Palestinian state; second, Mr. Arafat and Palestinian political leaders will be able, and will have the will, to convince their community that that goal will be achieved only if they give up violence, even against what they see as an illegal and oppressive occupation of their own land; third, that Mr. Sharon and his government will take action—for example, the dismantling of settlements—which will help Mr. Arafat accomplish the persuasive tasks assigned to him. Do we still believe that those propositions are true?

If there is to be the sort of settlement that will bring a permanent peace, then they need to be true, and if we have any doubts that they are, this only strengthens the case for greater engagement by the international community in pushing and shoving and harrying and cajoling both sides to move. The Europeans and the Arabs will need to be more assertive with the Palestinian leadership; but that will not work unless the United States is more prepared to act in the same way with Israel. It is, I am afraid, as crude as that.

Sequencing leads nowhere. Both sides need to be pressed to jump at the same time, a fundamental principle of the Road Map. Unless this happens, the bloodshed will continue, destroying the prospect of a better life for Palestinians and Israelis and poisoning relations between the United States, Britain, and some other European countries and the Arab world.

I come last to what for many observers will be the main test of the European Union's commitment to a pluralist and inclusive approach to Islam: not its relations with an Arab country but its approach to the question of Turkish membership of our Union—a question that has been asked, and received halting, embarrassed, and obfuscatory answers for more than thirty years. The question will be posed again when the EU has to decide whether it will finally open negotiations with Turkey, having conceded that it was, after all, a candidate for membership at the Helsinki European Council in December 1999.

The case that this is a pivotal moment in the EU's relationship with the Islamic world can be, and is, overstated. But our approach to Turkey does matter. It says a great deal about how we see ourselves, and want to be seen, in terms both of culture and of geopolitics.

Culture first, and perhaps most important. What does it take to be a member of the EU? According to the treaties, membership is open to any European country that respects the principles of liberty, democracy, respect for human rights and fundamental freedoms, and the rule of law. That naturally raises two questions: first, Is Turkey European? And second, Does it respect the principles that we hold dear?

Is Turkey European? If aspiration is any guide, the answer would have to be a resounding yes. Turkey has resolutely steered a European course ever since Ataturk decreed the end of the sultanate in 1922. The feeling runs deep and is promoted with unrelenting vigor by successive Turkish governments. The legacy of Ataturk, born in Thessaloniki and convinced, despite the condescension of the European powers of the day, that his country's future lay to the west, is ever present. And his presence is sometimes more than metaphorical. Any meeting in any Turkish government office takes place under the cool gaze of the Ghazi, immaculate in determinedly Western suit and tie.

Does Turkey respect our principles? This is where the legacy of Ataturk turns negative. Along with his many more positive achievements, he was also the creator of the Deep State. He saw ethnic and religious minorities as divisive. He established a key role for the military in politics. All of these were, and are, antithetical to the idea of Europe that we have been laboring to bring into existence since the Second World War. That was true in 1963, when we signed one of the then EEC's [European Eonomic Community] first ever Association Agreements, and it has remained true during times of often repressive military dictatorship ever since.

Walter Hallstein declared at the signature of that Association Agreement, "Turkey is part of Europe. This is the deepest possible meaning of this operation which brings, in the most appropriate way conceivable in our time, the confirmation of a geographical reality as well as a historical truism that has been valid for several centuries."

Many Turkish observers might be surprised if that were deemed to be less true now, under a government that has carried on and even redoubled a program of constitutional reform designed to entrench democracy, promote the protection of minorities, and limit the role of the military in government.

In their eyes, Turkey has grappled with the existential question, against a background of economic uncertainty and terrorist activity, and has unequivocally chosen the European course. Why, they ask, is that not recognized?

The answers to those questions matter to our own geopolitical interests. How much interest should we take in the fate of our southern neighbor and ally, bordered by Iraq, Iran, Syria, and the southern Caucasus? How welcoming should we be to a neighbor that has demonstrated the falsity of the case that Islam and democracy do not mix? When we do take an interest, should we recognize Turkey as a respected partner, or as a difficult pupil? These questions should preoccupy us all as the December European Council approaches, and we will no doubt come to different conclusions. I would submit, though, an example of what I think is almost exactly the wrong approach. In the aftermath of the conflict in Iraq, the American Deputy Secretary of Defense, Paul Wolfowitz, flew to Ankara to chide the Turkish generals for not intervening more forcefully to overturn the decision of the Turkish Parliament that Turkish troops should not be sent to Iraq. Happily for all of us, and especially for the people of Turkey, the generals did not intervene, and the parliamentary process was respected. The Turkish government acted creditably. Considering Iraq today, we can make our judgments about whether they acted wisely. But what if they had done otherwise, would the United States still have pressed us to accept Turkey as an EU member? Military interventions in politics are not one of our democratic criteria in Europe. We are not simply an alliance but a union in which democratic states share some of their sovereignty.

Turkey, then, lies on the cusp between the current EU and the Islamic world. Throughout its history Istanbul, Constantinople as was, has been a bridge between worlds. At one time, and particularly when Western Europe was a more savage place, Turkey and the Turks were the very incarnation of the threatening outsider. But that was when "Europe" and "Christendom" were synonyms. We've moved on from that, as I argued earlier. I should say in passing that the metropolitan of the Syrian Orthodox Church and the patriarchs of the Armenian Orthodox Church, among others, would be surprised to discover that they are outside the Christian club. The proposition that Europe can be defined by religion is a false one, not to say dangerous. In many ways, the European Union is a reaction against the idea that we can define ourselves by religion or ethnicity and thus define others as beyond consideration.

To be fair, the counterproposition, that saying no to Turkey for now would somehow turn the Arab world against us is also overstated. Turkey is not Islam, nor is it (as I have said) an Arab state. However, we cannot help but be conscious of the symbolism, at this time, of reaching out a hand to a country whose population is overwhelmingly Muslim. I look forward to the debate preceding the commission's opinion on the matter in the autumn. In making it, we will be conscious that we potentially pave the way for a very different EU—and that should be squarely and honestly confronted. It may well be politically difficult to envision and administratively gruelling to manage. But we need to open the debate, recognizing that the beginning of negotiations with Turkey, whatever the uncertainty of the outcome, would lead to a very different Turkey and very different relations between Europe and the Islamic world.

Provided we make the right policy choices in the four areas I have indicated, I believe we can avoid the clash between the West and Islam that some predict and a few pray and conspire for. The real clash is not between civilizations themselves but between civilizations and barbarism—the enemy of us all.

That is the struggle we need to define and win, working in the West with the leadership of the United States, whose military prowess we require for a peaceful world and whose moral leadership we need even more.

I opened a book critical of American foreign policy the other day—there is quite a cottage industry out there—which began with a stanza from a poem written by the author of "America the Beautiful," Katharine Lee Bates. Only an American could quote it, and I repeat it here not because I agree with it but because it contains an important sentiment: "And what of thee, O Lincoln's Land? What gloom / Is darkening above the Sunset Sea? / Vowed Champion of Liberty, deplume / Thy war crest, bow thy knee, / Before God answer thee."

Now there are three things that prevent me from shouting "Hallelujah" at the end of that. First, I am averse to dragging God into discussions of foreign policy; second, it is massively arrogant to demand humility of others; third, in a dangerous world we need America to don its war crest from time to time. Indeed, that makes it possible for us—a matter of shame for Europeans who still do too little for our own and the world's security—to be vauntingly sanctimonious. But I like the "Champion of Liberty" bit, and America has always been at its most convincing and effective when it has combined confident power with genial humility, as I seem to recall was once rightly said by a presidential candidate.

NOTES

1. Samuel P. Huntington, "The Clash of Civilizations," *Foreign Affairs* 72, no. 3 (Summer 1993): 22–28.

2. Bernard Lewis, *The Crisis of Islam: Holy War and Unholy Terror* (New York: Modern Library, 2003).

3. James J. Zogby, *What Arabs Think: Values, Beliefs, and Concerns* (Washington, D.C.: Zogby International, 2003).

4. Winston Churchill, *My Early Life, 1874–1904* (New York: Simon and Schuster, 1996).

hrx/98

(file 02-03)

Transitions from Terrorism to Modernity
Linking External and Internal Dimensions of Change

GREG MILLS

If we are just killing terrorists, we are not achieving anything. . . . I call them the leaves of a tree. As long as the tree is there, the leaves will keep growing.
—PRESIDENT PERVEZ MUSHARRAF, Stockholm, July 2004

Amid the theories and conspiracies around 9/11, the only two obvious common denominators about the nineteen terrorists were their religious identity and the fact that they had spent time in Afghanistan. Ironically, the link between the two was understood by and familiar to the U.S. government, which, in the course of the Cold War, had supported a war of Muslim fundamentalists against the Soviet Union in Afghanistan.

Many Arabs understandably bemoan their association with radicalism and backwardness. They prefer to stress the great achievements of Arab culture over the centuries, including such contributions as the arch, the zero, the preservation of Greek learning during the Middle Ages, and algebra. During Europe's Dark Ages, as Will Durant reminds us, Arabs "led the world in power, order and extent of government, in refinement of manners, in standards of living, in humane legislation and religious toleration, in literature, scholarship, science, medicine and philosophy."² But in the same breath, many Arabs lay the blame at the door of the West or Israel or both. It is inescapable, however, that Islamic movements have chosen to advertise the link between the gun and the Koran: Consider the names of Islamic jihad (holy war), Al-Dawa (The Calling), Hezbollah (Party of God), Al-Gama'a al-Islamiyya (Islamic Group), and the moniker *mujahideen* (holy warrior).

Three days after the war started in Iraq in March 2003, I attended a *diwaniya* in Kuwait City. While Kuwait is, at best, a limited democracy, there is a thriving civil society debate. Kuwaitis—or at least Kuwaiti men—regularly attend such public meetings. At this one I was surprised to hear the extent of the criticism of the emir and his ruling clique and of the absence of voting rights for women. While all present agreed that Saddam had to go, they were similarly concerned about the longer-term impact of the war on the Arab world. To deal with these negative perceptions, many felt that the United States has to promote reform and change wherever necessary, including in countries as diverse as Kuwait, Saudi Arabia, Egypt, Pakistan, and Indonesia.

98

Until 9/11, the rise of militant Islam—now considered the new global threat—was largely ignored by the United States and other international leadership. But is it possible to reform the societies in which this form of political-Islam is taking hold? Can one modernize regimes where small, insular, and often isolated cliques rule their populations with consideration only for their own survival? What is the role of leadership in this environment, and what shapes its choices?

The End of Isms?

Every morning promptly at nine o'clock, the green police van pulled up outside my window in Cairo's sleepy suburb of Zamalek to collect the ten policemen who had gathered there. My hotel's guard watched this event slumped apparently disinterested in his chair, fiddling with his AK-47, perhaps because the conclusion of his twelve-hour shift remained some way off.

Cairo is a contradiction between function and frenetic activity; a contrast between the deep-rooted knowledge and power that built the three Great Pyramids of Giza, and today's sprawling, uncontrolled, and poverty-stricken metropolis housing at least three times more people than its closest African rival, Lagos. Enveloped in pollution and dust, it emits a cacophony of noise from more than half a million cars and its fifteen million-or-so inhabitants, one-quarter of the country's population. Yet its people remain, for the most part, warmly hospitable and friendly—qualities for which the Arabs are renowned. It is, David Lamb notes, a paradox of civilization's birthplace and developing country status, a mixture of East and West, First and Third Worlds, and of old and new.[3]

But as might be expected of the nation living in such a thousand-year-old city where Plato once reportedly studied and for which Verdi composed *Aida*, Egyptians regard themselves as unique, "a cut above the rest of the Arab world." Or as Anwar Sadat's national security adviser, Hafiz Ismail, noted: "We Egyptians are Arab, and don't ever forget this—but we are not like other Arabs."[4]

Such self-belief founded in its pharaonic history combined with the knowledge that one in four Arabs is Egyptian granted Egypt leadership of the postindependence Arab world. This role was carefully cultivated and skilfully mastered by Gamal Abdel Nasser, who, preaching a mix of pan-Arabism, nationalism, anti-Zionism, and Arab socialism, developed a bold foreign-policy agenda emphasizing Egypt's strategic location in the overlapping worlds of Arab, African, nonaligned, and Islamic nations.

This recent history should not, however, overshadow important developments in Arab politics: increasing diversity between states and the shift over the past three decades toward Arab nationalism, a result principally of the devaluation of the other "isms," including socialism and anti-imperialism—even though this has not translated into a system of governance effective or efficient enough to meet the aspirations of their populations. The controversial reception of Francis Fuku-yama's thesis on the supposed "end of history" at the conclusion of the Cold War should be enough to deter those who attempt to extrapolate the importance of events as representing the "end" or the "beginning" of a period of history. Yet it is the struggle between Arab nationalism and the most potentially damaging of all the "isms"—Islamic radicalism—that may determine the direction of Middle Eastern politics and society—and possibly world history—for decades to come.

Bernard Lewis argues that the basic historical response of the Islamic world to its decay during the post-Renaissance period was to believe that the fault lay in its falling away from "good old ways, Islamic and Ottoman" and that the "basic rem-edy" was thus a return to them.[5] This "diagnosis and prescription," he argues, "still command wide acceptance in the Middle East." Absolutism combined with the identification of a Western threat to these traditional, "pure" values is a cock-tail for widespread violence and provides a credible philosophical vehicle for radi-cal leadership. Lewis is not alone, even though his (Western-origin) views have become targeted as "anti-Islamic." For example, the Lebanese scholar Faoud Ajami has also argued that some of the trouble in the Middle East comes from radical Islam rather than the widely held view that it is a response to U.S. policies.[6] But this explains Osama bin Laden's "Declaration of the World Islamic Front for Jihad against the Jews and the Crusaders" three years before September 11, in which he stated that "to kill Americans and their allies, both civil and military, is the individual duty of every Muslim who is able, until the Aqsa mosque [in Jerusa-lem] and the Haram mosque [in Mecca] are freed from their grip, and until their armies, shattered and broken-winged, depart from all the lands of Islam.[7] His objective is, however, the overthrow of Middle Eastern governments and the es-tablishment of Islamic states; the method, the undermining of the West's com-mitment to these states and the drawing of a link between Western influence and Middle Eastern rulers. There is nothing new here in terms of ambitions, except that now the main fight is taking place within the Muslim world.

Ironically, it is not only the failure of past "isms" but the emergence of new forces—including capitalism and globalism—that are seen today as potent threats to which the response is Islamic radicalism. The resultant tension—and con-flict—between individualism and fundamentalism, between modernity and tra-dition, manifest between and within states, will likely be a defining feature of international relations for the foreseeable future.

Thus the principal security challenges facing us today are twofold and interre-lated. One is the threat of terrorism, striking at rich and poor countries and popu-lations alike. The other is the threat of poverty and global exclusion to the bulk of the world's six billion people, 40 percent of whom are estimated to be living under the daily international poverty datum line of U.S. $1.

How can we meet these challenges?

The Challenge for Islamic States

Both the camel guide and carpet seller in Petra, Jordan, agreed that the reason for the lack of tourists in November 2003 was "the American Bush, Sharon, and Palestine." They agreed with the more sophisticated analysis of the Moroccan foreign ministry official who, in July 2004, said that success in the war on terror depended principally on settling the Israeli-Palestinian crisis, which in turn relied on greater pressure being exerted on the Israeli prime minister by the United States.

While no doubt the war in Iraq had led to a downturn in regional economies and tourism numbers, Arab states have routinely been fond of blaming others for their plight. Yet the UN Development Programme's *Arab Human Development Report 2003* suggests that Arabs have to take their share of responsibility for underdevelopment.[8] Moreover, Al Qaeda bombings in Saudi Arabia and Istanbul suggested that the war of terror is widening, pitching Muslim against Muslim and Arab against Arab.

There is an imperative for Muslims to ensure that the actions of Osama bin Laden and those around him do not define Islam. Yet it is important to acknowledge, that Islam is far from a monolithic religious force continentwide. Islam practiced in West Africa is dissimilar to that in East Africa, to that in North Africa, to that in southern Africa. Yet partnership is key in dealing with the threat of global Islamic terrorism.

As noted, Al Qaeda poses an existential threat to moderate Arab regimes. In this it is sometimes presumed that Saudi Arabia, given its role in funding Islamic causes, is at the core of a global terrorist problem rather than a co-victim and key partner in dealing with this blight. This is exactly the wedge that Al Qaeda and its allies want to drive between Riyadh and the West. Partnership between Saudi and the West is "indispensable" to the success of a counterterrorism strategy in which, if it fails, the House of Saud has the most to lose. As Magnus Ranstorp has noted, "the international community faces an Al Qaeda threat that does not emanate solely from Saudi Arabia but nevertheless requires its partnership to see this struggle through to a successful completion."[9]

The big wake-up call for Saudi Arabia was the fact that fifteen of the nineteen 9/11 hijackers were Saudi. This, combined with the bombings on May 12, 2002, meant, as U.S. deputy secretary of state Richard Armitage put it, "the scales fell from the eyes of the Saudis."[10] In response, the Saudi government moved to confront terrorism in four ways:

- First, by clamping down on militants and particularly on Al Qaeda. In August 2003, Crown Prince Abdullah described the battle against "deviant" and "misguided" terrorists, as a "conflict between the power of good and the power of evil."

- Second, by internal reform. In October 2003, the Saudi government announced that municipal elections would be held for the first time in the kingdom in 2004.
- Third, by playing a more active foreign-policy role, for example, in trying to assist in finding a solution to the Palestinian-Israeli impasse
- Fourth, by dealing with the teachings of intolerance in the religious schools—madaris—and mosques

But can democracy provide the answer?

Some predict that democracy can only lead to political takeovers by radicals from Palestine to Morocco, since this group is generally better organized and Islam better represents the frustrations of the underclass. For the more optimistic, however, with elections come certain rights as well as responsibilities. This is why analysts such as Shalom Harari, a colonel in Israeli military intelligence and an Arabist who has worked in the Palestinian areas for twenty years, stress the importance, for example, of staging open elections in the Palestinian Authority, in spite of the threat posed by Hamas and Islamic Jihad at the polls. Or as Saeb Erakat, the Palestinian chief negotiator has put it, "Anyone who says Arabs are not ready for democracy is a racist."[11] Democracy is key to insuring the sort of freedom and way of life that terrorism tries to destroy.

Establishing democracy will not be an easy task, however, as Iraq shows. There the coalition has seemingly put aside its Jeffersonian instincts, to opt instead for a speedy transfer to civilian power for Iraqis—for what analysts describe as "democracy in a regional theme," a sort of benevolent authoritarian regime in the style of Egypt, under which the opposition has a role and "can speak" but can never come to power.

The problem for external agents for change, in Iraq as elsewhere throughout the region, is that some Arab leadership does not want to see liberal democracy flourish but rather wants the status quo preserved and consolidated. Any long-term continued deterioration in the Iraqi situation will, as Efraim Halevy notes, give an "uplift to negative forces in the region." A combination of the upsurge in suicide attacks and the Iraqi situation has put into relief the stance of all regional actors on terrorism, an issue that one cannot be neutral about.[12]

The 2003 Riyadh and Istanbul bombings signaled a simultaneous widening of the war on terror and a deepening of cooperation in fighting it. No doubt much action will center on the Middle East. But care will have to be taken in the way in which the external powers engage in a region where the politics overlap with religion, ethnicity, geography, and personalities, and where political survival generally means physical well-being.

Ironically, despite the views of the carpet seller and camel rider, most of the tourists in Petra are American—certainly the bigger spenders are. The region cannot live without the global leviathan, but the United States and its allies will have to learn quickly to deploy their own power with care. As the Lebanese, Harvard-based academic Faoud Ajami has observed, a "great power should never wink at anyone in the Middle East. Small winks speak big things here. . . . They all want America's license, its resources and its green lights. . . . They like you big, but they want to send you back small; they like you a virgin, but they want to send you back a whore."[13]

Can the Military Provide the Answer?

A June 2003 edition of the influential *Jane's Defence Weekly* was headlined "The Death of Strategy." It argues that "effects-based operations dictate doctrine for the warfighter."[14] The use of effects-based operations (EBO) has seen a change in targeting strategy (and thus selection) from "linear" to "parallel" sequence: that is, a variety of leadership, air, troop, and other strategic targets can be attacked simultaneously. This targeting approach is enabled by the use of smart weapons employed in a "network-centric" real-time command-and-control battlefield system. EBO warfare, like that promoted by Sun Tzu, is about getting the enemy to fight according to your strategic interests. According to this line of reasoning, ultimately the United States can support a global military presence with fewer forces using air and space assets. EBO, it is argued, "may provide the answer to an otherwise insoluble conundrum: how to maintain a high degree of readiness in an era of declining resources."[15]

This statement, however, invites a strategic corollary. In the face of overwhelming U.S. military superiority, it should not be surprising that opposing nations and paramilitary nongovernmental groups should be attracted to the notion of asymmetric warfare. Whenever there has been a power with a clear advantage due to superior organization, doctrine, training, numbers, or equipment, its opponents seldom seek straightforward combat and instead try to avoid decisive confrontation. This has been the strategic guideline of guerrilla warfare since time immemorial. It largely explains why the world's largest power got so badly bogged down (and ultimately lost the war) in Vietnam, and how the cost to the colonial powers of continued occupation was made greater than any possible benefit in the wars of national liberation. It also explains the approach of the Iraqi resistance to coalition forces after the fall of Saddam.

The gap between conventional and guerrilla warfare has undoubtedly narrowed with the advent of complex, high-tech systems—not just laser-homing bombs but the whole package of satellites, reconnaissance aircraft, drones, intelligence, and analysis needed to locate enemy targets. Ironically, largely civilian-based information-technology skills have given the United States an enormous military edge. But the utility of strategies such as "rapid dominance" or "overwhelming force" (bywords of "shock and awe" and EBO adherents), the aim of which is to make it apparent to an opponent that it has no real alternatives other than to fight and die or to give up, are still insufficient in guerrilla operations.

Indeed, this is not enough to combat the sort of terrorist threat posed by Al Qaeda and other similar groups. Information technology can help prevent but cannot altogether stop terrorists of no known fixed abode or base armed with box cutters intent on suicide missions. For those who command these men and women, asymmetric warfare is much less bloody and costly than symmetrical war would be. How then can terrorism best be countered?

The Internal Dimension

Bernard Lewis's controversial volume on the rise and decline of the Islamic world, *What Went Wrong?* details how Muslims lost the leadership of civilization and re-treated from modernity.[16]

By the middle of the last millennium, Islamic control had expanded to the point of dominating much of Central and Eastern Europe, all of the Middle East and North Africa, a significant belt of sub-Saharan Africa, and much of Central Asia, South Asia, and Russia. Partly, their decline was posted by their inability to take advantage of the expansion in sea trade, and partly signaled by the increasing frequency of military defeats. Both these relative failings illustrated the shifting balance of power between Europe and the Ottoman Empire, itself a reflection of the advances made as a result of European innovation, invention, and experiment. Lewis notes that "usually the lessons of history are most perspicuously and un-equivocally taught on the battlefield, but there may be some delay before the les-son is understood and applied."[17] But are there other ways to achieve this, beyond violence?

The reasons behind radical acts are complex, ranging from the crypto-religious, to the even more nebulous relationship between hope and despair, social humilia-tion and powerlessness. The reality—and worse still, the prospect—of no jobs and no food in a mire of political repression, economic collapse, impoverishment, and corruption can lead citizens to grasp at the straws of radical solutions. In this environment, too, as Karl Maier observes with regard to Nigeria, "ethnic and reli-gious prejudices" find fertile ground "where there is neither a national consensus nor binding ideology" and where the state almost totally lacks in morality and le-gitimacy.[18] For those nations that are not even classifiable as "developing" but rather, in terms of their economic decline (such as Nigeria and, indeed, much of sub-Saharan Africa) are, in fact "underdeveloping," the absence of job and educa-tion opportunities bears particularly hard on the youth—as a result often a genera-tion seething with resentment and frustration.

The relationship between terrorism and poverty is, however, problematic. If terrorism is associated with the sort of acts perpetrated by Al Qaeda, then in the forty-nine countries currently designated by the United Nations as the least developed, hardly any terrorist activity occurs. If defined as a wider set of acts perpetrated by nonstate actors against a civilian population, then, of course, these societies are far from immune but rather the tragic centerpiece (at least in terms of lives lost) of terrorism today—think only of the loss of life in Rwanda or in Sierra Leone or the Congo, numbering in the millions rather than the thousands of the World Trade Center.

Also, many of the supporters of radicalism—and suicide bombings—are not poverty-stricken but rather middle-class. There is not an exact correlation either between political repression and terrorism, despite the almost wholesale absence of democracies in the Middle East. Historically, repressive regimes such as Stalin's Russia or Nazi Germany did not suffer terrorism. No doubt the closing of legitimate paths of debate and dissent has, in some countries, however, led citizens to seek alternative avenues for political expression.[19]

More exactly, terrorism is a product of fanaticism, where the contemporary "pride of place" is taken by Islamic zealots, surpassing sectarian forces like the Irish Republican Army and its Protestant loyalist counterparts or the more secular Baader Meinhof gang, with many of today's spin-offs of the Muslim Brotherhood.[20] Although the Brotherhood did not initially advocate violence, as a result of the influence of the ideologue Sayyid Qutb in the 1950s, by the 1970s the Brotherhood had spawned radical terrorist groups such as Takfir wa al-Hijra, whose Pol Pot-esque leader, Shukri Mustafa, believed that society was so corrupt that it had to be destroyed and built afresh.

This does not explain, however, why, even though acts are carried out in the name of Islam, some bombers are "as ignorant of Islamic jurisprudence" as they are "of Western liberal thought." For example, most of the Al Qaeda suicide hijackers had a technical education rather than religious background. And radicalism does not have a unique relationship with Islam. The Kurdistan Workers Party (PKK) and Liberation Tigers of Tamil Eelam (LTTE) have used suicide techniques, but they do not do so in the name of Allah. Walter Laqueur notes that with the LTTE, a combination of esprit de corps, personality cult, and "the feeling of racial or religious superiority and an eternal conflict between their race or religion and that of the enemy" motivate the suicide bomber. Indeed, he argues, the Muslim suicide bomber is not a psychotic but rather an introvert "looking for a spiritual anchor and a sense of certainties and community."[21] But even a religious motivation—despite its focus on preparation for the afterlife—is not enough. It demands an economic and political condition and is sometimes accompanied by a gender dimension as women, often marginalized and victimized, are seduced and sent off to die by men for the cause.

The Nexus in Meeting These Challenges

The short answer about how to do it—meet the challenge—is that every state is "experimenting." The Israelis have preferred to meet violence with still further violence. The coalition in Iraq has attempted to match the delivery of the hard security angle with the softer side of development efforts within a wider counterinsurgency-type campaign. Both tactics have done little to break, but may indeed have worsened, the cycle of violence in that region.

One key problem in dealing with radicalism in the form of terrorism relates to the absence of a common definition. As one Arab-based publication noted in 2004: "What is the real definition of terrorism . . . ? Is it what is happening in Spain or what is happening every day in Palestine?"[22] Thus, not only is one person's terrorist another's freedom fighter but another defense used is that governments routinely kill more people than terrorists, which undermines the "terrorist" label, often in dealing illicitly with political opponents from Tibetan Buddhists to the democratic opposition in Zimbabwe.

Understandings of radicalism and of dealing with its one manifestation, terrorism, have to hinge on questions of power. As Claude Ake notes with regard to Nigeria, "We have essentially relations of raw power in which right tends to be co-existensive with power and security depends on the control of power. The struggle for power, then, is everything and is pursued by every means."[23] The foundation for such radicalism is fundamentally in the nature of the state and its relationship with its citizens. In environments where the state is unresponsive to the basic needs of citizens, the strategic options facing leadership have ranged from divide and rule and patronage to the less-popular attempts to rise to the responsibility of management and what Chinua Achebe describes as "the challenge of personal example."[24] Political and religious radicalism can offer a useful diversion from criminal mismanagement of the economy, where the state serves less as a means of delivery free from fear or favor than as a tool of plunder and distribution by rulers to their supporters.

According to the legal adviser of the Israeli Ministry of Foreign Affairs, Alan Baker, the legal environment offers little guidance on how to deal with asymmetric threats such as suicide terrorism. Given their focus on interstate activity, there are no clear rules in the laws of armed conflict about how to deal with nonstate terrorists.[25] The Protocol to the 1977 Geneva Convention offers the last formal legal interpretation on terrorism in this regard. Article 51 states that "Acts or threats of violence the primary purpose of which is to spread terror among the civilian population are prohibited."[26]

As William F. Schulz observes, "the fact that history has rehabilitated reputations [of those once considered terrorists] is no excuse for evading moral judgment today. And the fact that governments have been responsible for massive

death and destruction offers no excuse for others' atrocities." While recognizing
the fallibility of states in supporting international law, his argument of the need
for an international treaty defining terrorism and outlining appropriate ways to
combat it, is not without merit.[27] After all, at its root, the deprivation of human
rights—financial and political—has the greatest appeal for those promoting radical disorder.

The Need to Instigate Modernity

Some of Islamabad's madaris[28] were, by 2004, advertising their services through
the Internet, contrary to their stereotype as hotbeds of Islamic radicalism. But
Pakistani authorities continue to view the religious schools as a key focus in the
war on terror.

Critics argue not only that Pakistan has been a failed state since its bloody birth
out of imperial India in 1947 but that today Washington's support for the Muslim
state highlights both the hypocrisy of U.S. foreign policy and the illegitimacy of
the rule of President Pervez Musharraf, the general who seized power by a military
coup in October 1999.

Such criticism overlooks the available options for change. Musharraf has his
hands full in trying to turn back simultaneously the tides of Islamic radicalization,
poverty, corruption, and poor regional relations while civilianizing his government: a tall order for any leader, let alone one trying to walk the fine balance between keeping onside with the United States and maintaining legitimacy at home.
As he put it in July 2004, "Muslim states are seen as the source of terrorism,"
warning of new "depths of chaos and despair" and of more "terrorism and an impending clash of civilisations" if the West, particularly the United States, and
Muslim countries fail to eradicate the root causes of anger and resentment.[29]

Whatever the four-year electoral mindset of U.S. (and many other) administrations, there is little doubt that dealing with the post-9/11 brand of Islamic terrorism will take at least a generation. Military means can remove leaders but,
as Iraq as shown, at best they will struggle to win the peace. In Pakistan, attempts
to confront Islamic militants through military clampdowns are complicated
by the self-governing system outside of Islamabad's control in the North West
Frontier Province. As the violent response to the army's 2004 operations in Wana
and Wazeristan also illustrates, there is considerable local sympathy for Al Qaeda
and other far-right religious groups in these tribal frontiers known as the *ilaqa
ghair*—lawless country—to local Pathans.

Several of Pakistan's Islamic parties are dedicated to the stricter enforcement of
Islamic Sharia law. These include Lashkar-e-Jhangvi, a Sunni Islamist militant
group banned in 2001 because of alleged links to Al Qaeda. A similar fate befell
Sipah-e-Sahaba Pakistan after the Sunni movement reportedly commenced a

program to recruit fifty thousand suicide bombers. So has the militant Shi'a group Tehrik-e-Jafria-e-Pakistan.

Both moderates and extremists claim the legacy of Pakistan's founder Mohammed Ali Jinnah, with radicals claiming that he wanted to build an Islamic state. Musharraf has to overturn the direct legacy of Major General Zia ul Haq, who ruled Pakistan from 1977 to 1988, and who introduced Islamic principles in most aspects of Pakistani life. Zia was ironically aided and abetted by U.S. support through the war against the Soviets in neighboring Afghanistan for which *mujahideen* fighters were groomed in his madaris and recruited to the struggle.

Key in this, as Colin Powell has argued, is the need to address some of the underlying causes, including education. For example, the U.S. secretary of state has denounced Pakistan's madaris as being "breeding grounds for terrorists."[30] No wonder that Musharraf has said that his country is involved in a "greater jihad (*'jihad-e-akbar'*) . . . a jihad against illiteracy, a jihad against poverty, backwardness, hunger."[31]

There are 1.7 million students in Pakistan's 10,430 madaris.[32] Many of them get drawn in for the food aid offered to students, with a bountiful supply of recruits for militant causes, given the economic conditions in much of South Asia. As Musharraf has put it, "They feed and house the poorest of the poor children."[33] In this way, poverty can cause terrorism.

Madaris highlight more fundamental problems with Arab education systems. These link to the use of language as much as they do the content of syllabi. When teaching at the University of the Western Cape, South Africa, in the early 1990s, I discovered most black students were terrifically disadvantaged by being taught—and having to respond—in English, what might have been their third or even fourth preferred language. In the same way, the formal Arabic medium— Nahaoui—that students are taught is light years away from street Arabic—or Dareg. Bridging this gap is critical to extending formal education and, in the view of local educationalists, moving away from today's rote learning of Arab systems.

While radicalization has a social dimension, analysis should not discount both the extent of religious ideological content and the organization behind it. This is what regional conflict specialists describe as "spiritual poverty."

As one influential Moroccan argues, radicalization relies on an archaic vision of the Sharia and an Islamic system based on the sanctification and legitimization of Allah. This use of God "is a political business—and it is not easy to challenge God in this way."[34] While some in the kingdom felt that they were previously immune to these tendencies, the Salafiyah al-Jihadiyah (Islamic Reform and Jihad) formed in the early 1990s is accused of involvement in bombings in Casablanca in May 2003, although responsibility for these acts was claimed by the Saiqah (Thunderbolt), a splinter of the radical Sirat al-Mustaqim (Correct Path).[35] As with Pakistan, many of these organizations have their origins in the radicalism and alienation brought home with returning *mujahideen* from the war against Soviet-run Afghanistan.

Countering this religious ideology demands, in turn, the identification of an alternative ideology and vision, in the Moroccan's words, "fusing national identity, tradition and modernisation, also restoring the legitimate place of God in society." Indeed, the Islamic world might say "we have been too silent, too shy, and too paralysed to deal with this because of the issue of religion. But why should God not be on our side too?"

This demands dealing with social conditions and poverty, transforming the system of education. In Pakistan, the madaris have been obliged to introduce four subjects: science, English, Pakistan studies, and mathematics, drawing them into the job markets outside of religion and into the mainstream of Pakistani society. But they will still graduate with a *Shahadatul-A'lamiya* (international degree) in Islamic and Arabic studies at the end of this five-year reform program, as they do today. Although the education budget has increased to 2.3 percent of GNP and one-third is now allocated to reforming the madaris, just two hundred have today received computers and teaching assistance for the new curriculum. Education reform will be a long slog. But in the words of my learned Moroccan, change also hinges on "speaking out, taking the floor and filling the ideological vacuum."[36] Yet this is not happening—or at least not happening fast enough.

Arab states did not intervene to remove Saddam. Nothing happened when Saddam invaded Iran, nor when he gassed his own people at Halabjah. Yet when he was removed by the coalition, the Arab world responded badly, perhaps because they were fearful of the impact on their own society and reform path (or lack of it). When faced with the abrogation of human rights by leadership in their midst, their resort has, until now, been to close ranks and genuflect to sovereign concerns. The excuse for not interfering is often to allow for regional, historical, or cultural differences in the pace at and the extent to which democracy can be instituted and followed.

A 2004 report of the U.S. RAND Corporation—"Civil Democratic Islam: Partners, Resources and Strategies"—argues that the West should help religious modernists in the Islamic world to prevent a clash of civilizations. It states: "It seems judicious to encourage the elements within the Islamic mix that are most compatible with global peace and the international community and that are friendly to democracy and modernity." It notes that modernists should be supported by, for example, assisting in education reforms, including getting their views into the Islamic curriculum and helping them in the new media world, which is dominated by fundamentalist and traditionalists.[37] This is not a million light years away from the response of other U.S. policy-thinkers—notably the so-called neo-cons—in attempting to counter the ideological component of Islam with an ideology not of containment but radical, revolutionary liberalization and democratization. Time will tell if this externalist strategy is successful, though events in post-Saddam Iraq are not promising. They are certainly light years away from early promises by President Bush on the impact of an Iraqi democratic revolution. In his speech to the National Endowment for Democracy in November 2003, for example, he argued, "The failure of Iraqi democracy would embolden terrorists around the world, increase dangers to the American people, and extinguish the hopes of millions in the region. Iraqi democracy will succeed—and that success will send forth the news, from Damascus to Teheran—that freedom can be the future of every nation. The establishment of a free Iraq at the heart of the Middle East will be a watershed event in the global democratic revolution."[38]

In the minds of local officials in both Morocco and Pakistan is the need for the West to assist in ending injustices against Muslims, including the conflicts in Palestine, Kashmir, and Chechnya. "Imagine," said one senior Pakistani foreign office official, "if the Russians responded in St. Petersburg as they have done in Chechnya? Would not the international community be outraged?" His point was that Muslims have somehow become dehumanised, and have resorted, in turn, to more and more radical acts of violence and counterviolence, including suicide bombings. Without such action to end these trigger conflicts, they would serve as draw-cards for international brigades like Al Qaeda in the same way as the Afghanistan conflict and, in earlier times, the Spanish Civil War had been a magnet for various causes.[39]

Of course, success cannot be instigated only from outside. Even though some Pakistanis dispute the right of militants to describe themselves as Muslims, it is impossible to ignore, in the words of a high-ranking officer in Pakistan's feared Inter-Services Intelligence (ISI) bureau, that "most terrorists are Islamic fundamentalists." One also cannot similarly ignore that Islamic fundamentalism is attractive to the affluent as well as those in the madaris. After all, as an ISI officer reminded us, American journalist Daniel Pearl's assassin was an LSE graduate.[40]

Responding to radicalism thus demands internal leadership in dealing with a wider struggle between modernists and traditionalists, which in most areas of the Arab and Islamic world remains unresolved. It demands an alternative ideology to radicalism. In Musharraf's terms, it requires "enlightened moderation" eschewing radicalism.[41]

This response should not be interpreted as an opposition to religion, however. Indeed, anything but. Rather, that many do not believe a commitment to religious values demands a truly Islamic state with laws based on the Koran but instead one in which Islam and democratic values co-exist. A long-term response dealing with radicalism also means essentially that local governments in the Arab and Islamic world have to get on with it themselves: leadership has to convince their populations that they are built for democracy and are acquainted with human rights, and vice versa. For example, the Saddam trial in Iraq would be a high-profile step in establishing the rule of law and due process, necessary also in remedying an intervention criticized from the outset for its dishonesty.[42]

One Pakistani summed up his country's challenges by stating: "It's not the people or the politicians, but the system." Musharraf is something of a singleton reformer. Indeed, his constant and most difficult challenge is to challenge and change this system, extending social benefits while gaining enough political support externally and internally from moderates and modernizers to head off the extremists.

Conclusion: Beyond Parody

It would be a mistake to dismissively parody the Bush administration as an aberration or underestimate international resolve in the war on terror. As John F. Kennedy noted over the Berlin Crisis in 1961, "We do not want to fight—but we have fought before. And others in earlier times have made the same dangerous mistake of assuming that the West was too selfish and too soft and too divided to resist invasions of freedom in other lands."[43]

A successful campaign—one where the war against terrorism and not only the battle is won—will thus have to involve military means with longer-term engagement. As U.S. Defense Secretary Donald Rumsfeld has said, "[The fight against terror] undoubtedly will prove to be more like a cold war than a hot war. If you think about it, in the Cold War it took 50 years, plus or minus. It did not involve major battles. It involved cooperation by a host of nations. It involved the willingness of populations in many countries to invest in it and to sustain it. It took leadership at the top from a number of countries that were willing to be principled and to be courageous and to put things at risk; and when it ended, it ended not with a bang, but through internal collapse."[44]

Dealing with radicalization is not, as many in Israel and Palestine have preferred to view it, about calculating percentages of territory or of solely debating the legality of responses. Solutions have to be considered within the wider political process, where the concerns of people rather than questions of legal principle are the focus. That is why debates around the legality or even the legitimacy (or not) of targeted killings are less than half the point—the real debate should be around rights of belonging, whether this be the right of the existence of the state of Israel or the creation of the state of Palestine.

Part of the answer to this conundrum lies also in altering the (human) tendency toward dehumanizing one's foe: whether this be "gooks" or "Charlie" in Vietnam, "ragheads" or "clothheads" in the Middle East, or "skinnies" in Somalia. But ultimately, terrorism and radicalism is a choice: It will thrive if it is not made a costly one or the only available policy selection. And the military can provide only part of the answer.

The difficulties faced by the coalition military in Iraq illustrate that military power alone is not enough to secure American—or Western—interests. But the contrarian appeal of terms such as "soft power" depends, too, on how these terms are defined. Sometimes soft power is viewed as the ability to persuade people to do America's bidding with various inducements, as opposed to forcing them through military power and threats. At other times, it refers to the soft power of culture. The problem is that the latter, while an attractive, nonmilitary option, is not a power in the sense that it can be directed and focused. Culture happens because of the market and communications. Put differently, it is difficult to use Michael Jackson and Michael Jordan in the same way that development aid can be employed. And in fact, to complicate matters further, the United States may be trying to use development aid to overcome the image that the two Michaels and other cultural phenomenon have given Americans.

Force and technology, however neat and sophisticated their splicing, are thus not enough to defeat terrorism. Here the answer lies partly in the shift in focus away from attempts to "defeat" the enemy toward a broader-based strategy attempting to "neutralize" the enemy. This strategy requires linking each act back to specific military and political objectives. But it requires more than the use of massive firepower aimed with precision in an effort to destroy everything: The success of guerrilla warfare depends on not destroying everything—and firmly linking military acts to a wider set of political objectives. But this demands nuance and an empathy with local conditions, aspects sometimes lost on the average GI, and for which intelligence and knowledge is key. Human rather than high-tech sensors are required for sustained regime change and reform. And in the Middle East in particular, defense and intelligence services will continue to have an important role to play in at least two respects: first, in terms of the defense of the realm, including society at large and the population; and second, and more controversially, as agents for change through an enlightened system of military governance.

NOTES

1. On the impact of Afghanistan, see George Crile, *Charlie Wilson's War* (New York: Atlantic Monthly Press, 2003).

2. Cited in David Lamb, *The Arabs: Journeys beyond the Mirage* (New York: Vintage, 2002), 131.

3. Ibid, 24.

4. Cited in Walter J. Boyne, *The Yom Kippur War* (New York: St. Martin's Press, 2003), 166.

5. Bernard Lewis, *What Went Wrong?* (New York: Perennial, 2002), 23.

6. Faoud Ajami, "The Falseness of Anti-Americanism," *Foreign Policy,* September 15, 2003, http://www.freerepublic.com/focus/f-news/983088/posts.

7. Peter David, "In the Name of Islam," *Economist,* September 11, 2003, http://www.economist.com/displaystory.cfm?story_id=2035107.

8. "Building a Knowledge Society," http://www.undp.org/rbas/ahdr/english2003.html.

9. Magnus Ranstorp, "Saudi Arabia and the global fight against Al-Qa'ida," *RUSI Journal,* February 2004, 32.

10. "Inside the Kingdom," Time, September 15, 2003. See also F. Gregory Gause III, "Saudi Arabia Over a Barrel," Foreign Affairs 79, no. 3 (May/June 2000): 80–94.

11. Both were interviewed in November 2003 in Herzliyah and Ramallah, respectively.

12. Discussion, Jerusalem University, Mount Scopus, November 2003.

13. Cited in Thomas Friedman, *From Beirut to Jerusalem* (London: HarperCollins, 1995), 209.

14. Nick Cook, "Cause and Effect," *Jane's Defence Weekly,* June 18, 2003.

15. Ibid., 54.

16. Lewis, *What Went Wrong?*

17. Ibid., 8–9.

18. Karl Maier, *This House Has Fallen: Nigeria in Crisis* (London: Penguin, 2000), xx–xxii.

19. See, for example, "Fighting Terrorism for Humanity" (conference report, Government of Norway with the International Peace Academy, September 22, 2003), esp. 6–7.

20. See Walter Laqueur, *No End to War: Terrorism in the Twenty-first Century* (New York: Continuum, 2003).

21. Ibid.

22. The AUI News (Ifrane, Morocco), May 2004.

23. Cited in Maier, *House Has Fallen,* xv.

24. Chinua Achebe, *The Trouble with Nigeria* (Oxford: Heinemann, 1983), 1.

25. Discussion, Sandton, South Africa, May 7, 2004.

26. Protocol 1, Additional to the Geneva Conventions, 1977, pt. 4: Civilian Population, sec. 1: General Protection Against Effects of Hostilities, chap. 1: Basic Rule and Field of Application, Article 51, Protection of the Civilian Population, http://deoxy.org/wc/wc-proto.htm.

27. William F. Schulz, "Security Is a Human Right, Too," *New York Times,* April 18, 2004.

28. Also known as madrasas.

29. *International Tribune,* July 6, 2004.

30. Ibid., March 11, 2004.

31. "U.S.-Pakistan Affirm Commitment against Terrorism: Remarks by President Bush and President Musharraf of Pakistan in Press Availability," Office of the Press Secretary, February 13, 2002, http://www.whitehouse.gov/news/releases/2002/02/20020213–3.html.

32. These figures were given in an interview in Islamabad with the Ministry of Education, July 14, 2004.

33. Ibid.

34. Interview with the author, Rabat, July 2004.

35. For details on these and the Moroccan Islamic parties, go to http://news.bbc.co.uk/1/hi/talking_point/3181815.stm.

36. Interview, Rabat Palace, June 7, 2004.

37. Paul Reynolds, "Preventing a 'Clash of Civilisations,' " BBC News online, http://news.bbc.co.uk/2/hi/americas/3578429.stm.

38. "President Bush Discusses Freedom in Iraq and Middle East: Remarks by the President at the 20th Anniversary of the National Endowment for Democracy, United States Chamber of Commerce, Washington, D.C.," Office of the Press Secretary, November 6, 2003, http://www.whitehouse.gov/news/releases/2003/11/print/20031106–2.html.

39. Interview, Pakistan foreign ministry, Islamabad, July 9, 2004.

40. Interview, ISI HQ, Islamabad, July 10, 2004.

41. The term "enlightened moderation" is used frequently by the Pakistani president and his officials. See, for example, Pervez Musharraf, "A Plea for Enlightened Moderation: Muslims Must Raise Themselves Up Through Individual Achievement And Socioeconomic Emancipation," *Washington Post,* June 1, 2004, A23, http://www.washingtonpost.com/wp-dyn/articles/A5081–2004May31.html.

42. See, for example, Patrick Bishop, "Saddam in the Dock," *Gulf News,* July 3, 2004.

43. "Radio and Television Report to the American People in the Berlin Crisis," July 25, 1961, available at http://www.jfklibrary.org/speeches.htm.

44. *Time,* October 15, 2001.

+ / p. 114 is blank

WHOSE VALUES? WHOSE JUSTICE?

x/p. 1116 is blank

The third cluster looks at the question whether the end justifies the means. In "From Just War to Just Intervention" Susan Atwood addresses a problem that has engaged theologians and ethicists since early Christian days. What constitutes the grounds for a just war? She discusses how the Just War Ethic has been used to define the just use of force, and how the Reformation, the birth of the nation-state, and the advent of the nuclear age (to name a few) have forced changes in our interpretation. After World War II, the United Nations became our authority on right intent and just cause. In the 1990s a number of interventions that took place were justified on humanitarian grounds. Now, after 9/11, the debate has changed radically. Can we justify preemptive interventions as "just"? The old Westphalian notion of sovereignty and nonintervention in the internal affairs of a state no longer holds sway.

No sovereign state has the right to murder its own citizens. How, then, do we balance the rights of sovereign states in a global world that recognizes the international primacy of human rights? When does oppression reach a point where forceful intervention on humanitarian grounds is justified?

Romeo Dalliare is an individual who chose to act—to intervene—in Rwanda. He acted outside of the mandate the United Nations had given him, and he eloquently tells us why. While we admire his personal strength and determination, his heroism will become a historical asterisk unless we find ways to create and fortify institutions that will exemplify such qualities and establish common agreement on their value, that is, on what is proper human behavior in moments of extremity.

The challenge of this new global century, Atwood concludes, "is to improve the implementation of humanitarian interventions and to define their mandate, as well as to clarify international human rights law. At a moment in history when, increasingly, even local conflicts have global implications, abandoning the pursuit of justice within or across state borders in an attempt to recapture an illusion of order is not an option." The Just War Ethic, Atwood asserts, must grow into an ethic of just intervention.

The Treaty of Rome established the International Criminal Court (ICC) in 1999, which acknowledges the grave human rights issues we face. The court's specific purpose: to hold accountable perpetrators of war crimes or crimes against humanity, whether they are individuals, governments, heads of state, or members of paramilitary groups. The court has jurisdiction in the territorial state, the state where the crime took place, or the state of nationality of the accused where those states are party to the statute or very significantly have accepted its jurisdiction on an ad hoc basis for that particular case. In addition, the court has jurisdiction over cases referred to it by the

Security Council. In October 2005, 141 countries had signed the treaty, which gave statutory effect to the court.

But the United States has not signed, citing reasons of sovereignty. No U.S. citizen will be tried in a foreign country for a war crime. Further, the United States continues to actively campaign to undermine the ICC by signing bilateral treaties with countries who agree not to sign the Rome Treaty in exchange for aid and other goodies.

Valerie Epps queries the democratic legitimacy of the court's claimed jurisdiction over states that are not party to the treaty. The ICC wields governmental authority as a judicial body to prosecute or punish individuals. At issue is the nature of the democratic linkage between this organ of governance and national governments. National states that are party to the treaty have representation through their own state's consent and through participation in the Assembly of States Parties, the governing body overseeing the court.

But Epps argues that there is no democratic basis for the ICC's power as applied to populations whose states have not consented on their behalf and are not represented in the Assembly of States Parties. Here, Epps says, it would be hard to claim democratic legitimacy for the ICC. Before the ICC can claim a legitimacy that is universally recognized this issue will have to be resolved satisfactorily, a claim the United States actively works to undermine.

In its quest for new allies in its war on global terrorism, Epps concludes, the United States has been willing to overlook human rights records. As a result, some countries with atrocious human rights records—Pakistan, Egypt, and Saudi Arabia—are welcomed aboard the war-on-terror wagon.

The bottom line, John Shattuck observes, is that the war on terrorism as it is now being conducted is "weakening, not strengthening, international security and undermining, not promoting, our national interests." Thus, the United States is losing the support of moderates all over the world who should be its allies, and it is strengthening the hand of authoritarian governments who crack down on reformers in the name of fighting terrorists. All of which, he maintains, increases the likelihood that terrorism will be bred by repression in places like Egypt and Pakistan, Chechnya, Uzbekistan, and Indonesia. "Above all," Shattuck concludes, "I believe we are destroying what Joe Nye has called 'our soft power,' our commitment to human rights, our commitment to democracy and the persuasion of people that those are values worth accepting, and replacing it with military force, our commitment to holding an increasingly hostile world at bay."

Both Epps and Shattuck delivered their remarks at the Tufts EPIIC Symposium in February 2003 on "Sovereignty and Intervention," roughly a month before the American invasion of Iraq when the administration was hyping the case for war.

Alfred McCoy's article "Cruel Science: CIA Torture Research and U.S. Foreign Policy" is an alarming example of the conflict between our need for security and our commitment to human rights and our American ideals.

McCoy details the process used by the CIA in 1963 to codify the practice of torture in its "Counterintelligence Interrogation" manual, which was disseminated to police in Asia, Latin America, and Central America. Following a ten-year hiatus at the end of the Cold War, the U.S. intelligence community, led by the CIA, revived the use of torture as a weapon against Al Qaeda in the war on terror. There is, therefore, a striking similarity in interrogation methods used by both American and allied security agencies from Vietnam in the 1960s, to Central America in the 1980s, all the way to Afghanistan and Iraq since 2001.

One of McCoy's most telling points is that democracies have great difficulty in dealing with torture (and rightly so). The media and the American public have been willing to blame a few bad apples rather than admit that many of the nation's standard methods are, under the UN convention, a form of torture. McCoy raises questions that cry for a serious debate. In 2005, the U.S. Congress, despite vociferous opposition from the Bush administration, overwhelmingly passed a law prohibiting the use of torture in any form in time of war. But the Bush administration did not give up, wanting an exemption for the CIA with regard to "soft" forms of torture, such as sleep deprivation and other techniques used to induce psychological disorientation.

The administration's assertion that terrorists are not prisoners of war and thus do not fall under the remit of the Geneva Convention threatens to undermine the basis of international law and is retrogressive in the extreme. Congress is trying to revoke protections provided by the Supreme Court in 2004 to detainees to access courts to challenge their detention at Guantánamo Bay, Cuba. Detention may be indefinite, detainees have limited or no access to legal representation, and allegations of mistreatment and abuse (a euphemism for "torture") are rampant. Detention itself, under these circumstances, becomes a form of torture, an assault on the rule of law in the name of protecting freedom. In November 2005 the UN Committee on Human Rights cancelled a visit to Guantánamo when the U.S. government refused to give it the access to prisoners it requested.

Abu Graib was dealt with to the satisfaction of the government agencies looking into these things, the executive was absolved, military trials were held, the few bad apples were sentenced to military jails; that is, justice was done. But whose justice?

For the Arab world, however, Abu Graib, so graphically captured in the photographs of sexual humiliation, degradation, and dehumanization, is an explosive depiction, now imprinted on its psyche. Abu Graib represents an invasion of their inner selves to destroy their connection to the core of their beings. It evokes in the collective subconscious their victimhood at the hands of the West. It is now part of the myth that sustains suicide bombers across the Middle East.

For the United States, the evidence surfacing of U.S. marines being involved in a cold-blooded massacre of Iraqis, including women and children, in Haditha in November 2005 and subsequent cover-up expose the contradictions between means and ends, values and justice that the administration brushed aside when it made the decision to invade. For Americans, perhaps this is the opportune moment to reflect on the huge rift between who we think we are and who we have become in the eyes of others.

Padraig O'Malley

From Just War to Just Intervention

SUSAN J. ATWOOD

The Just War Ethic, which traces its origins back to the medieval Christian Church, has faced many challenges regarding its relevance in different historical eras. But until today, it has remained the touchstone for defining the just use of force. It has done so by undergoing a number of evolutionary changes in focus, in response to fundamental shifts in world thinking and order—the Reformation, the birth of the nation-state, the advent of the nuclear age, to name but a few.

In 1945, the United Nations Charter drew directly on the Just War Ethic in its commitment to uphold world peace. But it also laid the groundwork for an expansion of right cause in the latter part of the twentieth century by its commitment to protect human rights. In that second part of the twentieth century, "states have generally sought to deal with threats to peace through containment and deterrence, by a system based on collective security and the United Nations Charter."[1] In terms of the Just War Ethic, the United Nations had, in the majority of cases, become the proper authority, the arbiter of right intent and just cause.

By the 1990s, however, we were no longer dealing with the tidy tableau of the Cold War, when the rules were laid down by the two superpowers; their nuclear balance of power defined world security as well as world vulnerability. New threats to global security began to emerge, posed by "rogue" states such as North Korea and Iraq; "failed" states such as Somalia; emerging nuclear powers such as India and Pakistan; and terrorists with potential access to weapons of mass destruction (WMD) such as the Al Qaeda network. The decade saw a number of multilateral "just" interventions on humanitarian grounds under UN or NATO auspices. These interventions stretched the capacities of the UN to its limits but seemed, however tentatively, to augur a nascent commitment to a multilateral approach to just humanitarian interventions.

The nature of the debate changed dramatically after the terrorist attacks of September 11, 2001. The United States went to war, first with the Taliban government of Afghanistan, then with Iraq, based on what it claimed to be potential threats to national security interests. The intervention in Afghanistan was justified by the Taliban government's refusal to cease harboring Al Qaeda. The Iraq intervention was justified, in part, as an effort to stop Iraq from transferring WMD to terrorists. In other words, it was preemptive.

Is the twenty-first century to be characterized by a doctrine of preemptive wars and interventions based on perceived threats to national interests? And, most im-

121

portant, are such interventions "just"? UN Secretary-General Kofi Annan fears that such an approach "could set precedents that resulted in a proliferation of the unilateral and lawless use of force, *with or without credible justification.*"[2] The nascent post–Cold War move to expand the definition of right cause to include humanitarian intervention within the borders of sovereign states finds itself abruptly, if temporarily, sidelined by this more fundamental challenge to the Just War view of proper authority, just cause, and right intent.

In this chapter I examine the changing nature of the debate about intervention through the lens of the Just War Ethic. I examine how we have responded to this new globalized world where the Westphalian notion of sovereignty and nonintervention in the internal affairs of a state are, after three hundred years, being reexamined in the light of such new threats as transnational terrorism, genocide, and failed states.

The Just War Ethic

Over the centuries, many people with different religious and cultural beliefs have contemplated the philosophical basis for war. In the early Middle Ages, around A.D. 400, Saint Augustine first formalized the Just War Ethic within the Christian Church. Augustine believed that war was a result of sin as well as a remedy for sin. The Christian view of love that he espoused requires at one and the same time that man do no harm, that man prevent harm to others, that he remove the source of harm, and that he do good to others. These different manifestations of love may conflict, creating significant internal tension and exhortations that lead in different directions. Augustine breaks this tension by saying that killing human beings is sometimes justified. This was a profound shift away from the pacifism of the early church. In the thirteenth century Thomas Aquinas subsequently specified three conditions for undertaking a Just War: proper authority, right intent, and just cause.

The emphasis throughout the Middle Ages in debating the Just War Ethic was on *jus ad bellum* (just cause for war), rather than *jus in bello* (just conduct in war). The "moral" arguments for a just war put forward from the Church by Augustine were furthered by Thomas Aquinas, who justified self-defense, as it is "the nature of being to preserve one's own life." Augustine had explicitly discounted self-defense as just cause. This was a huge change in the just war doctrine and one that prevailed.

Beginning in the sixteenth century, the world had become a different place. The Reformation split the Christian world in the West, and the Peace of Westphalia in 1648 opened the era of the rise of the modern state. No longer was there one "just authority" but many, both secular and religious. Prevailing wisdom held that it was the right of the state to defend itself against aggression by the use of force. Three thinkers—Hugo Grotius, a Dutch jurist, Francisco de Vitoria, a Spanish Dominican priest, and Francisco Suarez, a Spanish Jesuit priest, all of whom died in the century before 1648—saw the need to change the focus of the debate about a just war in order to preserve the ethic. Believing that war and politics must be constrained within the moral order, they took the lead in moving from discussion of just cause, *jus ad bellum,* to just means, *jus in bello.*

The concept of "simultaneous ostensible justice" was also introduced at this time—in other words, it was held to be possible that both sides could be ostensibly convinced of just cause and that there was likely some justice on each side. This was a move away from the medieval concept of the holy just war—the Crusades— where Christians believed that they had just cause, right authority, and right intent all on their side against the "infidels" (whether we have moved back to this mode of thinking under the George W. Bush administration is examined later). Now, one Christian state might find itself at war with another in defense of its territory. This was the period of the *droit de guerre* (right to war) and the emphasis was on *jus in bello,* the legal means by which to prosecute a just war. Just means included immunity for noncombatants and proportionality in the application of force, that is, the amount of force used must be in proportion to the problem encountered. From this period on, the two tracks, legal and moral, coexisted with some tension and some complementarity.

From the sixteenth to the early twentieth century, the focus was on order (that is, peace) over justice. The thinking behind the primacy of the sovereign state was that, to avoid an almost perpetual state of war, decisions about what was or was not just had to be decided within national boundaries. This was to change in the second half of the twentieth century, leading to the debate about just intervention in the internal affairs of a sovereign nation-state. The change marked a shift in emphasis of the debate from the legalist paradigm that "states should never intervene in the affairs of other states" to the moral underpinnings of this concept that allowed for exceptions to this principle.[3] As Michael Walzer argues, "humanitarian intervention is justified when it is a response (with reasonable expectations of success) to acts 'that shock the moral conscience of mankind.'[4]

The twentieth century was bloody. After World War II, the Just War Ethic came under extreme pressure with the advent of the nuclear age. Could any war be justified if the means used were nuclear and could presage the end of mankind? Was even nuclear deterrence moral when it threatened nuclear destruction and huge civilian casualties, violating the ethic of noncombatant immunity, which was codified in the 1929 Geneva Convention. How could nuclear war ever be proportional, that is, limited? In this way, deterrence came to be the principal weapon for preserving world peace.

Meanwhile, the United Nations, founded in 1945 by sovereign states to preserve world peace (that is, order), but also to protect human rights (that is, justice), was stymied by the Cold War mentality that prevented action in the spheres of influence of the two superpowers, the United States and the Soviet Union. But within their respective spheres of influence the two superpowers felt free to intervene in the internal affairs of countries, including Hungary, Czechoslovakia, Afghanistan, Grenada, and Panama. So intervention to preserve order went forward unsanctioned by the world community. The concept of "just" intervention—intervention to preserve justice and a return to the debate about just cause—was not yet on the radar screen.

The Just Intervention Debate

Saint Ambrose could be said to be the father of the doctrine of universal intervention when he stated, "He who knows about evil but does nothing is as bad as the evil doer." Intervention is not new. As we have seen, intervention was common practice during the Cold War. Colonialism in previous centuries might be seen as a form of long-term intervention. But the presumption of nonintervention, based on the Westphalian notion of the primacy of sovereignty and the inviolability of national borders (or, at least, of spheres of influence), remained the norm until the second half of the twentieth century. The rationale for nonintervention had broad support across a wide spectrum of ideology and belief. Its supporters included realists, liberals, and anti-imperialists.

The realist case for nonintervention emphasizes the primacy of order over justice. It draws from the Westphalian tradition of the sovereign state and noninterference into the internal affairs of states, which, after one hundred years of religious wars, brought order into the anarchical European world. The liberal position is somewhat more difficult to characterize. John Stuart Mill held that at times when a community struggles for its self-determination, the rest of the world should stay away and allow the combatants to prove the rightness of their cause through their own efforts. Only thus will it have validity. Other liberal thinkers, however, favor intervention to defend the rights of the oppressed. The anti-imperialist school of thought holds that the concept of justice gives carte blanche to strong and large states to dictate to the small, weak ones. So, the principle of nonintervention serves three needs: order, self-determination, and justice. In the period just before the Iraq war, we saw all these positions reexamined and, in some cases, reversed.

The second half of the twentieth century saw the beginning of a debate about just intervention, in other words, intervention on behalf of individual rights, a humanitarian intervention. In examining the precepts of this debate, it is helpful to revisit the basic philosophy of the just war tradition, which evolved over some sixteen hundred years. A just war requires proper authority, just cause, and right intent. Intervention, as distinct from war, consists of engagement in the internal affairs of a state. To cross this line from war to intervention, it had increasingly become accepted wisdom that proper authority should be multilateral, such as that of the United Nations. Just causes for intervention in the 1990s were held to include genocide, ethnic cleansing, and the collapse of state authority. Right intent, while remaining the restoration of peace, has moved from the vital interest of a state to defend its own civilian population to the national or international interest in justice for the victims of oppression.

Other just war criteria include the principles of proportionality, last resort, and moral possibility of success. These can also potentially guide the just intervention debate. Clearly, if the United States had intervened in Hungary in 1956, there would have been a risk of superpower confrontation escalating to nuclear war. Such an intervention would not, therefore, have been proportional. Although the nuclear threat has not disappeared (and indeed the number of countries in the nuclear club has increased) in the post–Cold War era, there is now little likelihood of catastrophic nuclear war between the superpowers because there is only one superpower left. But we are still faced with the problem of where intervention is likely to occur. From the perspective of proportionality, interventions are less likely to occur in large states such as China, or in the conflict in Chechnya, that would engage the Russians. Not surprisingly, therefore, the United Nations has witnessed more enthusiasm from the developed world for opening the debate on intervention and some outright opposition from developing countries who fear that they are the most likely targets of such interventions.

The principle of last resort also poses a dilemma. Sometimes, intervention can surely be more effective if it is not the last resort, thereby giving tyrants the time to carry out genocide or launch WMD. Indeed, this was one of the justifications employed by George W. Bush for the U.S. invasion of Iraq. In the case of intervention in a failed state, it is worth considering that failed states are likely to be exactly those states where the vital interests of the developed world are hard to define, and where intelligence on local conditions is poor. Under these circumstances, is there a moral possibility of success?

Other issues that have been hotly debated in the context of just intervention include the question whether intervention can be both limited and impartial. This is the question posed by Richard Betts in his article "The Delusion of Impartial Intervention."[5] He argues that if intervention is limited it has to be partial unless it is to prolong the conflict indefinitely. To be impartial and end the conflict presumes overwhelming both sides with force. For instance, in Bosnia, the United Nations was impartial. It is evident that its impartiality helped the stronger side, the Serbs. In addition, the presence of impartial peacekeepers on the ground inhibited NATO air strikes, again helping the Serbs.

In Kosovo, by contrast, the NATO intervention was partial and limited and brought a speedy end to ethnic cleansing. Betts argues that limited and impartial intervention "makes sense in old-fashioned UN peacekeeping operations, where the outsiders' role is not to make peace, but to bless and monitor a cease-fire that all parties have decided to accept. But it becomes a destructive misconception when carried over to the messier realm of "peace enforcement," where the belligerents have yet to decide that they have nothing more to gain by fighting."[6] The August 2000 Report of the Panel on United Nations Peace Operations states that impartiality remained one of the bedrock principles of UN peacekeeping but outlines exceptions to the principle "where one party to a peace agreement clearly and incontrovertibly is violating its terms." The panel further acknowledged, "No failure did more damage to the standing and credibility of the United Nations peacekeeping in the 1990s than its reluctance to distinguish victim from aggressor."[7]

Other questions concerning just intervention revolve around the type of mandate that is contemplated. In other words, is the mandate limited to stopping the killing after which the intervener leaves the country, or should it extend to supporting the establishment of democratic institutions and economic and social development?

The last type of intervention has been characterized as "nation building" and has come to have negative connotations, both for the developing world, which regards this as another type of imperialism, and for military personnel, who do not regard this as their role. George W. Bush came to the presidency pledging disdain for nation building. He embraced it when he began to make the case for intervention in Afghanistan and Iraq. There may well be a case to be made for the United States serving as the emergency response, stopping the killing and then leaving. The postconflict work, the peace building, might be better left to other, smaller nations and the United Nations whose motives are less likely to be interpreted as imperialist and thus less likely to politicize the situation further. But a situation where the rich, developed countries provide the money for intervention and the poor, developing countries provide the manpower, risks a further polarization of the whole concept of intervention.

So the question remains—given the complexities mentioned above, should the norm of nonintervention be modified and if so how? How would such a change translate into effective policy and international law? The current discussion resembles the post–World War II debate about the significance of nuclear weapons. First came a period of schizophrenia, from 1945 to 1958, when policymakers struggled to fit nuclear weapons into existing ideas about warfare and, at the same time, sought to remove them from the face of the earth. It was only in the late 1950s that a new strategy of deterrence for the nuclear age was undertaken. In the post–Cold War era, some fourteen years after the fall of the Berlin Wall, policymakers continue to struggle to determine whether the criteria of a just war still apply in the twenty-first century, and how they might be adapted to embrace the new challenges inherent in the concept of just intervention. If the "moral" decision is made to define what constitutes grounds for just intervention, a new policy and legal framework is needed. It is, however, worth noting that the Just War Ethic is the product of some sixteen hundred years of evolutionary thought, while the just intervention debate is in its infancy.

Before exploring further such a moral and legal framework for an ethic of just intervention, I will look at selected cases of intervention in the 1990s and early twenty-first century to examine the lessons they offer and the precedents that they may have set.

New Rules of Engagement?

The United States, in partnership with the United Nations, had barely a year to reflect on the challenges of the post–Cold War era before the Gulf crisis. In September 1990, President George H. W. Bush articulated his vision for a "new world order." President Bush stated, "Had we not responded to this first provocation with clarity of purpose; if we do not continue to demonstrate our determination; it would be a signal to actual and potential despots around the world." [8] This state- ment, made four months before the coalition went to war against Iraq, was followed, two weeks after the outbreak of the conflict, by another. Bush declared, "America was the only nation on this earth that could assemble the forces of peace." [9] Following the victory over Iraq, President Bush also alluded to the role of the United Nations in the new world order, "the United Nations, freed from cold war stalemate, is poised to fulfill the historic vision of its founders."

It is ironic that the first attempt to define a role for the United States in the post–Cold War era was, in fact, precipitated by a conflict that had all the elements of a traditional war in a prenuclear age, rather than an intervention. Iraq's aggression against a sovereign country, Kuwait, occasioned the conflict. The Alliance, led by the United States, in choosing to end the war after expelling Iraqi forces from Kuwait and not taking the war to Baghdad consciously sought to adhere to the traditional doctrine of a just war (respect for national boundaries) ethic rather than entering the still undefined territory of just intervention. President Bush's "new world order" was, in fact, a return to the vision of Woodrow Wilson, albeit under very different circumstances. Both visions foresaw:

- the guarantee of respect for sovereignty and territorial integrity
- insuring the safety of democratic societies by a universal system of collective security against the threat of arbitrary power
- a leadership role for the United States [10]

The real challenges in dealing with a new era characterized initially by intervention and then again by war were to fall to the next two U.S. administrations. And these challenges were very different. President Bill Clinton, on one hand, was

X / 128

confronted in short order by crises in Somalia, Rwanda, Bosnia, Haiti, and Kosovo. The U.S. response to these various crises was slow and painful and took place broadly within the framework of a debate on multilateral just intervention on humanitarian grounds. President George W. Bush, on the other hand, confronted by a direct act of aggression on U.S. soil, took immediate action, initially with UN approval, against Afghanistan and, subsequently, undertook a preemptive, unilateralist approach to war against Iraq. The rationale for the Iraq war was a curious mixture of just cause, posited in terms of defense of vital interests (that is, security against WMD) and right intent, in terms of the humanitarian suffering of the Iraqi people. Above all, it highlighted the tension surrounding the issue of last resort: Can a preemptive war be just? Is it "just" if evidence is subsequently found that "justifies" the intervention and therefore, to the contrary, if no evidence is forthcoming?

Judging Theory against Reality: Intervention in the 1990s

To President Clinton, inaugurated in January 1993, fell the task of actively defining the role of the United States in the post–Cold War era. The Gulf War that had inaugurated the new era did not presage the challenges that were to follow and this allowed the first Bush administration, while referring to a "new world order" to, in fact, conduct business very much as usual on its watch. The Gulf War was a traditional war, with a clear aggressor (Iraq) against a sovereign state (Kuwait), albeit the most high-tech one in history. U.S. casualties had been minimal, popular and congressional support high, and there was a sense that the United States had finally shed the burden of Vietnam.

Samuel Berger, Clinton's national security adviser, writes in *Foreign Affairs,* in late 2000: "Like no president before him, Bill Clinton has dedicated the power and passion of his presidency to peacemaking. Like most other presidents, he has had to contend with those who say America should do nothing about foreign conflict unless we are directly threatened. . . . We have worked for peace because we believe in defusing conflicts before, not after, they escalate and harm our vital interests."[11] His choice of the phrasing "vital interests" as distinct from national or international is interesting. Vital interests are usually defined as being those that directly threaten the security of the country and the safety of its civilian population. It is questionable whether intervention in a failed state, such as Somalia, would meet the traditional definition of vital interests.

Somalia

Somalia was the Clinton administration's immediate inheritance from the first Bush administration. The first UN peacekeeping forces, United Nations Operation in Somalia, arrived in Somalia in April 1992 in response to the collapse of civilian authority that had seen hundreds of thousands of Somalis dying of starvation and disease and fighting between rival clans. As the humanitarian crisis worsened, President Bush in December 1992 after his defeat at the polls announced the intention of the United States to deploy twenty-eight thousand U.S. troops as part of what was to become a thirty-seven-thousand-strong, U.S.-led Unified Task Force (UNITAF).[12] Bush stated, "Our mission is humanitarian, but we will not tolerate armed gangs ripping off their own people, condemning them to death by starvation." The seeds of confusion were already apparent in that statement and implied that, despite the humanitarian nature of the intervention, the United States would inevitably become involved in Somali politics.

For the United Nations, Resolution 794 of December 3, 1992, establishing UNITAF to implement humanitarian relief operations in Somalia, broke new ground. "This was the first time that an unambiguously internal and humanitarian crisis had been designated as a threat to international peace and security, thus justifying peace-enforcement measures."[13]

Somalia was to have a decisive impact on the just intervention debate for the wrong reasons—it was ultimately an unmitigated disaster. The death of eighteen U.S. soldiers in late 1993 led to the Clinton administration's decision to withdraw troops by March 1994, accompanied by all European troops. The UN forces withdrew completely by March 1995.

This experience tempered the approaches of both the United States and the UN to humanitarian intervention. The immediate loser was Rwanda where some eight hundred thousand people died as a result of genocide that began in April 1994 when the international community was still licking its wounds from Somalia and failed to intervene: "In Bosnia, UN peacekeepers under fire from or taken prisoner by Serb forces over the last two years were expected to turn the other cheek for fear of 'crossing the Mogadishu line' " (that is, abandoning neutrality and becoming involved in a civil war).[14]

But the lessons supposedly learned from Somalia, a failed state, where a successful intervention could never have been short-term, did not necessarily apply to the very different cases of Rwanda, where a rapid end to genocide would have been the rationale for just intervention, nor apply to Bosnia in the throes of a civil war, where ethnic cleansing in the heart of Europe made the case for just intervention on humanitarian grounds.

The retrospective lessons from Somalia, laid out by Clarke and Herbst in 1996, provide a much more constructive blueprint:

> This much is manifest: no massive intervention in a failed state—even one for humanitarian purposes—can be assuredly short by plan, politically neutral in execution, or wisely parsimonious in providing "nation-building" development aid. Nations do not descend into anarchy overnight, so intervenors should

expect neither the reconciliation of the combatants nor the reconstruction of civil societies and national economies to be swift. There is an inescapable reciprocity between civil and military goals. Military commanders cannot expect a failed state to become inherently peaceful and stable and their efforts to be worthwhile in the long run without the work of developmental and civil affairs experts. Likewise, humanitarian workers must recognize that the relief goods they handle in failed states can become the currency of warlords.[15]

By the time of the signing of the Dayton Peace Accord in November 1995, which brought an end to the four-year agony of Bosnia, the lesson had been learned that an intervention characterized by impartiality and limited in scope cannot suffice when a country has been devastated by civil war. But it came at a high price for the people of Bosnia. And it was of no help whatsoever to the eight hundred thousand who perished in the Rwandan genocide between April and July 1994.

Rwanda

The roots of the Rwandan tragedy in the 1990s can be found in the 1959–63 explosion of violence between the two rival groups, the Hutus and the Tutsis. In the late 1980s, Tutsi refugees in Uganda formed the Rwandan Patriotic Front that attacked the Hutu regime in Rwanda in 1990. After three years of conflict the Arusha Agreement was signed in August 1993. But the assassination of the president of Burundi, Melchior Ndadaye, a Hutu, October 1993, sparked mass killings first of Tutsis and then, in retaliation, Hutus. The subsequent death of President Juvenal Habyarimana of Rwanda and President Cyprien Ntaryamira of Burundi when their plane crashed on April 6, 1994, was used as a pretext by Hutu extremists to seize power and to attack all Tutsis and Hutu moderates.

Although it is arguable that the speed of the genocide, with the majority of the killings being carried out between April 3 and 20, 1994, would have rendered any intervention too little and too late, the lesson lies in the failure of foresight and preventive diplomacy. "U.S. intelligence agencies committed virtually no in-country resources to what was considered a tiny state in a region of little strategic value. During the genocide's early stages, the U.S. government actually received most of its information from non-governmental organizations."[16]

Other issues, raised by Romeo A. Dallaire, the Canadian commander of the UN forces on the ground, are the moral possibility of success and the role of nonmajor powers in intervention. He writes: "Yet a central, moral question remains unanswered: did the ineffectiveness of the UN mission in grasping the situation and poor handling of the political, humanitarian, and military response in extremis abet the genocide?" He answers in the affirmative. He goes on to say, "This gap between the intensely complex and desperately critical situation and the inadequacy of the resources provided to deal with it, raises a profound question of moral pragmatism. If the intervention comes to a point where it has little or no chance of being effective, should it have been withdrawn (or some might say undertaken) in the first place?"

Dallaire also reflects on the question of major power involvement:

> The US involvement in and around Rwanda presents a paradox that does not suit a global power. In my mind, it remains evident that even though US soldiers and field commanders were more than willing to do much more, they were ordered to stay out, avoid casualties and smile for the cameras. Of course, domestic politics have a direct influence on foreign policy, but when spin doctors slow and enfeeble relief efforts of the big powers well below the minimum of support required to stop the enormous suffering at hand, I believe we should look more closely at what middle powers and third world nations, which also had to balance moral assessments of support against risks of casualties, can ultimately do. Canada, Australia, the United Kingdom, Ghana, India, Ethiopia, and Tunisia all put their efforts inside Rwanda . . . right on the front line where they were needed most. These nations, some desperately poor, shamed the world by doing the right thing. So, do we pursue these middle powers to deploy up front and keep the world's first powers in reserve, in support of the operations? I believe this option merits serious study and review.[17]

So, by 1994, with Bosnia two years into its tragic war, the Clinton administration and the UN were already reeling from two ill-fated interventions in Africa. Although the United Nations High Commission for Refugees (UNHCR) had been heavily engaged in coordinating the UN humanitarian response to the refugee crisis in the former Yugoslav republics since November 1991, nothing that had gone before predisposed the UN or the United States to look with optimism on supplementing humanitarian intervention by military intervention in Bosnia.

Indeed, the decade of the 1990s that had opened with such high hopes for peace and prosperity in the post–Cold War era was no longer looking so bright. "In the 1995 edition of *Agenda for Peace,* the fundamental policy document on UN peacekeeping, Secretary-General Boutros Boutros-Ghali expressed less optimism about the possibilities for intervention than in the 1992 edition, largely because of the United Nations' searing experience in Somalia.[18] It would be left to his successor, Kofi Annan, to examine the legacy of the UN's peacekeeping role in the Brahimi report, issued in August 2000.

Bosnia

Bosnia was not a failed state (it was a brand-new one) such as Somalia; genocide was not being perpetrated as in Rwanda. Bosnia was an example of a civil war between the three major ethnic groups with outside aggression from Catholic Croatia and Orthodox Serbia. This outside aggression could have offered the international community the "just" option of intervening. But impartial intervention would have had to be massive to be effective and, therefore, unpopular in public opinion, whereas intervention on behalf of one side was not necessarily supported by member countries of the European Union (EU).

International reaction, therefore, was one of paralysis in the face of the unfolding crisis. This translated into a commitment to humanitarian assistance but little else. François Fouinat, Coordinator of the UNHCR Task Force for the Former Yugoslavia (deployed in November 1991), stated in October 1993, "It is not simply that the UN's humanitarian efforts have become politicized; it is rather that we have been transformed into the only manifestation of political will."[19] UNHCR itself came under severe criticism for allegedly facilitating ethnic cleansing by evacuating vulnerable civilian populations. UN High Commissioner for Refugees Sadako Ogata described the predicament as follows: "In the context of a conflict which has as its very objective the displacement of people, we find ourselves confronted with a major dilemma. To what extent do we persuade people to remain where they are, when that could well jeopardize their lives and liberties? On the other hand, if we help them to move, do we not become an accomplice to 'ethnic cleansing'?"[20]

The paralysis of the international community had several root causes. First, the United States, despite a growing debate about multilateral intervention, was still hostage to baggage from the Vietnam War and held to two central premises: that a government had ultimately to be able to survive without external support and that casualties had to be kept to a minimum. Too many elements of the Bosnian conflict resembled the quagmire of Vietnam with its guerrilla-type warfare and complex internal politics.

Profound difficulties arose as a result of deep-seated differences between the United States and the EU on interpretation of the root causes of the crisis and how to resolve it: "The US tended to see Serb aggression at the root of the conflict, while the Europeans (with the exception of Germany) tended to distribute blame more equally. The Europeans, therefore, approached the task more as mediators than as partisans. The Europeans were more inclined to believe that a solution would have to involve some form of separation while the Americans believed that a united, multiethnic Bosnia was not only desirable but also attainable."[21] The Dayton Peace Accord of December 1995 marked the final reluctant acceptance by the United States that, at least in the short term, Bosnia would be divided along ethnic lines. Dayton did, however, provide for assistance for the "right of return." Ironically, Dayton differed remarkably little in its lines of partition from an earlier peace plan put forward in February 1992 by the Europeans that provided for Bosnia to become a confederation of three states.

During the 1992 U.S. presidential election campaign, Democratic Party candidate Bill Clinton, "conveying a sense of moral outrage at Serb actions and

X /133

atrocities, was calling for a more interventionist US approach." [22] Once elected, N
however, the Clinton administration "expressed great concern for the Muslims'
plight, yet it was equally adamant [as the Bush administration] in ruling out a
combat role for US ground forces and was ambivalent even about helping to oversee the implementation of any peace accord." [23] However, the new administration N
immediately took a more active role in the negotiating process with the EU and
the UN and later joined with the United Kingdom, France, Germany, and Russia
to form the "Contact Group" in April 1994.

Bosnia highlighted the differences between the United States and its European
allies and underlined the absence of any clear definition of the principles for "just
intervention." Although the United States was rhetorically more inclined to intervene militarily in favor of the Muslims and against the Serbs, in practice it was not
prepared to commit ground troops to that end. The EU, inclined to seek a peace
accord based on ethnic partition and to deal in an even-handed way with the three
parties, had peacekeepers on the ground and was opposed to air strikes that would
jeopardize their safety. The UN meanwhile had been handed a mandate of peacekeeping that implied its neutrality. This ultimately contributed to strengthening
the strongest aggressor, the Bosnian Serbs.

The West at Dayton elevated President Slobodan Milosevic to the status of
peace maker. His popularity at home was undiminished. To the great disillusion-
ment of the Albanian population in Kosovo, a province of Serbia, the Dayton
Accord made no attempt to deal with its status. The human rights abuses against
Kosovo's Albanian majority population by the Serbs had long been seen as the
potential flashpoint for conflict in Europe. The groundwork was in place for the
evolution of the next crisis in Europe.

Kosovo

The crisis in Kosovo was hardly a surprise. Since 1989, when the province's autonomous status within Serbia was revoked, Balkans experts had been predicting that
Kosovo would be the tinderbox for another war in Europe.

In February 1998, clashes intensified between the Kosovo Liberation Army and
the Serbian security forces. The violence caused large numbers of Kosovars to flee
to Albania and Montenegro, provoking a large-scale refugee crisis that threatened
the fragile stability of those newly democratic governments.

Peace talks convened in Rambouillet, France, in February 1999 but when these
collapsed, NATO launched a seventy-eight-day bombing attack on Kosovo and
Serbia, as a "last resort." This action was taken without authorization from the
UN Security Council where Russian and Chinese vetoes were anticipated. The
NATO decision itself was hard fought and had provoked serious tensions within
the Alliance. Even though by autumn 1998, all NATO nations agreed that there

X /134

was a moral and political imperative to act, the members of the Alliance could not easily and unanimously find a legal ground for military action against Serbia. Six countries at least—Belgium, France, Germany, Greece, Italy, and Spain—had political and legal misgivings reflecting the unfinished state of international law concerning humanitarian intervention (using force)." [24]

Immediately prior to the NATO decision to begin its bombing campaign, the Russian Ambassador to the UN, Sergei Lavrov, asserted that to invoke "a humanitarian crisis in a country as a sufficient reason for unilateral intervention" would be "unacceptable and contrary to the foundations of the contemporary system of international relations and to the Charter of the United Nations." [25] Once the bombing campaign started, Chinese officials condemned the operation in even stronger terms and "warned of serious consequences if the bombing did not stop." [26] Western concepts about the evolution of the right of humanitarian intervention were, it appeared, by no means universal.

Kosovo was not a failed state; it was not a state at all. Aggression was being perpetrated by the government of the country on some of its (Albanian) citizens. Kosovo was the clearest example to date of the multilateral undertaking of just intervention in a sovereign state. Intervention in Kosovo was not impartial, because there were none of the doubts that accompanied the issue of intervention in Bosnia concerning which side was the aggressor.

The NATO air campaign caused an initial escalation of violence on the ground as Milosevic appeared intent on wrapping up his campaign of ethnic cleansing. Thousands of Kosovar Albanians were killed and some eight hundred thousand fled or were expelled from Kosovo after the start of the air campaign. [27] The NATO bombing was also responsible for the deaths of some refugees and of Serbian civilians in Belgrade and other major cities in Serbia proper, raising serious questions about noncombatant immunity and proportionality.

Was Kosovo an exception or would it set a precedent for just intervention? As the Clinton administration reached the end of its term, the next administration, under George W. Bush, seemed uninterested in grappling with the issue of just cause and just means with which to carry out interventions. In fact, it had publicly eschewed "nation building" during the election campaign and stated that it would begin to withdraw U.S. troops from Bosnia and Kosovo, a statement that it later recanted.

Iraq: An Old Reality Revisited?

Both the moral and legal framework for just intervention had been shown to be lacking in the 1990s, resulting in a number of interventions that lacked consistency in either the ways or means. Despite this, these interventions had some common features, in terms of proper authority (multilateral), just cause (humanitarian), and right intent (relief of suffering). The lessons they offered had been examined by the international community and the precedents they set have underlined the need to update and expand the evolving body of international law concerning humanitarian intervention. But in the aftermath of the September 11, 2001, attack on the World Trade Center, focus moved sharply away from humanitarian intervention and back to the more familiar territory of war.

Although the subject was more familiar, the players were different. The aggressor in this conflict was not a state, but nonstate actors with access to the type of resources and intelligence that traditionally had been out of their reach. The initial outpouring of sympathy and support for the United States from most of the world community reflected both the shock and the recognition that all states were potentially vulnerable to this type of attack. The rules of the game had been radically changed and the nature of the debates that followed reflected the disorientation of the major state players.

The Bush administration warned the Taliban government of Afghanistan that it should stop harboring Al Qaeda operatives. When it became clear that the Taliban would not oblige, the administration lost little time in going to war in Afghanistan. Although the United States took the lead itself, it enjoyed wide support both from UN member states and the U.S. public. By early 2003, Iraq had become the focus for the administration's concern. Saddam was deemed an "imminent" threat to U.S. vital security interests on the basis that he possessed WMD. The administration intimated that there was a strong connection between Saddam and the Al Qaeda network, the implication being that he could provide terrorists with WMD for use against the United States.

The administration initially worked through the UN Security Council, and Resolution 1441 was passed, bringing UN weapons inspectors back to Iraq. Despite their failure to locate any WMD and their requests for more time, the United States decided to take military action. When the UN declined to follow the U.S. lead, the administration, supported primarily by Britain, proceeded to take preemptive action and went to war, without UN proper authority.

The Bush administration cited the imminent threat to its vital national security interests as the main rationale for going to war with Iraq. It asserted the need to strike preemptively before Saddam Hussein could further develop and deploy WMD. But in an effort to depict the war in humanitarian terms that would be more palatable to a wider audience, it also made reference to rescuing the Iraqi people from oppression. Meanwhile, North Korea—another member of the Bush "axis of evil"—a country that was demonstrably closer to developing WMD than Iraq while continuing its domestic policy of oppression, was subjected to nothing more menacing than ongoing multilateral diplomacy. These two widely differing approaches led to inevitable speculation about the administration's hidden agenda, both by the American public and by the international community.

The administration floundered in its rhetoric, even as it moved decisively toward war. Terms such as "crusade" and "regime change" surfaced and then disappeared from the administration's official statements, but the harm was done. While some in the Bush administration saw Iraq as the first step toward creating a peaceful and democratic Middle East, other outside commentators speculated that for George W. Bush the real incentive was simply to get rid of Saddam Hussein, the man who had eluded and made attempts on his father's life.

The lack of one clearly stated and credible rationale for war with Iraq greatly damaged the international and national credibility of the Bush administration. It also provoked enormous strains with U.S. allies within the UN, particularly in Europe. The debate came to be less about the threat posed by Saddam and more about distrust of U.S. intentions.

Was the Iraq war a just war? In terms of proper authority, despite the UN's lack of sanction, the United States as a sovereign state has the right to defend itself from outside aggression, if such aggression actually was manifest. The cause would have been just if it was the destruction of WMD that could threaten the vital security interests of the United States—the problem was that no hard evidence was or has yet been found to support that claim.

As for right intent, the juxtaposition of so many conflicting reasons for war only raised doubts about intent. In terms of proportionality of means, although civilians were not explicitly targeted, there were many civilian casualties; however, the conduct of the war adhered to post–World War II norms for noncombatant immunity. The war itself could be judged proportional (that is, among other things, not likely to provoke wider conflict) if viewed as an attack on a small, rogue state by the U.S. superpower. But if the war against Iraq comes to be seen as a war by Christians against Muslims, a twenty-first-century crusade, it risks igniting the "Clash of Civilizations" predicted by Samuel Huntington. Seen in these terms, it does not meet the criteria of proportionality any more than did a U.S. intervention into Hungary in 1956. In addition, the war in Iraq appears to have distracted resources and attention from the fight against terrorism, as well as created new recruits for Al Qaeda. And far from offering hope for a wider Middle East peace, the war in Iraq threatens to further destabilize the region and to turn Iraq itself into a gathering point for terrorists. Certainly the Israeli-Palestinian conflict has only worsened in its aftermath.

There was a moral possibility, if not certainty, of military success. But in terms of the postconflict situation, there is no clarity of goals or timelines. The many different and conflicting reasons given for going to war have made it unclear what type of intervention the war in Iraq constitutes. Without benchmarks, it is impossible to judge success.

The Iraq war was not a war of last resort; it was a war of choice, not necessity. The conflict was also a radical departure from the "just" interventions of the

1990s. It bears more resemblance to the type of interventions carried out during the Cold War era by both superpowers into countries within their own spheres of influence to effect regime change or to restore order. In this sense, the Iraq war does not fit into the evolving framework for just intervention. It remains to be seen if the rest of the twenty-first century will follow the Iraq pattern with "coalitions of the willing," led by the United States, becoming the norm, or whether we will revert to multilateral just interventions under UN or other auspices. The current and growing unpopularity of the Iraqi occupation among the U.S. public may well determine the direction, particularly in the aftermath of Hurricane Katrina as the domestic political debate begins about the lack of resources and trained manpower available to aid the hurricane victims as a consequence of large scale National Guard deployments and expenditures on the Iraq war.

Lessons Learned from Interventions in the 1990s and in Iraq

UN Secretary-General Kofi Annan, in reviewing the record of intervention in the 1990s, has expressed the hope that two cases, those of Rwanda and Kosovo, are never repeated. The first case he characterizes as a moral failure on the part of the international community and the second as a legal failure, when the UN was simply bypassed and the air campaign launched without UN authorization. In the 1990s "expectations and assignments given to the United Nations outran its capacity for effective action." [28] The Brahimi report [29] was intended to review the record of the 1990s in the areas of peacekeeping and security and to make practical recommendations for the future.

In looking back on the decade, the panel stated:

> As the United Nations has bitterly and repeatedly discovered over the last decade, no amount of good intentions can substitute for the fundamental ability to project credible force if complex peacekeeping, in particular, is to succeed. But force alone cannot create peace; it can only create the space in which peace may be built. Moreover the changes that the Panel recommends will have no lasting impact unless Member States summon the political will to support the United Nations politically, financially, and operationally to enable the United Nations to be truly credible as a force for peace. [30]

Increasingly in the 1990s, the United Nations found itself deploying into situations where the warring parties had not signed a peace accord, or where a peace accord, such as the Arusha Agreement in Rwanda, had broken down. The UN, therefore, found itself in situations of ongoing conflict. Although the Brahimi Panel concurred that the "consent of the local parties, impartiality and use of force only in self-defense should remain the bedrock principles of peacekeeping," it went on to acknowledge that experience had shown that the norms of impartiality and self defense should be subject to exceptions. Thus, it should be understood that "where one party to a peace agreement clearly and incontrovertibly is violating its terms, continued equal treatment of all parties by the United Nations can in the best case result in ineffectiveness and in the worst may amount to complicity with evil."[31]

In addition, the panel recommends that the UN be authorized to stop violence against civilians in defense of the principle of noncombatant immunity. But the panel stresses that those UN missions charged with civilian protection should be given the appropriate resources with which to effectively carry out their mission—the moral possibility of success. This, most glaringly, did not happen in Srebrenica, Bosnia, where UN peacekeepers stood helplessly by while Bosnian Serb forces massacred Muslim civilians under UN protection in a designated "safe area."

The panel made a comprehensive list of recommendations to the UN. These focus on strengthening the UN's:

- intelligence gathering capacity;
- ability to deploy more rapidly by creating standby multinational brigades and on-call lists of military officers, civilian police, international judicial experts, penal experts, and human rights specialists;
- cooperation across military and civilian sectors through the creation of "Integrated Mission Task Forces"; and
- capacity of its headquarters to plan and support peace operations.

In commissioning this report, Annan showed courage and foresight. He recognized that the UN has become, de facto if not yet de jure, the primary institution charged, by its member states, with carrying out multilateral intervention, but that the record to date is a sorry one. In order for the UN to have the "moral possibility of success" in any future interventions, the lessons learned from the mistakes of the 1990s must be absorbed and measures taken to correct them.

Implementation of the panel's recommendations necessitates political will from its member states but also flexibility and creativity from UN bureaucrats. If successful, they will go a long way toward ensuring that interventions in the twenty-first century will benefit from a more coherent approach than those of the last decade. With enhanced planning, integration, means, and coherence of mandate, the UN may finally be in a position to carry out the vision of its founders. In conclusion, the panel called on the leaders of the world assembled at the Millennium Summit, "to commit . . . to strengthen the capacity of the United Nations to fully accomplish the mission which is, indeed, its very raison d'être: to help communities engulfed in strife and to maintain or restore peace."[32]

The Brahimi report was drafted to look at the hard lessons learned from the multilateral interventions of the 1990s. Kofi Annan recognized, however, that if the UN is to remain relevant in the new debate about the just use of force, it needs to continue to reform its structure and practices. Therefore, on September 23, 2003, Kofi Annan called on the Security Council to "begin a discussion on the criteria for an early authorization of coercive measures to address certain types of threats—for instance, terrorist groups armed with weapons of mass destruction."[33] He announced the formation of the High Level Panel on Threats, Challenges, and Change, charged with the following tasks: first, to examine current challenges to peace and security and to provide an analysis of potential future threats; second, to consider the contribution that collective action can make in addressing these challenges and assess existing approaches, mechanisms and instruments; and third, to recommend the changes necessary to ensure effective collective action.

The Secretary-General argued that a viable system of collective action "must protect millions of our fellow men and women from the familiar threats of poverty, hunger and deadly disease. We must understand that a threat to some is a threat to all, and needs to be addressed accordingly."

The panel issued a series of recommendations in its final report, including the need for preventive measures to combat poverty, ensure biological security, combat the spread of transnational organized crime and prevent the spread of nuclear and biological weapons. In terms of combating the threat of terrorism, the panel urged "the forging of a strategy of counterterrorism that is respectful of human rights and the rule of law."

In the sixtieth UN General Assembly beginning in September 2005, debate was dominated by discussion of the controversial enlargement of the Security Council. In this regard the panel made a strong recommendation that whatever the future composition of the Security Council (and it supported enlargement as a recognition of present-day realities), there should be a review of membership in 2020 that explicitly took into account the "point of view of the Council's effectiveness in taking collective action to prevent and remove new and old threats to international peace and security." But reform of the council's membership was blocked because of disagreement among current members and the failure of potential applicant states to reach consensus on a list of candidate countries.

In outlining the military measures that should be undertaken to combat threats, the Panel made an important contribution to moving the Just War/Just Intervention debate forward. The executive summary of the report includes the panel's endorsement of "the emerging norm of a responsibility to protect civilians from large-scale violence with force if necessary, though only as a last resort." The panel identifies five criteria that should determine whether or not to use military force: seriousness of threat, proper purpose, last resort, proportional means and balance of consequences. The last four criteria are directly drawn from the original Just War Ethic.

In seeking to identify seriousness of threat, the panel took a clear position in favor of moving the UN from an ethic of Just War to an ethic of Just Intervention in the twenty-first century. The report "endorses the emerging norm that there is a collective international responsibility to protect, exercisable by the Security Council authorizing military intervention as a last resort, in the event of genocide and other large scale killing, ethnic cleansing or serious violations of international humanitarian law which sovereign Governments have proved powerless or unwilling to prevent." The panel has rendered an important service by endorsing this norm, a reflection of international practice during the 1990s. The next step, described in the following section, is to transform the practice and the norm into international law.

On September 13, 2005, the General Assembly adopted a "statement of goals" that significantly watered down many of the panel's proposals, including language that the UN should assume a "responsibility to protect" civilian populations when governments are "unable or unwilling" to do so. The U.S. delegation took the lead in replacing this language with a weaker formulation that the UN "is prepared to take action" in such cases, thus removing any legal obligation to intervene.

Most recently, in an important move, on December 30, 2005, the United Nations approved the establishment of the Peacebuilding Commission. According to the UN Department of Public Information, the Peacebuilding Commission's mandate is to:

- Propose integrated strategies for postconflict peace building and recovery
- Help insure predictable financing for early recovery activities and sustained investment over the medium to longer term
- Extend the period of attention by the international community to postconflict recovery
- Develop best practices on issues that require extensive collaboration among political, military, humanitarian, and development actors

The establishment of this commission strengthens the UN mandate in postconflict situations and the reference to the need to insure predictable financing may enable this reform to have some real impact.

International Humanitarian Law

At the beginning of the twenty-first century, it is clear that there is as yet no new paradigm for "pro-democratic" or humanitarian intervention. Neither the moral nor legal framework fits the new reality. "International law governing the right of humanitarian intervention is incomplete. International practice has evolved swiftly during the 1990s. Yet the incipient political and moral consensus that intervention is sometimes necessary to prevent human rights violation on a major scale has not been formalized into a set of rules of international law. It is now urgent that this consensus should be transformed into international law."[34]

In the past decade, the moral practice of intervention has outstripped the current state of international humanitarian law. This must be addressed forthwith lest it lead to murderous delays or even be used as an excuse for indefinitely delaying intervention. The extreme confusion and different interpretations of the legal grounds for intervention surrounding the conflict in Kosovo are the most obvious example. China and Russia, as we have seen, accused the NATO members of violating the UN Charter, which requires Security Council authorization for intervention. The West Europeans, meanwhile, were equally conflicted. NATO Secretary-General Javier Solana justified the action by arguing that the use of force was the only way "to prevent more human suffering and more repression and violence against the civilian population of Kosovo."[35] This was a moral rather than legal argument and echoes Michael Walzer who, a prophet before his time, wrote in 1977, "Any state capable of stopping the slaughter has a right, at least, to try to do so. The legalist paradigm indeed rules out such efforts, but that only suggests that the paradigm, unrevised, cannot account for the moral realities of military intervention."[36]

The two bodies of law that are directly relevant in the debate on intervention are international human rights law and humanitarian law. The first of these is an offshoot of the UN's Declaration of Human Rights and deals with violations by states, and the second, which evolves from the older tradition of *jus in bello,* deals with violations by individuals. These two bodies of laws have increasingly overlapped as international tribunals on Former Yugoslavia (1993) and Rwanda (1994) and the International Criminal Court (1998) have been created in recent years. "But what is also common to international human-rights law and humanitarian law is that however sophisticated they are becoming in laying out sanctions, they are silent on preventive measures. Yet, it is precisely the prevention of massive human rights violations or humanitarian catastrophes that has become the basis of 'humanitarian intervention' practices in recent years. These practices have not yet been codified into law. The only certainty about them is that, increasingly, they give primacy to human rights over the sovereignty of states when the two principles conflict."[37]

As precedent is set in practice concerning just intervention within sovereign borders, international law is likely to follow. "The law evolves as practices become acceptable to most states in the international community."[38] Kosovo might therefore serve as a precedent rather than as an exception. One difficulty with using this precedent to establish universal practice is that Kosovo could be argued to be subject to the Organization for Security and Cooperation in Europe (OSCE) human rights principles that "allow states to interfere with one another's affairs well beyond what general international law permits."[39] It may be that Europe, through the OSCE, should take the lead in developing specific rules for humanitarian intervention with the hope that the rest of the world will follow.

Where To Now?

In the light of the lessons learned over the past decade, how should we construct a new ethic for the twenty-first century? The departure point should be to preserve nonintervention as the norm; intervention should be the exception that proves the rule. The Westphalian concept of state sovereignty did have some moral content in its goal of preserving order, in other words, peace. It also recognized that the first duty of a head of state is to his or her own people. Hence, the definition of vital interests as being those that relate directly to the security of the civilians of one's own state.

But in today's globalized world, conflict inside state borders now has the potential to threaten regional or international security with a speed and intensity that was unthinkable in the Westphalian age. In addition, with the end of the Cold War, the international community, for the first time in fifty years, has the chance to focus on issues of justice within states' borders and to reopen the discussion of just cause, as distinct from just means, that dominated the last four centuries. Vital interests retain their primacy but consideration of national and international interests now can and should be added to the equation. There must be consideration of contemporary causes that may override the presumption of nonintervention. In the 1990s, just cause for intervention included, in practice, genocide, failed states, and ethnic cleansing. Whereas it may be tempting to add to this list, it is a temptation that should be resisted.

In 2003, the Bush administration undertook intervention to prevent a state from developing WMD that, if employed, would threaten U.S. vital interests. An important line has been crossed here. A distinction should be drawn between the intent to use and the actual use which is qualitatively different—in other words, in nuclear terms, no first strike should be the rule for intervention. But such a distinction should not be applied to terrorist groups that may also acquire such weapons. Terrorist groups do not acquire WMD as a bargaining chip or to defend their own people; they acquire them with the express intent to use them against civilians of states that they seek to destroy. The U.S. intervention in Afghanistan to root out the terrorists who had, in this instance, already attacked American civilians on American soil, and the regime that sheltered them, was thus in a completely different category than its intervention in Iraq.

Another cause that some would like to see added to the list is abuse of human rights that falls short of genocide or ethnic cleansing, but to cross that line is to open a Pandora's Box. What country in the world do others at some point not see as committing human rights abuses? Such an approach also risks widening the philosophical divide between the West and the developing world that would likely be the target of most interventions of this type.

Diplomacy, including selectively applied sanctions, should remain the tool of choice in issues of prevention—in terms of dissuading states from acquiring WMD as well as in seeking to avert internal conflict. As we have seen, the intelligence gathering capacities of the United States and the UN should be strengthened, particularly in regions that have traditionally not been those of geo-strategic interest. Force should truly remain the last resort in terms of ending the aggression of whatever nature, otherwise the line become too easy to cross.

Interventions in the 1990s differed most notably from those of previous eras in their designation of proper authority. Multilateral intervention became the norm. A key building block for a new ethic of just intervention should be its multilateral nature. This would lessen fears that the United States or other major powers are acting in a hegemonic fashion and would give more credibility to claims of right intent. In the Cold War, the UN had a limited role. Now it has the chance to be the lead agency in the just intervention debate, but it must first resolve the paradox inherent in its own structure. Founded by sovereign states, it is also the home of the Charter of Human Rights. How does the UN balance these dual pressures? Secretary-General Kofi Annan has expressed the view that two crises of the 1990s must not be repeated. First, the failure to intervene in Rwanda (a direct consequence of the debacle in Somalia) and prevent mass genocide was a moral failure. Second, the decision to bypass the UN in the Kosovo intervention was a legal failure. Now the U.S. intervention in Iraq threatens to undermine the UN Charter and the Just War Ethic itself.

A preference for a multilateral approach, however, need not necessarily restrict the designation of proper authority to the UN. There may well be a case for recognizing that in certain circumstances when, as in the case of Kosovo, the Security Council threatens to veto intervention for political reasons, despite obvious just cause, NATO could be the designated authority. In other situations, the European defense force, should it materialize, might be the appropriate authority. The European defense initiative may also spur other regions such as Africa, Latin America, and Asia to examine the possible security role of their own regional associations, such as the African Union (formerly OAU)—as in Liberia, the Organization of American States, and the Association of South East Asian Nations. Such a role might be defined in terms of intervention to preserve peace in their own neighborhoods, preferably still under a UN mandate to avoid fears of the emergence of regional hegemons and, where appropriate, with U.S. involvement. This would lessen the direct burden on both the UN and the United States.

The debate at the UN about lessons learned in the 1990s should go a long way to addressing the issue of moral possibility of success. With a more coherent mandate and increased means, the question posed by Romeo Dallaire in Rwanda about whether it would have been better under the circumstances for the UN never to have deployed at all will, we hope, not have to be posed in future UN interventions.

Although the end of the Cold War and the consequent decreased likelihood of intervention provoking a nuclear response eased temporarily the justification of the principle of proportionality, the potential advent of terrorists acquiring WMD and of the danger of a Muslim-Christian global war should serve to keep this question at the forefront of any debate about just intervention.

The 1990s presented the international community with new challenges—in Kofi Annan's phrase, "problems without passports"—that required a serious review of the existing framework for the just use of force. In facing up to the hard lessons learned over the past decade, the dawning of the twenty-first century, despite the war in Iraq, holds out hope for the evolution of an ethic of just intervention, based on its much older counterpart, the Just War Ethic. The challenge of this next, global century is to improve the implementation of humanitarian interventions and to define their mandate, as well as to clarify international human rights law. At a moment in history when, increasingly, even local conflicts have global implications, abandoning the pursuit of justice within or across state borders in an attempt to recapture an illusion of order is not an option.

NOTES

1. Kofi Annan, September 23, 2003, address to the United Nations General Assembly.

2. Ibid. My emphasis.

3. Michael Walzer, *Just and Unjust Wars* (New York: Basic Books, 1977), 86.

4. Ibid., 107.

5. *Foreign Affairs* 73 (November–December 1994): 20.

6. Ibid.

7. United Nations Panel on Peace Operations, August 2000, ix (cited hereafter as Brahimi report, August 2000). The Brahimi report was commissioned by United Nations Secretary General Kofi Annan on March 7, 2000. The Panel on United Nations Peacekeeping Operations comprised Lakhdar Brahimi (Algeria), Brian Atwood (United States), Ambassador Colin Granderson (Trinidad and Tobago), Dame Ann Hercus (New Zealand), Richard Monk (United Kingdom), General (ret.) Klaus Naumann (Germany), Hisako Shimura (Japan), Ambassador Vladimir Shustov (Russia), General Phillip Sibanda (Zimbabwe), and Dr. Cornelio Sommaruga (Switzerland).

8. R. W. Tucker and D. C. Hendrickson, *The Imperial Temptation: The New World Order and America's Purpose* (New York: Council on Foreign Relations, 1992), 29.

9. Ibid., 30.

10. Ibid., 56–57.

11. *Foreign Affairs* 79 (November–December 2000): 29

12. United Nations High Commissioner for Refugees, *The State of the World's Refugees: Fifty Years of Humanitarian Action* (New York: Oxford University Press, 2000), 256.

13. James Mayall, ed., *The New Interventionism 1991–94* (New York: Cambridge University Press, 1996) 94.

14. W. Clarke and J. Herbst, "Somalia and the Future of Humanitarian Intervention," *Foreign Affairs* 75 (March–April 1996): 70.

15. Ibid., 71.

16. Alan J. Kupperman, "Rwanda in Retrospect," *Foreign Affairs* 79 (January–February 2000): 101.

17. Romeo A. Dallaire, "End of Innocence: Rwanda 1994," in *Hard Choices and Moral Dilemmas in Humanitarian Intervention,* ed. Jonathon Moore (Oxford: Rowman and Littlefield, 1998), 85–86.

18. Clarke and Herbst, "Somalia and the Future of Humanitarian Intervention," 71.

19. Ibid., 220.

20. Ibid., 222.

21. Maynard Glitman, "U.S. Policy in Bosnia: Rethinking a Flawed Approach," *Survival* 38 (Winter 1996–97): 68.

22. Ibid., 70.

23. Lawrence Freedman, "Why the West Failed," *Foreign Policy* 97 (Winter 1994–95): 61.

24. Ibid., 528.

25. Ibid., 531.

26. Ibid., 531.

27. United Nations High Commissioner for Refugees, *State of the World's Refugees,* 234.

28. J. Bryan Hehir, "Military Intervention and National Sovereignty: Recasting the Relationship," in Moore, *Hard Choices,* 49.

29. Brahimi report, August 2000.

30. Ibid., viii.

31. Ibid., ix.

32. Brahimi report, August 2000, xv.

33. Kofi Annan, September 23, 2003, address to the UN General Assembly.

34. Catherine Guicherd, "International Law and the War in Kosovo," *Survival* 41, no. 2 (Summer 1999): 29.

35. Ibid., 19.

36. Walzer, *Just and Unjust Wars,* 108.

37. Guicherd, "International Law," 22.

38. Ibid., 24.

39. Ibid., 30.

X / The Responsibility to Protect *Source*

ROMEO DALLAIRE   It is the aim of those us who have survived the catastrophe of the Rwandan genocide never to let it disappear. During the genocide
in Kigali in Rwanda, my mandate was self-defense. I was not authorized to protect
the forty thousand-odd people that we protected. That was done against orders.

We do not know how to resolve conflict today within these new, complex problems. We do not have the structures or instruments we need. We still insist on
solving them within two years—from the peace agreement to a democratic process
and elections in two years. That's impossible. In my country [Canada], we are still
arguing a problem between a minority and a majority that started in 1759. How
can we tell other nations how to solve their problem in two years? Where does that
pretentiousness come from? Why do the big international institutions impose
such milestones?

Ladies and gentlemen, humanitarian catastrophes are resolvable if we use a far
more mature premise of involvement.

The will to intervene is the problem. The instruments of intervention are there
in a spectrum that needs to be harnessed, then to be improved, and then made
usable in a systematic fashion. We need a whole new conceptual basis to conflict
resolution—multi-disciplined, political, diplomatic, military, humanitarian—all
working on one plan, not separate plans, and for a long time. We were in Cyprus
for forty years. Prosperity is there now, and maybe in twenty years the green line
will disappear. We have to acknowledge that we're in for the long haul in these
missions.

Ladies and gentlemen, I have no confidence in single-nation-led coalitions.
They are fundamentally not altruistic; they are fundamentally based on self-
interest. Their aims are not necessarily humanitarian. It is my opinion that we
must work through the UN—it is still the most transparent and impartial world
organization (with warts)—and that it can, in fact, grow if we want to use it.

Why should we worry about that 80 percent of the humanity that's in poverty?
Is it relevant to us? Is humanity in fact the 20 percent of the haves and the other
ones not? Within forty-eight hours of the start of the genocide, French, Italian,
Belgian, and American troops were landing in and around Rwanda, pulling out
about four thousand expatriates and leaving every black person behind: The people who had raised the kids of those who left were slaughtered in their houses. The

From the EPIIC Symposium at Tufts University, "Sovereignty and Intervention," February 2003 others left with banks full of gold and precious jewels and ivory. They even brought out their dogs. There were over two thousand of the best trained and equipped soldiers in the world in and around Kigali. But once the last white person was on the plane, they left and abandoned nearly two thousand ineffective (for the most part) UN troops. Bangladesh had received the order not to help or protect anyone. That's eleven thousand troops. The Belgians pulled out because of casualties and influenced everybody they could to pull out with them.

No one came. Weeks and weeks and weeks and no one came. Why? A staff officer from a power told me, "Sir, we're not going to come in to help stop this." And what were the reasons? One, Rwanda is of no strategic value in the world. Two, there is nothing here—no resources, certainly no strategic resources. He said, "The only thing here is humans, so we're not coming."

They died by the hundreds of thousands, there were more people killed, injured, internally displaced and made refugees in less than one hundred days in Rwanda than in the eight years of the Yugoslavian campaign. I couldn't keep troops on the ground, or feed the people, or give them water to keep them alive. There are still tens of thousands of troops in Yugoslavia. There are billions of dollars of aid going in there. What is the difference? Is the international community racist? Does it have a pecking order? Does it create orphan nations because there are only humans there? Ladies and gentlemen, humanity is made 100 percent of humans and every one of them counts.

They would stop convoys by putting children in the middle of the road. Children became instruments of war. As such they're efficient, they don't cost much, they are expendable. Walk them through the minefields first and then the elders can follow. And these kids in the middle of the road couldn't move because they would be shot if they moved off the road. The convoys would slow down, and they'd be attacked. NGO people who tried to move behind the lines or between the lines would be pulled out and slaughtered. Then one day there is a little three-year-old in the middle of the road. And so we slowed down and stopped. I had a couple of soldiers with me. We looked around and saw nobody there. We walked into the nearby huts: there are only dead bodies, decaying, and being eaten by dogs. As we're doing this the little boy disappeared. We found him in a hut among all the bodies of his family. So I brought him back into the middle of the road, and I looked at him, injured, bloated, full of vermin, and I looked in his eyes and discovered exactly the eyes of my three-year-old. They are both the same. They are both human. Circumstances are different and circumstances are the criteria still used in whether to intervene or not.

Are all humans human or are some more human than others?

Well, thank God, human rights have been in revival and NGOs are increasing exponentially. Today children learn about it, feel it, and live it. Human rights are the instrument by which Kofi Annan made the statement at the Millennium General Assembly in September 2000 in his speech "We the Peoples." He said, "This is the millennium of humanity." And I agree.

In the next millennium, it may take four, five, six, seven, eight centuries, but at the end of that we will stop these conflicts because of differences. Why? Because there is a momentum . . . in the western world there's a momentum and in different other parts of the world, that every individual counts, and as such, the expression and defense of human rights will some day override self-interest. I expect millions of innocent people still to die. It will take us decades and decades every day to bring forward the incredible power of those who are advancing and protecting child rights, human rights, individual rights, and the rights of women. And that effort will ultimately change the decision processes in the White House, in the Ottawa Parliament, and in other places around the world.

And so do not despair and do not be pessimistic. Time is not a factor. The responsibility of humanity is the responsibility of humanity, and those who do not use their capabilities in recognizing that every human is human, will carry the guilt of their self-interests into history.

So here on the verge of the Iraq war [February 2003] what do you think historians will say of the United States fifty years from now? That it was successful in securing itself and its allies? That it, in fact, brought in a new era of mature diplomacy, mature use of force, of a whole new set of humanitarian efforts in order to not find ourselves in the quandaries that we are currently living in? We are more insecure today than we were during the Cold War.

My sister and some of her friends are not going to have children for a few years yet because they are so concerned. I would contend that they are not alone.

Ladies and gentlemen, there is a responsibility; there is blood on the hands of people for the eight hundred thousand killed in Rwanda. Leaders who spend an hour or two in an airport with the engines running and promise billions of dollars to wash their hands of that blood . . . this simply will not do in the future.

Human Rights and the
International Criminal Court ✕ Service

JOHN SHATTUCK I must take you first into the heart of the U.S. government where I spent eight years. On one hand, there is a tremendous amount of lip service paid to the subject of human rights in the U.S. government, and values and norms of international law find their way into the discourse of leaders frequently. We know that President George Bush, when he appeared before the UN General Assembly last fall [2002], spent a great deal of time speaking about human rights in the context of Iraq. We also know, to be bipartisan about it, that my boss, President Bill Clinton, spent a great deal of time speaking about human rights in China during the campaign for the presidency in 1992.

On the other hand, the U.S. government is not a human rights organization. It is a vast collection of competing interests that are struggling with each other bureaucratically in every conceivable way; and human rights are often seen to be a threat by other elements of the bureaucracy because it limits the freedom of those other competing interests, be it trade with China or U.S. sovereignty in the context of the International Criminal Court. So there is a constant tug of war inside.

It is very important for human rights advocates inside to find ways of demonstrating how values and national interests coincide. The genocide in Bosnia and Rwanda, which were the two catastrophic events of the post–Cold War world, created major instability in central and southeastern Europe and central Africa, and millions of refugees, and the crisis became a national security interest to the United States even though in both cases it was not perceived to be so at the start. Human rights repression in Islamic countries today is a matter of national interest in the United States in that it blocks political expression and can be seen as the cradle of terrorism.

There are plenty of examples of what can happen when we ignore our values in pursuing what we may at that time think our interests are. Let me give you one example, a recently declassified 1990 State Department cable on Iraq, which begins: "Human rights and chemical weapons aside, the interests of the United States and Iraq are generally the same." Now even where international human rights values and national interests can be shown to be coincidental and the bureaucracy is willing to generally give lip service to it, there are bureaucratic impediments to actually moving forward and using the resources of the U.S.

From the EPIIC Symposium at Tufts University, "Sovereignty and Intervention," February 2003 government working with other governments to do such things as intervene in Bosnia or Rwanda to stop genocide.

There are five Washington syndromes that I would just quickly point out to those of you who are not familiar with the way the federal government works. First is what I call interagency gridlock, which is that consensus on a new policy is required before it can move forward and if one agency, the Pentagon for example, wants to block a new policy, such as the insertion of troops in Bosnia, that's what will happen.

Then there is the presidential decision-making syndrome. The only way to break the gridlock of the interagency process is to get a presidential decision; but you're not likely to get such a decision on a tough political issue that may have costs to the President without some degree of political support, which then leads you to what I would call the public opinion syndrome and, particularly in foreign affairs, the public is often not interested until there is presidential leadership. So the president is not going to act without the public behind him.

Then there is what I would call the Vietmalia syndrome, which is a combination of fears that come from Vietnam and the crisis of Somalia, when eighteen U.S. rangers were killed in a peacekeeping mission in October 1993. Somalia created tremendous fear in the bureaucracy that body bags were going to be accompanying various human rights adventures in the future.

Then there is the human rights catastrophe syndrome, which is that we need action before a crisis becomes severe; but that is often not likely because there is not enough attention paid to it until the horrors begin to flash across the television on CNN.

You can overcome these various bureaucratic gridlocks internally by, frankly, guerrilla warfare and those of you who are planning to go into the U.S. government in the foreign affairs area let me make some recommendations to you. Much of the government works on paper; paper is very important but paper is also very dangerous because it has to be cleared. It goes up through the system, that is, various other elements of the bureaucracy have to look at your paper in order to be able to get it up to the secretary of state or higher up and see whether they approve it. If they don't approve it, once again the interagency gridlock will settle in on you. So what you need to do is find your own channels. In the case of Bosnia in 1995, I established a channel with Richard Holbrooke [Chief U.S. Envoy to the former Yugoslavia] and on directly to the president. In the case of Haiti in 1994, a channel was established with the deputy secretary of state and on to the president. No paper whatsoever. Phone calls.

It is a cardinal rule in Washington that no subordinates' phone calls are ever returned. That is, if you want to make a phone call to your superior you have to make sure you have meetings with him or her because you're not very often going to get a phone call returned. But I did find that there was a way to get phone calls returned when I was trying to move through the bureaucracy and that was to travel to Sarajevo or Port au Prince or Beijing and then phone back to Washington with a report of what was happening or what I was doing or what I was seeing. Then I would get through right away.

Finally, meetings; the key rule in Washington is that the only important meetings are the ones to which you are not invited. That being the case, you have to figure out how to get yourself invited or figure out how to get your bureaucratic opponents who are on the same level as you disinvited or keep them out of the meeting in some way.

Now to be serious, beyond these bureaucratic struggles there are other impediments to human rights advocacy in the U.S. government. One in particular is U.S. exceptionalism. American exceptionalism is deeply rooted in our history and in our Bill of Rights in that we believe, and rightly so, that we have an outstanding system of justice and rights in our own country and therefore we do not necessarily have to adopt the rights systems that are in international law.

This is a position that has been picked up politically, particularly on the right side of the political spectrum, and I can tell you of many instances running across it when I was in the U.S. government. I made a report to the United Nations on the UN Convention on Civil and Political Rights, and I described in my report some of the efforts that the United States was engaged in to try to bring our own civil rights record to a higher level, particularly since there was a long history of past abuses. Well, there was a big fight inside the State Department and in the Congress over whether that report should be made because it involved an American government official going to the UN and saying we have our own human rights difficulties that we need to address.

That's the background. Let me then move to the context today, the struggle for human rights today. What is it all about? Let's cut to the chase; it's clearly about the crisis of human rights and terror, or more specifically human rights in the context of the U.S.–led war against terrorism and how that is beginning to play out. The background that I think we need to know in looking at this is that before September 11 in the whole decade of the post–Cold War reality, the world fundamentally changed and yet in some ways Americans did not realize that. We were self-absorbed. The Cold War was over, communism was dead, we had every reason to focus on domestic issues. President Clinton ran on a campaign, "It's the economy, stupid."

But there were two great forces that were at work in the world throughout that decade leading up to September 11. There were the forces of integration, and those were the forces that, in fact, reflected the end of the Cold War, the fall of the Berlin Wall, and the victory over apartheid in South Africa. They also reflected the triumph of market economics and the technology boom, the communications revolution, and the fall of various borders, leading some commentators to call this the end of history.

Those were the forces that we counted on in the nineties, but there were equally powerful forces of disintegration. As the repression of the Cold War was lifted and states failed, such as Yugoslavia in particular, there was growing ethnic and religious conflict, there were economic disparities, and there was the rise of terrorism, leaving some commentators to refer to this as the clash of civilizations.

Throughout the nineties U.S. policy was largely focused on promoting the forces of integration, and surely that was a correct policy; but almost as an afterthought we were also trying to contain the forces of disintegration, and nowhere near enough resources, political and otherwise, were going into that struggle. It was very hard to build domestic support to address crises in far away places, such as Bosnia and Rwanda, and the Washington syndromes that I referred to earlier often kicked in to prevent the kind of action that could have been taken.

But there were major warning signals throughout the decade and these warning signals were showing where the forces of disintegration were going. Five million civilians killed in internal conflicts in the decade after the Cold War, according to statistics of the UN; massive regional instability, in the Balkans, Central Africa, certainly the Middle East; thirty million refugees by the end of the decade; soaring costs of humanitarian assistance; and terrorist bombings and attacks in 1998 on American embassies; and the growth of terrorism leading to September 11.

September 11 was certainly a powerful statement of what those forces were about and it had two immediate consequences. Americans violently were awakened by and now no longer saw them as simply operating in faraway places. I think the second result was that the underlying conditions that spawn terrorism became visible to everyone in places like Afghanistan, Egypt, Saudi Arabia, Pakistan, the Sudan. These were all human rights disasters where there was religious intolerance, repression of civil society, torture, and other kinds of gross human rights abuses.

The Bush administration pushed human rights off the agenda largely after September 11. There were three reasons for this and three manifestations of it. First, the administration characterized again and again the war against terrorism as a zero sum game—you were either with us or you were against us. There's a cartoon that I think speaks more than any analysis can of this, which is that a U.S. official in Guantánamo is explaining to an Al Qaeda prisoner that international law does not apply to his case, and the prisoner responds by saying, "Don't worry, we understand, we would have done the same thing to you if we had won."

The second reason, and real manifestation I think, is that in order to assemble a coalition to deal with the immediate after-effects of the terrorism and effort to go into Afghanistan, the administration began to condone human rights crimes of any country that was with us. In Russia, Chechnya no longer was an issue of concern. In the central Asian republics we winked at most of the repression that was going on there, in Pakistan, in China, in Saudi Arabia, in Egypt more than usual.

Then the third manifestation, was the Bush/Ashcroft war on civil liberties at home as part of the war on terrorism around the world where we had seen the round-up of prisoners, often of foreigners based on their national background, brought under surveillance in great secrecy, mistreatment of prisoners, and the like.

The bottom line in my view is that the war on terrorism as it is now being conducted is weakening, not strengthening, international security and undermining, not promoting, our national interests. We are losing the support of moderates all over the world who should be our allies. We are strengthening the hand of authoritarian governments who are cracking down on reformers in the name of fighting terrorists. We are increasing the likelihood that terrorism will be bred by repression in places like Egypt and Pakistan, Chechnya, Uzbekistan, and Indonesia. Above all, I believe we are destroying what Joe Nye has called "our soft power," our commitment to human rights, our commitment to democracy and the persuasion of people that those are values worth accepting, and replacing it with military force, our commitment to holding an increasingly hostile world at bay.

Let me conclude by moving to strategies for peace. I believe there is another way. I believe there are other approaches that could be taken. I think an orientation of our approach to policies needs to be fundamentally different. We need to connect our interests with our values. Surely there are those within the administration who say that what they are planning with respect to Iraq is precisely that, but let me come to that in a moment. We need to recognize that terrorism and the forces of disintegration cannot be stopped without a strategy for promoting human rights, and this is a strategy for peace and it requires a different approach. It draws on the lessons that we have learned in the human rights wars of the 1990s, most of which we lost, I would say because we were not paying sufficient attention or because we were diverted by the relative calm in the domestic situation.

There are seven key points to this strategy. First, it needs leadership from the top. The only way to break out of those gridlocks I described earlier is to get that kind of leadership. The president should announce that it is an explicit goal of the United States to work with other countries to promote international human rights and standards at home and abroad, a statement of policy that is clear and filters down to the bureaucracy. There is no question that that is the only way to mobilize the bureaucracy in the United States; presidential leadership has been shown again and again to be important in human rights. Unfortunately, there are too many examples in the wrong direction. Certainly President Bush after September 11 with the U.S.A. Patriot Act is an example of the wrong kind of signal on human rights. After the Somalia disaster, President Clinton issued a new policy restricting

U.S. peacekeeping understandably because he felt the political pressures as a result of the disaster of Somalia, but that in many ways led to our disengagement from some other disasters, particularly Rwanda.

Second, the strategy must be multilateral. U.S. unilateralism is indeed one of the main causes of the world's distrust of our motives and objectives in the war on terrorism. When it comes to human rights, a multilateral approach always increases the legitimacy of the argument and a unilateral approach always raises suspicions that it is being pursued only for national political reasons.

Third, we need a strategy for preventing or heading off human rights catastrophes before, not after, they lead to genocide. Here we need to work with other governments and we have plenty of tools at our disposal. We can jam hate radio; we can engage in aerial photography of areas that we think are raising serious human rights problems. We can freeze foreign assets of human rights violators. We can impose sanctions. We can issue arms embargoes; we can withdraw aid; we can expel ambassadors; we can do many, many things short of actual military intervention.

Fourth, when prevention fails, we need to be able and prepared to join with other countries to intervene, as a last resort, militarily. This is a tricky area, to be sure, especially after what I've said about my concerns on Iraq. There is now an evolving doctrine of humanitarian intervention. It comes out of the interventions in human rights wars in Haiti, in Bosnia, in Kosovo, in East Timor, but we need to be very careful about the criteria that are used for intervention in the context of a human rights crisis of the kind that President Bush has characterized Iraq to be.

There are four criteria that I would set forth. First, genocide and crimes against humanity should be very much the cause of the intervention; that is, they are being committed. Second, it should be multilateral. There should be involvement of other countries in a significant way, the UN being the forum in which that involvement should occur. Third, there should be regional support and no risk of a wider war. And fourth, there should be no risk that more lives will be lost than will be saved in the context of such an intervention.

In my view the Iraq intervention does not meet three out of four of the criteria. It's not likely to be broadly multilateral and clearly there is a risk of a wider war because there is very little regional support, and it's certainly very likely that more lives will be lost than will be saved. We may trigger the very things that we are trying to stop, the use of more terror, certainly in Iraq, the tensions with Kurdistan and that regional crisis, the nuclear weapons crisis in Iran, and the terrorist attacks that might result in the United States and Europe. All of these, I think, are especially high if the goal, as we are now hearing, is to occupy and transform the entire Middle East by military force.

Fifth, there can be no peace without justice. This needs to be an element of the strategy. There are three basic reasons why it is essential to hold accountable those who commit massive human rights crimes like genocide. We need to stop the spiral of revenge that goes on and we saw go on in the Balkans, for otherwise it will never stop. We need to lift the cloud of collective guilt so that a whole society is not accused of the crimes that the leaders were instigating, and we need to create a deterrent against future crimes because, without the rule of law, terrorism inevitably becomes acceptable.

I think over the past decade we've made great progress in this direction, with the establishment of the two International Criminal Tribunals, and now the International Criminal Court, controversial as it is. The issues that are keeping the United States on the sidelines and in some respects very hostile with respect to the International Court are issues of sovereignty. They are also issues of international hegemony. The fact of the matter is that this administration does not want an international institution to have any authority to judge the actions of the United States.

Now, a close reading of the statute of the International Criminal Court will show that the primary jurisdiction is in the nation-state, it's not in the International Criminal Court, and that if the nation-state is investigating human rights crimes it will not be brought, nor any of its citizens, before the International Criminal Court.

The only point I want to make here is that I'm afraid what we see is a wholesale assault on international law and treaty wherever it seems to impede the freedom of unilateral action, that is, the large theme that we're seeing in the justice area. There's a huge cost to this. It costs the United States interests, it sends a signal that any other country can do this, and I think it weakens the fifty-year structure of international treaties and laws that have been built up that insured some degree of stability and conflict resolution in the world.

There are two other broad topics that I will just mention and then conclude. We need to commit ourselves to nation building, peace building, after a war has ended. We need to be prepared to stay for the long term, not militarily, but we need to engage much more with development assistance. We need to be prepared to meet the humanitarian crises that are going to unfold after that and all too often we have focused on our exit strategy, rather than our long-term commitment.

Finally, we must work with other countries to find new ways of challenging the forces of repression that block political expression and turn people into terrorists. That is a strategy looks to address the conditions in which terrorism emerges.

Let me end with a message by an Egyptian democracy activist, Saad Eddin Ibrahim, who said to the world when he was sentenced for challenging the authorities in his country, "Civil society as a space for liberty is an essential condition for sustained development. Perhaps we are being persecuted today because we have dared to speak openly what millions of others think privately." Now I think Egyptian democracy activists like Saad Ibrahim are sending us a message of hope and a message related to human rights, but frankly it is also a warning. It is a warning that if we allow the sacrifice of human rights in the name of fighting terror, in the long run we will only reap more terror and that, I fear, is exactly what will happen if we storm into Iraq without broad international support and try to transform the Islamic world by military force alone.

VALERIE EPPS   Ambassador Shattuck touched on two themes relating most directly to the issues surrounding the International Criminal Court; the importance of human rights generally and more specifically the importance of democracy in insuring and fostering human rights. This duo of human rights and democracy arises in quite a problematic context in relationship to the International Criminal Court (ICC). Specifically, I think that the ICC poses a tension between two different sorts of accountability, the legal accountability of perpetrators of grave human rights abuses on one hand, and the democratic accountability of the ICC itself, on the other hand.

I am going directly to the accountability of the ICC itself in terms of its democratic credentials and legitimacy. In effect, I find a tension embodied within the ICC treaty between the human right to freedom from violent abuse and a human right to a representative government.

The relationship between the ICC and national courts is to be governed by the so-called complementarity regime embodied in its own treaty. Under the system of complementarity, the ICC may exercise jurisdiction only if states are unable or unwilling to do so. As Article 17 of the treaty states, a case shall not be admissible before the ICC if the case is being investigated or prosecuted by a state with jurisdiction over the case unless that state is unable or unwilling genuinely to prosecute or investigate. So in this way, complementarity gives priority to states rather than to the ICC in the development and enforcement of humanitarian law. But the system embodied in the treaty also provides the ICC with the authority to conduct prosecutions when states are unable or unwilling to do so. If the state where the crime is alleged to have occurred, the territorial state, is a party to the treaty then the ICC would have authority to prosecute even if the defendant's state of nationality were not a treaty party and had not consented to jurisdiction of the ICC. This is the ICC's so-called jurisdiction over nonparty nationals.

This jurisdiction over nonparty nationals has been central to the controversy concerning the ICC's jurisdiction, particularly within the United States. I don't want to rehearse the whole legal debate about nonparty jurisdiction here but I would like to discuss what I think is the underlying meaning of that controversy. What I think is ultimately at stake, is the tension between the human rights embodied in humanitarian law and the human rights of democratic governance. The ICC may in some circumstances prosecute an individual even without the consent of that defendant's state of nationality.

Now the very clear advantage of this ICC power to prosecute is that all too often the state is the problem. States often collude in genocide, war crimes, and crimes against humanity and then tend to shield the perpetrators of those crimes. If the ICC requires the consent of the defendant's state of nationality before it can prosecute, then the court's purpose would be largely defeated. An international court is needed most when the perpetrator acted for, or is shielded by, a government. For that reason the ICC needs, and has to have genuinely supranational powers, powers that are to be used in those particular cases where a state is unable or unwilling to render accountability. So where the territorial state consents to ICC jurisdiction, the ICC has the authority under the treaty to prosecute a defendant without the consent of his or her state of nationality. In essence it's a supranational solution to the problem of national transgressors.

This kind of supranational authority is a new departure, a new step. Even while complementarity comports with and supports the authority of the state in a state-based international system, it also goes beyond state authority and makes an exception. Where crimes of genocide, war crimes, or crimes against humanity have been committed or are alleged, there is now to be an authority higher than the state and this is a genuine innovation.

There is a feature of this innovation, however, that has gone seriously unexamined. We've created a supranational judicial authority but have not really carefully examined its democratic legitimacy. This stands in stark contrast to our experience with, for instance, the World Trade Organization, where the debate has very much focused on the so-called democratic deficit of that international organization. By contrast with the ICC, we've created a powerful new international institution but oddly we have had virtually no discussion of the democratic features of this new court's power.

The ICC will wield governmental authority as a judicial body to prosecute or punish individuals. What is the democratic linkage then between this organ of governance and the governed? For national states that are party to the treaty, their representation comes through their own state's consent to become a party to the treaty and it continues through participation in the Assembly of States parties, the governing body overseeing the court.

But what then about nonparty nationals? What is the democratic basis for the ICC's power as applied to populations whose states have not consented on their behalf and are not represented in the Assembly of States parties? Here it would be hard to claim democratic legitimacy for the ICC. If that's the case or if that's even arguable, it raises the question, Why have we heard no clamor about it or even discussion of the democratic credentials of the ICC? I think that we can identify the reason.

The implicit unarticulated assumption seems to be that if there is any democratic loss at all it's negligible because the court's mandate is so thin and circumscribed. The implicit reasoning seems to be that, first, the ICC's jurisdiction over nonparty nationals is an exception that gives the ICC authority to act only when states fail to do so, and, second, that the exceptions to state prerogative is thin because, unlike the World Trade Organization, the ICC is not intended to make law and policy; rather the ICC mandate is to apply clear, uncontroversial standards that exist in international law. Genocide, war crimes, and crimes against humanity are crimes, nobody debates that, and so the argument goes, there is no democratic or undemocratic decision making to discuss.

But here the reasoning breaks down. It's true that the prohibitions of genocide, war crimes, and crimes against humanity are unquestionable, but applying that law will inevitably turn out to be far more complex and politically fraught than are the court's prohibitions. There will be questions, large and small, about the content and interpretation of the law, even with the elements of crimes in place relative to the ICC statute. For example, a question could be before the ICC relative to the war crime of causing excessive death, injury, or damage about whether countries with the resources to use precision-guided munitions are obliged to use those weapons in order to minimize collateral damage, rather than using much less expensive ordinary kinetic weapons? Or relative to that same war crime of causing excessive death, injury, or damage, whether belligerents who have not invested in, or cannot afford night-vision goggles, are prohibited from fighting at night because excessive collateral damage could be avoided with the goggles? Or relative to the crime of genocide, what is the intent requirement for command responsibility for genocide? Where the commander knows of the subordinate's genocidal intent but does not entertain that intention himself or herself, does he or she have the necessary mental element for conviction for genocide? Relative to the war crime of attacking civilian objects, what is the status of dual use targeting where the targets are objects like a bridge, television station, or electrical grid that is partially in military use and partially in civilian use?

These difficult questions are not answered by the ICC statute, and they entail enormous political and even moral issues and controversies. They go to the issue of how much needs to be spent for a given degree of military strength, to basic issues of North/South politics, to issues of which countries can afford to fight with which allies and coalitions and what would be the cost of warfare, including humanitarian intervention. Each of these questions involves areas where the law is indeterminate and the politics are complex and do not require anything like the mere application of the law to the fact.

So, inevitably, the ICC will be a feature and an organ of global governance as it makes and applies international law and policy. As a consequence, we cannot avoid the question of the democratic legitimacy of the ICC by supposing that there's no policy making or law making that will be done there.

It's also no answer to the problem of democratic governance to say that the solution is for each state to become a party to the ICC treaty and thereby to gain a voice in the Assembly of States parties. Insofar as the states parties will govern the court through voting in the Assembly of States parties, the assembly system involves the form of governance by majority rule and states cannot and should not be forced into a majority rule system. A system based on the consent of the government requires that that consent be meaningful, that it be optional, that there will be the option of alternatively not consenting. The question of majority rule in any form at the international level is notoriously complex. The related issues concerning global democracy, within or outside the UN system, are enormous.

What is clear, however, is that as we move forward in constructing international institutions that will wield governmental power, we ought to be paying very careful attention to democratic control. I don't trust governments; I presume that you don't either. Indeed, if we did, we wouldn't have any need for human rights safeguards. As we construct organs of international governance, we need to be every bit as attentive to the needs for checks on power and mechanisms for accountability as we would be at the national level. In fact, we may need to be more careful because, while states may provide checks on each other, a global government would have no such natural checks and balances.

There are two different things that we want here, the human right to freedom from violent abuse and a way to achieve representative government. Neither can be sacrificed. Quite obviously we cannot countenance the abuse the innocent, nor can we acquiesce in the erosion of democratic governance. In fact, the two ultimately are linked; the erosion of democracy leads eventually to violent abuse.

X/ Cruel Science
CIA Torture and U.S. Foreign Policy

ALFRED W. MCCOY

In April 2004, the American public was stunned when CBS broadcast photographs from Abu Ghraib prison showing Iraqis stripped naked, blinded by bags, and contorted in humiliating positions while U.S. soldiers stood smiling.[1] As the scandal grabbed headlines around the globe, Secretary of Defense Donald Rumsfeld assured Congress the abuse was "perpetrated by a small number of U.S. military," whom columnist William Safire soon branded "creeps."[2] Other commentators, citing the famous Stanford prison experiment, attributed the abuse to a collapse of discipline by overstretched American soldiers.[3]

These photographs are snapshots, however, not of simple brutality or a breakdown in discipline but of Central Intelligence Agency (CIA) torture techniques that have metastasized over the past fifty years like an undetected cancer inside the U.S. intelligence community. A close study of this half-century history leads, most immediately, to the conclusion that the CIA was the lead agency at Abu Ghraib, enlisting, as it often has, U.S. Army intelligence to support its mission. Indeed, these photographs from Iraq illustrate standard operating practices inside the global gulag of secret CIA prisons that have operated, on executive authority, since the start of the War on Terror. Thus, the seven soldiers facing courts-martial for the abuse at Abu Ghraib were simply following prescribed practices. Responsibility for their actions lies higher, much higher, up the chain of command.

At a deeper level, this controversy over Abu Ghraib is a product of a contradictory U.S. policy on torture evident since the start of the Cold War. At the UN and other international forums, Washington has opposed torture and advocated a universal standard for human rights, but the CIA has, in contravention of these same conventions, propagated torture during these decades. Several scholarly essays have noted this "ambiguity" in U.S. human rights policy without understanding the reason: a persistence of the torture prerogative within the intelligence community.[4] Moreover, the agency's attempt to conceal these programs from later executive and legislative review has required that it operate quasi-covertly in its own society through clandestine techniques, such as disinformation and destruction of incriminating documents.

From 1950 to 1962, the CIA conducted massive, secret research into coercion and human consciousness that cost a billion dollars per annum.[5] After experiments with hallucinogenic drugs, electric shocks, and sensory deprivation, this research produced a new method of torture that was psychological, not physical, perhaps best described as "no touch torture." The agency's discovery was a counterintuitive breakthrough—indeed, the first real revolution in this cruel science in three centuries.

For over two thousand years interrogators have found that mere physical pain, no matter how extreme, often produced heightened resistance or unreliable information. By contrast, the CIA's psychological paradigm used two new methods, sensory disorientation and self-inflicted pain, to make victims capitulate. A week after the Abu Ghraib scandal broke, General Geoffrey Miller, U.S. prison commander in Iraq, offered an unwitting summary of this two-phase torture. "We will no longer, in any circumstances, hood any of the detainees," the general said. "We will no longer use stress positions in any of our interrogations. And we will no longer use sleep deprivation in any of our interrogations."[6]

"No touch torture" leaves deep psychological scars on both victims and interrogators. The victims often need long treatment to recover from trauma, and perpetrators can suffer a dangerous expansion of ego, leading to escalating cruelty and lasting emotional disorders. These procedures have led to unimaginable cruelties, physical and sexual, that were often horrific and only occasionally effective. Every gulag has its masters who take to the task with sadistic flair, abhorred by their victims and valued by their superiors.

Just as interrogators are often seduced by a dark, empowering sense of dominance over victims, so their superiors can succumb to the idea of torture as an all-powerful weapon of control. Among all the practices of the modern state, torture is the least understood, the least rational—one that seduces its practitioners, high and low, with fantasies of dominion. Our contemporary view of torture as aberrant and its perpetrators as abhorrent ignores its pervasiveness as a Western practice for over two millennia and the perverse psychological appeal of both its practice and practitioners. Once torture begins, its perpetrators, plunging into the uncharted recesses of culture and consciousness, are often swept away in reveries, frenzies of power and potency—particularly in times of crisis. "When feelings of insecurity develop within those holding power," one CIA analysis of the Soviet state applicable to post-9/11 America reads, "they become increasingly suspicious and put great pressures on the secret police to obtain arrests and confessions. At such times, police officials are inclined to condone anything which produces a speedy 'confession' and brutality may become widespread."[7]

Any modern state that sanctions torture, even in a very limited way, thus runs the risk of becoming increasingly indiscriminate in its application. Just four years after the CIA published its 1963 torture method for use against a few key counterintelligence targets, its agents were operating forty interrogation centers in South Vietnam that killed over twenty thousand suspects and tortured several hundred thousand more. Just a few months after CIA interrogators began torturing top Al

Qaeda suspects at Kabul in 2002, its agents were leading U.S. Army intelligence in the torture/interrogation of hundreds of Iraqi prisoners. As its most troubling legacy, the CIA's psychological method, with its legitimating scientific patina and avoidance of obvious physical brutality, has provided, for the past forty years, a pretext for the preservation of torture as an acceptable practice within the U.S. intelligence community.

Torture is so powerfully seductive that its perpetrators refuse, in defiance of evidence and rationality, to recognize its limited utility and high political cost. At least twice during the Cold War, the CIA's torture training would contribute to the destabilization and de-legitimation of two key American allies, Ferdinand Marcos and the shah of Iran. Yet the agency would not see that its psychological torture was destroying the allies it was designed to defend.

After codification in its "KUBARK Counterintelligence Interrogation" manual in 1963, the CIA disseminated its new torture method first through the Office of Public Safety (OPS), a division of the United States Agency for International Development, to police in Asia and Latin America and, after 1975, through the U.S. Army Mobile Training Teams active in Central America during the 1980s. Following a ten-year hiatus during the 1990s, the U.S. intelligence community, led by the CIA, revived the use of torture as a weapon against Al Qaeda in the War on Terror. These four decades explain the striking similarity in interrogation methods used by both American and allied security agencies in Vietnam in the 1960s, in Central America during the 1980s, and in Afghanistan and Iraq since 2001.

Indeed, much of the torture synonymous with authoritarian rule in Asia and Latin America seems to have originated in the United States. Though these dictatorships would no doubt have tortured on their own, U.S. training programs provided sophisticated techniques, new equipment, and moral legitimacy for the practice, producing a clear coincidence between U.S. Cold War policy and the extreme state violence of the authoritarian age. Torture spread globally with the proliferation of U.S. training programs and then receded when America turned resolutely against the practice with the end of the Cold War. In its pursuit of torturers across the globe for the past forty years, Amnesty International has been, in a certain sense, following the trail of CIA torture-training programs. In these same troubled decades, U.S. leadership in the global fight against torture and inhumanity has waxed and waned. After World War II, American diplomats played a central role in drafting the UN's Universal Declaration of Human Rights and the Geneva Conventions on treatment of prisoners—documents that ban torture in both principle and practice. During the Cold War, however, Washington withdrew from active support of international human rights, ignoring or rejecting several major conventions.

At the close of the Cold War, Washington resumed its advocacy of universal principles, participating in the World Conference on Human Rights at Vienna in

1993 and, a year later, ratifying the UN Convention Against Torture. On the surface, the United States had resolved the tension between its principles and practices. But, by failing to repudiate the CIA's propagation of torture, while adopting a UN convention that condemned its practice, the United States left this contradiction buried like a political land mine to detonate with phenomenal force, years later, in the Abu Ghraib prison scandal. In effect, the CIA's creation of torture techniques, through a somewhat confused, chaotic process at the height of the Cold War, created a covert capacity that the executive could deploy at times of extraordinary crisis, whether in South Vietnam in the late 1960s or Iraq in 2003.

In battling communism, the United States adopted some of its most objectionable practices—subversion abroad, repression at home, and torture. While other covert agencies synonymous with Cold War repression such as the Securitate, the Stasi, and the KGB have disappeared, the CIA, survives—its archives sealed, its officers decorated, and its crimes forgotten.

Even now, more than a decade after the Cold War's close, the American public has only a vague understanding of these CIA excesses and the scale of its massive mind-control project. Yet almost every adult American carries fragments of this past—LSD drug experiments, Vietnam Phoenix program, assassination attempts on Fidel Castro and Patrice Lumumba, murder of an American police adviser in Montevideo, and, of course, Abu Ghraib photographs. But few fit these fragments together. There is a willing blindness, a studied avoidance of a deeply troubling topic, akin to that which shrouds this subject in postauthoritarian societies.

Now, with the controversy over Abu Ghraib, incidents that once seemed isolated gain a new significance. They form a mosaic of a clandestine agency manipulating its government and deceiving its own citizens to propagate a new form of torture throughout the Third World. Those Americans willing to consider torture a necessary expedient in the War on Terror should pause to consider its powerful symbolism within Western culture. For nearly two millennia, torture's practice has been identified with tyrants and empires. For the past two centuries, its repudiation has been synonymous with the humanist ideals of the Enlightenment and democracy. For any modern state to compromise its majesty by willfully torturing even a few victims leaves a stigma profoundly corrupting of its integrity. More than any other act, torture can destroy the legitimacy of a regime or a ruler. During the Cold War the CIA's propagation of torture among U.S. allies soon delegitimated the very regimes it was designed to defend.

Cold War and Human Rights

In the decade after World War II, competing priorities within Washington's foreign policy produced a sharp contradiction between a public commitment to human rights and covert torture research. Meeting at New York in 1948, the

United Nations' delegates, led by former first lady Eleanor Roosevelt, adopted the Universal Declaration of Human Rights—the foundation for later UN humanitarian conventions.[9] Among its many idealistic provisions, this covenant specified in Article 5 that "no one shall be subjected to torture or to cruel, inhuman, or degrading treatment." But the declaration provided few specifics and no mechanism for enforcement.[10]

A year later, the United States ratified the Geneva Convention III Relative to the Treatment of Prisoners of War with similar prohibitions against torture. Article 13 states that "prisoners of war must at all times be humanely treated," while Article 87 bars "corporal punishment, imprisonment in premises without daylight and, in general, any form of torture or cruelty." Article 89 offers an unambiguous ban on harsh treatment, saying: "In no case shall disciplinary punishments be inhuman, brutal or dangerous to the health of prisoners of war."[11] Similarly, under Geneva Convention IV Relative to Protection of Civilian Persons in Time of War, the United States accepted the broad language of Article 31 that: "No physical or moral coercion shall be exercised . . . to obtain information from them or from third parties."[12]

By the mid 1950s, a confluence of pressures, legislative and clandestine, led Washington to suspend its support for human rights. The founding of the UN had raised the threatening specter of "world government" for American conservatives, inspiring a movement in Congress for the "Bricker Amendment," which would limit executive authority over foreign affairs—a threat the Eisenhower administration defeated by suspending its support for human rights at the UN.[13] Less visibly, the CIA's massive mind-control project may have created internal pressures dampening Washington's support for human rights.

Two Thousand Years of Torture

Under the pressures of the Cold War, the CIA developed torture techniques that were a fusion of ancient and modern methods. Through basic research into human psychology in the 1950s, experimentation on human subjects in South Vietnam during the 1960s, and refinement in the 1970s, the CIA made what was arguably the most important modern advance in the practice of torture.

Through its use in judicial interrogation, torture played a central role in European law for over two millennia. While ancient Athens had limited torture to extraction of evidence from slaves, imperial Rome extended the practice to freemen for both proof and punishment. "By *quaestio* [torture] we are to understand the torment and suffering of the body in order to elicit the truth," wrote the third-century jurist Ulpian. Ulpian also recognized that torture was a "delicate, dangerous, and deceptive thing," often yielding problematic evidence. "For many persons have such strength of body and soul that they heed pain very little, so that there is no means of obtaining the truth from them," he explained, "while others are so susceptible to pain that they will tell any lie rather than suffer it."[14]

With the rise of Christian Europe, judicial torture faded for several centuries. Torture was antithetical to Christ's teachings and Pope Nicholas I banned the practice.[15] But after a Church council abolished trial by ordeal in 1215, European civil courts revived Roman law with its reliance upon torture to obtain confessions—a practice that persisted for the next five centuries.[16] With the parallel rise of the Inquisition, Church interrogators also used torture for both confession and punishment, a procedure that was formalized under Pope Innocent IV in 1252. In Italy by the fourteenth century, the Inquisition used the *strappado* to suspend the victim from a beam with ropes in five degrees of escalating duration and severity—a scale preserved in modern memory by use of the phrase "the third degree" to mean harsh police interrogation.[17] The absolutist regimes of the sixteenth and seventeenth centuries employed torture. "Military torture was prodigious," wrote Alec Mellor of sixteenth-century Europe, "religious torture was regularized; and judicial torture was enriched daily by new varieties."[18]

But in the eighteenth century, free judicial evaluation of evidence replaced forced confessions, allowing the abolition of torture across Europe by the end of the century.[19] In the nineteenth century, moreover, modern European states replaced torture's symbols—the Tower, Bastille, and public execution—with the apparatus of a scientific criminology that included police, courts, and prisons. The respite proved short-lived for, in the years following World War I, rival authoritarian states—Hitler's Third Reich and Stalin's Soviet Union—revived the practice, applying modern methods to expand the diversity and intensity of physical pain.[20]

In the 1920s, torture thus reappeared in Europe as "an engine of the state, not of law." After taking power in 1922, Italy's dictator, Benito Mussolini, declared "man is nothing" and used his OVRA [Organizzazione di Vigilanza Repressione dell'Antifascismo] secret police to torture the enemies of his all-powerful state. Similarly, Hitler's Gestapo engaged in limited, largely concealed torture during the regime's first years, relying on protracted isolation, crude beatings, and humiliation to break political opponents, whether communist or gypsy, Catholic, or Jew.[21] Then, in June 1942, SS chief Heinrich Himmler ordered that interrogation would use a "third degree" of beatings, close confinement, and sleep deprivation. At the Dachau concentration camp in the late 1930s, SS doctors under Dr. Kurt Plotner tested mescaline on Jews and gypsies, finding it caused some to reveal their "most intimate secrets." But the Gestapo "was not ready to accept mescaline as substitute for their more physical methods of interrogation."[22] At war's end, the United States prosecuted the so-called Nazi doctors at Nuremberg, producing

x / 166

principles known as the Nuremberg Code prescribing, under Article Four, that all medical experiments "should be so conducted as to avoid all unnecessary physical and mental suffering."[23]

Despite the Third Reich's defeat in 1945, its legacy persisted in the former occupied territories, notably among French officers who used torture in colonial Algiers. The 1955 Wuillaume Report excused the army's systematic torture of Algerian rebels saying: "The water and electricity methods, provided they are carefully used, are said to produce a shock which is more psychological than physical and therefore *do not constitute excessive cruelty*. . . . According to certain medical opinion, the water-pipe method . . . involves no risk to the health of the victim." In contrast to this exculpatory approach, the classical scholar Pierre Vidal-Naquet argued, in his study of the French experience in Algeria, *Torture: Cancer of Democracy,* that public indifference to torture had the long-term effect of eroding a democratic society's civil liberties.[24]

CIA Torture Research

America's contact with torture came, ironically, through wars against its proponents. To fight fascism during World War II, the United States created the Office of Strategic Services (OSS), and then used it at war's end to collect Nazi scientists who could assist in its struggle against the Soviet Union—including those who had directed the Nazi's experiments into human physiology and psychology. Under Operation Paperclip, the American agent Boris Pash recruited Nazi scientists, such as the same Dr. Kurt Plotner who had tested mescaline on Jewish prisoners. After the OSS was reborn as the CIA in 1947, the agency continued Nazi-inspired experiments with LSD and THC for interrogation of suspected spies and double agents.[25] As the iron curtain came down across Europe in 1948, the human mind was becoming a key Cold War battleground.

From its founding in 1947, the CIA was disturbed by the Soviet ability to extract public confessions. In 1950, a CIA analysis of Stalin's 1937 show trials of fellow communists found that "the style, context and manner of delivery of the 'confessions' were such as to be inexplicable unless there had been a reorganization and reorientation of the minds of the confessees." Such changes, the analysis concluded, "cannot be brought about by the traditional methods of physical torture," raising the disturbing possibility that the Soviets had discovered "newer or more subtle techniques," including psycho surgery, shock method, or "psychoanalytic methods." In late 1950, moreover, Edward Hunter, a CIA propagandist working undercover at the *Miami News,* aroused public hysteria about Chinese Communist "brain-washing." A few years later, public confessions by American soldiers captured in Korea seemed to confirm this concern. "There is ample evidence," reported the chief of CIA Medical Staff in 1952, "that the Communists were utilizing drugs, physical duress, electric shock and possibly hypnosis against their enemies. With such evidence, it is difficult not to keep from becoming rabid about our apparent laxity. We are forced by this mounting evidence to assume a more aggressive role in the development of these techniques."[26]

In later testimony before the U.S. Senate, one CIA officer recalled, "We were literally terrified" by reports of Soviet experiments with LSD "because this was the one material that we had ever been able to locate that really had potential fantastic possibilities if used wrongly."[27] The officer who had directed the agency's drug experiments, Dr. Sidney Gottlieb, said that "the impetus for going into the LSD project specifically rested in a report, never verified . . . , that the Russians had bought the world supply."[28]

In response to this communist challenge, the CIA would spend several billion dollars over the next decade to probe two key aspects of human consciousness—the mechanisms of mass persuasion and the effects of coercion upon individual consciousness. This complex, at times chaotic, mind-control project, had two goals: improved psychological warfare to influence whole societies and better interrogation techniques for targeted individuals.[29] Gradually, these two strands diverged. Psychological warfare research explored mass persuasion through the U.S. Information Agency and the academic field of mass communication. By contrast, interrogation research, which probed the impact of drugs, electrical shock, and sensory deprivation upon individual psychology, moved inside the intelligence bureaucracy and into the laboratories of its medical allies.

U.S. national security agencies were determined to match their enemy weapon for weapon. "It is now clear that we are facing an implacable enemy whose avowed objective is world domination by whatever means," read the Hoover report on government operations in 1954. "We must learn to subvert, sabotage, and destroy our enemies by more clear, more sophisticated, and more effective methods than those used against us." Offering a prediction that proved, sadly, accurate, the report adds: "It may become necessary that the American people will be made acquainted with, understand and support this fundamentally repugnant philosophy."[30] If Moscow had the KGB, Washington would create the CIA; if Russian scientists manipulated human behavior, then their American counterparts must follow. After 150 years without a clandestine service, the U.S. government passed the National Security Act in July 1947, creating both the National Security Council as a top-level executive agency and the CIA as its instrument—effectively removing foreign intelligence from congressional control.[31] In the Cold War crisis of the day, this act contained a brief clause allowing this new agency to perform "other functions and duties relating to intelligence affecting the national security" that the president, through the National Security Council, might direct—in effect, investing executive agents with extraordinary authority to operate outside the law, whether for covert operations, assassinations, or torture.[32] Five months after the agency's founding, the National Security Council (NSC) promulgated NSC 4-A, a "top secret" authorization for the CIA to conduct overt propaganda programs that "must be supplemented by covert psychological operations."[33]

The Rise of MKUltra

In retrospect, the CIA's mind-control research moved through two distinct phases: first, esoteric, often bizarre experiments with hallucinogenic drugs from 1950 to 1956; and then more conventional research into human psychology until 1963 when the agency finally produced its basic interrogation manual.

In April 1950, CIA director Roscoe Hillenkoetter launched "Operation Blue-bird" to discover more effective methods for interrogation by using teams with a psychiatrist, a polygraph expert, and a hypnotist. Under this project, Boris Pash, formerly employed in Operation Paperclip, reviewed Nazi studies of interrogation techniques including "drugs, electro-shock, hypnosis, and psycho-surgery." Blue-bird also conducted the first CIA experiments with LSD, testing doses on twelve subjects before expanding the program to seven thousand unwitting U.S. soldiers at Maryland's Edgewood Chemical Arsenal.[34]

A year later, the agency's Office of Scientific Intelligence started "Project Arti-choke" to explore interrogation through "the application of tested psychiatric and psychological techniques including the use of hypnosis in connection with drugs." While Bluebird experimented on captured North Koreans, Artichoke used Amer-ican subjects, notably seven patients at the U.S. drug treatment center in Lexing-ton, Kentucky, who were kept on dangerous doses of LSD for seventy-seven days straight.[35] Although Project Artichoke used unwitting human subjects, the agency imposed "medical and security controls which would ensure that no damage would be done to individuals volunteering."[36]

In April 1953, the CIA gathered this growing array of mind-control research into the MKUltra project within its Technical Services Division (TSD) under Dr. Sidney Gottlieb—who, in turn, reported to Richard Helms, the assistant deputy director of plans, a euphemism for covert operations. Helms would, for the next twenty years, protect behavior-modification research from internal review and external attack. Until its funding, totaling some $25 million, was curtailed in 1963, MKUltra supervised 149 projects and 33 more subprojects focused on con-trol of human consciousness. The work continued at a reduced level until 1973 when then-CIA director Helms, fearing a damaging exposé, terminated the proj-ect and destroyed its files.[37]

The MKUltra researchers were given extraordinary powers to probe the limits of human consciousness. At its outset, Helms proposed, and CIA director Allen Dulles agreed, that 6 percent of the budget for TSD could be spent "without the establishment of formal contractual relations." Helms noted that key researchers "are most reluctant to enter into signed agreements of any sort which connect them with this activity since such a connection would jeopardize their professional reputations."[38] Helms ran the program covertly within the agency, avoiding oversight by the CIA director, since he and his collaborators "felt it necessary to keep details of the project restricted to an absolute minimum number of people."[39]

Under MKUltra, the CIA's mind control project reached out into civil society, its universities and hospitals, to involve "physicians, toxicologists, and other specialists" during both "the basic research phase" and later "intensive tests on human subjects."[40] In a 1963 internal investigation, the CIA's inspector general found that the project's initial "research and development" phase was structured to conceal "the interests of the CIA" from all but "key individuals."[41] In the late 1950s, for example, respected researchers ran LSD experiments at Boston Psychopathic, Mount Sinai, and Columbia University Hospitals, reporting superficial results in medical journals and covert applications to the CIA.[42] Through this combination of basic university research and its own field tests, the CIA launched a serious, albeit covert, national effort to develop a new method of psychological torture.

Of the several billion dollars expended on this mind-control effort in the 1950s, the government allocated $7 million to $13 million for academic research to leading universities by channeling its support through private foundations, some legitimate and others fronts: the Ford Foundation, Rockefeller Foundation, and the Josiah Macy Foundation. One of the main CIA conduits for this research was the Bureau of Social Science Research (BSSR), which was established at American University in 1950. Albert Biderman's *A Study for Development of Improved Interrogation Techniques* analyzed communist methods under an Air Force contract to find that psychological torture seemed "the ideal way of 'breaking down' a prisoner" because "the effect of isolation on the brain function of the prisoner is much like that which occurs if he is beaten, starved, or deprived of sleep."[43]

Two respected neurologists at Cornell Medical Center in New York, Lawrence Hinkle and Harold Wolff, undertook a seminal study of communist interrogation done for the CIA's TSD in 1956. In a sanitized version published in the *Archives of Neurology and Psychiatry,* the authors reported that successful communist interrogation relied not on esoteric "brain washing" with drugs or electro-shocks but on standard "police practices" that the KGB had inherited from its czarist predecessor. After four weeks of "isolation, anxiety, lack of sleep, uncomfortable temperatures, and chronic hunger," most Russian prisoners suffered "profound disturbances of mood" that made them willing to cooperate with their KGB interrogators. The KGB simply made victims stand for eighteen to twenty-four hours—producing "excruciating pain" as ankles double in size, skin becomes "tense and intensely painful," blisters erupt oozing "watery serum," heart rates soar, kidneys shut down, and delusions deepen. After seizing power in 1949, Chinese Communists adopted most of the Soviet procedures, though they employed manacles and leg chains no longer used by the KGB. Significantly, the authors found no reason to differentiate these nonviolent KGB methods "from any other form of torture."[44]

This Cornell report may have contributed to the agency's shift from the search for a miracle mind-control drug to the exploration of human psychology. Indeed, when the agency's two-stage torture method was finalized seven years later, it would follow many of the KGB's tactics.

CIA Behavioral Experiments

The CIA's MKUltra and allied projects spent some $25 million from 1953 to 1963 to fund human experiments by 185 nongovernmental researchers at eighty institutions, including forty-four universities and twelve hospitals.[45] At the outset, CIA director Allen Dulles stated, "We have no human guinea pigs to try these extraordinary techniques."[46] To overcome this critical shortage of human subjects, the agency's research adopted methods marked by cruelty, illegality, and, with surprising frequency, failure.

To test drugs on unsuspecting subjects, the CIA injected North Korean prisoners, spiked drinks at a New York City party house, paid prostitutes to slip LSD to their customers for CIA cameras at a San Francisco safe house, and attempted behavior modification on inmates at California's Vacaville Prison. For "terminal experiments" that pushed to potentially fatal limits, the agency trolled Europe for dubious defectors or double agents deemed "expendable."[47]

As a part of these early drug experiments, the CIA's chief scientist, Gottlieb, did his own LSD tests on unsuspecting subjects, once spiking the drinks of colleagues at a meeting in 1953. One of his fellow scientists, Dr. Frank R. Olson, suffered a mental breakdown and apparently jumped from the tenth floor of New York's Statler Hotel, where the agency had confined him for observation—a crime that the CIA covered up for the next twenty years by reprimanding Gottlieb quietly for "poor judgment" and reporting the death to the family as a "suicide." After the 1975 Rockefeller report into the CIA revealed that the death was induced by LSD, President Gerald Ford apologized to Olson's family, setting in motion release of classified CIA documents and a congressional payment of $750,000.[48]

By 1956, these esoteric drug experiments had failed to produce useful results, and the agency began to focus on psychology research, particularly innovative work being done in Canada. After several U.S.-UK-Canadian meetings to discuss Soviet mind-control in the early 1950s, Dr. Donald O. Hebb, former chair of Human Relations Research on the Canadian Defense Research Board, received a Canadian Defense grant of $10,000 to study sensory deprivation. Using student volunteers at McGill University, where he was chair of Psychology, Heb found that after just two to three days wearing headphones and wrapped in foam "the subject's very identity had begun to disintegrate." But when Parliament grumbled about such wasteful research, Canada's Defense Board canceled the funding and Hebb delivered his data to unidentified American contacts. As it happened, one of Hebb's colleagues in Psychiatry at McGill, Dr. Ewan Cameron, then president of the American Psychiatric Association, had claimed that he had been able to duplicate "the extraordinary political conversions . . . in the iron curtain countries," in one case "using sleeplessness, disinhibiting agents [drugs], and hypnosis."[49]

Starting in March 1957, CIA director Allen Dulles provided Dr. Cameron with funding for secret experiments on his patients at the Allan Memorial Institute in Montreal. Although the funds were laundered through a foundation, the CIA designated Dr. Cameron's research MKUltra Subproject 68 and placed it under Dr. Gottlieb's direct supervision. Between 1957 and 1963, approximately one hundred patients admitted to Allan Institute with moderate emotional problems became unwitting, often unwilling subjects. A young psychiatrist, Dr. Mary Morrow, who agreed to routine tests when she applied for a staff position, was drugged and subjected to weeks of electro-shocks and sensory deprivation. A young housewife, Jeanine Huard, who had sought help for ordinary postpartum depression, became a subject for experimentation with drugs, electrical shock, and protracted sleep deprivation. In these CIA-funded experiments, Dr. Cameron used his patients to test a three-stage method for "depatterning"—first, drug-induced coma for up to eighty-six days; next, electro-shock treatment to the brain three times daily for thirty days; and, finally, a football helmet clamped to the head for up to twenty-one days with a looped tape repeating messages such as "my mother hates me." In contrast to Dr. Hebb's six-day maximum of voluntary isolation, Cameron confined one patient, known only as Mary C., in his sensory deprivation "box" for thirty-five days. At the end of his CIA funding in May 1960, Dr. Cameron told a U.S. Air Force conference that he had moved beyond Dr. Hebb's earlier experiments with "self-imposed" sensory deprivation to discover that indefinite "strict sensory isolation," with patients treated as prisoners, was "much more disturbing."[50]

The Allan Institute's follow-up study in 1967, three years after Dr. Cameron had resigned, found that 60 percent of the seventy-nine subjects who reached stage three of his depatterning still suffered persistent amnesia and 23 percent had serious physical complications. In 1980, after press exposés of CIA funding for Dr. Cameron, nine former subjects filed a civil suit against the agency in Washington. Two litigants, Mary Morrow and Jeanine Huard, were still suffering from prosopagnosia, a brain disorder that blocks recognition of faces or common objects. After a federal judge rejected a CIA motion to dismiss in 1988, the agency settled out of court for $750,000.[51]

The CIA pressed ahead with its research. Stripped of its bizarre excesses, Dr. Cameron's experiments, building upon Dr. Hebb's earlier breakthrough, laid the scientific foundation for the CIA's two-stage psychological torture method. Cameron had found that initial sensory deprivation disoriented subjects, broke down their resistance, and made them susceptible to suggestion.[52]

After these experiments, the CIA was ready to move beyond research to application. Most important, this research had convinced agency scientists that "esoteric" methods with "drugs or mind-altering conditions" simply did not work. "By 1962 and 1963," CIA psychologist Dr. John Gittinger later told the Senate, "The general idea we were able to come up with is that brain-washing was largely a process of isolating a human being, keeping him out of contact, putting him under long stress in relationship to interviewing and interrogation, . . . without having to resort to any esoteric means."[53]

That same year, the CIA's inspector general came across the super-secret MKUltra project in a routine audit and compiled a twenty-four-page report for the director condemning these experiments for putting "the rights and interests of all Americans in jeopardy." The report noted that "research in the manipulation of human behavior is considered by many authorities in medicine . . . to be professionally unethical." Significantly, he added, "some aspects of MKUltra raise questions of legality" within the CIA's charter.[54] The inspector general was particularly critical of the program's drug testing on unwitting subjects, since the agents were "not qualified scientific observers" and had no way of treating subjects who became seriously ill.[55] In response to the report, the CIA suspended MKUltra. But powerful backers, such as Richard Helms, objected, saying that "for over a decade Clandestine Services has had the mission of maintaining a capability for influencing human behavior" and warning that the suspension threatened the agency's "positive operational capability to use drugs."[56]

After more than a decade of research and field trials, the CIA issued a report in 1963, titled "KUBARK Counterintelligence Interrogation"—findings that would define the agency's interrogation methods and be propagated throughout the Third Word for the next forty years. The report's "fundamental hypothesis" is that successful interrogation, coercive and non-coercive, involves a "method of inducing regression of the personality to whatever earlier and weaker level is required for the dissolution of resistance and the inculcation of dependence."

Thus, all interrogation techniques "are essentially ways of speeding up the process of regression." In words that would echo in later CIA interrogation manuals, KUBARK suggested non-coercive techniques involving "persistent manipulation of time, by retarding and advancing clocks and serving meals at odd times" would be "likely to drive him [the subject] deeper and deeper into himself, until he is no longer able to control his responses in an adult fashion." The principal techniques for coercive interrogation were "arrest, detention, deprivation of sensory stimuli through solitary confinement, . . . threats and fear, debilitation, pain . . . , hypnosis, narcosis, and induced regression." Citing Albert Biderman's BSSR study on coercion approvingly, the KUBARK manual argues that "the threat to inflict pain . . . can trigger fears more damaging than the immediate sensation of pain." Significantly, in assessing Biderman's major research, *The Manipulation of Human Behavior,* KUBARK comments critically that its "contribution consistently demonstrates too theoretical an understanding of interrogation" and has "practically no valid experimentation."[57] This deficiency, the lack of verifiable results from human subjects, would soon be resolved in Vietnam.

Through the KUBARK manual and its application in Asia and Latin America, the CIA developed a two-stage method of psychological torture designed to make victims cooperate with their interrogators. In the method's first stage, interrogators employed simple, nonviolent techniques to disorient the subject, such as hooding or sleep denial. To intensify disorientation, interrogators used attacks on personal identity, often involving sexual humiliation. To render their threats credible, interrogators would inflict physical pain through beatings, electric shock, or more elaborate methods. Once the subject was disoriented, interrogators could move on to a second stage, self-inflicted discomfort, such as standing for hours with arms extended. In this latter phase, the idea was to make victims feel responsible for their own pain and thus induce them to alleviate it by capitulating.

Under actual field conditions, agency and allied interrogators, whether out of simple cruelty or a need to accelerate the psychological breakdown, added physical methods reminiscent of the Inquisition's trademark tortures. At the CIA's center on Bagram air base near Kabul in 2002, American interrogators forced prisoners "to stand with their hands chained to the ceiling and their feet shackled" with an effect similar to the Italian Inquisition's *strappado.* At Abu Ghraib Prison in late 2003, U.S. Military Police paraded Iraqi prisoners naked with plastic sandbags over their heads, combining psychological humiliation with the physical pain of restricted breathing—just as medieval victims were displayed in town squares with iron donkey masks clamped on their heads, suffering both "imagined ridiculousness" and "physical torture through obstruction of the mouth or the nose." Yet agency techniques did away with the old iron implements to make the pain feel self-inflicted. Although the Paris Inquisition's "water question" and the CIA's "water boarding" at Kabul both forced water down the throat to induce a sense of drowning, the Church sought to purge and punish, while the agency tried for psychological dominance. The Inquisition used an iron-framed "crippling stork" to contort the victim's body, while CIA interrogators made their victims assume similar "stress positions" but without any external mechanism, again aiming for a psychological effect of self-induced pain.[58] For thirty years after completion of the KUBARK manual, the CIA would disseminate this method globally, working through overt U.S. police and military training programs.

(file 03-04)

Vietnam and Human Subjects

From 1962 to 1974, the CIA worked through OPS, the division of USAID that assigned public safety advisers to police in developing nations.[59] Established by President Kennedy in 1962, USAID's public safety program grew, in just six years, into a global counter-insurgency effort with an annual budget of $35 million and over four hundred U.S. police advisers worldwide. By 1971, the program had trained over a million policemen in forty-seven nations, including eighty-five thousand in South Vietnam and a hundred thousand in Brazil.[60] CIA torture research would become evident as the agency disseminated its psychological model to allied security agencies across the Third World—particularly in South Vietnam, Uruguay, Iran, and the Philippines.

To implement its new doctrine of "counter-insurgency," the Kennedy administration formed a powerful, interagency Special Group (CI) whose members—General Maxwell Taylor, national security adviser McGeorge Bundy, CIA director John McCone, and undersecretary of state U. Alexis Johnson—could cut across bureaucratic boundaries to get the job done.[61] As a 1962 National Security Action memorandum indicates, "the President [Kennedy] desires that careful consideration be given to intensifying civil police programs in lieu of military assistance where such action will yield more fruitful results in terms of our internal security objectives."[62] Even though "the police program is even more important than Special Forces in our global C-I effort," said committee staffer Robert Komer in an April 1962 memo, the first problem was to find a "congenial home" for such a hybrid program.[63] The problem was how to expand USAID's police program to serve as a cover for a more aggressive CIA internal-security effort among Third World allies.

The solution, apparently, was to expand the existing program within USAID while simultaneously placing it under the control of CIA personnel—notably the program's head, Byron Engle.[64] During his decade as OPS chief, Engle recruited CIA personnel for the program and provided a close coordination with the CIA's intelligence mission.[65]

The hybrid nature of OPS allowed CIA field operatives a cover to disseminate new interrogation techniques. In South Vietnam, for example, Public Safety was incorporated into the Phoenix program in 1967 and trained Vietnamese police in what the chief adviser called "stringent wartime measures designed to assist in defeating the enemy." At the provincial level, Vietnamese National Police Field Forces, trained by OPS, worked with CIA mercenaries in seizing civilians for interrogation.[66] In Latin America, the CIA used Public Safety to recruit local police for training at a clandestine center in Washington, International Police Services, that operated behind a blind provided by USAID's International Police Academy (IPA). In its audit of OPS in 1976, the General Accounting Office reported that "there were allegations that the [International Police] academy . . . taught or encouraged use of torture," but its investigation did not support the allegations.[67]

Amnesty International, however, documented widespread torture, usually by police, in twenty-four of the forty-nine nations that had hosted OPS police-training teams.[68] Staffers for Senator James Abourezk (D-S.D.) also found evidence of torture training at the IPA by examining student graduation theses. In his 1968 essay, for example, Nickolas V. Fotinfpfulos of Greece described "the psychological tactics and techniques of an effective interrogation of reluctant witness by means of instrumental aids or drugs."[69] A year later, after devoting four pages of his fourteen-page thesis to a history of European torture, Luu Van Huu of the South Vietnam Police summarized lessons learned, saying, "We have 4 sorts of torture: use of force as such; threats; physical suffering, imposed indirectly; and mental or psychological torture."[70] In his 1971 paper, Le Van An of the South Vietnam Police defended torture, saying, "Despite the fact that brutal interrogation is strongly criticized by moralists, its importance must not be denied if we want to have order and security in daily life."[71]

More broadly, the CIA worked through U.S. Public Safety advisers in Brazil and Uruguay to provide local police with training and interrogation equipment. Through its field offices in Panama and Buenos Aires, the agency's TSD, the unit responsible for psychological research, shipped polygraph and electro-shock machines in diplomatic pouches to Public Safety offices across the continent.[72]

The Vietnam War was the ultimate test of the CIA's mind-control program, allowing the agency to overcome the shortage of human subjects that had slowed past research. Although OPS advisers had tried to transform Vietnamese police into an effective counter-insurgency force, it was clear by 1963 that they were failing. Arriving in Saigon in December, the CIA station chief, Peer DeSilva, recalled in his memoirs, "The Viet Cong were monstrous in their application of torture and murder." Inspired by a doctrine of counter-terror, DeSilva began a campaign "to bring danger and death to the Vietcong functionaries themselves, especially in the areas where they felt secure." This vision of an effective counter-terror, psychological and physical, launched the CIA on a path toward the Phoenix.[73]

After organizing South Vietnam's Central Intelligence Organization, the CIA built the organization's Saigon headquarters, the National Interrogation Center, in early 1964 and then assigned four agency advisers to train the Vietnamese by interrogating the hundreds of prisoners confined inside its concrete walls. Within a year, under DeSilva's leadership, each of the forty-plus provinces in Vietnam had a Province Intelligence Coordination Committee and a concrete Provincial Interrogation Center (PIC) of its own. By 1965–66, the CIA had thus developed a nationwide intelligence-collection system that reached from the National In-terrogation Center in Saigon down to the provincial PICs. The CIA sent "experts . . . , most of whom had worked on Russian defectors" from its Technical Services Division to train the Vietnamese interrogators.[74]

The program expanded in 1967 when the CIA established a centralized pacification bureaucracy, CORDS, and drew the U.S. counter-insurgency operations into the unified Phoenix program—making Phoenix a secret war on the Viet Cong underground within the larger Vietnam war. In Saigon, the program used sophisticated computer information banks to centralize all data on the Vietcong infrastructure, identifying communist cadres for interrogation or elimination. In the countryside, Phoenix established the 146-man counter-guerrilla teams called Provincial Reconnaissance Units (PRU) attached to each of the CIA's forty Provincial Interrogation Centers.[75]

After the PRU brought in suspected communists, PIC interrogators, under CIA supervision, tortured the alleged agents, often summarily executing them without trial or due process. Although many early recruits were well motivated, the PRUs began to attract social outcasts, including convicted criminals, who embraced their basic task, murder, by tattooing themselves "Sat Cong" (Kill Communists).

Phoenix and allied programs apparently allowed the CIA to continue its more extreme research into the effects of coercion on the human mind. No longer restricted to isolated drug trials or simulated psychology experiments, the CIA was now operating a nationwide network of interrogation centers that used torture to generate intelligence. Under this program, the CIA gained a limitless supply of human subjects. In mid 1966, the agency sent a Page-Russell electro-shock machine and three psychiatrists, two of its own staff and a private California practitioner, Dr. Lloyd H. Cotter, to conduct experiments at Bien Hoa Mental Hospital just north of Saigon. In effect, they were testing, under field conditions, whether Cameron's "depatterning" could actually alter behavior. As he later wrote in the *American Journal of Psychiatry,* Cotter applied electro-convulsive treatment three times weekly and withheld food to force patients to work, finding himself "impressed" with the results. Meanwhile inside a walled compound on the hospital grounds, the two CIA doctors subjected one Vietcong prisoner to a dozen shocks the first day and sixty over the next seven days until he died. Two weeks later when the last prisoner died, the CIA men packed up their machine and flew home without fully breaking any of the Vietcong.[76]

Congressional Investigations

After nearly four years of secret operations, Congress and the press exposed the Phoenix Program in 1970. William Colby, a career CIA officer and chief of pacification in Vietnam, testified before the Senate Foreign Relations Committee that in 1969 Phoenix had killed 6,187 members of the 75,000 strong Vietcong Infrastructure. Although admitting some "illegal killings," Colby rejected Senator J. William Fulbright's suggestion that it was "a program for the assassination of civilian leaders."[77]

Despite mounting congressional opposition, in 1971 the U.S. command, according to a *New York Times* report, launched a pacification effort aimed at "neutralization" of 14,400 communist agents by killing or capture.[78] In the wake of this exposé, the House Operations Subcommittee conducted the first wide-ranging congressional probe of CIA pacification operations, finding that Phoenix had killed 9,820 Vietcong suspects in the previous fourteen months. "I am shocked and dismayed," said Representative Ogden R. Reid. "Assassination and terror by the Vietcong or Hanoi should not, and must not, call forth the same methods by Saigon, let alone the United States, directly or indirectly."[79]

Several days later, William Colby told the committee that Phoenix had killed 20,587 Vietcong suspects since its inception in 1968.[80] When Representative Reid charged that Phoenix was responsible for "indiscriminate killings," Colby defended the program as "an essential part of the war effort" that was "designed to protect the Vietnamese people from terrorism." Though the CIA had started the program, the agency, Colby explained, had already transferred the apparatus to the Vietnamese National Police so that it was now, in his words, "entirely a South Vietnamese program."[81] In these same hearings, a Military Intelligence veteran, K. Barton Osborn, who worked with the CIA's Phoenix program in 1967–68, described, "the insertion of the six-inch dowel into the six-inch ear canal of one of my detainee's ears and the tapping through the brain until he died. The starving to death of a Vietnamese woman who was suspected of being part of the local [Vietcong] political education cadre." He also recalled "the use of electronic gear such as sealed telephones attached to . . . [the] women's vagina and the men's testicles . . . [to] shock them into submission." During his eighteen months in the Phoenix program, not a single VC suspect survived CIA interrogation. All these "extralegal, illegal, and covert" procedures were, Osborn testified, found in the *Defense Collection Intelligence Manual,* issued to him during his intelligence training at Fort Holabird.[82]

As the Vietnam War wound down, public opinion, disturbed by impending defeat and reports of the CIA's questionable role, created a climate for reform. In December 1974, the *New York Times* reporter Seymour Hersh published a front-page story that the CIA's "Operation Chaos" had conducted illegal mail interception and phone tapping against antiwar activists. In response to these revelations, President Ford appointed Vice President Nelson Rockefeller to investigate, and both houses of Congress formed special inquiries. Instead of stonewalling as Helms had done with the MKUltra files, Colby skillfully restrained these inquiries by feeding investigators just enough information to convince them that they were uncovering the truth.[83]

Not surprisingly, the Rockefeller Commission found that the CIA, in monitoring U.S. citizens, had done things that "should be criticized" but concluded that the agency had already reformed itself. Alone among these inquiries, the U.S. Senate Committee, led by Senator Frank Church, held hearings into CIA assassinations. But the author of a critical history of the CIA found that the Senate's inquiries into MKUltra and subsequent torture training did not go beyond the anecdotal.[84] Two years later, Senator Edward Kennedy tried to repair this oversight with hearings into Olson's death from LSD. But Gottlieb was granted immunity from further prosecution in exchange for some "exceedingly obscure" testimony that blocked all subsequent prosecution.[85] Though the Senate hearings inspired four well-documented books on the CIA's mind-control experiments, there has been no official investigation or criminal prosecution of culpable officials. "I thought in 1978 when our books were appearing, when we were doing media work all over the world," Alan Scheflin, author of *The Mind Manipulators*, recalled, "that we would finally get the story out, the vaults would be cleansed, the victims would learn their identities, the story would become part of history, and the people who had been injured could seek recompense. Instead, what happened was the great void."[86]

Our Man in Montevideo

Although the Phoenix program was the largest CIA interrogation effort, it was OPS-sponsored police training in Latin America that prompted a Senate attempt to end U.S. torture training. Ironically, it was the murder of an American police adviser in Uruguay that exposed the OPS involvement in torture and contributed to that agency's abolition.

The story broke in August 1970 when the *New York Times* reported an American police adviser, Dan A. Mitrione, had been kidnapped by Tupamaro guerrillas in Montevideo. The report described Mitrione as a family man from Indiana, and head of the U.S. Public Safety program in Uruguay aimed at encouraging "responsible and humane police administration." In an inadvertent hint of Mitrione's actual mission, the report added that he "unquestionably knew more about the Tupamaro operations than any other United States official."[87]

In reporting Mitrione's point-blank execution, the paper noted that Mitrione "was considered to have contributed materially to the Government's anti guerrilla campaign." Nonetheless, an accompanying editorial expressed the paper's "shock and horror," saying: "Only diseased minds could see in the gunning down of this father of nine from Indiana the weakening of the capitalist system or the advancement of social revolution in the Americas."[88]

Mitrione's burial in Richmond, Indiana, was an emotional tribute to an American hero. Nine thousand people paid their respects. A cavalcade of 125 cars moved through a city decorated with black-bowed roses to the cemetery where Secretary of State William Rogers and President Nixon's son-in-law David Eisenhower listened as the Uruguayan ambassador Hector Luisi warned that the "masterminds" of this crime would "reap the wrath of civilized people everywhere."

Only days after this emotional funeral, the story of Mitrione's mission began to emerge. A senior Uruguayan police official, Alejandro Otero, told the *Jornal do Brazil* that Mitrione had used "violent techniques of torture and repression." On August 15, a U.S. Embassy spokesman in Montevideo called the charge "absolutely false."[89] Eight years later, however, a Cuban double-agent, Manuel Hevia Cosculluela, who had joined the CIA and worked with Mitrione in Montevideo, published a book alleging that the American adviser had tortured four beggars to death with electrical shocks at a 1970 seminar to demonstrate his techniques for Uruguayan police trainees. "The special horror of the course," Hevia added, "was its academic, almost clinical atmosphere. Mitrione's motto was: 'The right pain in the right place at the right time.' A premature death, he would say, meant that the technique had failed." Over drinks at his home, Mitrione once gave Hevia a summary of his methods that showed the influence of the CIA's psychological paradigm: "He said he considered interrogation to be a complex art. . . . The objective was to humiliate the victim, separating him from reality, making him feel defenseless. No questions, just blows and insults. Then silent blows." Significantly, the Cuban charged that Mitrione's deputy in the Public Safety office was William Cantrell, a CIA agent.[90]

Only three months before Mitrione's death, the unsettling coincidence of police torture and U.S. police training in Brazil finally raised questions, albeit muted, in the U.S. Congress about torture. In May 1971, the Senate Foreign Relations Committee summoned the chief U.S. Public Safety adviser for Brazil, Theodore D. Brown, and scrutinized his program. Brown's statement that OPS taught "minimum use of force, humane methods" sparked a dialogue that led to an affirmation by all, senators and police adviser alike, that America would not, could not train torturers. In his questioning of Brown, Senator Claiborne Pell (D-R.I.) had the uncommon insight to recognize the de-legitimizing impact of torture on the regimes it was designed to defend, asking "Why is it the Brazilians . . . use torture as a police method when it will alienate their friends and allies around the world?" Yet Pell also followed up with a question revealing the mistaken assumption that psychological torture was not really torture, asking, "But from a police viewpoint, you would agree that psychological, nonphysical methods of interrogation can be just as effective as the physical, as torture?"[91]

Four years after these denials and the hero's funeral for Dan Mitrione, Congress investigated the Public Safety program and curtailed its operations. Led by Senator Abourezk, congressional investigators found widespread allegations that the program was training torturers within the Latin American police.[92] Congress, concerned about these persistent allegations of torture, finally cut all funds, effective July 1975, for "training or advice to police, prisons, or other law enforcement"—in effect, abolishing the Office of Public Safety. Many of the USAID public safety officers soon found themselves disavowed, discredited, and unemployed.[93]

Though these reforms were well-intentioned, Congress had failed to probe for the source of the torture training. Although these investigations had exposed the CIA's mind control project, there was no public pressure to restrain the agency's propagation of psychological torture. By the time Congress began investigating this office in 1971, the CIA had already stopped using it as a cover for its foreign agents, and shifted its torture training to the U.S. Army's Military Adviser Program.[94]

CIA and Savak

In the turmoil of the late 1970s, Iran showed the long-term instability fostered by U.S. tolerance of an ally's torture and human-rights abuse. After launching a coup in 1953 that restored the shah to direct rule, the CIA, in the decades that followed, helped consolidate his control. By 1959, U.S. and Israeli advisers were involved in the reorganization of the "Iranian secret police." Most important, the CIA helped establish the shah's main secret police unit, the Savak, and trained its interrogators.[95]

In 1962, for example, the Kennedy administration's top-level Special Group (CI), which included CIA director John McCone, approved $500,000 in riot control equipment to expand the Iranian capital's contingent from 350 to 500 men.[96] Consequently, in early 1964, the U.S. State Department reported that "with the arrival of most of the AID-programmed riot-control equipment for the Tehran police," training was now starting that would allow the Gendarmerie "to deal with any likely and foreseeable civil disturbance in Tehran."[97]

The former CIA analyst Jesse Leaf recalled that senior agency officials had trained Savak in interrogation methods that "were based on German torture techniques from World War II." Although no Americans participated in the torture, Leaf recalled "people who were there seeing the rooms and being told of the torture. And I know that the torture rooms were toured and it was all paid for by the U.S.A."[98] As opposition to the shah grew in the 1970s, Savak tortured dissidents cruelly and indiscriminately, fueling angry Iranian student protests in Europe and the United States against the brutality of the shah's police and his detention of fifty thousand political prisoners.[99] Defending his regime in an interview with *Le Monde,* the shah spoke candidly: "Why should we not employ the same methods as you Europeans? We have learned sophisticated methods of torture from you. You use psychological methods to extract the truth: we do the same."[100] After the shah fell from power in 1979, Savak's torture and the CIA's role were heavily publicized, both in Iran and the United States. One former CIA analyst told the *New York Times* that the agency had sanctioned the torture.[101] Writing in *The Nation*, the Iranian poet Reza Baraheni claimed that "at least half a million people have . . . been beaten, whipped, or tortured by Savak"—a cruelty that he illustrated with gruesome autopsy photos of mangled bodies, scabbed and scarred.[102]

The Islamic revolutionary government's prosecution of former Savak agents for torture and murder received extensive international coverage, including several reports in the *New York Times*. At his trial in June 1979, a former Savak interrogator, Bahman Naderipour, confessed in "excruciating detail" to years of "interrogation, torture, and killing." Despite such coverage, there was little public reaction in the United States to revelations about the CIA's ties to the shah's brutal secret police. Yet Iran provided an important cautionary tale. By buttressing the shah's rule with riot police and ruthless interrogation, the CIA had unwittingly contributed to the rising opposition that eventually toppled his regime. After training his police, Washington underestimated the stigma attached to torture and stood by, confused, while the regime slowly lost legitimacy. The lesson was clear: Torture introduced to defend the shah had helped discredit and destroy the shah.

Training Filipino Torturers

In the slow unwinding of the Cold War in the mid 1980s, a democratic uprising in the Philippines toppled an entrenched dictator and plunged the country into four years of abortive coup attempts by a restive military. Though overlooked by the international media, this instability exposed the corrosive effect of the agency's psychological torture paradigm on allied armies trained in its techniques. The CIA had long tried to discourage simple brutality by allied agencies, but its psychological torture had, as the Philippines demonstrates, a more corrupting long-term impact upon perpetrators than its crude physical variant.

Under President Ferdinand Marcos (1972–86), torture became a key instrument in the maintenance of authoritarian rule. Marcos's rule had rested on a theatrical terror. His military officers who administered this torture were not impersonal cogs in a military machine. They were actors who personified the violent capacities of the state. If the president had written a script of terror for his "new society," then these young officers were his players. When he ordered mass arrests of his political opponents, it was the military, particularly the young officers of the Philippine Constabulary, who carried out these orders and came to personify the violent capacity of Marcos's authoritarian state.[103]

After a decade of dictatorship, a group of middle-echelon officers, hardened by these extra-legal duties formed a clique called the Reform the Armed Forces

Movement, or RAM, and then spent a decade plotting to seize state power. Led by officers who had been involved in torture, RAM plotted a coup d'état against Marcos in 1986 and, failing to take power, launched five more against his successor Corazon Aquino.

Within the Philippines, RAM represents, above all, a breakdown in military socialization. Most of its members were regular officers who had graduated from the Philippine Military Academy during the 1970s. There, for four years, they were drilled in obedience and indoctrinated into a belief in civilian supremacy over the military. These future rebels graduated into Marcos's martial-law military and served as junior officers, often in the Philippines Constabulary, fighting a civil war in Mindanao or interrogating dissidents in Manila. Then, as torture and extra-judicial killings rose, they became the instruments of state terror. For them, torture proved transformative, freeing them from military socialization and inspiring a will to power.

Under Marcos, torture was usually more psychological than physical. Some of his officers proved innovative practitioners of psychological torture, using a theatrical variant that seemed lifted from a leaf in the CIA interrogation manuals. Indeed, these Philippine practices are so similar to CIA techniques that we must ask: Did the agency train Marcos's interrogators?

There are indications that the answer may be yes. In 1978, a human rights newsletter reported that the regime's top torturer, Lieutenant-Colonel Rolando Abadilla, was studying at the U.S. Command and General Staff College, Fort Leavenworth. A year later, another group claimed that his understudy, Lieutenant Rodolfo Aguinaldo, was going to the United States "for six months to one year for additional training under the Central Intelligence Agency." [104] Were these officers given training in either tactical interrogation or torture?

Definitive answers must await release of classified documents. But as revealed by victims' accounts, the methods of the Filipino interrogators, and particularly the theatricality of the future RAM officers, seem similar to the spirit of the CIA interrogation manual technique.

A rural priest tortured by one of the future RAM leaders offers us the most acute insight into their methods. Arrested for subversion in October 1982, Fr. Edgardo Kangleon was subjected to two months of constant interrogation before breaking down. In his confession, he admitted to being a communist agent and named his fellow clergy as subversives—charges that the Marcos regime seized upon to harass the Church. [105] Throughout his long confinement, the priest suffered only limited physical abuse and was instead psychologically terrorized by his chief interrogator, Lieutenant Colonel Hernani Figueroa, a Philippine Constabulary commander who later became chairman of the RAM faction.

Only a week after his release, Fr. Kangleon composed a twenty-five page memoir. Though damning himself as a "stinking coward" and "traitor" who broke

X/183

under interrogation, his statement describes the theatricality of psychological torture. In his account, the cell becomes studio, the inquisitors actors, and the detainees audience for a psychological drama crueler than physical pain.

Most significant, in Fr. Kangleon's account, his 1982 interrogation seems drawn, in almost every detail, from the "Human Resources Exploitation Manual—1983" that the CIA was using to train Honduran officers on the other side of the Pacific. As the manual recommends, the Filipino colonel enters with a thick file, maintains a controlling calm, starts with psychological rather than physical techniques, and makes the shift to coercive methods seem the victim's fault. As his underlings begin the physical phase of his interrogation, they speak not of simple brutality but a praxis they call "counter-terror."

On his fifty-first night of detention, Fr. Kangleon was brought before Lieutenant-Colonel Figueroa, a name synonymous with terror on Samar Island. At the start, the colonel entered like an actor striding to center stage, carrying a prop signifying his role as inquisitor:[106]

> The entry of the dreaded chief intelligence officer, who came in with a thick pile of documents, dashed to the ground the last bit of my hopes to get out of there "unscathed." His initial declaration: "Father, the general has decided that we start interrogating you tonight" was enough to unleash that fear that was building up inside me for these past two months. I felt cold sweat, sweat broke all over my body and I thought I was going to faint.
>
> For several hours, predator and prey fenced around verbally, one sizing up the other. Questions were posed and answers of innocence were given. Suddenly the "chairman" changed his approach. He said that since I would not answer his questions without my lawyer's presence, it would suffice if I would just give my biodata. And readily I fall for it. . . . I had fallen into a trap. I was already talking. Hastily, I tried to correct it by sticking to innocent or safe answers.
>
> Sensing that I had caught up to what he was up to and, irritated with the futility of that encounter, Ltc. Figueroa finally said: "Since you refused to cooperate, Father, we will be forced to use other means. We cannot allow ourselves to be taken for fools."

At the colonel's command, the priest was blindfolded before being taken to the nearby offices of the Military Intelligence Group. There, Fr. Kangleon discovers a metaphor central to our understanding of these Filipino officers and their psychological torture:[107]

> Inside I was made to sit on a stool. I felt a small table being placed in front of me. Then, I heard voices—new voices! Three or four of these voices—the more commanding ones—took their places around me. And with actors in their places, the most crucial stage of my detention started to unfold.
>
> "Now, Father, you are going to answer our questions!"
>
> "As the [communist] NPA utilizes terrorism, we are also willing to use counter-terror. . . . Every time you preached against us, I wished at that time to just shoot you there at the altar."

"What's the name of that sister you used to visit at the Sacred Heart College? She is your girlfriend, *ano*? You are fucking her? How does it feel?. . . "

"For me, he is not a priest. Yes, your kind is not worthy of a respect of a priest."

"OK, take off his shirt. Oh, look at that body. You look sexy. Even the women here think you are macho. You are a homosexual, *ano*?"

"Let's see if you are that macho after one of my punches." A short jab below my ribs.

"Hey, don't lean on the table. Place your arms beside you. That's it." Another jab.

"You, take that stool away from him." I stood up. A blow landed behind my ears. I started to plead that they stop what they are doing to me. I started to cower. More blows.

"You better answer our questions or else you will get more of this." With that, a short blow landed in my solar plexus.

I was already quaking with fear. The psychological and physical aspect . . . of my interrogation had finally taken its toll. I finally broke down. "Yes. Go call Ltc. Figueroa. I am now willing to cooperate."

As Fr. Kangleon implies by calling the interrogators "actors," his torture is a theater of humiliation. After blindfolding, stripping, and insulting the priest, the soldiers communicate their dominion by beating him, almost playfully, and forcing him to assist in his own degradation. He is beyond the help of courts and the law.[108] And, in the end, as the CIA manual predicts, the priest capitulates and calls out the name of his torturer as his savior.

What is the impact of such torture on the torturer? For a young lieutenant to degrade and dominate society's leaders—priests, professors, and senior officers—may well induce a sense of mastery, even omnipotence. By breaking their superiors through psychological manipulation, these officers gained a sense of their society's plasticity, fostering an illusion that they could break and remake the social order at will. Through their years of torturing priests and professors for Marcos, these officers learned the daring to attack Marcos himself. Clearly, their preference for psychological methods had important political consequences for the Philippines.

In the enclosed arena of the safe house, the future RAM officers played the lead in countless dramas of their own empowerment, rehearsing for a later moment on the national stage—a moment that brought six abortive coup attempts to the Philippines between 1986 and 1990. If this Philippine experience is any guide, the CIA's psychological torture proved particularly damaging to any armed force that adopted it, breaking down military discipline and fostering political instability. As in Iran, torture's complex psychopathology had led to its almost uncontrolled spread among the Philippine armed forces, corroding military discipline and contributing to the downfall of the regime it was designed to defend. Once again, the CIA ignored the long-term impact of its torture training and showed no cognizance of its role in destabilizing another key American ally.

(file 03-05)

CIA Torture Manual

At the height of the Cold War in the 1970s and 1980s, the CIA trained military interrogators in Latin America, propagating and legitimating the systematic torture that became the hallmark of the region's military dictatorships. In retrospect, it seems the CIA, denied access to Latin American police after the abolition of OPS in 1975, began working through U.S. military advisers to train the region's armed forces.

Though the agency trained military interrogators across the continent, our knowledge of the actual torture techniques comes from a single document, the CIA's "Human Resources Exploitation Manual—1983." After completing a training session for Honduran military interrogators in early 1983, an anonymous agency instructor combined this field experience with the agency's psychological paradigm to produce the most detailed statement of the CIA's interrogation methods.[109] Five years after the manual was written, a front-page *New York Times* exposé of Honduran military torture prompted a secret U.S. congressional inquiry that uncovered this document.

This 1983 manual provides indications of a clear continuity between CIA training in Latin America and the agency's original 1963 KUBARK interrogation handbook. At the outset, this anonymous CIA instructor emphasizes that his manual will explain two types of "psychological techniques," the coercive and non-coercive. "While we do not stress the use of coercive techniques," the agent tells his Honduran students, "we do want to make you aware of them and the proper way to use them."[110] In his review of non-coercive techniques, the agent explains that they "are based on the principle of generating pressure inside the subject without application of outside force. This is accomplished by manipulating him psychologically until his resistance is sapped and his urge to yield is fortified."[111] Thus, when a questioner uses threats, "it should always be implied that the subject himself is to blame using words as, 'You leave me no other choice but to . . .' He should never be told to comply or else."[112]

To establish control at the outset the questioner should, the CIA instructor continues, "manipulate the subject's environment, to create unpleasant or intolerable situations, to disrupt patterns of time, space, and sensory perception. The subject is very much aware that the 'questioner' controls his ultimate disposition." In these manipulations, "the number of variations in techniques is limited only by the experience and imagination of the 'questioner.'"[113] Among the many techniques that might spring from such an imagination, the subject should be arrested at a time selected to "achieve surprise and the maximum amount of mental discomfort," particularly, early morning when "most subjects experience intense feelings of shock, insecurity, and psychological stress,"[114] should immediately be placed in "isolation, both physical and psychological,"[115] should be "completely stripped and told to take a shower" while blindfolded before a guard,[116] and should be "provided with ill-fitting clothing (familiar clothing reinforces identity and thus the capacity for resistance)."[117] To convince the subject that much is already known and resistance is futile, the questioner should enter with a thick dossier, "padded with extra paper, if necessary, to give the illusion that it contains more data than is actually there."[118] If the subject proves resistant, then there are a "few non-coercive techniques which can be used to induce regression."[119]

A. Persistent manipulation of time
B. Retarding and advancing clocks
C. Serving meals at odd times
D. Disrupting sleep schedules
E. Disorientation regarding day and night
F. Unpatterned "questioning" sessions
G. Nonsensical questioning
H. Ignoring half-hearted attempts to cooperate
I. Rewarding non-cooperation

Though the report's overall approach is psychological, the CIA trainer points out that coercion still plays an important role in effective interrogation. "The purpose of all coercive techniques is to induce psychological regression in the subject by bringing a superior outside force to bear on his will to resist," the CIA trainer explains. As coercion is applied, the subject suffers "a loss of autonomy, a reversion to an earlier behavioral level."[120]

There are, the manual states, three basic coercive techniques—debility, disorientation, and dread. "For centuries," the CIA trainer explains, " 'questioners' have employed various methods of inducing physical weakness . . . [on the] assumption that lowering the subject's physiological resistance will lower his psychological capacity for resistance."[121] While disorientation can "destroy his capacity to resist," sustained dread also "induces regression."[122] Thus, the trainer explains: "The threat of coercion usually weakens or destroys resistance more effectively than coercion itself. For example, the threat to inflict pain can trigger fears more damaging than the immediate sensation of pain."[123]

But even within the CIA's psychological torture paradigm, such threats, including those involving physical pain, must be both made and carried out. "Threat is basically a means for establishing a bargaining position by inducing fear in the subject," the CIA trainer explains. "A threat should never be made unless it is part of the plan and the 'questioner' has the approval to carry out the threat."[124] In his concluding sections, the CIA trainer reiterates his emphasis on the psychological over the crudely physical. "The torture situation is an external conflict, a contest between the subject and his tormentor," he explains. While pain inflicted on the victim "from outside himself may actually intensify his will to resist," pain that "he feels he is inflicting on himself is more likely to sap his resistance."[125]

The success of these CIA techniques relies ultimately on the psychological empowerment of the interrogator. "Remember," this CIA trainer told his Honduran students, "the 'questioner' always has the advantage in 'questioning. . . . He creates, modifies, amplifies, and terminates the subject's environment. He selects the emotional keys upon which the 'questioning' will proceed. The subject is acutely aware that the 'questioner' controls his ultimate disposition."[126] Significantly, the agency did indeed warn that physical torture weakens the "moral caliber of the [security] organization and corrupts those that rely on it." But the CIA missed an important point that would emerge, time and again, in Iran and the Philippines: psychological torture has a far more corrupting impact upon perpetrators than its physical variant.[127]

Only five years after the manual was written, a cover story in the *New York Times Magazine* exposed CIA training for Honduran torturers, producing another cycle of public shock and official indifference. As civil war intensified in Honduras during the late 1970s, the CIA brought in Argentine officers to train Honduran interrogators. "I was taken to Texas with 24 others for six months between 1979 and 1980," Sergeant Florencio Caballero told the reporter. "There was an American Army captain there and men from the CIA." The chief agency instructor was "Mr. Bill," who had served in Vietnam. Sergeant Caballero recalled the American officers "taught me interrogation in order to end physical torture in Honduras. They taught us psychological methods—to study the fears and weaknesses of a prisoner. Make him stand up, don't let him sleep, keep him naked and isolated, put rats and cockroaches in his cell, given him bad food, served him dead animals, throw cold water on him, change the temperature."

One of those tortured by Sergeant Caballero's unit, Ines Murillo, recalled her "psychological" interrogation at a secret prison near Tegucigalpa where her questioners "gave her raw dead birds and rats for dinner, threw freezing water on her naked body every half hour for extended periods and made her stand for hours without sleep and without being allowed to urinate." Her "worst torturer" was Lieutenant Marco Tulio Regalado, another alumnus of the CIA's Texas training program. Though American CIA agents visited these prisons and observed interrogations, it is not clear whether they knew of these excesses and tolerated them as an acceptable level of coercion. Though Sergeant Regalado said the "Americans didn't accept physical torture," the CIA backed the rise of Colonel Gustavo Alvarez Martinez, the Honduran police commander, and his deputy Alexander Hernandez, even though a brother officer denounced them as death squad leaders in 1982.[128]

When the U.S. Senate's Select Committee on Intelligence, responsible for legislative oversight of the CIA, met in closed session for hearings into the *New York Times* report, committee chair Senator David Boren (D-Okla.) stated CIA's review of these allegations had uncovered several training manuals used in Central America. The techniques were in Boren's view, "completely contrary to the principles and policies of the United States."[129]

In his top secret testimony to the committee, Director for Operations, confirmed the essential accuracy of the *New York Times* story, saying that: "[Sergeant] Caballero did indeed attend a CIA human resources exploitation or interrogation course [excised] from February 8th to March 13th, 1983."[130] Though this CIA trainer had written the interrogation manual after a 1983 training session in Honduras, the basic techniques, Stolz said, apparently referring to the KUBARK report, were "assembled back in March of 1964."[131]

Suddenly, Senator Frank H. Murkowski (R-Alaska), reflecting Congress's reluctance to explore these issues during the Cold War, interjected: "Mr. Chairman, I feel very uneasy about getting into these areas. I mean this is the report and we're going through it. . . . I really question the propriety. I mean, hell, there's a million reports." When Senator William S. Cohen (R-Maine) objected that this was no mere press report but an actual CIA manual, Murkowski repeated, "I just want to note that this Senator feels very uncomfortable."[132]

Deftly evading any discussion of past CIA research into interrogation, Deputy Director Stolz explained that in 1985 senior agency officers had ordered revisions to this manual and related CIA training policies. The new text banned "interrogation which results in the use of force, mental or physical torture, demeaning indignities or exposure to inhumane treatment of any kind as an aid to interrogation."[133]

But Senator Alan Cranston (D-Calif.) pointed out that the manual stated explicitly "there are times when you should use coercive methods." Nonetheless, Stolz insisted that "we were not talking anything about the kind of coercive methods that was alleged" in the *New York Times* article. Stolz added, "we are talking about . . . sitting in a chair on a stool for a long period of time, some sensory deprivations, sounds . . . and some techniques that while it might appear harsh were certainly not anything like what was alleged in the article." Then, Senator Bill Bradley (D-N.J.) launched into an aggressive cross examination of this CIA witness about the article's accuracy, revealing the committee's ignorance of the CIA's long involvement in torture research and training.[134]

> *Senator Bradley:* Denying sleep?
> *Mr. Stolz:* Yes, there was some denied sleep.
> *Senator Bradley:* Making them stand up?
> *Mr. Stolz:* Yes.
> *Senator Bradley:* So making him stand up, denying him sleep—keeping him
>   naked?

Mr. Stolz: No. Definitely not.

Senator Bradley: Rats?

Mr. Stolz: No rats.

Senator Bradley: Where it says: the CIA taught us psychological methods, to study the fears and weaknesses of the prisoner, make him stand up, yes; don't let him sleep, yes. Keep him naked and isolated—

Mr. Stolz: No.

Senator Bradley: Isolated?

Mr. Stolz: Well, yes—the answer is yes.

Senator Bradley: Naked no. Isolated yes.

Mr. Stolz: Right.

Senator Bradley: Put rats and cockroaches in the cell, no. Give him bad food?

Mr. Stolz: No. Bland food but not bad food . . .

Senator Bradley: Serve him dead animals.

Mr. Stolz: No.

Senator Bradley: Throw cold water on him.

Mr. Stolz: No, sir.

Senator Bradley: Changed the temperature?

Mr. Stolz: I don't know the answer to that. That's not impossible.

A moment later, apparently aware that he had stumbled onto something larger than a few training manuals, Senator Bradley interjected, demanding to know, "who was in charge of all this? Prior to 1984?" Mr. Stolz's four-line reply is blacked out.[135]

In a follow-up question, Senator Cohen, revealing the committee's ignorance of the CIA's long history of torture research, said, "I am not sure why in 1983 it became necessary to have such a manual." More pointedly, Cohen asked "why the word questioning is always in quotes in the manual itself" and suggested that the CIA might be "sending subliminal signals that say this [coercion] is improper, but by the way, you ought to be aware of it." Nonetheless, the senator, seemingly unaware that Stolz had lied to conceal the CIA's long history of torture research, praised the agency for being "most cooperative." In his closing remarks, Stolz assured the senators the CIA's inspector general would conduct a prompt review of these allegations—a report that, if completed, has not been released.[136]

Although the country's leading newspaper had published a detailed report of CIA torture training, Congress was, as this committee demonstrated, unwilling to expose the agency's human rights violations. Under the pressures of the Cold War, CIA torture training had again eluded serious reform.

After the Cold War

Although the United States was tacitly tolerant of torture by its allies during the Cold War, the international community worked to oppose this abuse by police and military across the Third World. As military regimes using systematic torture proliferated, the international community reacted with treaties to ban the practice and therapy to treat its victims. In 1972, Amnesty International, realizing the limitations of its lawyerly practices of documentation and petition, appealed to the medical profession for support. A group of Danish doctors responded by examining Greek and Chilean refugees for "forensic medical evidence about the after-effects of torture," discovering a pernicious form of post-traumatic stress disorder. "When you've been tortured," explained one of the Danish researchers, Dr. Inge Genefke, "the private hell stays with you through your life if it's not treated." But the victims did respond well to therapy. These discoveries inspired, in 1982, the foundation of Copenhagen's Rehabilitation and Research Centre for Torture Victims (RCT). Within a decade, the RCT built a network of ninety-nine treatment centers in forty-nine countries and pioneered a therapy that treated 48,000 victims in 1992.[137]

These efforts broadened medical understanding of torture and built international support for its abolition. In December 1984, the UN General Assembly adopted the Convention against Torture. Significantly, this convention, under Article 1, defined torture broadly as "any act by which severe pain or suffering, whether physical or mental, is intentionally inflicted on a person for such purpose as obtaining from him or a third person information or a confession."[138]

After the UN General Assembly adopted the Torture Convention by a unanimous vote, creating enormous international pressure for compliance, President Ronald Reagan sent it to Congress in 1988 with a ringing invocation of "our desire to bring an end to the abhorrent practice of torture." Simultaneously, however, the administration proposed a record nineteen reservations that stalled the convention's ratification in the Senate for the next six years.[139] Among these nineteen reservations, the Reagan administration focused, above all, on the issue of psychological torture. As Assistant Attorney General Mark Richard explained, both State and Justice found an "unacceptable level of vagueness" in the convention's definition of mental pain. To correct this vagueness, the State Department drafted a four-part definition of psychological torture as "prolonged mental harm caused by (1) the intentional infliction or threatened infliction of severe physical pain or suffering; (2) the administration . . . of mind-altering substances; (3) the threat of imminent death; or (4) the threat that another person will imminently be subjected to death . . . or other procedures calculated to disrupt profoundly the senses or personality."[140] Significantly, this narrow definition excluded sensory deprivation (hooding), self-inflicted pain (stress positions), and disorientation (isolation and sleep denial)—the very techniques the CIA had refined at such great cost over the past forty years.

Why this impassioned concern about a single word, "mental," in a UN convention that covers twenty-six printed pages? Was this objection a response to some conservative ideological concern, or, more likely, the result of CIA maneuvering

X
−191

through State and Justice to protect its psychological torture from legal sanction? Whatever the cause, the State Department's four-part definition did, if narrowly interpreted, exempt the CIA's two-phase psychological method from the UN Torture Convention as recognized and ratified by the United States. Once drafted, this narrow definition of torture would soon find its way, verbatim, into two later U.S. criminal laws and thus become the basis for Washington's policy on prisoner interrogation during the War on Terror fifteen years later.

With the end of the Cold War the United States resumed its active participation in the international human rights movement. In 1991, Congress passed the U.S. Protection for Victims of Torture Act to allow civil suits in U.S. courts against foreign perpetrators who enter American jurisdiction—adopting the same narrow definition of "mental pain" the State Department had drafted in 1988.[141] Three years later, Congress finally ratified the UN Torture Convention by amending the U.S. Code, under Section 2340–2340A, to make torture, as narrowly redefined by the Reagan administration in 1988, a crime punishable by twenty years' imprisonment.[142] And, at the 1993 Vienna Human Rights conference, Washington resumed its vigorous advocacy of a universal standard, opposing China and Indonesia's idea of exceptions for "regional peculiarities."[143]

Capping this process three years later, President Clinton announced that he was "pleased to sign into law" the War Crimes Act of 1996 as "an important reaffirmation of American leadership in the development of law for the protection of victims of war." Indeed, this law provides that any American, civilian or military, who "commits a grave breach of the Geneva Conventions," including all later protocols ratified by the United States, shall be punished by imprisonment or even the death penalty "if death results to the victim."[144]

Media and Memory

As the Cold War ended, public advocacy of human rights and official secrecy over their violation collided in press revelations over torture training at the School of the Americas, a training facility for Latin American officers operated by the U.S. Army in Panama since 1949.[145] As part of the U.S. withdrawal from Panama, the School moved to Fort Benning, Georgia, in 1984.[146] As the Cold War waned and the press began to report on U.S. torture training in Central America, critics charged the School with making torturers and called for its abolition.

Reacting to these allegations, the Defense Department launched a formal investigation, which indicates that the CIA's mind-control research permeated the national security establishment and had been transmitted to military forces in Latin America. In March 1992, the assistant secretary for intelligence oversight informed the secretary of defense that a review of his department's training had found seven intelligence manuals, compiled in the mid 1980s, that "contained material that either was not or could be interpreted not to be consistent with U.S. policy." U.S. Army Mobile Training Teams had used these manuals, all written in Spanish, in five Latin American nations from 1987 to 1989, and U.S. Army instructors used them to train soldiers from ten Latin American countries at the School of the Americas from 1989 to 1991.

The handbook on "Handling of Sources" was clearly influenced by the CIA's psychological paradigm. Reflecting the CIA's early mind control experiments, this handbook recommended use of drugs and hypnotism during interrogation. Indeed, the assistant secretary's report stated that these seven manuals "were based in part, on material dating back to the 1960s from the Army's Foreign Intelligence Assistance Program, entitled 'Project X.' "

This report indicates that the Defense Department had somehow lost control of its Latin American program, and army trainers were operating in clear violation of U.S. military regulations. Had the CIA detached officers from the normal chain of command and integrated them into a covert program that used the agency's standard extra-legal procedures? Significantly, the assistant secretary noted: "It is incredible that the use of the lesson plans since 1982, and the manuals since 1987, evaded the established system of doctrinal controls." Interviews with army intelligence personnel who had used these manuals found that they were under the false impression that regulations on "legal and proper" interrogation "were applicable only to U.S. persons and thus did not apply to the training of foreign personnel." As a corrective, the assistant secretary's office had tried to recover all copies of these manuals from Latin American governments and recommended that all so recovered "should be destroyed." [147]

Eight years after the Cold War's end, the CIA's torture training was finally exposed to public scrutiny. In January 1997, the *Baltimore Sun, Washington Post,* and *New York Times* published extracts from the CIA's "Human Resources Exploitation Manual—1983," describing it as the latest edition of a thousand-page manual distributed to Latin American armies for twenty years. Under the damning headline "Torture Was Taught by CIA" the story begins: "A newly declassified CIA training manual details torture methods used against suspected subversives in Central America during the 1980s, refuting claims by the agency that no such methods were taught there." [148]

Though the descriptions of torture were chilling, the public reaction was muted. At the peak of the longest economic boom in the nation's history, Americans were generally content. Citizens and civic groups were silent. Editorials did not call for investigation. Congress did not react. The CIA's budget continued to grow.

Handwritten top: (file 03-06)

Torture Debate after 9/11

In the ten-year hiatus between the last known use of CIA torture manuals in the early 1990s and the questioning of Al Qaeda suspects after September 2001, torture has been handled by allies. This second-hand torture was evident at Manila in 1995, for example, where Philippine National Police (PNP), working with the CIA, discovered plans for a wave of trans-Pacific aircraft bombings. As the successor to the Philippine Constabulary, the PNP had ties to the CIA dating back to the 1960s, including some exposure to the agency's torture training.

In the post-9/11 American media, this incident, recounted in a very particular way, was cited over and over to justify the use of torture. Its significance makes it worth recounting in some detail. In a security sweep before the Pope's 1995 visit, Manila police found bomb-making materials in the apartment of an Arab tourist, Abdul Hakim Murad. For two days, Murad "taunted his captors" at PNP Intelligence Command until police, "racing for time" to protect the Pope, did "what they did best to a prisoner at crunch time." After weeks of physical and psychological torture by beating, water boarding, "lighted cigarettes to his private parts," and threats of rape, all while blind-folded, Murad supposedly cracked and confessed to a plot to blow up eleven trans-Pacific aircraft and kill four thousand passengers and crew. Although advised of the arrest, U.S. Embassy officials delayed extradition for months while, as one Filipino officer put it, "we did the dirty job for them." After three months in the hands of Filipino police, Murad was finally sent to New York to face trial for his role in the 1993 World Trade Center (WTC) bombing.[149]

In the public debate after the September 2001 attacks on the WTC, this Manila incident, with certain key facts omitted, would be cited time and again to support a growing consensus for torture. In October, the *Washington Post* reported FBI frustration with four suspected terrorists arrested after 9/11. "We're into this thing for 35 days and nobody is talking," said a senior FBI official, adding that, "frustration has begun to appear." With surprising frankness, the agent admitted that the FBI was considering torture: "We are known for humanitarian treatment. . . . But it could get to that spot where we could go to pressure . . . where we won't have a choice, and we are probably getting there." One "law enforcement official" suggested suspects be extradited to Morocco where, of course, King Hassan's CIA-trained interrogators were notorious for their tortures.[150] A week later, the *Los Angeles Times* reported serious discussion of torture in U.S. intelligence circles. "A lot of people are saying we need someone at the agency who can pull fingernails out," said one thirty-year CIA veteran. "Others are saying, 'Let others use interrogation methods that we don't use.' The only question then is, do you want to have CIA people in the room?"[151]

These musings inside the intelligence community inspired support for torture by media commentators across the political spectrum. Writing in the *Wall Street Journal,* the historian Jay Winnick, twisting the facts of Murad's Manila torture to portray the results as timely and valuable, asked: "What would have happened if Murad had been in American custody?"[152] In *Newsweek,* columnist Jonathan Alter wrote: "In this autumn of anger, even a liberal can find his thoughts turning to torture." Citing the Filipino success with Murad he added, "some torture clearly works." Alter advocated psychological torture or transfer of suspects to "our less squeamish allies."[153] When a panelist on PBS Television's *McLaughlin Group* asked fellow columnists where they would send Al Qaeda suspects for torture, *National Review* editor Rich Lowry bellowed, "The Turks!" Host John McLaughlin shouted out, "The Filipinos!"[154]

Adding gravitas to this media swagger, Harvard Law professor Alan M. Dershowitz, writing in the *Los Angeles Times,* argued that judges should be allowed to issue "torture warrants" for "non-lethal pressure" in a "ticking bomb" case when "a captured terrorist who knows of an imminent large-scale threat refuses to disclose it." Elaborating these views in a book several months later, Dershowitz cited the "lifesaving information" that Manila police beat out of Murad to argue that torture can sometimes "prevent harm to civilians."[155] Reviewing the book for the *New Republic,* U.S. Judge Richard A. Posner cited this "telling example" from Manila to argue that civil liberties are no more than a "point of balance between public safety and personal liberty." When the balance is tipped by a ticking nuclear bomb in Times Square, then, the judge ruled, "torture should be used."[156] But Dershowitz's Harvard colleague Philip B. Heymann, a former deputy U.S. attorney general, challenged this chimera of limited, judicially controlled torture, saying judges would prove indiscriminate and "torture will spread," compromising worldwide "support for our beliefs."[157] Does the public silence that greeted this media chatter indicate that the American people condone torture in the War on Terror?

But this enthusiasm for harsh methods was based on misinformation and ignorance of the complex psychopathology of torture. In fact, as the *Washington Post* reported in the midst of this media debate, Manila police got all important information from Murad in the first few minutes when they seized his laptop with the bomb plot and evidence that led the FBI to the World Trade Center bomber Ramzi Ahmed Yousef in Pakistan. Most supposed details gained from the sixty-seven days of torture that followed were, as one Filipino officer testified in New York, police fabrications that Murad mimed to end the pain.[158] In weighing personal liberty versus public safety, all these "pro-pain pundits" were ignorant of torture's complexly perverse psycho-pathology that leads to both uncontrolled proliferation of the practice and long-term damage to the perpetrator society. In advocating torture, moreover, these American pundits seemed utterly unaware of the CIA's long history of torture and thus had no inkling that they were reactivating a ruthless apparatus that had only recently been restrained.

The CIA Gulag and Abu Ghraib

While the public debated, the Bush administration was moving quickly to make torture Washington's secret weapon in the War on Terror. On September 11, 2001, right after his evening address to a shaken nation, President George W. Bush gave his White House counter-terrorism staff wide latitude for retribution, saying "any barriers in your way, they are gone." When Defense Secretary Donald Rumsfeld interjected that there were legal restraints on such action, the president shouted back, "I don't care what the international lawyers say, we are going to kick some ass." Indeed, two months later on November 13, the president ordered detention of Al Qaeda suspects under "such other conditions as the Secretary of Defense may prescribe" and denied these detainees access to any court, whether U.S. or international.[159]

According to a *Newsweek* investigation, conservative administration lawyers soon translated their president's directive into U.S. policy. In late 2001, the Justice Department gave the CIA a narrow interpretation of the UN anti-torture convention that sanctioned use of "sleep deprivation . . . and deployment of 'stress factors' " for interrogating Al Qaeda suspects—as long as it did not reach "severe physical or mental pain." On January 9, 2002, John Yoo of the Justice Department's Office of Legal Counsel wrote a forty-two-page memo arguing that the Geneva Conventions did not apply to the Afghanistan conflict, sparking a strong rebuttal from the State Department. "In previous conflicts," wrote State's legal adviser William H. Taft IV, "the United States has dealt with tens of thousands of detainees without repudiating its obligations under the Conventions."[160] On January 11, as the first captives from Afghanistan arrived at the Pentagon's Guantanamo detention center in Cuba, Secretary Rumsfeld denied them legal status as prisoners of war, saying, "Unlawful combatants do not have any rights under the Geneva Convention."[161]

Similarly, on January 18, 2002, White House legal counsel Alberto R. Gonzales informed President Bush that the Justice Department "had issued a formal legal opinion concluding that the Geneva Convention III on the Treatment of Prisoners of War does not apply to the conflict with Al Qaeda." That same day, the president decided that "the war against terrorism is a new kind of war" that "places a high premium on . . . the ability to quickly obtain information from captured terrorists . . . to avoid further atrocities against Americans." Accordingly, Bush ordered that the Geneva Convention "does not apply to al Qaeda and the Taliban" and their members "are not prisoners of war" under the convention.[162]

Four days later, on January 22, Assistant Attorney General Jay S. Bybee sent counselor Gonzales a detailed, thirty-seven-page legal road map for practicing harsh interrogation without legal complications, arguing that "neither the federal War Crimes Act nor the Geneva Conventions would apply to the detention conditions of al Qaeda prisoners." More important, Bybee added that the president has "the plenary constitutional power to suspend our treaty obligations toward Afghanistan during the period of the conflict." Significantly, on February 2, the administration's top lawyers, with the exception of State and the Joint Chiefs, approved Justice's position that the Geneva Conventions did not apply to the Afghan war. This same memo noted, in the words of the *New York Times,* that the CIA had "asked for an explicit understanding that the administration's public pledge to abide by the spirit of the conventions did not apply to its operatives." [163]

Responding to a strong protest over the decision to waive the Geneva Convention from Secretary of State Colin Powell, counselor Gonzales advised the president that "this new paradigm renders obsolete Geneva's strict limitations on questioning of enemy prisoners and renders quaint some of its provisions." The president's formal waiver of the Convention, Gonzales continued, "substantially reduces the threat of criminal prosecution under the [U.S.] War Crimes Act," particularly for violations of Geneva's ban on "outrages against personal dignity" and "inhuman treatment." [164] But Secretary Powell, after warning that setting aside the conventions would "have a high cost in terms of negative international reaction" and "undermine public support among critical allies," won a very partial victory. On February 7, the White House announced Geneva would apply to the Afghan war but not to its Taliban or Al Qaeda prisoners—a large loop-hole that would allow torture. The next day, Secretary Rumsfeld reiterated his position, in a Pentagon briefing, that "the current war on terrorism is not a conflict envisioned by the framers of the Geneva convention," and the Taliban do not "qualify for POW status." In sum, the White House policy, in *Newsweek's* assessment, "set the stage for the new interrogation procedures ungoverned by international law." [165]

Less visibly, the administration began building a global gulag for the CIA. Sometime in late 2001, Secretary Rumsfeld, working with CIA and allied agencies, launched a "special-access program" under the "most stringent level of security" to pursue the top Al Qaeda leadership—outfitting this covert operation with prior authorization for assassination and torture, selected troops from the elite Navy SEALs and Army Delta Force, and a network of secret CIA detention centers. According to Seymour M. Hersh, the program was authorized by President Bush, known to fewer than two hundred operatives and officials, and directed by Rumsfeld's trusted aide Stephen Cambone, who later became undersecretary of defense for intelligence. After the president signed a secret order giving the agency "new powers," Washington negotiated agreements for secret CIA interrogation centers in Thailand, Jordan, Diego Garcia Island in the Indian Ocean, and

X/197

Bagram air base near Kabul. To avoid U.S. Air Force planes, the agency created a charter airline to shuttle prisoners secretly among its own centers and allied intelligence agencies, including those of Jordan and Morocco, which both had ties to the CIA and bleak records of sadistic torture. To keep these prisoners beyond the reach of the International Red Cross, Defense Secretary Rumsfeld agreed, at the request of CIA Director George Tenet, to create some thirteen "ghost detainees"—arrested in Pakistan, Indonesia, Morocco, Thailand, Iraq, and elsewhere—by holding them without the registration numbers that are required by the Geneva Convention. By mid 2004, the *New York Times* estimated that the CIA was holding some twelve to twenty-four top Al Qaeda suspects in its secret gulag who had never been visited by "a lawyer or a human rights organization." The respected British newspaper the *Observer* reported an estimated three thousand Al Qaeda suspects were being held in both CIA centers and, through an illegal process called "rendition," allied prisons across the Middle East.[166]

Initially, the CIA used its gulag to focus on the top Al Qaeda leaders, leaving lesser suspects to the U.S. Army. In April 2002, the agency captured one of its first targets, Abu Zubadaydah, chief recruiter for Al Qaeda, in Pakistan, and flew him to its secret base in Thailand for interrogation. Although he had been shot several times during his capture, the CIA denied Abu Zubadaydah painkillers during this interrogation. In general, the Bush administration was pleased with the yield from Zubadaydah's torture since he helped identify another top Al Qaeda operative, Khalid Shaikh Mohammed, as a principal in the 9/11 attacks, and he was the main source for discovery of Jose Padilla's supposed "dirty bomb" plot in Chicago. In June, moreover, Indonesian agents working with the CIA captured Al Qaeda's top Southeast Asian operative, Omar al-Faruq, and the agency flew him to its Bagram base for an interrogation. In the words of the *New York Times,* Faruq was, for three months, "left naked most of the time, his hands and feet bound," while "subjected to sleep and light deprivation, prolonged isolation, and room temperatures that varied from 100 degrees to 10 degrees." One Western intelligence official said this treatment was "not quite torture, but about as close as you can get." In the end, Faruq gave detailed information about Al Qaeda's operatives and projected operations in Southeast Asia. But these methods were so harsh that they sparked concern among FBI agents and a debate within the CIA over possible violations of U.S. anti-torture laws, prompting correspondence between the agency and the Justice Department "over the legality of specific techniques."[167]

To calm these concerns and let the brutal interrogations continue, Assistant Attorney General Bybee delivered a detailed, fifty-page memo to White House counsel Alberto Gonzales in August 2002 providing "sweeping legal authority" for a wide range of harsh interrogation techniques. By carefully parsing key words in the UN anti-torture convention and its parallel U.S. legislation, USC §§ 2340–2340A, Bybee concluded that U.S. law limited the crime of torture to "acts inflicting, and . . . specifically intended to inflict, severe pain or suffering, whether mental or physical." To constitute torture under U.S. statute, the physical pain must "be equivalent in intensity to the pain accompanying serious physical injury, such as organ failure, impairment of bodily function, or even death." In parsing both Reagan's original four-part reservation to the UN anti-torture convention back in 1988, and the first Bush administration's ratification and enabling legislation six years later, Bybee found his primary grounds for exculpating CIA torturers in a clause that defined torture as "an act [that] must be specifically intended to inflict severe physical or mental pain." In effect, an interrogator who tortured, but later claimed his aim was information instead of pain, was not guilty of torture. Then, further limiting the ambit of CIA culpability, Bybee concluded that psychological torture could become a crime only if there were three tightly linked conditions: (a) the "specific intent" to cause (b) "prolonged mental harm . . . such as posttraumatic stress disorder" solely by (c) committing one of the four forms of mental torture (with threats or drugs) specified in the 1994 law. In sum, the U.S. statute, in Bybee's analysis, "prohibits only extreme acts." Significantly, the "sensory deprivation techniques," long central to the CIA's paradigm, did not, in his view, "produce pain or suffering of the necessary intensity to meet the definition of torture." More broadly, any limitation on commander-in-chief powers to order interrogations would "represent an unconstitutional infringement of the President's authority to conduct war."[168]

In effect, by emphasizing "specific intent" as a necessary precondition for criminal torture, Bybee narrowed the definition of psychological torture in the 1994 U.S. legislation, which had, in turn, both narrowed and muddled the starkly clear prohibition on physical and psychological torture in the UN convention's original language. Through this linguistic legerdemain, the Justice Department granted the CIA de facto authority to use torture techniques, excepting only "the most heinous acts" that brought maiming or death. When the White House released this memo two years later, prominent legal scholars mocked its transparently tendentious reading of the law. "If the president has commander-in-chief power to commit torture," said Yale Law dean Harold Hongju Koh, "he has the power to commit genocide, to sanction slavery, to promote apartheid, to license summary execution." But there was no such criticism inside the Bush administration back in 2002 and Bybee's logic, though clearly flawed, became U.S. policy.[169]

While this clandestine gulag grew, use of the CIA's Cold War torture techniques revived, surfacing first in the agency's Bagram Collection Point near Kabul in late 2002 where the United States held many of its two hundred to three hundred high-value Afghani detainees. In December, the *Washington Post* reported that prisoners inside the Bagram interrogation center, hidden in an abandoned airport hangar, were subjected to "standing or kneeling for hours in black hoods or spray-painted goggles," and forced into "awkward, painful positions and deprived of sleep with a twenty-four-hour bombardment of lights." According to American eyewitnesses, captives were "softened up" by U.S. Army Military Police and Special Forces "who beat them and confine them to tiny rooms." In response to this report, Human Rights Watch warned that Washington was violating "the most fundamental prohibitions of international human rights law."[170] Two months later, the *New York Times* reported two Afghan prisoners had been found dead in their cells at Bagram in December 2002, and a Pentagon pathologist, Major Elizabeth A. Rouse, ruled the death of a twenty-two-year-old Afghani named Dilawar "homicide" after finding "blunt force injuries to lower extremities."

In late 2002, the Defense Department issued instructions for harsher military interrogation after assigning Major General Geoffrey D. Miller to command its Guantanamo detention center that November. A month later, Guantanamo commanders asked the Pentagon for more latitude to interrogate potential assets like Mohamed al-Kahtani, a twenty-six-year-old Saudi branded the twentieth hijacker—claiming, in the words of Southern Command chief General James T. Hill, that "some detainees have tenaciously resisted our current interrogation methods." In support of his request, General Hill attached a memo from Guantanamo's Joint Task Force 170 recommending harsher methods such as "stress positions [such as standing] for a maximum of four hours," "isolation facility for up to 30 days," "deprivation of light and auditory stimuli," hooding, "use of 20-hour interrogations," and "wet towel and dripping water to induce the misperception of suffocation." Consequently, Secretary Rumsfeld "approved" eighteen procedures beyond the U.S. Army's standard interrogation manual, which had been based on psychological methods written to comply with the Geneva Conventions. The secretary, referring to the standing designer desk in his office, added a jocular handwritten note signaling his tolerance for a tough interpretation of these guidelines, saying: "However, I stand for 8–10 hours a day. Why is standing limited to 4 hours?"[171]

In the following months, however, some officials reported that the harsh methods extracted little information from al-Khatani, who "had been most forthcoming under more subtle persuasion." In mid January 2003, Rumsfeld suspended these new procedures until his Pentagon Working Group produced a memo in March with a narrowly drawn definition of torture and a broad interpretation of executive power quite similar to Assistant Attorney General Bybee's views a year earlier. In April, therefore, the secretary restored the wide latitude for Guantanamo interrogators with seven methods beyond the army's interrogation manual—including "environmental manipulation," "reversing sleep cycles from night to day," and isolation for up to thirty days. Under General Miller, Military Intelligence units at Guantanamo thus adopted a "72-point matrix for stress and duress" strikingly similar to the CIA's original torture paradigm, using "harsh heat or cold; withholding food; hooding for days at a time; naked isolation in cold, dark cells for more than 30 days, and . . . 'stress positions' designed to subject detainees to rising levels of pain."[172] By mid 2004, over seven hundred detainees from forty-four nations, some as young as thirteen, would pass through Guantanamo, with still uncounted numbers subjected to such harsh interrogation.[173]

When this March 2003 Working Group memo thus became Pentagon policy, a delegation of senior officers from the Judge Advocate General's (JAG) Corps paid an unofficial visit to Scott Horton, then head of the Human Rights Committee of the New York City Bar Association. Concerned that their exemplary, fifty-year history with the Geneva Conventions was ending, the JAG officers warned that "conditions are ripe for abuse, and it's going to occur," and urged Horton's committee "to challenge the Bush administration about its standards for detentions and interrogation." Others outside the military feel that these concerns were, in retrospect, well grounded. "We believe that this memo," Jamie Fellner of Human Rights Watch said, "shows that at the highest levels of the Pentagon there was an interest in using torture as well as a desire to evade the criminal consequences of doing so."[174]

These interrogation policies, originally used only against top Al Qaeda operatives, soon proliferated under the pressure of the Iraq occupation. In August, Iraq suffered a wave of terror bombing that detonated the Jordanian Embassy with nineteen deaths and blasted the UN headquarters, leaving twenty-three fatalities including its head, Sergio Vieria de Mello. A U.S. military study soon found that the lethal roadside bombings were "the result of painstaking surveillance and reconnaissance," and the rebels drew their intelligence from sympathizers in both Iraqi police and the secure U.S. Green Zone in downtown Baghdad. In striking contrast to the rebels, the U.S. command suddenly found it had no real intelligence to counter these terror attacks. As American casualties surged and the U.S. occupation was engulfed in spreading violence, Secretary Rumsfeld reportedly acted with characteristic decisiveness by ordering his "special-access program" operatives into Iraq, inserting them into Abu Ghraib with authority for harsh interrogation beyond army regulations. The nominal commander of Abu Ghraib, General Janis Karpinski, recalled seeing mysterious interrogators at the prison in late 2003, "disappearing ghosts" who concealed their identities with aliases and civilian clothes. Apart from the usual psychological tactics, these CIA and "special-access program" interrogators reportedly brought new methods of forced nudity and explicit photography based on a sophisticated cultural theory that "Arabs are particularly vulnerable to sexual humiliation."[175]

Despite the Bush administration's assurance that the Geneva Convention applied to Iraq, the CIA and its collaborators in Military Intelligence began torture/interrogation at Abu Ghraib and other camps with high-value detainees. In early September, Guantanamo's commander, General Miller, inspected Iraqi prisons with "a team of personnel experienced in strategic interrogation," recommending, in his classified report, "It is essential that the guard force be actively engaged in setting the conditions for successful exploitation of internees." In the following weeks, the U.S. commander for Iraq, Lieutenant General Ricardo S. Sanchez, authorized much of what General Miller had proposed, including harsh procedures earlier banned at Guantanamo such as sleep deprivation, stress positions, and manipulation of "lighting, heating . . . , food, clothing, and shelter." To improve the intelligence yield from Abu Ghraib, veteran army interrogators from the 519th Military Intelligence Battalion, led by Captain Carolyn A. Wood, arrived from service at the CIA's Bagram center in Afghanistan with more aggressive methods that had already produced several Afghani fatalities. Consequently, from October to December 2003, military police in the security blocks at Abu Ghraib began to soften up dozens of detainees for CIA and Military Intelligence interrogation with harsh methods documented, in the words of a later army report, by "numerous photos and videos portraying in graphic detail detainee abuse by Military Police." [176]

To intensify this already tough interrogation, on November 19, 2003, the 205th Military Intelligence Brigade under Colonel Thomas M. Pappas took command of Abu Ghraib prison and the top-secret facility near Baghdad airport known as Camp Cropper. During the months of most intense abuse in late 2003, Colonel Pappas was summoned to periodic grillings by General Sanchez and pressed hard to deliver more intelligence. As prescribed in the CIA's psychological method, military police were now responsible for the first phase of intensive disorientation to prepare detainees for later interrogation by CIA, Military Intelligence, and private contractors, producing what the army's investigation later called "numerous incidents of sadistic, blatant, and wanton criminal abuses . . . on several detainees." In the words of Major General Antonio Taguba's later investigation, this abuse involved "punching, slapping, and kicking detainees" and "keeping them naked for several days at a time." In the escalation that often comes with psychological torture, this treatment soon moved beyond sleep and sensory deprivation to sexual humiliation marked by "photographing naked male and female detainees; forcibly arranging detainees in various sexually explicit positions . . . ; forcing groups of male detainees to masturbate while being photographed." Dismissing the idea of such behavior as simply aberrant, General Taguba's inquiry found that "Military Intelligence (MI) interrogators and Other U.S. Government Agency's (OGA) [that is, CIA] actively requested that MP guards set physical and mental conditions for favorable interrogation." [177]

Then, in a second, still unexamined phase prescribed in the agency's torture method, trained Military Intelligence and CIA operatives administered the requisite mix of interrogation and self-inflicted pain—a process that evidently took place outside the frame of these now famous photographs. Under the 205th Military Intelligence Battalion, forced nudity became a standard interrogation procedure to humiliate and break prisoners at Abu Ghraib. There were, moreover, increasing incidents of capricious cruelty. In November 2003, for example, five Iraqi generals suspected of instigating a small prison riot were manacled, blindfolded, and beaten by guards "until they were covered with blood." Although the prison's Detainee Assessment Branch filed at least twenty reports of serious abuse with General Sanchez and his intelligence chief, Major General Barbara Fast, the army command, did not intercede. Significantly, General Taguba later found that Colonel Pappas and his deputy, Lieutenant Colonel Steven L. Jordan, chief of the Joint Interrogation and Debriefing Center, were "directly or indirectly responsible" for the prisoner abuse at Abu Ghraib.[178]

In contrast to General Taguba's succinct, dispassionate descriptions, a February 2004 Red Cross report offers explicit details of U.S. interrogation techniques, both psychological and physical, that are very similar to the methods recommended in earlier CIA torture manuals. Throughout these months of harsh interrogation in late 2003, the International Committee of the Red Cross (ICRC) made twenty-nine visits to U.S. detention facilities across Iraq, exercising their right to arrive unannounced for unrestricted inspections. While conditions for most detainees were satisfactory, those "under supervision of Military Intelligence were at high risk of being subjected to a variety of harsh treatments ranging from insults, threats and humiliation to both physical and psychological coercion, which in some cases was tantamount to torture." Significantly, some coalition military intelligence officers told the ICRC that "between 70 percent and 90 percent" of detainees in Iraq, which reached about forty thousand at peak, "had been arrested by mistake." In their visits to Abu Ghraib's military intelligence section, several U.S. officers told the ICRC that "it was part of the military intelligence process to hold a person . . . naked in a completely dark and empty cell for a prolonged period [and] to use inhumane and degrading treatment, including physical and psychological coercion." In words that could have been lifted almost verbatim from past CIA interrogation manuals, the ICRC detailed the forms of "ill treatment" that U.S. Military Intelligence used "in a systematic way to . . . extract information" from Iraqi detainees:[179]

- Hooding, used to prevent people from seeing and to disorient them, and also to prevent them from breathing freely . . . ;
- Beatings with hard objects (including pistols and rifles) . . . ;
- Threats (of ill-treatment, reprisals against family members, imminent execution . . .);
- Being stripped naked for several days while held in solitary confinement . . . ;
- Being paraded naked outside their cells in front of other persons . . . ;
- Being attached repeatedly over several days, for several hours each time, with handcuffs to the bars of their cells door in humiliating (i.e. naked or in underwear) and/or uncomfortable position causing physical pain;

• Being forced to remain for prolonged periods in stress positions such as squatting or standing with or without the arms lifted.

During a visit to Abu Ghraib in October, the ICRC discovered detainees "completely naked in totally empty concrete cells and in total darkness, allegedly for several days." The Red Cross medical staff determined that prisoners so treated were suffering from "memory problems, verbal expression difficulties, incoherent speech, acute anxiety reactions, . . . and suicidal tendencies." In sum, the ICRC found these practices "are prohibited under International Humanitarian Law."[180]

By late 2003, after several months of prisoner abuse, the CIA reportedly tired of this seamy sexual torture of ordinary Iraqis and, on advice of its lawyers, withdrew from Secretary Rumsfeld's top-secret "special-access program" at Abu Ghraib. But after Saddam Hussein's dramatic capture on December 13, the military sent a dozen of the aides arrested with him to Abu Ghraib, creating new pressures for tough interrogation. To exploit these assets in the apparent absence of CIA interrogators, the Iraq command's intelligence chief, Brigadier General Barbara Fast, authorized a "special projects team" to use harsh methods beyond the army manual, including reduced diet, sleep deprivation, isolation cells for thirty days, and military dogs. In contrast to the very slender results from the past three months of torture at Abu Ghraib, the yield from Saddam's entourage was rich, leading to the arrest of Baath Party officials, ex-generals, and tribal leaders involved with the resistance. But just four weeks later, on January 13, 2004, a young MP named Joseph Darby delivered a CD with those now notorious photographs to the army's Criminal Investigation Division, setting in motion General Taguba's investigation in February and the later leak of his findings to the news media.[181]

As the Abu Ghraib scandal intensified in May 2004, the Pentagon, after months of delays, suddenly issued death certificates for twenty former prisoners, including twelve cases of homicide or unexplained death. The Defense Department had long attributed one of these deaths, that of the former Iraqi air defense chief, Major General Abed Hamed Mowhoush, to "natural causes." But after the *Denver Post* published his U.S. military autopsy, the Pentagon admitted that the general had, in fact, died from suffocation and "blunt force trauma" after CIA interrogation in November 2003. Indeed, this harsh treatment had produced that unsettling color photo of the general's badly bruised death mask now circulating worldwide on the Internet along with other indelible images from Abu Ghraib.[182]

Responding to this deepening scandal in May and June 2004, the Bush White House issued pro-forma apologies while scrambling to depict events at Abu Ghraib as "abuse," not torture. At a Pentagon press conference on May 4, Secretary Rumsfeld stated that "what has been charged thus far is abuse, which I believe technically is different from torture." When pressed, the secretary said, "I'm not going to address the 'torture' word." On May 10, after the Senate condemned the prisoner abuse by a 92 to 0 vote, President Bush offered an oblique apology, stating there would be "a full accounting for the cruel and disgraceful abuse of Iraqi detainees." Four days later, General Sanchez announced an end to all coercive interrogation in Iraq, though, on questioning by reporters, his spokesman admitted that the general still reserved the right to hold prisoners in isolation cells for more than thirty days. Speaking to the U.S. Army War College on May 24, President Bush promised to demolish Abu Ghraib prison because it had become "a symbol of disgraceful conduct by a few American troops who dishonored our country and dishonored our values" and announced plans for "a modern, maximum security prison . . . as a fitting symbol of Iraq's new beginning."[183]

In the weeks that followed, however, a torrent of leaked executive documents showed that officials up and down the chain of command had condoned torture, from White House and Justice Department law officers who defined "torture" narrowly to allow abusive interrogation to Secretary Rumsfeld, who personally ordered harsh measures, next to senior CIA and army officials who ignored reports of cruelty and even death to press subordinates for better intelligence, all the way down to middle-ranking officers and ordinary soldiers who carried out these commands, often with a steely professionalism, occasionally with a psychopathic abandon. As Congress probed the scandal, the Bush administration, in the words of the *New York Times,* "spent nearly two months obstructing investigations and stonewalled senators over dozens of Red Cross reports that document the horrible mistreatment of Iraqis at American military prisons." In particular, the paper branded Rumsfeld's prevarication over release of Red Cross reports "the most outrageous example of the administration's bad faith on the prison scandal."[184]

In early June 2004, the UN Office of the High Commissioner for Human Rights in Geneva condemned the "willful killing, torture and inhuman treatment" in Iraq, calling it a "grave breach" of international law that "might be designated as war crimes by a competent tribunal." The scandal was, the commissioner added, recognized by even Coalition leaders as "a stain upon the effort to bring freedom to Iraq." When President Bush visited the Vatican on June 4, Pope John Paul II, referring to the Abu Ghraib scandal, spoke publicly of "deplorable events . . . which have troubled the civic and religious conscience of all."[185] Two weeks later, UN Secretary-General Kofi Annan rejected a U.S. request for immunity of its troops from the International Criminal Court, calling the move deplorable "given the prisoner abuse in Iraq." Faced with certain defeat in the UN Security Council, Washington was forced to withdraw its request for immunity, in large part because former supporters like China were, in the words of its ambassador, "under pressure because of the scandals and the news coverage of the prisoner abuse." As international outrage mounted, U.S. Attorney General John

Ashcroft, long a militant supporter of harsh interrogation, announced the indictment of a CIA contract employee, David A. Passaro, who had "brutally" beaten
an Afghani detainee to death with hands, feet, and flashlight for two days in June
2003.[186]

Closing a month of rapid-fire repudiation of the Bush administration's policy
toward prisoners of war, on June 28 the U.S. Supreme Court affirmed the right of
"enemy combatants" held at Guantanamo to due process under law, flatly rejecting the Bush administration's insistence on unchecked, unlimited detention of all
prisoners in the War on Terror, whether aliens or U.S. citizens. The Abu Ghraib
scandal, though not mentioned explicitly, cast a heavy shadow over the court's
deliberations. In oral arguments for *Rumsfeld v. Padilla* on April 28, Justice Ruth
Bader Ginsburg challenged the executive's claim to exemption from judicial oversight, asking, "So what is it that would be a check against torture?" When the
Deputy Solicitor General, Paul D. Clement, tried to evade the question with a
bland assurance that military violators would be prosecuted, the Justice pressed
harder, asking: "Suppose the executive says mild torture we think will help get this
information." To quiet that concern, the deputy solicitor insisted that "our executive" would never tolerate torture, adding that in wartime "you have to trust the
executive to make the kind of quintessential military judgments that are involved
in things like that."[187]

Only hours after the government said it could be trusted not to torture, CBS
televised the first photographs of U.S. soldiers torturing prisoners at Abu Ghraib.
In the weeks following, moreover, the press published leaked copies of secret Bush
administration memos, including the August 2002 report by Bybee, arguing that
the president had the legal authority to order torture. Then, just two months after
hearing oral arguments, the court handed down in its decisions in these three
cases, ruling, in sum, that "war is not a blank check when it comes to the rights of
the Nation's citizens." Writing for the plurality in an essentially six-to-three decision that Yaser Esam Hamdi, a Saudi-American arrested in Afghanistan, was entitled to due process, Justice Sandra Day O'Connor said "indefinite detention for
the purpose of interrogation is not authorized." She added, "An unchecked system
of detention carries the potential to become a means for oppression and abuse of
others." Dissenting from the court's finding that it had no jurisdiction over Jose
Padilla, the so-called dirty bombe" confined in a Navy brig, Justice John Paul
Stevens argued that it was of "no consequence" whether information extracted
from indefinite detention "is more or less reliable than that acquired by more extreme forms of torture." In a minority opinion joined by three other justices, Justice Stevens added pointedly: "For if this nation is to remain true to the ideals
symbolized by its flag, it must not wield the tools of tyrants even to resist an assault
by the forces of tyranny." Suddenly, the Pentagon's plans for endless detention of
six hundred Guantanamo detainees, without any judicial oversight, were thrown

into disarray, and the Bush administration was faced with the mass transfer of hundreds of cases to U.S. federal courts.[188]

Clearly, the Abu Ghraib scandal has been a heavy blow to U.S. international prestige, sparking strong domestic and international pressures for both reform and punishment. If a fuller, future inquiry does establish that the Red Cross was accurate in its description of what happened at Abu Ghraib, then these seven military police now facing courts-martial are just ordinary American soldiers following orders within standard CIA and military interrogation procedures. Whatever the guilt of these soldiers, their prosecution is likely to become the first step in an investigation that may, under U.S. and international pressure, move up the chain of command to the Pentagon, CIA, and White House. While these inquiries may well produce a mountain of executive memos and Dantesque details of torture, they will not, in all likelihood, probe deep for the bureaucratic roots of the interrogation methods, leaving these practices buried, unchecked and unexamined, deep inside the CIA and its intelligence community to resurface in some future crisis.

Conclusion

Strong democracies, far more than post-authoritarian societies, have difficulty dealing with torture. Even after all of the explicit photos at Abu Ghraib, the United States, like France and Britain before it, has struggled to cope with the realization that its security forces have been using systematic torture to fight a counterinsurgency campaign. In the weeks following release of the Abu Ghraib photographs, the United States has moved quickly through the same stages, as defined by John Conroy, that the United Kingdom experienced after revelations of British Army torture in Northern Ireland during the early 1970s—first, minimization of the torture with euphemisms such as "interrogation in depth"; next, justification on grounds that it was necessary or effective; and, finally, burial of the issue by blaming "a few bad apples."[189]

Indeed, the Bush administration and much of the U.S. press have studiously avoided the word *torture* and focused the blame on those bad apples, the seven accused military police. In July, the army's Inspector General, Paul T. Mikolashek, delivered his 321-page investigation attributing 94 incidents of abuse, including 20 homicides, not to "system failures," but to "an individual failure to uphold Army Values." Indeed, he reported all "observed commanders, leaders, and soldiers treated detainees humanely," and even recommended regulations be loosened to allow "commanders to more effectively conduct intelligence exploitation in a non-linear battlespace."[190] In his appearance before Congress, several senators faulted Mikolashek for failing to investigate General Taguba's earlier report of "systemic and illegal abuse of detainees"—a finding corroborated by the Red

X   Cross determination that humiliating sex acts were "done in a systematic way." Although the *New York Times* called his conclusions "comical" and his report a "whitewash," General Mikolashek's exculpatory approach seems a fair indicator of what we can expect from the six ongoing military investigations.[191]

Indeed, Mikolashek's conclusions seem to resonate with an emerging conservative consensus. "Interrogation is not a Sunday-school class," said Senator Trent Lott (R-Miss.). "You don't get information that will save American lives by withholding pancakes." Two months after release of the Abu Ghraib photos, an ABC News/Washington Post poll found that 35 percent of Americans felt torture was acceptable in some circumstances.[192]

Then in August 2004, Major General George R. Fay released his report on the role of Military Intelligence, blaming not the seven bad apples but the interrogation procedures at Abu Ghraib. After finding army interrogation doctrine sound, the general confronted an uncomfortable question: What was the source of the aberrant practices? In its short answer General Fay's report blames a flouting of military procedures by CIA interrogators that "eroded the necessity in the minds of soldiers and civilians for them to follow Army rules." Specifically, the army "allowed CIA to house 'Ghost Detainees' who were unidentified and unaccounted for in Abu Ghraib," thus encouraging violations of "reporting requirements under the Geneva Conventions." Freed from military regulations, CIA interrogators moved about with a corrupting "mystique" and extreme methods that "fascinated" some army interrogators. In sum, General Fay seems to say that the CIA compromised the integrity and effectiveness of the U.S. military. He might have added that the sensory deprivation, stress positions, and cultural shock of dogs and nudity were plucked from the pages of past CIA torture manuals.[193]

Almost simultaneously, in June 2004 the International Red Cross completed an investigation of U.S. military interrogation at Guantanamo that, along with General Fay's report of Abu Ghraib, provided strong corroboration that once-covert CIA torture techniques had now become official U.S. doctrine. Through periodic inspections of Guantanamo's Camp Delta, the Red Cross determined that the psychological techniques used on the 550 detainees were, under international law, "tantamount to torture." In particular, the Red Cross objected to the U.S. military's use of medical personnel, particularly psychologists on the Behavioral Science Consultation Team, to advise military interrogators on more effective methods calling the practice "a flagrant violation of medical ethics." Moreover, medical personnel who treated the detainees conveyed information about their patients to interrogators through the Behavioral Team, creating an "apparent integration of access to medical care within the system of coercion." Between its first visit to Guantanamo in January 2002 and its most recent in June 2004, the Red Cross found that these psychological techniques had grown "more refined and repressive," involving "humiliating acts, solitary confinement, temperature extremes, use of forced positions." The Red Cross concluded, in uncharacteristically blunt language: "The construction of such a system, whose stated purpose is production of intelligence, cannot be considered other than an international system of cruel, unusual, and degrading treatment and a form of torture." When the *New York Times* published extracts on November 30, Guantanamo's commander, General Jay W. Hood, insisted the detainees have "not been tortured in any way." Speaking for the Bush administration, Secretary Rumsfeld's spokesman, Lawrence Di Rita, said simply and dismissively that the Red Cross had "their point of view"—one the White House clearly did not share. In effect, this public rejection of a finding by the Red Cross, an impartial international agency, that U.S. psychological methods were "a form of torture" resolved that contradiction, evident since the early 1950s, between Washington's secret propagation of torture and its public embrace of international conventions, barring the practice. After a half-century of the CIA's secret use of psychological torture, the U.S. government now defied the international community by publicly defending these distinctive methods and denying they constituted torture.[194]

Clearly, the American public, its government, and its media have failed to examine U.S. interrogation tactics closely to discover that they are, apart from their modern psychological twist, strikingly similar to the classic European tortures used for nearly a thousand years, from the Inquisition to the Soviet KGB. Indeed, the CIA's psychological torture method has become so widely accepted within the U.S. intelligence community that military interrogators today seem unaware or unwilling to admit that many of their standard methods are, under the UN convention, a form of torture. This acceptance of psychological torture in defiance of the UN Convention also gained surprising currency among public intellectuals after 9/11. Writing in the *New York Times Magazine* just days before release of the Abu Ghraib photos, Harvard professor Michael Ignatieff argued, in words that could have been plucked from a CIA torture manual, for legislation to permit "forms of sleep deprivation that do not result in lasting harm to mental or physical health, together with disinformation and disorientation [such as keeping prisoners in hoods] that would produce stress."[195]

In keeping with their advocacy of torture after 9/11, these same intellectuals, if one can speak of them collectively, seemed conflicted in the light of Abu Ghraib. After seeing the actual photos of what their words had wrought, some suddenly reversed their support for torture—as Ignatieff did very publicly, repudiating his very recent advocacy of "permissible duress." "At Abu Ghraib," he wrote in late June, "America paid the price for American exceptionalism, the idea that America is too noble, too special, too great to obey international treaties like the Torture Convention." Continuing in words that seem self-referential, he argued: "Enthralled by narcissism and deluded by servility, American lawyers forgot their own constitution and its peremptory prohibition of cruel and unusual punishment."[196]

This is not, of course, the first American debate over torture in recent memory. From 1970 to 1988, the U.S. Congress tried repeatedly, without success, to expose elements of this CIA torture procedure in four major investigations. But on each occasion the public showed little concern, and the practice persisted inside the intelligence bureaucracy. Like post-authoritarian societies in Asia and Latin America, the United States seems to suffer from a culture of impunity over this sensitive topic that has barred both self-examination and serious reform in the fifteen years since the Cold War's end.

But now, through these photographs from Abu Ghraib, ordinary Americans have seen the interrogation techniques that the U.S. intelligence community has propagated and practiced for nearly half a century. The American public can join the international community in repudiating a practice that, more than any other, represents a denial of democracy. Or, in its desperate search for security, the United States can continue its clandestine torture of terror suspects in the hope of gaining good intelligence without negative publicity.

In the likely event that Washington adopts the latter strategy, it will be a decision posited on two false assumptions: that torturers can be controlled; and that news of their work can be contained. Once torture begins, its use seems to spread uncontrollably, particularly in times of crisis, in a downward spiral of fear and empowerment. With the proliferation of digital imaging—on cell phones, personal computers, and micro cameras—we can anticipate, in five or ten years, more chilling images and more devastating blows to America's international standing. Next time, however, the American public's moral concern and Washington's apologies will ring hollow, producing even greater damage to U.S. prestige.

NOTES

Acknowledgments: For the research and editing of this essay, I am indebted Professor Jeremi Suri, a generous colleague at the University of Wisconsin–Madison, Ellen Jarosz, my research assistant, Matthew Gildner, a doctoral student in History at the University of Texas–Austin, my mother Margarita P. McCoy, professor emerita at California Polytechnic University–Pomona, and my wife, Mary E. McCoy, a dissertator at Northwestern University. My initial work on this project with Matthew Gildner was funded by a Hilldale joint faculty-undergraduate research grant from the University of Wisconsin–Madison.

1. *New York Times,* May 1, 2004; Seymour M. Hersh, "Torture at Abu Ghraib," *New Yorker,* May 10, 2004, 42–47.

2. *New York Times,* May 8, 2004, May 12, 2004.

3. Ibid., May 6, 2004, May 7, 2004, May 9, 2004.

4. Hans-Peter Gasser, "An Appeal for Ratification by the United States," *American Journal of International Law* 81 (1987): 912–45; David P. Forsythe, "The United States, the United Nations, and Human Rights," in Margaret P. Karns and Karen A. Mingst, eds., *The United States and Multilateral Institutions* (Boston: Unwin Hyman, 1990), 261–84; Kenneth Roth, "The Charade of U.S. Ratification of International Human Rights Treaties," *Chicago Journal of International Law* (Fall 2000): 347–53.

5. Christopher Simpson, *Science of Coercion: Communication, Research, and Psychological Warfare, 1945–1960* (New York: Oxford University Press, 1994), 9.

6. *New York Times*, May 7, 2004.

7. Lawrence E. Hinkle Jr. and Harold G. Wolff, "Communist Interrogation and Indoctrination of 'Enemies of the States': Analysis of Methods Used by the Communist State Police (A Special Report)," *Archives of Neurology and Psychiatry* 76 (1956): 135.

8. United Nations, Department of Public Information, *Outlawing an Ancient Evil: Torture. Convention Against Torture and Other Cruel, Inhuman, or Degrading Treatment or Punishment* (New York: United Nations, Department of Public Information, 1985); Ahcene Boulesbaa, *The U.N. Convention on Torture and the Prospects for Enforcement* (The Hague: Martinus Nijhoff, 1999), 1–2.

9. David Forsythe, "Human Rights in U.S. Foreign Policy: Retrospect and Prospect," *Political Science Quarterly* 105 (1990): 435–54.

10. United Nations, *Human Rights: A Compilation of International Instruments of the United Nations* (New York: United Nations, 1973), 1–3.

11. Adam Roberts and Richard Guelff, eds., *Documents on the Laws of War* (Oxford: Oxford University Press, 2000), 243–44, 250, 278–79, 361, 368. Legal commentary published by the International Red Cross makes it clear that, under Article 87 of Convention III, "the lighting must be sufficient to enable them [prisoners] to read and write without difficulty." See Jean de Preaux, *The Geneva Conventions of 12 August 1949. Commentary. Geneva Convention III Relative to the Treatment of Prisoners of War* (Geneva: International Committee of the Red Cross, 1960), 431–32.

12. Roberts and Guelff, *Documents,* 312. In the view of International Red Cross lawyers, Article 31 represented a marked expansion of Article 44 of the 1907 Hague Regulations and now covered "all protected persons, thus including even civilian aliens on the territory of a party to the conflict." See Oscar M. Uhler et al., *The Geneva Conventions of 12 August 1949: Commentary; Geneva Convention IV Relative to the Protection of Civilian Persons in Time of War* (Geneva: International Committee of the Red Cross, 1958), 431–32.

13. David P. Forsythe, "The United Nations and Human Rights, 1945–1985," *Political Science Quarterly* 100 (Summer 1985): 249–52.

14. Edward Peters, *Torture* (Philadelphia: University of Pennsylvania Press, 1985), 1, 14–18, 25–33, 35; Malise Ruthven, *Torture: The Grand Conspiracy* (London: Weidenfeld and Nicolson, 1978), 25, 30–31.

15. Ruthven, *Torture,* 43–48.

16. John Langbein, *Torture and the Law of Proof* (Chicago: University of Chicago Press, 1977), 7; Peters, *Torture,* 40–62.

17. Peters, *Torture,* 62–67; Ruthven, *Torture,* 57–59.

18. Alec Mellor, *La Torture: Son histoire, son abolition: Sa réapparition au XXe siécle* (Paris: Horizons Litterraires, 1949), 105–15; Mitchell B. Merback, *The Thief, the Cross, and the Wheel: Pain and the Spectacle of Punishment in Medieval and Renaissance Europe* (Chicago: University of Chicago Press, 1998), 158–70.

19. Langbein, *Torture and the Law of Proof,* 10–12, 60–69; Ruthven, *Torture,* 12–15.

20. Ruthven, *Torture,* 218–78; Peters, *Torture,* 102–40.

21. Ernst Winkler, *Four Years of Nazi Torture* (New York: D. Appleton-Century, 1943), 1, 42–43, 57–59, 71, 75–77, 124–26.

22. Peters, *Torture,* 103, 121–25, 138–39; John Marks, *The Search for the "Manchurian Candidate": The CIA and Mind Control* (New York: Times Books, 1979), 8–10.

23. George J. Annas and Michael A. Grodin, eds., *The Nazi Doctors and the Nuremberg Code: Human Rights in Human Experimentation* (New York: Oxford University Press, 1992), 2, 102–7.

24. Peters, *Torture,* 138–40.

25. Alexander Cockburn and Jeffrey St. Clair, *Whiteout: The CIA, Drugs, and the Press* (New York: Verso, 1998), 145–54.

26. U.S. Senate, 94th Cong., 2nd sess., Select Committee to Study Governmental Operations with Respect to Intelligence Activities, *Foreign and Military Intelligence, Book I: Final Report,* Report No. 97–775 (Washington, D.C.: U.S. Government Printing Office, 1976), 393; John Ranelagh, *The Agency: The Rise and Decline of the CIA* (New York: Simon and Schuster, 1986), 202–4; Marks, *Search for the "Manchurian Candidate,"* 125–26, 223.

27. U.S. Senate, *Foreign and Military Intelligence, Book I,* 392–93.

28. Ted Gup, "The Coldest Warrior," *Washington Post Magazine,* December 16, 2001.

29. Simpson, *Science of Coercion,* 8–9.

30. U.S. Senate, Select Committee to Study Government Operations with Respect to Government Activities, *Foreign and Military Intelligence, Book I: Final Report* (Washington, D.C.: U.S. Government Printing Office, 1975), 9; Loch K. Johnson, "On Drawing a Bright Line for Covert Operations," *American Journal of International Law* 86 (1992): 293–94; *New York Times,* June 10, 2004.

31. James L. Sundquist, *The Decline and Resurgence of Congress* (Washington, D.C.: The Brookings Institution, 1981), 107; Loch K. Johnson, *A Season of Inquiry: The Senate Intelligence Investigation* (Lexington: University Press of Kentucky, 1985), 7.

32. Ranelagh, *The Agency,* 110–11; *New York Times,* June 10, 2004.

33. Simpson, *Science of Coercion,* 38–39.

34. Marks, *Search for the "Manchurian Candidate,"* 22–23; Cockburn and St. Clair, *Whiteout,* 153–61.

35. Marks, *Search for the "Manchurian Candidate,"* 62–64; Ranelagh, *The Agency,* 204–8, 575–76, 778.

36. U.S. Senate, Select Committee to Study Government Operation with Respect to Government Activities, *Foreign and Military Intelligence, Book I: Final Report,* 387–88.

37. Ranelagh, *The Agency,* 204–8, 575–76, 778; Harvey M. Weinstein, *Psychiatry and the CIA: Victims of Mind Control* (Washington, D.C.: American Psychiatric Press, 1990), 129–30.

38. U.S. Senate, *Foreign and Military Intelligence, Book I,* 4–5.

39. Ibid., 406–7.

40. Ibid., 390–91.

41. Ibid., 422.

42. Marks, *Search for the "Manchurian Candidate,"* 58–61.

43. Simpson, *Science of Coercion,* 4, 9, 72, 81–82, 134, 156–57; Albert D. Biderman and Herbert Zimmer, eds., *The Manipulation of Human Behavior* (New York: John Wiley & Sons, 1961), 29.

44. Weinstein, *Psychiatry and the CIA,* 32–34; Marks, *Search for the "Manchurian Candidate,"* 127–30, 147–63; Hinkle and Wolff, "Communist Interrogation and Indoctrination," 116–17, 128–30, 134–35.

45. Weinstein, *Psychiatry and the CIA,* 130, 179–80.

46. Marks, *Search for the "Manchurian Candidate,"* 31, 131.

47. Ibid., 31–32, 88–95; Cockburn and St. Clair, *Whiteout,* 189–208.

48. Ranelagh, *The Agency,* 208–10; *New York Times,* July 22, 1975, July 23, 1975; Gup, "Coldest Warrior"; Weinstein, *Psychiatry and the CIA,* 130; Marks, *Search for the "Manchurian Candidate,"* 84–85.

49. Weinstein, *Psychiatry and the CIA,* 99, 117–20, 135, 139–40, 274.

50. Elizabeth Nickson, "My Mother, the CIA, and LSD," *Observer* (London), October 16, 1994, 48–52; Weinstein, *Psychiatry and the CIA,* 110–20, 140–41; Gordon Thomas, *Journey into Madness: Medical Torture and the Mind Controllers* (London: Bantam Press, 1988), 176–77; Marks, *Search for the "Manchurian Candidate,"* 135–39.

51. Nickson, "My Mother, the CIA, and LSD," 48–52; *Mrs. David Orlikow et al. v. United States of America,* 682 F. Supp. 77, U.S. District Court, District of Columbia, January 18, 1988; Weinstein, *Psychiatry and the CIA,* 142, 158–59, 166–67, 250, 268–69.

52. Nickson, "My Mother, the CIA, and LSD," 50; Thomas, *Journey into Madness,* 164–65; Marks, *Search for the "Manchurian Candidate,"* 134–35.

53. U.S. Senate, 95th Cong., 1st sess., *Project MKUltra: The CIA's Program of Research in Behavioral Modification.* Joint Hearing Before the Select Committee on Intelligence and the Subcommittee on Health and Scientific Research of the Committee on Human Resources (Washington, D.C.: U.S. Government Printing Office, 1977), 51–52.

54. U.S. Senate, *Foreign and Military Intelligence, Book I,* 390–91.

55. Ibid., 400–403.

56. Cockburn and St. Clair, *Whiteout,* 208–09.

57. "KUBARK Counterintelligence Interrogation" (July 1963), File: Kubark, box 1: CIA Training Manuals (National Security Archives, Washington, D.C.), 1–2, 41, 45, 76–77, 84–85, 90–91, 93–94, 98–99, 111–12.

58. Aldo Migliorini, *Tortura Inquisizione Pena de Morte* (Siena: Lalli Editore, 1997), 56, 118; Mellor, *La Torture,* 77–80; Susan Sontag, "Regarding the Torture of Others," *New York Times Magazine,* May 23, 2004, 25–26; *New York Times,* March 9, 2003, May 5, 2004, May 13, 2004.

59. *New York Times,* February 16, 1986.

60. Michael T. Klare, *War Without End: American Planning for the Next Vietnams* (New York: Alfred A. Knopf, 1972), 241, 245, 247, 250; Thomas David Lobe, "U.S. Police Assistance for the Third World" (Ph.D. diss., University of Michigan, 1975), 82.

61. Lobe, "U.S. Police Assistance for the Third World," 42–44.

62. Ibid., 46.

63. Robert Komer, Memorandum to McGeorge Bundy and General Taylor, "Should Police Programs be Transferred to the DOD?" Secret (Declassified), April 18, 1962.

64. A. J. Langguth, *Hidden Terrors* (New York: Pantheon, 1978), 47–52, 124–26, 300.

65. Lobe, "U.S. Police Assistance for the Third World," 56–57, 60–61, 72.

66. Klare, *War Without End,* 241, 245, 247, 250, 260–65.

67. U.S. General Accounting Office, *Stopping U.S. Assistance to Foreign Police and Prisons* (Washington, D.C.: U.S. General Accounting Office, 1976), 14.

68. Klare, *War Without End.*, 382–83; Amnesty International, *Report on Torture* (London: Duckworth, 1975), 114–239; R. Matthew Gildner, "Torture and U.S. Foreign Policy" (honor's thesis, Department of History, University of Wisconsin–Madison, 2001), 2.

69. U.S. Senate, *Congressional Record,* 93rd Cong., 2nd sess., 1974. Vol. 120, pt. 25, 33474.

70. Ibid.

71. Ibid., 33475.

72. Langguth, *Hidden Terrors,* 125–28, 138–40, 251–52.

73. Klare, *War Without End,* 261–64; Douglas Valentine, *The Phoenix Program* (New York: William Morrow, 1990), 59–60.

74. Valentine, *Phoenix Program,* 63, 77–85. On p. 84, Valentine identifies the CIA officers who trained the Vietnamese Special Branch as "experts from the CIA's Support Services Branch." In other accounts, this unit is identified as Technical Services Division (Langguth, *Hidden Terrors,* 138–40).

75. I an McNeill, *The Team: Australian Army Adviser in Vietnam, 1962–1972* (St. Lucia: University of Queensland Press, 1984), 385–411.

76. Lloyd H. Cotter, "Operant Conditioning in a Vietnamese Mental Hospital," *American Journal of Psychiatry,* 124 (July 1967): 23–28; Thomas, *Journey into Madness,* 281–82.

77. *New York Times,* February 18, 1970.

78. Ibid., April 7, 1971.

79. Ibid., July 16, 1971.

80. Ibid., July 20, 1971; August 2, 1971.

81. Ibid., July 20, 1971, August 2, 1971; U.S. House of Representatives, 92nd Cong., 1st sess., Subcommittee of the Committee on Government Operations, Hearings on August 2, 1971, *U.S. Assistance Programs in Vietnam* (Washington, D.C.: Government Printing Office, 1971), 349.

82. U.S. House of Representatives, *U.S. Assistance Programs in Vietnam,* 319–21, 327, 349; U.S. Senate, 93rd Cong., 1st sess., Committee on Armed Services, Hearings on July 2, 20, 25, 1973, *Nomination of William E. Colby to be Head of Central Intelligence* (Washington, D.C.: U.S. Government Printing Office, 1973), 101–17.

83. Ranelagh, *The Agency,* 571–77, 585, 589.

84. Ibid., 571–76, 584–99.

85. Cockburn and St. Clair, *Whiteout,* 194.

86. Ibid., 210–11.

87. *New York Times,* August 1, 1970.

88. Ibid., August 11, 1970.

89. Ibid., August 16, 1970; Langguth, *Hidden Terrors,* 252–54, 285–88.

90. *New York Times,* August 5, 1978.

91. U.S. Senate, 92nd Cong., 1st sess., Committee on Foreign Relations, Subcommittee on Western Hemisphere Affairs, *United States Policies and Programs in Brazil* (Washington, D.C.: U.S. Government Printing Office, 1971), 17–20, 39–40.

92. Langguth, *Hidden Terrors,* 299–301.

93. Ibid., 301; U.S. Senate, 93rd Cong., 2nd sess., Committee on Foreign Relations, *Foreign Assistance Act of 1974: Report of the Committee on Foreign Relations United States Senate on S. 3394 to Amend the Foreign Assistance Act of 1961, and for Other Purposes* (Washington, D.C.: U.S. Government Printing Office, 1974), 42.

94. Langguth, *Hidden Terrors,* 415, 421. Lobe, "U.S. Police Assistance for the Third World," 415, 421.

95. Darius M. Rejali, *Torture and Modernity: Self, Society, and State in Modern Iran* (Boulder, Colo.: Westview Press, 1994), 77–79.

96. Special Group (CI), Memorandum for the Record, Subject: Minutes for Meeting of Special Group (CI), 2 p.m., Thursday, August 9, 1962, Collection: Iran Revolution, National Security Archive.

97. John D. Jernegan, "Memorandum from the Acting Assistant Secretary of State for Near Eastern and South Asian Affairs (Jernegan) to the Special Group (Counterinsurgency), Washington, March 2, 1964," in Nina D. Howland, ed., *Foreign Relations of the United States, 1964–68,* vol.22, *Iran* (Washington, D.C.: U.S. Government Printing Office, 1999), 15.

98. *New York Times,* June 11, 1979.

99. Ranelagh, *The Agency,* 649–50.

100. Amnesty International, *Amnesty International Briefing: Iran* (London: Amnesty International, 1976), 9.

101. *New York Times,* June 11, 1979.

102. Reza Baraheni, "The Savak Documents," *The Nation,* February 23, 1980, 198–202.

103. Harold W. Maynard, "A Comparison of Military Elite Role Perceptions in Indonesia and the Philippines" (Ph.D. diss., American University, 1976), 461–62. For a detailed discussion of the impart of torture on the Philip-

pine Armed Forces, see Alfred W. McCoy, *Closer Than Brothers: Manhood at the Philippine Military Academy* (New Haven: Yale University Press, 1999).

104. "Torturer in U.S. for Training," *Tanod* (Manila) 1, no. 3 (September 1978): 3; Task Force Detainees, Association of Major Religious Superiors in the Philippines, *Pumipiglas: Political Detention and Military Atrocities in the Philippines* (Manila: Task Force Detainees of the Philippines, 1980), 106–7.

105. Alfred W. McCoy, *Priests on Trial* (New York: Penguin, 1984), 212–15.

106. Fr. Edgardo Kangleon, "A Moment of Uncertainty" (December 8, 1982), enclosed in letter "To: Dear Papa/Mama/Rey," September 30, 1983 (copy furnished by Fr. Niall O'Brien, St. Columban's Mission Society, Bacolod City). An excerpt of this letter was published in Promotion of Church People's Rights (PCPR), *That We May Remember* (Quezon City: PCPR, May 1989), 168–73.

107. Kangleon, "A Moment of Uncertainty," 13–16.

108. Church People's Rights, *That We May Remember,* 172–73.

109. U.S. Senate, Select Committee on Intelligence, "Transcript of Proceedings Before the Select Committee on Intelligence: Honduran Interrogation Manual Hearing," June 16, 1988 (box 1: CIA Training Manuals; folder: Interrogation Manual Hearings, National Security Archives), 14–15.

110. CIA, "Human Resource Exploitation Training Manual—1983," June 8, 1988 (box 1: CIA Training Manuals; folder: Resources Exploitation Training Manual," National Security Archives), I-D.

111. Ibid., K–1.B.

112. Ibid., I–22.

113. Ibid., K–1.F–G.

114. Ibid., F–1.A.

115. Ibid., F–5.E.

116. Ibid., F–14.F.

117. Ibid., F–15.H.

118. Ibid., K–5.D.

119. Ibid., L–17.

120. Ibid., L–1, L–2.

121. Ibid., L–3.

122. Ibid., L–3, L–4.

123. Ibid., L–11.D.

124. Ibid., L–21.

125. Ibid., L–12–E.

126. Ibid., I–26.III.

127. *Baltimore Sun,* January 27, 1997; *Washington Post,* January 28, 1997; *New York Times,* January 29, 1997.

128. James LeMoyne, "Testifying to Torture," *New York Times Magazine,* June 5, 1988, 45–47, 62–65.

129. U.S. Senate, Select Committee on Intelligence, "Transcript of Proceedings Before the Select Committee on Intelligence: Honduran Interrogation Manual Hearing," June 16, 1988 (box 1: CIA Training Manuals; folder: Interrogation Manual Hearings, National Security Archives), 3–5.

130. Ibid., 14.

131. Ibid., 21–22.

132. Ibid., 23–24.

133. Ibid., 24, 30.

134. Ibid., 25–27.

135. Ibid., 28–29.

136. Ibid., 33–35.

137. *New York Times,* July 9, 1996; William Rees-Mogg, "The Torture Industry," in Rehabilitation and Research Centre for Torture Victims, *Annual Report 1995* (Copenhagen: Rehabilitation and Research Centre for Torture Victims, 1996), 5–6; Inge Genefke, "Some Steps Towards a World with Less Torture," in Rehabilitation and Research Centre, *Annual Report 1995,* 15–16; Rehabilitation and Research Centre, *Annual Report 1995,* 21–23, 32–34; Keith Carmichael et al., "The Need for REDRESS," *Torture* 6, no. 1 (1996): 7; Helena Cook, "The Role of Amnesty International in the Fight against Torture," in Antonio Cassese, ed., *The International Fight against Torture* (Baden-Baden: Nomos Verlagsgesellschaft, 1991), 172–86.

138. Erik Holst, "International Efforts on the Rehabilitation of Torture Victims," in June C. Pagaduan Lopez and Elizabeth Protacio Marcelino, eds., *Torture Survivors and Caregivers: Proceedings of the International Workshop on Therapy and Research Issues* (Quezon City: University of the Philippines Press, 1995), 8–14, 190–91, 291–316, 356–57.

139. U.S. Senate, 100th Cong., 2nd sess., Treaty Doc. 100–20, *Message from the President of the United States Transmitting the Convention Against Torture and Other Cruel, Inhuman or Degrading Treatment or Punishment* (Washington, D.C.: U.S. Government Printing Office, 1988), iii–iv; Boulesbaa, *U.N. Convention on Torture,* 19.

140. Boulesbaa, *U.N. Convention on Torture,* 19; U.S. Senate, 101st Cong., 2nd sess., Committee on Foreign Relations, *Convention Against Torture: Hearing Before the Committee on Foreign Relations* (Washington, D.C.: U.S. Government Printing Office, 1990), 1, 12–18, 34, 35, 40–43, 66–69, 70–71.

141. U.S. Senate, 102nd Cong., 1st sess., Report 102–249, Committee on the Judiciary, *The Torture Victims Protection Act* (U.S. Senate, Calendar No. 382, 26 November 1991), 6–7; *Torture Victims Protection Act* P.L. 102–256, 106 Stat. 73 (1992), 28 USC§ 1350; *Congressional Record,* 102nd Cong., 1st sess., 1991. Vol. 137, pt., 1991 (November 25), 34785; *Congressional Record,* 102nd Cong., 1st sess., 2nd sess., 1992. Vol. 138, pt. 3 (March 3), 4176–78.

142. *Congressional Record.* 103rd Cong., 2nd sess.. 1994. Vol. 140, pt. 1 (February 2), 827; *Foreign Relations Authorization Act,* PL 103–236, Title V, Sec. 506, 108 Stat. 463 (1994), 18 USC§ 2340–2340A.

143. *New York Times,* June 6, 1993.

144. *Weekly Compilation of Presidential Documents* 32, No. 34 (Washington, D.C.: U.S. Government Printing Office, 1996), 1482; *Congressional Record* 104th Cong., 2nd sess., 1996. Vol. 142, pt. 14, 19562–63.

145. Klare, *War Without End,* 300–304; *New York Times,* June 24, 2001.

146. Werner E. Michel, Assistant to the Secretary of Defense (Intelligence Oversight), Subject: Improper Material in Spanish-Language Intelligence Training Manuals, March 10, 1992 (box 2: Intelligence Training Source Manuals; folder: untitled, National Security Archives).

147. Ibid.

148. *Baltimore Sun,* January 27, 1997; *Washington Post,* January 28, 1997; *New York Times,* January 29, 1997.

149. Marites Dañguilan Vitug and Glenda M. Gloria, *Under the Crescent Moon: Rebellion in Mindanao* (Quezon City: Ateneo Center for Social Policy and Public Affairs, 2000), 222–23, 224, 227.

150. *Washington Post,* October 21, 2001; Thomas, *Journey into Madness,* 348.

151. *Los Angeles Times,* October 28, 2001.

152. *Wall Street Journal,* October 23, 2001.

153. Jonathan Alter, "Time to Think of Torture," *Newsweek,* November 5, 2001, 45.

154. Steve Randall, "Pro-Pain Pundits," *Extra!* January/February 2002, http://fair.org/extra/0201/pro-pain.html (accessed December 22, 2002).

155. *Los Angeles Times,* November 8, 2001; Alan M. Dershowitz, *Why Terrorism Works* (New Haven: Yale University Press, 2002), 136–39.

156. Richard A. Posner, "The Best Offense," *New Republic,* September 2, 2002, 28–31.

157. *Boston Globe,* February 16, 2002.

158. Vitug and Gloria, *Under the Crescent Moon,* 222–24, 229–30, 232; Matthew Brzezinski, "Bust and Boom," *Washington Post Magazine,* December 30, 2001, 16.

159. Richard A. Clarke, *Against All Enemies: Inside America's War on Terror* (New York: Free Press, 2004), 24; George W. Bush, "Notice: Detention, Treatment, and Trial of Certain Non-Citizens in the War against Terrorism," White House, November 13, 2001, 66 *Federal Register* (FR) 57833, http://www.law. uchicago.edu/tribunals/docs/exec_orders.pdf (accessed June 14, 2004).

160. John Barry et al., "The Roots of Torture," *Newsweek,* May 24, 2004, 29–30.

161. Human Rights Watch, *The Road to Abu Ghraib,* June 9, 2004, 5, http://www.hrw.org/reports/2004/usa0604/.

162. Alberto R. Gonzales, Memorandum for the President, Subject: Decision Re. Application of the Geneva Convention on Prisoners of War to the Conflict with Al Qaeda and the Taliban, January 25, 2002, DRAFT 1/25/2002—3:30 p.m., http://www.msn.com/id/4999148/site/newsweek/ (accessed May 24, 2004).

163. Jay S. Bybee, Assistant Attorney General, Office of Legal Counsel, U.S. Department of Justice, Memorandum for Alberto R. Gonzales, Counsel to the President, and William J. Haynes II, General Counsel of the Department of Defense, January 22, 2002, 37, http://www.washingtonpost.com/wp-srv/nation/documents/012202 bybee.pdf (accessed June 28, 2004); Barry, "Roots of Torture," 31; *New York Times,* June 8, 2004.

164. Gonzales, Memorandum for the President, January 25, 2002, 2.

165. Colin L. Powell, Memorandum, To: Counsel to the President, Subject: Draft Decision Memorandum for the President on the Applicability of the Geneva Convention to the Conflict in Afghanistan, n.d., http://msnbc.com/modules/newsweek/pdf.powell_memo.pdf (accessed June 20, 2004); George Bush, "Memorandum for the Vice President," Subject: Human Treatment of al Qaeda and Taliban Detainees, 7 February 2002, http://www.washingtonpost.com/wp-srv/nation/documents/0207026bush.pdf (accessed June 28, 2004); Barry, "Roots of Torture," 31; *New York Times,* June 8, 2004; *American Forces Information Service News Articles,* February 8, 2002, http://www.defenselink.mil/news/Feb2002;t02082002_t0208sd.html (accessed July 1, 2004).

166. *Washington Post,* 26 December 2002; *New York Times,* November 23, 2002, March 9, 2003, June 17, 2004, June 18, 2004; Barry, "Roots of Torture," 31–33; Seymour M. Hersh, "The Gray Zone: How a Secret Pentagon Program Came to Abu Ghraib," *New Yorker,* May 24 , 2004, 38–39; *Observer* (London), June 13, 2004.

167. *New York Times,* March 3, 2003, March 7, 2003, March 9, 2003, June 27, 2004, June 28, 2004.

168. Jay S. Bybee, Memorandum for Alberto R. Gonzales, August 1, 2002, 1–2, 8, 16–22, http://www.washingtopost.com/wp-srv/nation/documents/dojinterrogationmemo20020801.pdf (accessed June 20, 2004); *New York Times,* June 27, 2004, June 28, 2004.

169. *New York Times,* June 25, 2004.

170. *Washington Post,* December 26, 2002, December 28, 2002; *Toronto Star,* December 28, 2002.

171. *Washington Post,* December 26, 2002; *New York Times,* November 23, 2002, March 9, 2003, June 21, 2004, June 22, 2004, June 23, 2004; Barry, "Roots of Torture," 31–33; *Boston Globe,* June 24, 2004; William J. Haynes II, General Counsel, Department of Defense, For: Secretary of Defense, Subject: Counter-Resistance Techniques, 27 November 2002, http://www.washingtonpost.com/wp-srv/nation/documents/dodmemos.pdf (accessed June 28, 2004).

172. *Washington Post,* December 26, 2002; *New York Times,* November 23, 2002, March 9, 2003, 21 June 2004, 22 June 2004, 23 June 2004; Barry, "Roots of Torture," 31–33; *Boston Globe,* June 24, 2004; Donald Rumsfeld, Memorandum for the General Counsel of the Department of Defense, Subject: Detainee Interrogations, January 15, 2003, http://www.washingtonpost.com/wp-srv/nation/documents/011503rumsfeld.pdf (accessed June 28, 2004); Working Group Report on Detainee Interrogations in the Global War on Terrorism: Assessment of Legal, Historical, Policy, and Operational Considerations, 6 March 2003, http://www.informationclearinghouse.info/pdf/military-0604.pdf (accessed June 14, 2004); Donald Rumsfeld, Memorandum for the Commander, U.S. Southern Command, April 16, 2003, http://www.washingtonpost.com/wp-srv/nation/documents/041603rumsfeld.pdf (accessed June 28, 2004).

173. Human Rights Watch, *Road to Abu Ghraib,* 13.

174. *New York Times,* June 8, 2004; Hersh, "Gray Zone," 42.

175. Hersch, "Gray Zone," 41–42.

176. M. G. Antonio M. Taguba, Article 15–6 Investigation of the 800th Military Police Brigade, February 26, 2004, 7, 8, 15, http://www.cbsnews.com/htdocs/pdf/tagubareport.pdf (accessed May 10, 2004); *New York Times,* May 24, 2004, May 26, 2004, June 22, 2004; Human Rights Watch, *Road to Abu Ghraib,* 32–33.

177. Taguba, Article 15–6 Investigation of the 800th Military Police Brigade, 16, 18; *New York Times,* May 19, 2004.

178. Taguba, Article 15–6 Investigation of the 800th Military Police Brigade, 18, 21, 38, 45–46; *New York Times,* June 4, 2004, June 8, 2004, June 14, 2004.

179. Report of the International Committee of the Red Cross (ICRC) on the Treatment by the Coalition Forces of Prisoners of War and Other Protected Persons by the Geneva Conventions in Iraq During Arrest, Internment and Interrogation, February 2004, 3–4, 6, 8, 11, 12, http://www.redress.btinternet.co.uk/icrc_iraq.pdf (accessed May 12, 2004); *Newsday,* May 5, 2004.

180. Report of the International Committee of the Red Cross, February 2004, 13, 15, 17–18.

181. Hersh, "Gray Zone," 42; *New York Times,* July 3, 2004.

182. *New York Times,* May 31, 2004; Human Rights Watch, *Road to Abu Ghraib,* 28–29.

183. NewsHour with Jim Lehrer, May 4, 2004, http://www.pbs.org/newshour/bb/military/jan-june 04/abuse1_05_04.html (accessed June 14, 2004); *New York Times,* May 11, 2004, May 15, 2004, May 25, 2004; United Nations, Commission on Human Rights, *Report of the United Nations High Commissioner for Human Rights and Follow Up to the World Conference on Human Rights* (Geneva: Commission on Human Rights, 61st Session, E/CN.4/2005/4, Advance Edited Edition, June 9, 2004), 18; "President Outlines Steps to Help Iraq Achieve Democracy and Freedom," May 24, 2004, http://www.whitehouse.gov/news/release/2004/05/print/20040424-10.html (accessed June 14, 2004).

184. *New York Times,* June 30, 2004.

185. Bertrand Ramcharan, *United Nations High Commissioner for Human Rights and International Humanitarian Law,* Program on Humanitarian Policy and Conflict Research, Harvard University, Occasional Papers, no. 3, Spring 2005, http://www.hpcr.org/pdfs/OccasionalPaper3.pdf; *New York Times,* June 5, 2004.

186. *International Herald Tribune,* June 19–20, 2004; *New York Times,* June 18, 2004, June 24, 2004.

187. Supreme Court of the United States, Oral Arguments, *Donald H. Rumsfeld v. Jose Padilla,* No. 03–1027, http://www.supremecourtus.gov/oral_arguments/argument_transcripts/03-1027.pdf (accessed July 5, 2004); *New York Times,* July 4, 2004.

188. *New York Times,* June 29, 2004, July 1, 2004, July 4, 2004; Supreme Court of the United States, *Yaser Esam Hamdi, et al. v. Donald Rumsfeld, Secretary of Defense, et al.,* no. 03–6696, http://caselaw.lp.findlaw.com/cgi-bin/getcase.pl?court=US&navby=case&vol=000&invol=03–6696 (accessed July 5, 2004).

189. John Conroy, *Unspeakable Acts, Ordinary People: The Dynamics of Torture* (New York: Alfred A. Knopf, 2000), 112–13, 244–47.

190. *New York Times,* July 23, 2004; Department of the Army, Inspector General, *Detainee Operations Inspec-*

2/6

tion (July 21, 2004), forward, 13, 22, 31, 38, http://www.washingtonpost.com/wp-srv/world/iraq/abughraib/detaineereport.pdf (accessed July 28, 2004).

191. *New York Times,* July 24, 2004; *Los Angeles Times,* July 23, 2004; Taguba, Article 15–6 Investigation of the 800th Military Police Brigade, 16.

192. Deborah Solomon, "Questions for Trent Lott," *New York Times Magazine,* June 20, 2004, 15; Michael Ignatieff, "Mirage in the Desert," *New York Times Magazine,* June 27, 2004, 14.

193. MG George R. Fay, "AR 15–6 Investigation of the Abu Ghraib Detention Facility and 205th Military Intelligence Brigade (U)," 7–9, 29, 42, 44, 45, 55, 118, http://www4.army.mil/ocpa/reports/ar15–6/ar15–6.pdf.

194. *New York Times,* November 30, 2004, December 1, 2004.

195. Michael Ignatieff, "Lesser Evils," *New York Times Magazine,* May 2, 2004, 86.

196. Ibid.

SHAPING A NEW WORLD

x/ p. 218 it blank

The final cluster focuses on global responsibilities to protect and how to deal with the growing phenomenon of failed states, among them those most poor and purported to be the most likely sources of terrorism. Global institutions relating to these matters fail us, and while a considerable portion of the blame can be attributed to the unwieldy, inefficient, and bureaucratic nature of these institutions, nation-states tend to make global declarations and then pursue narrow sovereign state interests. We speak globally, act parochially—even when it is in the perceived interests of all to act together in the face of a perceived threat, such as climate change.

And this is essentially true with regard to problems such as massive income and wealth disparities between North and South, the marginalization of Africa, the proliferation of weapons of mass destruction, and the problems represented by increasing numbers of failed states. The old rules governing nation-states are outmoded, the concept of the sovereignty of the nation-state has run its course, but the isms that underpin it are rooted in our institutions and resilient in our identity.

Cornelio Sommaruga, Ram Damodaran, Robert Jackson, and Gwyn Prins discuss, one month before the United States invaded Iraq in March 2003, the forms that global challenges might take in the context of an evolving globalization. They emphasize the norms being established for both international humanitarian and military intervention in conflicts that erupt in sovereign states, thus signaling a post–Cold War paradigm shift in the UN's conception of its role in keeping the peace. Although the UN Charter expressly declares the sanctity of the principle of nonintervention, the UN has, in recent years, begun to set limits on that sanctity.

The International Commission on Intervention and State Sovereignty (ICISS) sets out the principles for international military intervention in failed, about to fail, or rogue states where conflict is about to erupt or has already erupted: the right intention, the last resort, proportional means, and reasonable prospect. Most important, the ICISS was unambiguous in two regards: the principle of nonintervention yields to the principle to protect and with intervention comes the principle to rebuild. Thus, one of the major consequences of our interdependence is the recognition that a threat to peace must now include the "feared adverse international consequences of civil conflicts involving humanitarian catastrophes." But no intervention can occur unless it has the sanction of the Security Council.

Robert Weiner examines how the UN has tried to adapt to a post–Cold War era, and now to a post 9/11 era. It was poorly equipped to do either. He notes the dichotomy in the UN Charter—although the UN was created to prevent war, member states could not agree that there should be a permanent UN international army, thus requiring it to

improvise ways to deal with wars. Peacekeeping—never mentioned in the charter—
had to be invented.

Weiner proposes that for the UN to become a viable instrument for the prevention
of conflict, it will have to democratize the Security Council, which continues to reflect
a Cold War composition, and develop a flexible military peacekeeping capability that
will enable it to prevent conflicts from developing and escalating out of control. But
the problem dogging UN peacekeeping operations is that "member states . . . are not
yet ready to surrender their sovereignty over the troops that they contribute to UN
peacekeeping operations, which would be entailed in the creation of a UN standing or
more permanent type of force."

Brian Urquhart and Michael Glennon discuss other forms of inertia—the failure of
the international community to agree on the best way to handle relatively new threats
like large-scale terrorism or nuclear proliferation, rogue states, or even humanitarian
intervention. The larger the UN, the slower its ability to respond to imminent crisis.
Darfur attests to endemic inertia.

Without the authority to intervene in a timely way, the UN will continue to remain a
primarily deliberative body, without clout other than moral suasion, which is worth
less after the Volcker Commission's report on the Iraq Oil for Food scandal revealed a
degree of breathtaking corruption among senior officials.

The UN looked hard at the reforms it would have to implement to meet the challenges of the twenty-first century but balked at taking the necessary steps to give expression to their intent. A plethora of diverse interests gutted real reform and settled
for cosmetics. The challenges of the twenty-first century were firmly earthed in the
power relations of the mid twentieth.

In November 2003, UN Secretary-General Koffi Annan set up a high-level panel of
eminent personalities to assess the UN's role in dealing with new global threats. The
panel endorsed "the emerging norm of a responsibility to protect civilians from large-
scale violence with force if necessary, though only as a last resort," in effect telling the
UN that it should adopt an ethic of Just Intervention. The report also endorsed "the
emerging norm that there is a collective international responsibility to protect, exer-
cizable by the Security Council authorizing military intervention as a last resort, in the
event of genocide and other large-scale killing, ethnic cleansing or serious violations of
international humanitarian law which sovereign Governments have proved powerless
or unwilling to prevent."[1]

The panel also addressed and reached near agreement on one of the most intrac-
table issues: the composition of the Security Council. The present council, consisting
of five permanent veto-wielding members (the victors of World War II plus China) and
ten others, elected for short durations on a regional basis, would be replaced by an
expanded twenty-four-member council of three tiers: the existing five permanent
members (the United States, China, Britain, France, and Russia); a second tier of seven
or eight semipermanent members on renewable terms of four or five years (Brazil,

Germany, India, and South Africa, for example), and a third tier of rotating regional members elected as at present for nonrenewable two-year stints. Only the permanent five would have a veto.

The panel recommended that the UN reorient its work to meet global threats into several categories: interstate conflict; internal violence including genocide; social and economic threats, such as poverty and disease; terrorism; and organized crime and corruption. The Security Council would have the power to authorize a preventive use of force, but only after "a serious and sober assessment" of the threat based on "clear and compelling evidence," the office of the Secretary-General would have authority to act without having to have the sanction of the General Assembly for next to inconsequential decisions.

In September 2005, on the sixtieth convening of the General Assembly, the document Koffi Annan had carefully crafted out of the commission's report and for which he had secured the basis of consensus was gutted, primarily, but not exclusively, by the United States. The General Assembly adopted a "statement of goals" that significantly watered down many of the panel's proposals, including language that the UN should assume a "responsibility to protect" civilian populations when governments are "unable or unwilling" to do so. The United States took the lead in replacing this language with the weaker formulation that the UN "is prepared to take action" in such cases, thus removing any legal obligation to intervene.

Expanding the Security Council (SC) was shelved, primarily at the insistence of the United States. But it would be unfair to place blame on the United States alone. Proponents of reform, themselves touted as likely members of an expanded SC, could not agree on how many additional member states should sit on a new SC, and their regional distribution could not resolve competing claims within regions or decide which member states should be permanent and which nonpermanent. Africa scuppered reform at that level when the African Union insisted that permanent African members of the SC should have the power of veto.

Some member states were unwilling to cede power to the Secretariat because it might diminish their influence in the assembly; others aligned themselves with regional interests. The United States already dismissive of the UN worked hard to ensure that it would become a body the United States could be even more dismissive of.

The General Assembly rejected Annan's language on nonproliferation. Annan called the action a disgrace.[2] Again, the developing world, working on the simple principle that what is good for the goose is good for the gander, balks at any proposal that seeks to limit nuclear capacity to countries that already have it, especially when efforts to do so are led by countries who simultaneously rewrite the goals of the Millennium Conference. The failure to decouple issues of preeminent concern ensures that compliance with the nonproliferation treaty opens the way to proliferation.

In the new post-Iraq geopolitical world, where the Bush administration no longer seems invulnerable, there is a new global dance card. States pick their partners on specific issues in search of oil or regional influence, often contrary to the U.S. agenda. Europe is turning to Russia for its energy supplies and as its dependency increases, the rhetoric about human rights and democratization is losing its punch. North Korea, China, and South Korea perceive their interests as different from Japan's and the United States'. Iran's continued enrichment of uranium has become a matter of pivotal global concern. Russia's, India's, and China's interests are different from those of Europe and the United States. And unlikely as it appears, Pakistan and India both oppose penalizing Iran. Coalitions are becoming fluid, opposition to American hegemony often making for unlikely dancing partners and dancing partners more likely to switch in mid-dance.

It is easy to argue that the world is a better place because the UN is there—the statement cannot be challenged since there is no other "world" against which to measure its performance. Some institutions work well (the World Health Organization, the International Atomic Energy Agency, the World Food Program, the United Nations Children's Fund, for example). But things fall apart in the areas of conflict prevention and intervention. Big-power politics stymie action, effective authority to enforce the peace is absent, resources are scant.

The institution is too bloated, too bureaucratic, too set in its ways, too vast, out of managerial control, accountable only to its own inadequate structures for assessing accountability, without adequate performance monitors. Perhaps we have to accept that "best" tinkering is the best we can hope for, given the existing wide divergences of interests that uneasily coexist within the UN. Within the Assembly, power has shifted to coalitions of newer members and the developing world is perceptive of its numbers, given the requirement of a two-thirds majority to enact change. Increasingly it is prepared to use that power to thwart the SC, which it perceives as a relic of colonial domination. Likewise, the SC is reluctant to share its exclusive powers with others.

Divergence of interest will increase in the next fifty years as the economic and demographic structures of international relations change and strategic concerns take precedence over old alliances. Since concerted and common action generally follow a catastrophe, it seems likely that if a catastrophe of some magnitude occurs, perhaps the explosion of a limited WMD, where we see the global wreckage such an event produces, only then will our minds become sufficiently concentrated.

Reform is entirely dependent on members' resolve. But if we use their willingness to meet their financial commitments as a gauge of intent, resolve is wanting. The determination to put effective global institutions in place to prevent conflict or to intervene will not emerge until the United States takes the lead. Only when it agrees to give over power to the UN and only when it actively embraces the measures proposed by the panel will the UN emerge as the world's policeman with the authority and appropriate institutions to punish miscreants. This, of course, goes to the heart of how the United States perceives its role in the world, and to the nature of national sovereignty.

Jonathan Moore addresses the crisis of failed states in blunt, forceful terms: They stay "failed" because the international community's response to their staggering needs is inadequate. Needs are not addressed simultaneously, although they are mutually interdependent. Donor countries tend to define needs in terms of what they are willing to invest, thus distorting the complexity and scale of the problem. The investment required to create and maintain sustainable development, which successful peace building requires, is rarely forthcoming and never adequate. The powerful nations who set the agenda for peacekeeping supply band-aids for symptoms of disintegration but are unwilling to commit the resources for radical surgery to remove the causes of disintegration.

And sometimes, there is an innate intractability to postconflict divided societies in the process of transition. In June 1999, after NATO bombing helped to drive Serbian forces from Kosovo, thousands of international civil servants and policemen—eleven thousand at one point—poured into Kosovo as part of the UN mission at an estimated annual cost of $1.3 billion. They built ministries, a parliament, local councils, courts, customs, police services, and the media. In 2001 their efforts to build a modern democratic state were hailed as an example for nation building elsewhere. But in 2006, they had begun to withdraw: The process had stalled—hamstrung, according to international experts by "the inability of foreigners to adopt solutions that addressed the needs of the people who live all their lives in Kosovo."[3]

Moore's conclusions echo the mantra of this collection: We lack the collective institutional capacity to deal with these problems. We lack a collective vision, a common commitment. We drag our feet when we should be running at full speed. And unfortunately, with such institutional inertia, developed countries, with few exceptions, sit on their rich hind sides doling out aid in stingy amounts and invariably to their "own" countries from which they will receive a benefit in return for the aid. Aid given in insufficient dollops, in haphazard and unconnected ways—unconnected to the region in which a country subsists may be worse than no aid—the aid is simply siphoned off in corruption, projects that will collapse because there is no infrastructure to sustain them.

The rich North continues postcolonial forms of exploitation, despite its own prognosis of the consequences—failing countries faltering more rapidly, opening the way to intraterritorial conflict, famine, disease, narcotics trafficking, and the resentments of the have-littles and have-nots. Rather, the North poaches from their small pools of developing skills, stealing their new professionals to meet its needs.

When the millennium was approaching with the possibility of a Y2K crash of computers, power and communications systems, as well as a possible global economic meltdown, there was a gnawing global anxiety (at least in the developed world) and a global response. Countries coordinated their efforts to prevent such an outcome, there were reassurances to the public, and a measure of "togetherness" as we waited for the clock to strike twelve. In contrast, we are today confronted with the possibility that a lethal avian influenza virus, H5N1, may kill from fifty to one hundred million. For now our fears are inarticulate. Experts are alarmed at the inadequacy of national and international plans to deal with such a pandemic. Only now, belatedly, are we beginning to see the international coordination that was a hallmark of the Y2K "crisis." It remains inadequate. Should avian flu virus infect humans anytime soon, potential disaster will become an actual reality, with deaths in the tens of millions, perhaps even in the hundreds of millions.

The World Health Organization warned in November 2005 that an H5N1 flu pandemic was "unavoidable," not in a decade but in the near future. The way in which the global community mobilizes resources to manage such a catastrophe, whether nations will act cooperatively or close borders to protect their own might well determine how we deal with the threats of war and conflict during the rest of the century. For a crisis of this potential magnitude will redefine our understanding of the rights and obligations of nation-states in an age of global interdependence, not least finding that the concept itself as we have understood it in the twentieth century is obsolete in the twenty-first.

Padraig O'Malley

NOTES

1. United Nations, *A More Secure World: Our Shared Responsibility,* Report of the High-level Panel on Threats, Challenges and Change (New York: United Nations, 2004), par. 203, http://www.un.org/secureworld/report3.pdf.

2. *New York Times,* September 15, 2005.

3. Nicholas Wood, "UN Effort to Rebuild Kosovo Loses Steam," *International Herald Tribune,* September 30, 2005.

Globalization
New Challenges

At a time when the information revolution has largely freed economics from the reins of politics, when globalization has indeed brought economic growth and liberated innovation, there is a need to also globalize responsibility. The state is being undermined by the assertion of so many different identities.

CORNELIO SOMMARUGA

Globalizing responsibility implies, I believe, the improvement of human security, that is, the security of individual persons—their physical safety, their economic and social well-being, respect for their dignity and worth as human beings, and the respect of human rights and fundamental freedoms, namely, those of religious choice. There is a growing recognition worldwide that the concept of security must include people as well as states. This is particularly evident after the dreadful terrorist attacks on New York and Washington and the events that have followed September 11, 2001.

The interrelated challenges to human security and peace require an international multilateral response of the whole world system, and this calls for increased cooperation between international organizations with enhanced authority for the UN. Security can be obtained only on the basis of a just and sustainable world order. International cooperation must also include a strong, well-respected judicial element like the International Criminal Court. No country, whether large or small, can protect itself from global threats by itself.

Let me insist that attacking only the symptoms of terrorism will address neither its systematic nature nor its underlying causes. The most effective response is to establish universal good governance and secure human rights for all. Civil liberties, the rule of law, must be respected in any response to terrorism and such response measures must always conform to international law, especially international humanitarian law. I also strongly believe that globalizing responsibility implies a responsibility to protect and, as the International Commission on Intervention and State Sovereignty (ICISS) has firmly stated, the responsibility to protect includes the accompanying responsibility to prevent. It is more than high time for the international community to be doing more to close the gap between rhetorical support for prevention and tangible commitment. Yes indeed, the prevention of conflicts and other forms of manmade catastrophes is first the responsibility of

From the EPIIC Symposium at Tufts University, "Sovereignty and Intervention," February 2003, roughly one month before the March 20, 2003, U.S. invasion of Iraq.

225

sovereign states and the communities and institutions within them. A firmer national commitment to insuring fair treatment and fair opportunities for all citizens provides a solid basis for conflict prevention. Efforts to insure accountability and good governance, to promote social and economic development, and to insure a fair distribution of resources are also part of conflict prevention, as are the containment of corruption and of small arms and light weapons transfers and humanitarian demining programs.

An important aspect of the ICISS report about the so-called right of humanitarian intervention is the determined shift in focus to the responsibility to protect. We have wished to avoid ambiguities, to prevent the possible militarization of humanitarian action, and particularly with a responsibility to protect, to be closer to victims. We also wanted to make clear that the humanitarian objective cannot be used as a shield for operations that have other objectives. It also permitted the development of principles for military intervention while requesting that less intrusive and coercive measures be conceded before such an intervention. The just cause was defined in a very restrictive way, mentioning, on one side, large-scale loss of life, and, on the other side, large-scale ethnic cleansing. There are four major precautionary principles: the right intention, the last resort, proportional means, and reasonable prospect. The commission also spent some space to indicate the right authority.

There is no better or no more appropriate body than the UN Security Council to authorize interventions for the purpose of human protection, and in the ICISS report, we tried to show how to make the Security Council work better. Let me, however, insist on the necessity for action by the Security Council in cases where, in a conscience-shocking situation, the responsibility to protect appears evident. Should the Security Council not act, individual states may conduct a military intervention without the constraint and discipline that would be inherent in a UN authorization. Inaction by the Security Council followed by an armed intervention by a coalition of the willing that would appear to be legitimate, while illegal, would have serious negative consequences for the UN as an organization.

It is, finally, a responsibility of the whole international community, including civil society, to take action to protect human beings in danger, and the purpose of the action of our ICISS, particularly in a situation of threatened mass killing or ethnic cleansing. This is also why I consider of particular importance the part of the report devoted to operational principles where reference is made to rules of engagement that should involve total adherence to international humanitarian law and maximum possible coordination with humanitarian organizations, and the responsibility to rebuild; the quest to provide full assistance with recovering, reconstruction, and reconciliation, addressing the causes of the harm the intervention was designed to halt.

Let me recall that state sovereignty implies responsibility and that the primary responsibility for the protection of its people lies with the state itself. In front of serious suffering of the population because of insurgency, civil war, repression, or state failure, when the state itself is unwilling or unable to halt it, the principle of nonintervention yields to the international responsibility to protect. To limit violence is part of the globalization of responsibility. This is essential for prevention, and I believe that humanitarian actors could do better to create a hate-free, fair, and greed-free world. We have all to be convinced that the world cannot continue leaving one-fifth rich, two-fifths in abject poverty, and another two-fifths struggling for a decent life. Each of us has to take responsibility to act in order to enhance human security.

Up to now I have not referred to the feelings of hopelessness on the part of the vast majority of world people confronted with the inevitability of war. Going to war, any war, is always a step back; a failure for democracy, development, and understanding; a defeat for the whole of humanity. A war against Iraq will cause more deaths, misery, and desperation to a population already depressed. The UN, I am convinced, is working seriously in all its main bodies and sectors to find diplomatic solutions to a real crisis because of the absolute unreliability of the Iraqi regime but also in order to contain a certain arrogance of power and the tendency toward unilateral action. The international community must exercise its common responsibility to insure Iraqi compliance with Security Council resolutions, but the exercise of this responsibility must be moral as well as legal. Religion cannot be used to justify what is illegal or immoral.

In this context I—a friend of the United States, a friend of this great nation, a friend of all U.S. citizens—I would wish to see the United States fully committed to building solid peace, real justice, and sustainable development. Their responsibility throughout the world and before Easter lies in a response to the tremendous problem to which we are confronted worldwide, and this should occur in a spirit of solidarity, justice, and aid. Humanity needs and expects winning the peace rather than winning the war. Through the collective security organization of the UN, let us work for the reasonable balance between we the people and you the governments of the world.

ROBERT JACKSON   There are two doctrines that exist in some conflict and contradiction at present. There is the post-1945 doctrine of nonintervention that was established at San Francisco at the end of World War II. That conference had noted, among other things, that causes of the war had involved interventions that were deemed to be unjustified and so the doctrine of nonintervention was at the center of the concerns of the founders of the UN. You find it at the heart of the UN Charter. That is the first doctrine.

The second doctrine is a contemporary doctrine that has taken on reality, a life of its own, since the end of the Cold War. This is a contemporary, more positive doctrine to relax the rule or restriction of nonintervention in relation to states when certain conditions are present. Let me briefly run through these two doctrines and then offer a few comments on them.

The first doctrine is essentially a negative doctrine. I am referring explicitly to Article 2 of the UN Charter, which affirms, I think it is fair to say, the fundamental norm of the charter, which is, equal sovereignty, territorial integrity, and nonintervention. That doctrine holds that the inviolability of sovereign states can be overridden or trumped only by two other basic norms of the charter. The first of these is what I consider to be the primordial norm of the whole arrangement and that is the state right of self-defense, Article 51. The second one is the Security Council's fundamental responsibility to defend international peace and security, which is spelled out in Chapter 7.

In the conventional view, this article is the basic norm of post-1945 international society. It can be characterized as a doctrine of state responsibility to uphold and respect the sovereignty of all states. That doctrine is not qualified or modified by any conditions that apply to the domestic institutions or domestic policies of sovereign states, which is deemed to be a purely internal affair and not an international affair.

The second doctrine that has emerged in the past dozen years is the more expansive, positive doctrine of intervention. Since 1990 the Security Council has authorized a number of military interventions in various failing or failed states torn apart by violent civil conflict. I refer to UN–authorized interventions in postwar Iraq in 1991, the former Yugoslavia in 1991 and onward, Somalia in 1991–92, Haiti in 1993, Rwanda in 1994, and Kosovo in 1998. But let me add a little asterisk for Kosovo. The UN Security Council, of course, authorized the intervention after it occurred. Then there was East Timor in 1999, Afghanistan in 2001. There may be one or two others I have forgotten, but I think that's most of them.

Now all of these cases exist because they escaped veto by any permanent member of the Security Council. If a veto had been cast, they would not have happened the way they did. This is simply a footnote to the present controversy. At this time [prior to the 2003 U.S. invasion of Iraq], I understand the Russians are considering exercising the veto. They have a full constitutional right to do it and, in fact, the veto exists to avoid major conflict between the permanent members. We should not forget that.

Let me then briefly run through this new practice that has been emerging. The heart of the practice is in a series of resolutions by the Security Council. In those resolutions the Security Council has been reframing the definition or the understanding of international peace and security, and they have been doing that in particular by looking at the notion of a threat to international peace and security in working it out. There is here, built right into the heart of the UN in its resolutions, an assumption of preemption in matters of intervention. The notion of a threat to peace has been expanded and loosened to include what might be characterized as the feared adverse international consequences of civil conflicts involving humanitarian catastrophes—such destabilizing refugee flows produced by war-torn societies as happened in postwar Iraq in 1991 and in Kosovo in 1999, among others. The original notion of a threat to peace, namely, a palpable danger of international war involving the military forces of states in conflict has been relaxed, reinterpreted, and expanded. In my opinion, this recently constructed norm of humanitarian intervention is a significant departure from the normative order spelled out at San Francisco in 1945.

At the background of my remarks today is a most careful, thoughtful, and balanced report of these cases, published by the Danish Institute of International Affairs, the main think tank of the Danish Ministry of Foreign Affairs. It is a cool, rational assessment. The doctrine of responsibility to protect has been crafted in a clear way by a report originated by the Canadian Ministry of External Affairs and in particular a former Canadian foreign minister, Lloyd Axworthy, and it has produced another report, a report of the International Commission on Intervention and State Sovereignty, which in my view expresses this better than any other report. This is a notion that when individual human beings are at risk in significant numbers wherever they live, that risk, that hazard, ought to be addressed not only by individuals in a voluntary way but by states. It ought to be their responsibility as sovereign states. I quote from a report: "Sovereign states have a responsibility to protect their own citizens from avoidable catastrophe, from mass murder and rape, from starvation, but when they are unwilling or unable to do so," and this is the key, "that responsibility must be born by the broader community of states."[1]

They deconstruct this notion of a responsibility to protect in three ways, along three dimensions. The responsibility to prevent these humanitarian catastrophes from arising in the first place, preventive diplomacy and that sort of thing; the responsibility to react when it does occur; and third, and I think in some ways most interesting and provocative, the responsibility to rebuild. In short, as members of the international community, sovereign states are understood to be bound by a norm of human rights protection. More important, the responsibility to protect is seen to trump the responsibility to respect and uphold the sovereign immunity of all international peace-loving states if and when these two basic norms come into conflict.

This is basically a doctrine of international community, international involvement, and intervention. I believe it is a controversial doctrine. It introduces the normative criterion or standard of international legitimacy that draws a rather sharp distinction between two classes of countries, namely, constitutional democracies on one hand and the rest. The standard is reminiscent of an earlier standard of civilization that used to be applied by European countries in their dealings with the rest of the world as a justification of intervention, occupation,

X /230

and reconstruction—the colonial era. The best example I can come up with of that earlier doctrine is found in the General Act of the Berlin Conference of 1884–85 when the European powers, the imperial powers, partitioned Africa and occupied it and governed it for a further period of seventy or eighty years.

This doctrine has, therefore, hints of trusteeship and paternalism in it, and I put it in that way because the 1945 doctrine is based on antipaternalism, anticolonialism, restriction on outside involvement where there is no violation of the right of self-defense or collective security under the UN.

So what we have here in my view is a conflict of two basic values, the old norms of nonintervention and this new doctrine of responsibility to protect. I think at certain points that conflict can be massaged and one hopes it won't arise in many places, but the possibility of its arising is always there, which raises the question of what do you do when it happens. I cannot tell you my answer to that question because I think that question is largely bound by circumstances. But I wish to point out that both of these normative orders or arrangements produce good consequences and bad consequences, and in international affairs we cannot have our cake and eat it.

RAMU DAMODARAN   The first prime minister of my country, Jawaharlal Nehru, had said very loftily in 1947 that the real test of a nation's freedom comes in its conduct of foreign affairs, all else is local autonomy. But if you go to an Indian today and ask whether the degree of local autonomy that we have had for the past fifty-five years has brought us the genuine fruits of independence for which Nehru and his comrades struggled in the thirties and forties, I think you would get a mixed answer.

An Erosion of Norms

The real challenge before us in addressing the reconciliation between sovereignty and globalization is to find areas where they can coexist. Is it, as Dr. Cornelio Sommaruga argues, really in the responsibility to protect? If it is in the responsibility to protect, who is there to monitor the protectors? Is it in the capacity to delineate a set of finite goals, which the UN and its leaders have tried to do in terms of the development goals that they have set for 2015? Does that exercise other nations' sovereignty to pursue domestic, economic policies that are essential to realizing multilaterally agreed ends mean an enhancement or an abridgement of sovereignty?

The challenge now is in the definition of an internationally accepted and internationally articulated set of norms, because what we have seen, ironically enough, in the half century since the UN was created, is a steady erosion of global norms and a steady misinterpretation or reinterpretation of just what those norms mean.

We have come to a point, for instance, when we no longer talk of, say, disarmament as a goal in itself. We have replaced talk of disarmament by talk of nonproliferation, or the nonspread of weapons. So a core value has gone.

In order to attain the goals of halving the world population that is living on less than a dollar a day by 2015, you will require a rise in the national income of countries on the order of 3.7 percent, which one-third of the world's population in 127 countries have not been able to do in the past ten years. Do we not allow our consciences to be shocked by the fact that in sub-Saharan Africa today the life expectancy has come down to forty-five years from forty-seven years while on the continent of Europe we are looking forward to an old Europe where more than 60 percent of the population will be pensioners in another twenty-five years? How do we reconcile these without allowing it to offend our conscience?

And so we come back to the question, Where does the global responsibility for global citizens end and the responsibility of a state to protect its citizens from that intrusion begin? When a multinational company decides, for instance, to come to India and manufacture an item of immediate consumer appeal, say, lipstick, is the government obliged to regulate that company so that the resources that its citizens might otherwise invest or spend in productive areas is not diverted by enlarging their areas of choice? Or is that an intrusion upon the sovereignty of the individual?

The Sovereignty of the Individual

We must realize that the sovereignty of the state or the globalized order of the world in which we live today becomes entirely peripheral until we accept the sovereignty of the individual. It is a sovereignty of the individual, which means, clearly, that genocide does not begin in the thousands, it begins with the death of one person. It is the primacy of the individual that recognizes that terrorism is not encapsulated in one particular newspaper headline but is in the stark fact that a person who goes to work quite normally on a clear blue day in September does not live for two hours beyond taking that first train. Once you come down to the level of the individual—and this I think is what the UN in particular has now to do, and by the UN I mean its member states—then a lot of these problems come back into a coherent form in which you can tackle them, otherwise the danger with which we are faced is globalization like the Internet—it is something that is all around us but no one can really control it—a situation where you will not allow the fundamental responsibility of governments to their citizens to be addressed and therefore you will negate the very widespread enhancement of global democracy that has occurred since 1989 by which governments are no longer responsive to the people who put them in power in the first place but are more anxious to protect their physical security from neighbors around them.

Sovereignty and Ethics

Sovereignty, in a sense, is the cornerstone of ethics, and the UN is a coalition of fractious states. But in any community of 190-odd members, discussions are bound to be fractious. I do not see a problem in that. But if they are going to be inconclusive or, worse still, if they are going to divert from the central agenda at hand, then I think we endanger the entire multilateral system on which globalization ultimately depends. As we have legitimate governments now, you will have increasingly self-assertive legitimate opposition in the form of civil society groups. Are these groups legitimate? Is the degree of opposition sanctioned? This is a question that we have to ask. Certainly there are powerful nongovernmental organizations that have really worked, as the International Committee for the Red Cross has, and have become synonymous with international humanitarian action.

But my point is that you cannot allow your sovereignty to be challenged by, or your globalization to be facilitated by, crises alone. It has to be much more mundane, much more day-to-day. And therefore, to my mind, the very fact that we can set up a monitoring body, as the UN has set up in the case of specific human rights treaties, as the UN has done in the case of the Organisation for the Prohibition of Chemical Weapons, or the Ottawa Coalition on Landmines, or, indeed, the International Criminal Court—if we can extend that into the social sector by which governments are responsible not only to their citizens for what they are doing for their benefit but are accountable to a larger international system as well, then you will genuinely be able to reconcile the sovereignty of states with the imperatives of globalization.

This is clearly not impossible. In the last year in Brazil, the evolution of the system of citizens participating in civic budget-making has led to a re-appropriation of resources to the extent of 98 percent increase for water services and 85 percent increase for sanitation services, which was not possible when the budgets were being drawn up by government planners alone. In Uganda as a result of Jubilee 2000 and the debt relief measure that followed, there is a national Uganda debt network; in each school there is a blackboard demonstrating how the eradication of national debt has translated into specific funds for specific projects in that community and in that school.

This is where our energies should be focused. Without it we will have a UN, as it has been compelled to be in the last half century—a source of international peace and security without realizing what exactly constitutes that peace. The lowest common denominator is the individual, and we must make sure that whatever the UN does or whatever member states are responsible to the UN for, is something that will affect that individual not only in times of peril or crises but also in his day-to-day life.

GWYN PRINS We are living at a time where we see the transfer of primary political responsibility from the states—the nation-states, this curious and special creation of the last 230 years—to individuals. This is occurring in the rather special and complex risk environment of the modern world.

For the rich world, this transfer is occurring in what the director of the London School of Economics, Tony Giddens, calls, rather helpfully, the transformation of intimacy. You may know of an advertisement for watches often seen in fashion magazines: A rather elegant, impossible looking lady says, "Who will I be today?" Living in this society, we can wake up in the morning and decide who we're going to be. Why? Because we are hugely empowered as individuals. Compared with previous generations, it is quite astonishing. And we now take it all for granted.

We have all made telephone calls and sent e-mails without thinking twice about it. And this gives us in our society, as individuals, a heightened sense of ourselves and of our self-importance. But there is a paradox here, because that heightened awareness has coupled with it a profound anomie, a profound sense of alienation. The evidence for this is all around us in all mature democracies where we have seen for the past twenty years a consistent pattern of withdrawal from formal politics. The present British government—just to take my own country as the example—was elected on the smallest number of votes that have been cast from the total potential electorate since the Khaki election of 1918, and this is a pattern that you find across all of the mature democracies. Portmanteau political parties are being replaced by politics of a different sort, consumer politics—people who vote through the way that they spend their money in the supermarket. It is arguably quite sensible as a strategy.

In our world we see another absolutely decisive characteristic: a rising age and a declining birth rate. Young women living in this society wrestle a tension resulting from the fact that their bodies tell them that the age at which they should have children is far earlier than the age at which their careers and their other obligations tell them that they want to do it. We have seen a rise in the average age of first birth to the late twenties to early thirties, and this is coupled with a spectacular decline in the birth rate. Also, we see an epidemic of stress and depression. Look only at prescription rates for Prozac and other sorts of antidepressants to know that this is the case.

But most people, of course, don't live like this. Two-thirds of the human family has never made a telephone call, and two-thirds live in conditions where there is a structural disempowerment of individuals. That is because they are living in a world where we see the increasingly quick collapse of the postcolonial state settlement that was put in place at the end of the last round of formal empires in the middle of the twentieth century. Those people live, therefore, in one way rather ahead of those of us in the rich world because they do not withdraw from formal politics) They have never entered them. If you look at the pattern of electoral behavior in most postcolonial societies, it is absolutely consistent. You get a sudden introduction of people voting, usually in the pre-independence election and maybe the one after, and then the participation disappears. Why? Because most parts of the world run on patronage politics, and they always have done. In a sense they are proof therefore against this change.

We also see in the poor world a rising birth rate because when you are denied the benefits of public goods, that is, all things like running water and refrigerators and insurance policies and things that we take for granted, and if you are poor, what do you have to substitute for all of those functions? The answer is only one thing: children. You have to have children to haul water, to do the cooking, to look after you in your old age because you don't buy an insurance policy.

Therefore we have seen the rising birth rate in much of the poor world, which is now being tempered very visibly by the epidemic of two things, of genocide, on one hand, which is the pathological killing of their own people by governments, and of pandemic disease, on the other. People who are poor, particularly women, are put in conditions where they at risk of pandemic disease of which the AIDS/HIV epidemic is one example. We are now in the middle of the African epidemic that is going to be followed by a much bigger Indian one, and that will then be followed by a Chinese one of a rather different nature.

In this deeply riven world, we face three structural dilemmas. First, we no longer have a common matrix of institutions that lies equally across the whole of the human family. The 1945 settlement out of which the UN principle of sovereign equality came is now shattered, and not all sovereign states are equal. But, and here's the structural dilemma, at the same time that we see this happening, we see an increasingly firm matrix of universal principle arising: Robert Kagan recently and famously enraged Europeans by informing us that Americans came from Mars and we came from Venus. We Europeans lived in a sort of Kantian world where history had stopped, but the poor old Americans live in a Hobbesian world and still deal with all the nasty things that happen. The Europeans, although they did not seem very grateful for this, were only able to play their splendid Kantian games because the Americans kept the world that way for them. And the Europeans were furious, not least, of course, because it's clearly quite correct. We do live in that sort of a world.

I prefer, in fact, a different way of formulating this breaking of the common matrix, and that has been put by one of our most senior diplomats, Robert Cooper in the Foreign Office, who observes that we live in a world with modern, premodern, and postmodern states. Europeans on the continent of Europe, some of them, live in postmodern societies where sovereignty of the state seems less important. Much of the poor world lives in premodern conditions and, importantly, two large countries are modern where the notion that security and state sovereignty are tightly tied together with the identity of the individual. And those are, respectively, China and the United States. The United States is preeminently a modern society because *e pluribus unum*. What holds people together? It's the flag, it's the sense that everybody is different but everybody is an American.

Another feature is the rise of human rights. This is the new principle that is being laid across the human family. It is expressed in the ICISS "just cause principle," which is becoming, therefore, a basis of customary international law. And it has three implications. First, we are now in a world where universal human rights mean exactly that. The lowest common denominator of rights attaches itself to each individual. Much of the modern debate, the twenty-first-century debate, has a familiar ring because it is the unfinished conversation that was being held by philosophers of the late eighteenth century. The discussion was prematurely terminated when the French Revolution insured that individual identity would be fused into that of the state.

We also see the rising significance of obligation-driven actions. That is because much of the human family have no rights that they can enforce upon us, the rich and powerful. If we take action to look after those who are at risk, particularly if they are at risk from genocidal and brutal tyrants like Saddam Hussein, then the only way they can call upon us is by speaking to our sense of obligation and duty. It is a very old-fashioned, Kantian thing.

This leads me to the next structural dilemma: As far as sovereignty is concerned, in a modern world we can see that the Peter Principle is at work. To those who have, more will be given; and from those who have not, some will be taken away. This is merely the return of the world to business as usual in the conduct of international affairs. If you take a thousand-year perspective, we are now entering again an imperial era. The United States is the most important imperial power since Augustan Rome in the second century A.D.. We see the implications of this in front of our eyes this week, if you're watching the newspapers [February 2003]. We see power draining simultaneously from all three of the major mid twentieth-century multilateral institutional creations. NATO is, of course, already dead. It was accidentally assassinated after September 11. The European Union, although it is not noticed very publicly yet, is also in its last days (the present conduct of French policy is, in my view, quite likely to lead to the withdrawal of many countries, including my own, from what used to be a consensual view about the European future). And the UN now is clearly at the Abyssinian moment. As Mr. Bush quite accurately and eloquently put it, the choice is between being a continuing relevant body, which will actually fulfill what it said it wanted Saddam to do in Resolution 1441, or not. And if not, then we will know that the UN will be like the League of Nations, and it will go the same way. But that does not have to be its future. The UN can steer a useful course into the new future. In thinking about what the UN actually stands for, I would suggest that rather than looking at

Article 2 you look for where the spirit of the UN is expressed, which is not in any of the clauses but in the preface. In the preface there is a very useful sentence where you see that the hierarchy that puts men and women before states is explicitly expressed.

As for the ways forward, they are increasingly clear. After Saddam has been removed from Iraq, there will be a need for the UN to play a role through a reawakening of sleeping chapters and clauses in the charter, notably Chapter 12 and Article 84, which are the ones that deal with trusteeship. We are now, as I said, back in an imperial age, and the international community will have an important role to play after the period of the U.S. government and military occupation in creating (recreating) a circumstance for civil society in that country. That will have important implications for the continuing cancer in international affairs—the Israel/Palestine conflict, which will depend upon the UN imposing a partition. That will happen only if the Palestinians can see that the successful operation of trusteeship in Iraq can be applied to them in the short term, which I think is not impossible.

Another implication that you should note is one that is uncomfortable for the International Committee of the Red Cross (ICRC) and other multilateral non-governmental institutions, for in this new world what used to be called humanitarian space is being remorselessly squeezed to the point of extinction. The ICRC knows this very well.

Which brings us to the final structural dilemma, which is actually rather an amusing one. As we sit here in the New World, we have to be aware that the New World is much older than the Old World. What I mean by that is that the United States, which always thinks of itself as a new country is actually a rather old country—old in the sense that matters for this discussion. This is the only country in the world of any significance that is operating a pre-French Revolutionary constitution. What we see is the indispensability of the United States as the prime actor and shaper of this imperial era into which we move. The only game in town, ladies and gentlemen. We have a great advantage here because as you well know, when you go down to the reflecting pool, when you go into the Jefferson Memorial and you look at those great bronze panels, what is the word that you do not find? That word, of course, is "America" or "Americans" because this was a country that was not set up for Americans; it was set up for the principles and rights of man, meaning everyone. This is extremely helpful, You have a country whose self-defining image and whose founding myths are in congruence with the requirements of this loosely structured new twenty-first century into which we are going. We collectively in this world are very fortunate that the imperial hegemon happens to have those values within itself.

Of course, they are not the only forces in this society. Heaven knows there are many negative forces in contention. But the name of the game, if we are going to ensure that the sovereignty of the individual is going to be protected around the world, something that I strongly hope, is going to depend on the degree to which we can speak to and activate that sense of itself, which this reluctant new imperial hegemon has so centrally in its own self-image.

NOTE

1. *The Responsibility to Protect,* Report of the International Commission on Intervention and State Sovereignty, IDRC 2001, http://www.idrc.ca/en/ev-9436-201-1-DO_topic.html.

X / The United Nations and War in the Twentieth and Twenty-first Centuries

ROBERT WEINER

The United Nations was created in 1945 to prevent another world war. It was designed, as the preamble to the UN Charter states, to eliminate the scourge of war that had befallen humanity twice in the first half of the twentieth century. The United Nations, as the successor to the failed experiment of the League of Nations, embodied Wilsonian idealism. It represented the liberal internationalist approach to world politics, which offered an alternative model to realism,[1] dealing with the central problem of international relations—the avoidance of world war. From a realist perspective, there were elements in the British government that saw the League as a means of bringing the United States into the security structure of Europe.[2] France was also interested in using the League as an instrument to resolve its security dilemma vis-à-vis a revenge-seeking Germany in the future. Unfortunately and tragically for Woodrow Wilson, the United States never joined the League of Nations because of the resurgence of isolationist sentiment after the Great War.[3]

The United Nations was based on the neo-liberal assumption that international institutions can make a difference in preventing and resolving wars in the international system.[4] The centerpiece of the war-prevention and conflict-resolution system of the United Nations was the philosophy of collective security, which was supposed to offer an alternative method of maintaining international order, in comparison with the amoral, Machiavellian, balance-of-power politics that had led to the collapse of the international system twice in the twentieth century and had brought untold suffering to humanity.[5] More important, the United Nations was supposed to represent the best impulses of world civilization, in the sense that it would prevent another Holocaust and genocidal slaughter of the innocents, plunging humanity into the dark ages once again.

Collective Security

To accomplish this objective, the central principle on which the United Nations was based, as had been the League of Nations before it, was that of collective security, to represent the will of the international community to deter and punish acts of aggression committed in interstate conflict. "Evil doers" who committed acts of aggression would be faced with the overwhelming might and righteous wrath of the international community.[6] It is very important to point out, in connection with this, that the United Nations was not originally designed to deal with internal or intrastate wars, which have emerged as the major form of conflict since the end of the Cold War, but rather was designed to deal with interstate conflicts.[7] Indeed, Article 2, Section 7 of the UN Charter prohibits the United Nations from intervening in matters that fall within the domestic jurisdiction of a state, unless there is a Chapter VII enforcement action under way there.[8] But this article may need to be rewritten and adapted to a new concept of sovereignty that has emerged in connection with the recent trend toward humanitarian intervention (two recent cases are Kosovo and East Timor in 1999), which has been driven by the neo-liberal philosophy that the international community has a responsibility to protect human rights that takes precedence over the traditional Westphalian notion of state sovereignty, which is based on the idea that a government can do whatever it wants to on its own territory.[9] On one hand, as Michael Walzer writes, "humanitarian intervention is a response to acts that shock the moral conscience of mankind."[10] On the other hand, an obstacle to humanitarian intervention stems from the developing nations that object to international intervention in matters that are perceived as falling within the domestic jurisdiction of a state.[11]

The idea of collective security is based on a number of assumptions, the basic features of which could be attributable to Wilsonian idealism and its precursors. Collective security is supposed to represent the organized will and power of the international community, which in a Manichean sense, from a moral point of view, would personify the forces of good. Those forces would oppose any real or potential aggression, which was depicted as synonymous with the forces of evil. The use of force by the international community in this fashion was collectively legitimized, even though a hegemonic power like the United States could turn a collectively legitimized action to its own national interest, as in the case of the UN "police action" in Korea in 1950[12] or the "coalition of the willing" led by the United States in the Gulf war in 1990–91. The organized power of that nebulous entity known as the "international community," according to the philosophy of collective security, would be superior to that, it was assumed, of any real or potential aggressor(s). Furthermore, it was assumed that the international community would have no difficulty in marshalling an overwhelming amount of force to deter or compel an aggressor to comply with the norms of international law. Even collective security, as idealistic as it was, was in the final analysis rooted in the process of making calculations about the application of the mechanics of power in international politics.

Supposedly, the power of the international community would be sufficient to deter a potential aggressor from making a miscalculation[13] in engaging in risk-taking behavior that could unleash the dogs of war. It was erroneously assumed that through rational calculation, a potential aggressor would add up the costs and benefits of starting a war and would be deterred by the prospect of having to face the overwhelming force of the mobilized international community. But as numerous studies by political scientists have shown, wars often start because the aggressors either underestimate or overestimate the intentions and capabilities of their opponents.[14] In addition, it is more often that a divided and weak international community, rather than deterring aggression, encourages it because it lacks the resolve and will to deal decisively with aggression, as the reaction of the international community to the wars of the Yugoslavian succession from 1991 onward have amply demonstrated. In 1991, the United States did not believe at first that its vital interests were involved in Yugoslavia, and as a distant, offshore balancer, left it up to the Europeans to deal with the disintegration of that state.[15] Yet the United States was ready to lead a UN-sanctioned "coalition of the willing" against Iraq in 1991, because its policy makers responsible for defining national interest believed that the country's vital interests were at stake.

In keeping with the theory of neo-liberal institutionalism, it was also assumed that collective security must operate within the framework of international institutions, such as the League of Nations or the United Nations, in order for it to be implemented effectively. International institutions were to constrain the behavior of potential international law–breakers through the application of a series of sanctions (found in Article 16 of the League of Nations and Article 41, Chapter VII, of the UN Charter) ranging from diplomatic actions to economic steps, to the ultimate sanction of the use of force by the international community.[16] Ideally, from the neo-liberal institutionalist perspective, states, by participating in international institutions, would learn to cooperate with one another and resolve their disputes through peaceful means and thereby prevent the outbreak of wars in the first place. Neo-liberal institutionalists believe that there is a direct connection between the domestic source of the foreign policy behavior of a state and the prevention of the outbreak of war.[17] There was faith in the age-old idea of Immanuel Kant expressed in 1795, that if "constitutional republics" would become the prevalent form of government, then international institutions consisting of such states would guarantee "Perpetual Peace," contrary to Helmuth von Moltke's notion that "Perpetual Peace is a dream . . . and war is an integral part of God's ordering of the universe."[18] As the world experienced various waves of democratization, beginning in the eighteenth century, this notion was also echoed in Wilson's idea of justifying American participation in the First World War, that is, to make the world "safe for democracy," and in the post–Cold War Grand Strategy of the United States, of expanding the zone of democracy, and therefore the zone of peace.[19] This is based on the assumption that liberal democracies are less war-prone and have less of a tendency to go to war against each other, although generally speaking, liberal democracies are no less war-prone than nondemocracies. The democratic peace theorist argues that it is the internal makeup of a state that matters and therefore challenges the realist paradigm of world politics.[20] According to the democratic peace theorist, liberal democracies have less of a tendency to go to war against other liberal democracies because they are constrained from doing so by institutional or structural factors, such as check-and-balance systems and a political division of power in the government. There is also a sharing of cultural factors such as the commonality of democratic values, which inhibit liberal democracies from waging war against each other.[21] Exceptions to the rule that democracies do not wage war against other democracies, such as Athens versus Sparta, the War of 1812, the U.S. Civil War, and the Spanish-American War of 1898, is explained by the fact that one of the states in each of these conflicts was not a genuine liberal democracy. Critics of democratic peace theory argue that it does not explain a number of "near misses," such as the U.S.–British dispute over the borders between Venezuela and British Guyana in 1895. In that instance, it is argued, the United States and Britain drew back from war not because they were liberal democracies but because of realist power calculations.[22] Given the popularity of democratic peace theory after the end of the Cold War, though, it has been the Western liberal model of democracy that has served as the paradigm for the UN's postconflict peace-building strategy that has formed such an essential component of its comprehensive approach to multidimensional peacekeeping.

Since the ultimate sanction of collective security is force, international institutions needed to set up some kind of arrangement in which military force could be brought to bear against a recalcitrant lawbreaker, as a last resort, if necessary.

Consequently, the United Nations was created in San Francisco in 1945 by the international community, identified as the victorious wartime allies (the term United Nations itself was coined in 1942 to refer to the allied wartime coalition formed to defeat the Axis powers), with the purpose of having yet another try at devising a world organization that would maintain stability through collective security in the international system.[23] President Franklin Roosevelt hoped that the wartime Grand Alliance between the Soviet Union and the United States would continue to function in the postwar world. The "Big Two" would operate as the policemen of the world, according to the Rooseveltian scheme of postwar international order. The type of international military force provided to the UN to accomplish this task was based on the model that had successfully led the Allied wartime coalition to victory in World War II. A permanent military force was supposed to be created as the enforcement arm of the Security Council, drawn from its five permanent members, that would supply national contingents on the basis of agreements that would be negotiated according to Article 43 of the UN Charter. The Military Staff Committee, a subordinate unit of the Security Council that consisted of the military representatives of the five permanent members of the council, was entrusted with the responsibility for drawing up the blueprint for the permanent army. But by 1947, it was clear that the outbreak of the Cold War had made this impossible. Therefore not only did the United Nations lack the permanent international military force that the founders had envisioned in the agreements but the agreements themselves were never negotiated.[24]

Unfortunately, the whole principle of collective security itself was actually embedded in a realist conception of international order, which rested on the idea that the fundamental principle of international relations was that of state sovereignty, with the state functioning as the primary unit of the international system.[25] This principle was reflected in the structure and distribution of power in the Security Council of the United Nations, with each one of its five permanent members being allocated a special voting right known as the veto, which allowed it to protect its national interest, virtually guaranteeing that the United Nations would not function as an effective instrument of collective security.

The failure to agree on the structure and the composition of a robust permanent international military force meant that over the next half century the United Nations had to improvise in dealing with wars.[26] The very term *peacekeeping* is not even mentioned anywhere in the charter, and during the next five and a half decades the United Nations engaged in over fifty peacekeeping (Chapter VI) and enforcement (Chapter VII) operations, which encompassed a wide variety of different forms.

Peacekeeping and Enforcement Operations

Peacekeeping or Chapter VI-operations usually deal with a conflict situation in which the consent of the host state or states where the force is to be deployed has been secured.[27] More often than not, these consent-type forces were mandated under Chapter VI, which deals with peacemaking, within the framework of third-party mediation of a conflict, rather than Chapter VII, which deals with enforcement action, which does not require the consent of the parties to a conflict. There has been a significant upsurge of enforcement operations since the end of the Cold War.[28] Chapter VII mandates an enforcement operation to go into an area without the consent of the government or parties to the conflict, before a cease-fire or an armistice has been achieved. The enforcement-type operation therefore is far riskier than the traditional consent-type of operation that was the prevalent model of peacekeeping during the Cold War. The consent-type of operation usually went into an area after a cease-fire or armistice agreement had already been negotiated, to function as a kind of buffer force to keep the belligerents apart.[29] In contrast, in the post–Cold War age of increased "ethno-political conflict," placing lightly armed blue helmets into the middle of a vicious civil war and with rules of engagement that allow them to use their weapons only for self-defense (as in the former Yugoslavia) has resulted in situations in which peacekeepers have been attacked with impunity, killed, or taken hostage and stripped of their weapons.[30] States, especially industrialized democratic states, have become increasingly reluctant to expose their troops to this kind of treatment, as "donor fatigue" has set in.[31]

The Evolution of UN Peacekeeping

UN peacekeeping has undergone a process of evolution from more simple buffer-type forces imposed between belligerents to uphold a cease-fire to more complex multidimensional types of operation that may include the peace building of failed states. Although it should be stressed that a traditional Cold War peacekeeping force like ONUC, the United Nations Operations in the Congo (1960–64), was in many ways a precursor for current operations that find themselves embroiled in a civil conflict in the post–Cold War world.[32]

The evolution of UN peacekeeping can be divided into four generations: the first generation consisted of the classical or traditional Cold War peacekeeping operation; the second, of transitional operations that were devised as the Cold War was winding down; and the third phase of peacekeeping consisted of complex multidimensional post–Cold War operations that mostly involved humanitarian intervention in civil conflicts, such as the former Yugoslavia, Somalia, and Rwanda.[33] The latest and fourth generation consists of UN-sanctioned multinational forces designed to engage in robust military action under the command of one or more "lead" states, to be followed by a UN peacekeeping stabilization force when it is possible to secure collective legitimation from the Security Council to do so. Further, the evolution of generations of UN peacekeeping does not necessarily proceed in a unilinear fashion, but more traditional forms of peacekeeping can coexist with newer forms.

In the late 1980s and early 1990s, there was an explosion of UN peacekeeping activities that unrealistically raised expectations that the United Nations, having broken free of the Cold War, would now be able to function in the manner that its founding fathers had intended, as a significant actor in the international system, since it would no longer be marginalized by American-Soviet Cold War competition.[34] This false hope may have been fed by the success of the United States in leading a UN-sanctioned "coalition of the willing" to deal with the Iraqi invasion of Kuwait in 1990–91 (somewhat similar to what had occurred in Korea in 1950–53), and American triumphalism that a new world order was in the making.

The Clinton administration also initially advocated a policy of "assertive multilateralism," that is, strong support of international institutions like the UN, as a central tenet of its foreign policy. The support of the U.S. "hyper-power" was considered critical to the success of the UN, even though the United States has tended at times to function as a hegemonic power in its relationship with the world organization, that is, use it for purposes to advance its own national interest, rather than the interests of the international community. But the hopes that the United Nations would be able to function as an effective actor on the world stage in the realm of peacekeeping suffered major setbacks in the former Yugoslavia (1991–95) and in Rwanda in 1994, especially as the world organization failed to prevent genocide and ethnic cleansing from taking place. With very limited resources and military advisers, the UN Secretariat was placed virtually in the impossible situation, often in the early 1990s, of having to put UN peacekeeping forces together in an ad hoc and improvised fashion. This usually had to be done in a very short time, often driven by the desire of the permanent members of the Security Council to appear to be "doing something" in reaction to outraged international public opinion to genocide and ethnic cleansing.

Rwanda and Srebrenica

In a discussion of the evolution of UN peacekeeping, two cases stand out among the more than fifty since 1945 and therefore require special attention: the genocide that occurred in Rwanda in 1994, and the massacre of about eight thousand Bosnian Moslems in Srebrenica, Bosnia, in 1995.[35] These horrific events occurred when the current Secretary-General, Kofi Annan, was the Under-Secretary-General for UN Peacekeeping. They were both turning points in the post–Cold War history of UN peacekeeping.

One of the greatest peacekeeping failures of the United Nations in the twentieth century was its inability to prevent genocide from taking place in Rwanda. The UN is still wrestling with the legacy of the enormity of this evil, which put to the test the very meaning of the existence of the organization as a factor of justice in world civilization. As former Secretary-General Boutros Boutros-Ghali wrote, "the genocide in Rwanda in 1994 was one of the greatest tragedies since the Second World War."[36] As the Independent Commission of Inquiry that was set up by Secretary-General Kofi Annan in 1999 to investigate the genocide in Rwanda stressed, "the international community did not prevent the genocide, nor did it stop the killing once the genocide had begun."[37] In a short period of one hundred days in 1994, about eight hundred thousand members of an ethnic community known as the Tutsi were slaughtered (along with Hutu moderates) by Hutu extremists.[38]

In terms of the historical background to the civil conflict that took place in Rwanda, it should be pointed out that the Tutsi, long favored by the colonial powers (Germany and Belgium) that had ruled Rwanda, were subsequently overthrown by the majority Hutus in 1959, as periodic bloodbaths marked the relations between the two ethnic groups. The descendents of the Tutsi who had been forced into exile launched an invasion of Rwanda in 1991, and in 1993 the UN became involved in arranging a cease-fire there. It is necessary to point out that the conflict in Rwanda was also caused by the poor state of the political economy of the country, since Rwanda, primarily an agricultural country, was one of the most overcrowded countries on the Continent.[39]

The UN Security Council had authorized a UN peacekeeping force for Rwanda, known as UNAMIR (the United Nations Assistance Mission in Rwanda) in 1993, to oversee a peace agreement (the Arusha Accords) that had been negotiated between the two warring ethnic groups there. UNAMIR was entrusted with the mission to set up a secure zone in the Rwandan capital city of Kigali.

The entire UN operation in Rwanda, however, suffered from a distinct lack of political will (perhaps with the exception of the French, who wanted to maintain a Francophone sphere of influence in Africa) among the permanent members of the Security Council.[40] This was especially true of the United States since the debacle in Somalia, when eighteen U.S. soldiers were killed in Mogadishu in October 1993.[41] Even though the soldiers were operating under U.S. and not UN command, the United States retreated from its policy of "assertive multilateralism."[42] Public opinion and Congress turned against U.S. participation in UN peacekeeping, except under extraordinary conditions, especially when the national interest of the country was involved. This, combined with the reluctance of the Pentagon to place U.S. troops under foreign command, resulted in a sharp reversal of the Clinton administration's policy. A new Presidential Decision Directive (PDD 25) was issued right in the middle of the Rwandan crisis, which sharply constrained the ability of the United States to participate in future peacekeeping operations.[43] Consequently, we also see a shift in the U.S. position in which Washington evidences a preference for high-risk military operations to be undertaken within the framework of regional military alliances such as NATO, rather than by multilateral institutions such as the UN, thereby for example, setting the stage for the U.S. option to engage NATO rather than the UN in Kosovo in 1999.

This translated into a reluctance to provide UNAMIR with the financial resources and equipment that it needed. General Romeo Dallaire, the Canadian general who was placed in command of UNAMIR, argued that a military force of about forty-five hundred was necessary to properly carry out UNAMIR's mission, while the United States proposed the deployment of a UN force of about one hundred. The permanent members of the Security Council, in a clear-cut case that cried out for the need for humanitarian intervention, were even reluctant to use the term genocide, which would acknowledge the planned, systematic extermination of the Tutsi minority.[44] Indeed, there was even a forewarning that extremist advocates of Hutu power in the inner circle of the president of Rwanda were deliberately planning the extermination of the Tutsis. This was based on information that was received as early as January 1994 by General Dallaire from a highly placed informant in the Rwandan government.[45] Dallaire believed that if

UNAMIR had numbered about five thousand, it would have been possible to prevent the genocide.[46]

The Security Council did not provide UNAMIR with the resources that it needed to accomplish its mission and consequently UNAMIR was unable to protect the civilians and the refugees (as was the case with UNPROFOR—the United Nations Protection Force—a year later in Srebrenica) that sought refuge with it.[47] Furthermore, the original mandate of UNAMIR also limited its ability to protect people because it was a traditional peacekeeping force created within the terms of Chapter VI, and therefore it could not use force except in conditions of self-defense. Additionally, the mandate of UNAMIR was not adjusted to take into account the rapidly changing circumstances in Rwanda. As it became apparent (on April 21, 1994) that mass killings were occurring, the Security Council reduced UNAMIR down to a force of only 270 with a mandate to mediate an end to the dispute.[48] Moreover, in 1993, the attention of the Security Council was also diverted by the fact that it was overseeing two other major operations in Bosnia and Somalia, where the bulk of UN forces were committed.[49] Because of its setback in Somalia, the United States was not willing to become involved in a much more horrendous war in Rwanda. Therefore, Secretary-General Boutros-Ghali believed that the United States shared a considerable amount of the responsibility for the genocide in Rwanda. Given Boutros-Ghali's complaint that the Security Council was paying too much attention to Europe and not enough to Africa, it is not surprising that the United States prevented him from being elected to a second term as Secretary-General.[50] By the time it was clear that genocide was being committed, the Security Council finally replaced UNAMIR with UNAMIR II, a larger force of about fifty-five hundred, which also was a traditional Chapter VI force but it never was fully deployed. Later, the Security Council also authorized the French to launch "Operation Turquoise" with a Chapter 7 mandate that, although designed to serve French interests and influence in the region, nonetheless did save lives.[51]

In conclusion, the lessons learned from one of the darkest moments in the history of the twentieth century, apart from the obvious lack of will on the part of the United States to commit itself to assertive multilateralism, is the necessity for the UN to possess the political analytical capabilities and an early warning system to detect and act on an impending genocide, and to strengthen its capacity for preventive diplomacy and the prevention of conflicts. But this cannot compensate or substitute for the lack of political will, or the conclusion by a great power that it is not in its national interest to act even in the face of genocide. The Independent Commission of Inquiry created by Secretary-General Kofi Annan concluded that genocide prevention should comprise an essential component of any UN peacekeeping operation (where relevant), and the International Tribunal for Rwanda, with a lot of difficulty, has proceeded to convict individuals for committing genocide there. Thousands of individuals in Rwanda have also been arrested and placed on trial as well, although there is also much to criticize in the application of this model of transitional justice.

One of the most devastating setbacks in the entire history of UN peacekeeping occurred in July 1995, in the former Yugoslavia, with the fall of the city of Srebrenica, Bosnia, to Serbian forces.[52] In one of the greatest horrors of "ethnic cleansing" (designated as genocide by the International Tribunal for the Former Yugoslavia) that occurred during the wars of the Yugoslavian succession, approximately eight thousand Bosnian men and boys were executed in a brutal fashion, described as "truly scenes from hell, written on the darkest pages of human history."[53] This occurred while a Dutch contingent of UNPROFOR was on the scene. Srebrenica, along with several other Bosnian cities and towns had been designated as a safe area by the UN in 1993, based on the model of the safe area created in northern Iraq to protect the Kurds from the Iraqi government following the Gulf War. The concept of "safe-area" was not clearly defined and could be viewed as an ill-conceived response by the Security Council to international public opinion to "do something." The application of the concept of the "safe area" in Bosnia was an unmitigated disaster, because the members of the UN did not have the political will to provide UNPROFOR with the resources that it needed to adequately protect the civilians who sought refuge in the "safe areas." Bosnian Serb forces directly attacked this "safe area" of Srebrenica, as well as the Dutch troops there, with impunity, taking some of them hostages as well. An independent inquiry by the United Nations did not spare the UN itself from sharp criticism for that disaster, one of the major factors that contributed to the withdrawal of UNPROFOR from the former Yugoslavia and its replacement by a robust NATO military force in 1995, as part of the Dayton Peace Accords.

One reason for the failure of the UN to protect the Bosnians, it is argued, is that supposedly the UN never imagined that the Serbs would behave with such barbarism (although atrocities were committed by all sides in the conflict) and cruelty, exhibiting a brutality that Europe had not seen since the Second World War.[54] Probably one of the most telling criticisms of the inability of the UN to protect the Bosnians was the UN's failure to effectively use NATO airpower to stop the advancing Serb troops, as they moved in on Srebrenica.[55] As UN peacekeeping operations became more complex, the coordination of military with civilian decision-making became more difficult. The Special Representative of the Secretary-General also had to deal with the UN bureaucracy in New York in making a decision to use airpower. Furthermore, Boutros-Ghali, Secretary-General at the time, also writes in his memoirs that the Dutch minister of defense vetoed the use of NATO air power because of the fear that the Dutch troops who had been taken hostage by the Serbs would be injured.[56] In addition, there was a fear that if robust air power were used, it would jeopardize the chances of reaching a peaceful settlement to the conflict. Boutros-Ghali also blames the Americans for encouraging the Bosnians to turn down the Vance-Owen Pact, which called for the division of Bosnia into a number of cantons.[57] This move provided the Bosnian Serbs with an incentive[58] to attack the "safe areas" that had been designated in Bosnia by the UN Security Council in 1993 (which were poorly conceived and ill-defined concepts in the first place) to gain more territory.[59] Furthermore, as the UN's own investigation pointed out, another reason for the failure in Srebrenica was the institutional ideology of the UN, which stressed the avoidance of becoming involved in a militaristic "culture of death," since the UN traditionally was supposed to function as an impartial force that was not to engage in war making.[60] According to Boutros-Ghali, "the UN forces in the 'safe areas' were there as peacekeepers, and they had neither the authority nor the means to do battle with the parties to the conflict."[61] The rules of engagement and mandate of the UN forces on the scene needed to be changed to allow them to engage in robust military action, but neither the will nor the resources of Dutchbat, which consisted of about three hundred combat soldiers at the time, was sufficient.[62] The Dutch forces were not sufficient to deter the one to two thousand heavily armed Serbs who advanced on Srebrenica, or to prevent the slaughter that took place. But in August 2001, the International Tribunal for the former Yugoslavia at The Hague convicted Bosnian Serbian General Radislav Krstic of genocide in Srebrenica and sentenced him to over forty years in prison. This was the first conviction for the acts of genocide that were committed at Srebrenica. Former Yugoslavian President Slobodan Milosevic, who was ousted by the Serbs in a revolution in October 2000, was also delivered to The Hague and placed on trial for the crimes committed in Srebrenica, among other charges.

Resurgence of UN Peacekeeping

During the 1990s, after the failures in Rwanda and the former Yugoslavia, the number of blue helmets in the field was reduced from over seventy thousand to fourteen thousand. But the new millennium brought a sudden surge in demand for UN peacekeeping, and a willingness by Secretary-General Kofi Annan to meet these challenges. The Secretary-General's surprising expansion of UN peacekeeping efforts reversed the previous trend in downsizing. In the last few years of the twentieth century, the UN faced a surge in traditional and postconflict peacekeeping demands in places like Kosovo, East Timor, Sierra Leone, the Democratic Republic of the Congo, Ethiopia and Eritrea, Southern Lebanon, and Palestine (where the Palestinians unsuccessfully requested that the UN send an international observer force into the occupied territories).[63]

Following NATO intervention in Kosovo, the Security Council adopted Resolution 1244, which authorized the creation of UNIKOM (the United Nations

Interim Administration Mission in Kosovo), and the UN, supported by NATO forces, stepped in to administer the province as a sort of international protectorate and to prepare it for "substantial autonomy."[64] NATO supposedly intervened in Kosovo in 1999 to engage in a humanitarian mission designed to rescue the Albanian minority that was being subjected to horrific ethnic cleansing by Serbian forces.[65] As the conflict unfolded, there initially were unsubstantiated estimates that as many as one hundred thousand Albanians had been killed, but a more realistic figure was between five thousand and ten thousand.[66] Kosovo raised the question of when a humanitarian intervention should take precedence over the traditional notion of sovereignty, and whether a regional military alliance like NATO had an obligation to act when the Security Council could not because it was divided. UNIKOM was given the task of rebuilding civil society, supervising the return of refugees, disarming the Albanian National Liberation Army and incorporating them into a civilian police force, and overseeing elections along with the OSCE (the Organization for Security and Cooperation in Europe) and EU (European Union), backed by the KFOR forces of NATO. But now, seven years later, UNIKOM's peace-building efforts in Kosovo, buttressed by an International Civilian Police force, have been far from successful, as the Albanians there have engaged in their own version of ethnic cleansing of the Serbian minority, and extremist Albanian forces reportedly used Kosovo as a base of operations to launch an attack on the neighboring government of the Former Yugoslav Republic of Macedonia in 2001. A European Union force was dispatched to Macedonia in 2003 to help maintain the Ohrid peace agreement that had brought an end to the conflict.

These new challenges at the end of the millennium called for forms of humanitarian intervention as well as the expansion of or deployment of peacekeeping and peace-enforcement forces of a more traditional nature.[67] Humanitarian intervention is based on the Annan doctrine of the "two sovereignties," in which the UN Secretary-General argues that the sovereignty of the individual should take precedence over the sovereignty of the state.[68] This doctrine is based on the need for the international community to intervene within a state to protect the human rights of minorities from gross and massive violations committed against them by their own government.

Besides the more complex and multidimensional humanitarian intervention, the UN also found itself involved in more traditional peacekeeping operations. For example, the UN was called on to put together a force of about four thousand observers to oversee an armistice and maintain a temporary security zone that had been established between Ethiopia and Eritrea, hoping to help bring an end to the conflict that had been raging there since 1998.[69] The Secretary-General also had to quickly expand UNIFIL (the United Nations Force in Lebanon) in 2000, a force that had been deployed in Southern Lebanon since 1978. It was necessary

x/250

to do this because of the precipitous Israeli withdrawal from the area in 2000, which created a power vacuum right at the Israeli-Lebanese demarcation line, the Blue Line, that had been filled by fundamentalist Islamic groups such as the Hezbollah, raising the danger of increased clashes with Israeli forces, although by 2003, UNIFIL also was downsized.

The Regionalization of UN Peacekeeping

One approach that has developed to compensate for the ineffective peacekeeping record of the UN, as the UN has found itself overstretched and starved of resources, is the regionalization of peacekeeping. In the 1990s, as the UN engaged in more complex, multidimensional peacekeeping operations, it found itself increasingly relying on regional and subregional organizations and arrangements to maintain peace and security and restore order in zones of turmoil by stabilizing the spate of regional conflicts (some of them protracted conflicts that had been going on for years) that had erupted at the end of the Cold War.[70] Regionalism has always been an important ingredient of the UN system.[71] According to the UN Charter, regional organizations can act in self-defense, but they must report to the Security Council, and they cannot engage in action without the authorization of the Security Council. NATO, however, which was involved in a number of peacekeeping operations in the Balkans in the 1990s as it redefined itself and underwent a transformation from a collective defense to a collective security organization, claims that legally it is not considered a regional organization but rather is a military alliance, which does not need the authorization of the Security Council to engage in humanitarian intervention.[72] Peacekeeping by regional and subregional organizations and arrangements has both advantages and disadvantages, as does reliance on "coalitions of the willing" led by regional hegemons. "Coalitions of the willing" (in place of traditional peacekeeping forces) have been led by regional/global hegemons such as the United States in Haiti, France in Rwanda (as well as in the Ivory Coast and the Democratic Republic of the Congo in 2003), Russia in the Commonwealth of Independent States, and Australia in East Timor.[73] More recently, the EU has become more active in out-of-area peacekeeping operations. An EU police force replaced the UN in Bosnia, and an EU force led by France was deployed in the eastern part of the Democratic Republic of the Congo in the summer of 2003. This EU mission, which was approved by the Security Council at the end of May 2003, officially terminated its mission on September 1, 2003. This was the first time that an EU mission had been sent outside of Europe.

"Coalitions of the willing," however, may not be a good solution to the *problematique* of effective peacekeeping, because they seem rather reminiscent of the old colonial practice of dividing the world into spheres of influence, which allow global and regional hegemons to assert their dominance of adjacent geographical areas.[74] Furthermore, a "coalition of the willing" sent to deal with a conflict in a region can take place outside the framework of an existing regional organization.

Sanctions

What some would consider to be the failure of UN peacekeeping and peace enforcement in the 1990s resulted in an increased reliance on sanctions, which can be seen as a form of coercive diplomacy and which represents a negative form of action that can be used for purposes of both deterring and compelling. For example, a conflict considered to be ended may restart, and efforts at postconflict peacekeeping may suffer a setback, making it necessary to impose or reimpose sanctions on a state or substate actor, such as the leaders of a revolutionary organization, to attempt to coerce them to comply with a cease-fire or peace agreement that they already signed.

As far as the implementation of collective security is concerned, sanctions are, according to Inis Claude Jr., "the first line of attack."[75] All members of the UN are expected to comply with sanctions, since according to Article 25 of the charter, they are obligated to carry out decisions of the Security Council. The United Nations has discovered in the post–Cold War period, however, that it further needed to refine and improve upon the application of sanctions to deal with the growing "culture of impunity" that characterized the behavior of sundry war criminals and governments who flouted the norms and the will of the international community. Sanctions constitute the heart of a collective security system of an organization like the United Nations and provide for a graduated series of measures that can be applied against international lawbreakers. Sanctions involve economic measures, including such as trade and financial restrictions as the freezing of the foreign assets of targeted elites and leaders, and the interruption of relations with the international community by air and sea (as applied against Libya and Afghanistan), as well as the imposition of travel restrictions on the targeted leaders and their families.[76] A number of developing countries, however, object even to the use of smart sanctions, because they believe that they are used to advance the hegemonic interests of states like the United States, especially against states identified by Washington as rogue states.

At first, economic sanctions were seen as a relatively humane means of trying to force an international lawmaker to comply with the will of the international community, but in reality the application of economic sanctions against a society can be quite devastating in terms of the effects it may have on innocent civilians; hence, the need for "smart sanctions." Sanctions can be rather indiscriminate in their effects, a problem that Annan refers to as the "paradox of sanctions."[77] But a tyrannical regime may deliberately manipulate the effects of sanctions to gain the sympathy of international public opinion. In the case of Iraq, for example, the

UN decided for humanitarian reasons to provide relief to Baghdad in the form of the "oil for food" program, which allowed Iraq to sell its oil abroad under conditions monitored by the UN, to buy food and medical supplies, although some of the income earned from the sale of Iraqi oil was also used to compensate claims against the Iraqi government stemming from the Gulf War.[78] But at times, Iraq withheld the sale of oil as a pressure tactic on the UN, to protest the prolongation of the sanctions regime, which had been in place for over a decade.[79] After the second Gulf War, the UN made arrangements to phase out the "oil for food" program.

The War against Terror, Afghanistan, Iraq, and UN Peacekeeping

Following 9/11, the UN had expressed its sympathy to the United States, and UN Resolution 56/1 condemned the terrorist attacks against the United States. The United Nations urged it member states to take action on the national level to deal with terrorism. The Security Council Committee on Counter-Terrorism was created to monitor the actions that members were taking to deal with terrorism.[80] Members of the United Nations were also urged to ratify the twelve existing so-called sector conventions, dealing with terrorism, that had been adopted by various UN agencies over the past four decades. They deal with such issues as the hijacking of aircraft, attacks against diplomats, the taking of hostages, acts of terrorism on the high seas, and the protection of nuclear materials, among other things. After 9/11, the UN General Assembly also considered the adoption of a comprehensive convention dealing with terrorism. But given the rather controversial nature of arriving at a mutually acceptable definition of terrorism, not every member of the international community was solidly behind the adoption of an omnibus resolution in the General Assembly. By 2005, it still remained to be adopted.

As we have seen, the inability of the UN to deal effectively with ethnic cleansing and genocide in Bosnia and Rwanda had weakened its role further as an instrument of peacekeeping in the world political system. Moreover, the UN was also marginalized when the United States functioned as a global hegemon in waging the war against terrorism, seeking, if possible, legitimation for its military operations but prepared to act unilaterally or in concert with some of its closest allies in a "coalition of the willing."

In the case of Afghanistan, a "coalition of the willing" had been sanctioned by a UN mandate in the form of Security Council Resolution 1386(2001) as Secretary-General Kofi Annan had made it clear that the United Nations did not have the resources to put a UN peacekeeping force into Afghanistan. In December 2001, mostly U.S. forces and the British, with the aid of various groups and warlords in Afghanistan, such as the Northern Alliance, had temporarily crushed the

Taliban and Al Qaeda in the war. After some equivocation about the possibility of restoring the exiled Afghan King Mohammad Zaher Shah to power, a conference was held by the international community in Bonn, Germany, on December 5, 2001. The supposed purpose of the so-called Bonn process was to create a government that could enjoy the support of the diverse ethnic and tribal groups in Afghanistan, especially one of the most important tribes known as the Pashtuns. Most important for our purposes here, the Bonn process also called for the creation of an international security force to be deployed in the Afghan capital of Kabul and the surrounding areas. Therefore, in December 2001, the Security Council voted unanimously for the creation of a multinational force (not a UN peacekeeping force) that was dubbed the International Security Assistance Force (ISAF).[81] The United States, however, opposed giving ISAF the mandate to operate outside of Kabul and its environs, because Washington did not want the force to interfere with its operations in Afghanistan. This provided a model of two separate forces operating in the country. The United Kingdom played a key role in assembling the force, which by mid August 2003 numbered about five thousand.[82] ISAF was to be commanded by a "lead" nation, or nations, that rotated every six months.[83] The force was originally led by the United Kingdom and Turkey, and then by Germany and the Netherlands. It was also considered to be of critical importance that Turkey participate in the force, to underscore the fact that the military action in Afghanistan should not be interpreted as a war against Islam, cast in the mold of Huntington's war of civilizations. It is important to point out that the ISAF was not a traditional UN force but fit into the model of a new "generation" of multinational forces, authorized by the Security Council.

In June 2003, the Under-Secretary-General for Peacekeeping argued that ISAF should be expanded throughout the country and that expanding would be easier to do under NATO command.[84] At the time, it also appeared that the central Afghan government, led by Hamid Karzai, was losing control of some of the regions of the country, for it became increasingly more dangerous for the UN Mission in Afghanistan to operate in parts of the country that had reverted to the control of Afghan warlords, some quite hostile to the United States and to the central government. The growing chaos, as Afghanistan struggled to put together a national army capable of maintaining order, further undermined efforts to hold elections, draw up a constitution, and engage in reconstruction. Moreover, the full amount of the financial aid that had been promised to Afghanistan at the Bonn conference was never forthcoming.

On August 11, 2003, ISAF was placed under the command of NATO, ostensibly to eliminate the difficulties of finding states that were willing to serve as lead states commanding the multinational force.[85] The transformation of ISAF into a NATO force provided the military alliance with a base in central Asia, close to the Caspian Sea and the Middle East.

The ability of the United Nations to function as an effective instrument of war prevention and peacekeeping was seriously tested in the spring of 2003, when the United States launched what it dubbed a preemptive (but really preventive) war against Iraq. The avowed purpose of the war was to engage in "regime change" in order to disarm Iraq of its weapons of mass destruction (WMD), which Washington claimed posed a threat to the national security of the United States. Saddam Hussein was demonized and painted as an evil tyrant who had used WMD not only against Iran during the Iraqi-Iranian war (1980–88) but also against his own people. As the United States tried to make the case before the international community, the main rationale for the war was that it was an essential part of the "war against terror." But the Bush administration was never able to provide the facts to establish that a definitive link existed between Hussein and Al Qaeda.[86] The war against terror was presented by Washington as an unconventional and asymmetrical war that was global and was aimed at destroying Al Qaeda's terrorist networks and cells around the world, which reportedly were operating in approximately sixty countries. According to Washington, the war against terror was not to be confined to Afghanistan but was extended as well to states that the administration claimed were protecting and aiding terrorists. Washington was following the new strategic doctrine of preemption that had been unveiled in the National Security Strategy of September 2002. This replaced the decades-old doctrine of deterrence and containment, which essentially was a Cold War doctrine designed to prevent a nuclear war between the United States and the Soviet Union.

Because the main rationale for the war presented by the United States was the need to disarm Iraq of its WMD, which supposedly posed a threat not only to the national security of the United States but to the maintenance of international peace and security as well,[87] an effort was also made to portray the war as a "just war."[88] A U.S. military buildup in the Gulf region in 2002 put tremendous pressure on Iraq to accept the return of a team of reconstituted UN inspectors known as UNMOVIC (the United Nations Monitoring, Verification, and Inspection Commission), led by Hans Blix as its executive chairman, to replace the inspectors who had to leave Iraq in 1998. The application of U.S. coercive diplomacy resulted in negotiations between Iraq and the UN in Vienna in which the return of the inspectors was agreed to. UNMOVIC was to deal with chemical and bacteriological weapons as well as missiles, while the IAEA would deal with Iraq's nuclear weapons program. The Bush administration placed an enormous amount of pressure on the Security Council to make an effective system of inspections work, which would ensure that Iraq was in compliance with all of the relevant resolutions that had been adopted by the Security Council since the first Gulf War. In his speech to the United Nations on September 12, 2002, President Bush, in effect, threw down the gauntlet to the Security Council, claiming that Iraq had ignored all of the previous Security Council resolutions adopted over the past twelve years.[89] This could also be seen as an effort by Washington to buy time until its military forces were ready to attack Iraq. But before launching a "preemptive" strike, Bush was prevailed upon by the Secretary of State Colin Powell to give the UN one last chance before the dogs of war were unleashed.[90]

The majority of the international community opposed a war against Iraq. Most of the members of the UN emphasized that every diplomatic opportunity should be exhausted to resolve the crisis, and that war should be considered only as a last resort. Furthermore, in the debate that took place in the Security Council on October 17, 2002, a number of delegates, especially the French, also stressed the broader ramifications of the manner in which the crisis was resolved not only for the United Nations but for the entire international system as well.[91] Clearly, the authority and the credibility of the United Nations were at stake, and there was the fear that the United Nations had failed to maintain international order just as the League of Nations had failed as an instrument of collective security in the interwar period.

The "last chance" for Iraq, took the form of the adoption of Security Council Resolution 1441 on November 8, 2002, which was the product of about two months of intensive negotiations.[92] It stated that Iraq was in "material breach" of previous Security Council resolutions and that "serious consequences" would follow if Baghdad did not cooperate fully with the enhanced and strengthened UN and IAEA inspection teams, which were expected to function in an impartial and objective manner. Resolution 1441 provided the inspectors with unimpeded access to sites such as the presidential palaces, which had previously been off limits. Inspectors also had the right to interview Iraqi experts who had been involved in the development of WMD, although they encountered a fair amount of obstruction from the Iraqi government. Furthermore, Iraq was given thirty days from the date of the adoption of the resolution to issue a declaration providing accurate information on the status of its programs of WMD. Any falsehood or misrepresentation in the declaration would be considered as a "material breach" and therefore could be followed by "serious consequences," which were not defined anywhere but everyone assumed that it meant the application of military force.

The United States, although a co-sponsor of the resolution, had been reluctant to bring the matter back to the Security Council in the first place, but the negotiations involved in the drafting of the resolution probably did allow it to buy some further time to continue its military buildup in the region. The unanimous adoption of the resolution was designed to convey to Iraq the sense of unity of the Security Council and the international community. The resolution was also based on the idea expressed by a number of delegations that all diplomatic means had to be exhausted before military force could be used. France, in particular, stressed that the resolution set up a two-step process that did not include an automatic trigger that would authorize the use of military force.[93] According to Washington, though, "material breaches" of Security Council resolutions 678 and 687 had already nullified the cease-fire that had been in place since 1991. According to the French interpretation of Resolution 1441, the first step of the resolution defined the conditions that Iraq had to meet, setting up the "rules of the game," based on full proactive Iraqi cooperation with the inspectors who would report back to the Security Council. The second step would consist of holding another Security Council meeting to consider the course of action in the face of Iraqi material breach and noncompliance, which even the French conceded would not exclude "any alternative." The Secretary-General hailed the adoption of the resolution as a decision that had strengthened the role of the Security Council and the United Nations in the international system.[94] But he also added that "this is a time of trial for Iraq, for the United Nations, and the world."[95]

In contrast to the United States and the United Kingdom, the three other permanent members of the Security Council (France, China, and Russia) were opposed to the Security Council's adopting a follow-up resolution authorizing the United States to use military force and lead a "coalition of the willing" against Iraq. At the time, the unanimous adoption of Resolution 1441 was hailed by most members of the UN as a step that showed the resolve and unity of the international community and strengthened the role and the credibility of the UN as an actor in the international system. In broader terms, it also fit in with the overall strategy of states like France, a grand strategy designed to use UN institutions such as the Security Council as part of a plan to construct a multipolar balance of states in the international system to check the power of the United States as a global hegemon.

From the U.S. point of view, however, a twelve-thousand-page declaration that was issued by Iraq on December 7, 2002, that purported to comply with the terms of Resolution 1441 was not satisfactory. Washington claimed that it was inaccurate and contained material from previous reports, as the Iraqi government continued to argue that it possessed no WMD.

At the same time, Hans Blix of UNMOVIC seemed to be at loggerheads with the Bush administration on this issue. On January 27, 2003, the Security Council met to consider the reports of Blix and Mohamed ElBaradei, the director-general of the International Atomic Energy Agency. For example, Blix stated on January 27, 2003, that the Iraqi declaration contained "a good deal of new information," which dealt with "missiles and biotechnology."[96] He also focused on some problems that needed to be resolved from the previous war, such as the disposition of anthrax and vx and other biological weapons, as well as chemical weapon shells.[97] Blix also expressed his concern about the production of missiles by Iraq that exceeded the permissible UN range of 150 kilometers[98] (although Iraq later destroyed some of them). But Blix also stressed that Iraq was cooperating with the

UNMOVIC inspectors and that the inspectors should be given more time before there was a rush to war.

Mohamed ElBaradei also flatly stated, in stark contrast to the Bush administration, in his testimony before the Security Council on January 27, 2003, that his "agency had found no evidence that Iraq had revived its nuclear weapons programme since the elimination of the programme in the 1990s."[99] Given time, the IAEA could provide "credible assurance" that Iraq was not involved in a nuclear weapons program. Furthermore, ElBaradei disagreed with the Bush administration that aluminum tubing that had been purchased by Iraq could be used to construct nuclear centrifuges.[100]

Nonetheless, on February 5, 2003, Secretary of State Colin Powell presented the U.S. case that Iraq was continuing its WMD program in defiance of the international community, and that Iraq was therefore in material breach of Resolution 1441, as well as previous UN resolutions that had been adopted on the matter.[101] A series of arguments were presented by the Bush administration about why it was thought necessary to launch a preemptive war against Iraq. Powell argued that "Saddam Hussein was determined to keep his weapons of mass destruction and make more,"[102] and that the "United States could not take the risk that these weapons would be used against the American people at some point."[103]

But in March 2003, the United States was unable to secure the adoption by the necessary majority of nine out of fifteen votes of a draft resolution (co-sponsored by Spain and the United Kingdom) authorizing military action as a follow-up to Resolution 1441. This represented an unsuccessful American effort to secure collective legitimacy for the launching of a preemptive war against Iraq. A number of leading international lawyers argued that such an attack would constitute a violation of international law and a violation of the obligations it held under the charter as a member of the UN. For instance, Article 2, Section 4 of the charter prohibits the use or the threat of the use of force against a state.[104]

One of the arguments made by the supporters of the Bush administration was that the United States, as a sovereign state, had the right to engage in self-defense. Indeed, Article 51 of the UN Charter establishes this right, which gives a state the right of self-defense against an armed attack but stipulates that this has to be subsequently approved by the Security Council.[105] But as also stipulated in Article 51, self-defense could be exercised only after an armed attack had occurred, as opposed to the doctrine of anticipatory self-defense that was presented by the Bush administration to justify military action undertaken against an imminent threat.[106]

In March 2003, though, there was no evidence that Iraq had been involved in the 9/11 attack on the United States. At least in the eyes of its critics, the United States had not definitively established the existence of ties between Iraq and Al

Qaeda.[107] The Bush administration also argued that Iraq was in material breach of Security Council Resolutions 678 and 687.[108] Washington believed apparently that the charge of material breach provided it with the justification to argue that the cease-fire that had been established in Resolution 678 should be considered suspended, and that it could use all means necessary to deal with the breach as called for in that resolution. Spain, which had been one of the staunchest supporters of the Bush administration and one of the co-sponsors of the draft resolution calling for military action as a follow-up to Resolution 1441, also argued in the Security Council on March 19, 2003, that Resolution 687, legitimizing all means necessary to insure Iraqi compliance was still in effect and had been held in abeyance only since the adoption of the cease-fire called for in Resolution 678.

But the Russian Federation, France, and China, plus nonpermanent member of the Security Council Germany opposed the use of military force to secure Iraqi compliance.[109] German Foreign Minister Joschka Fischer, after pointing out that Germany had willingly participated in the "war against terrorism" in the ISAF in Afghanistan, raised the question whether "the problem which the UN encountered in working towards the disarmament of Iraq, should seriously be regarded as grounds for war with all of its terrible consequences."[110] Germany further argued that there was "no basis in the UN Charter for regime change by military means."[111] The German foreign minister concluded, "We do not live on Venus but rather we are survivors of Mars."[112] The Russian Federation stressed that Resolution 1441 gave "no one the right to the automatic use of force."[113] France threatened to veto any resolution that authorized the use of military force against Iraq, stressing that "war can only be a last resort, while collective responsibility remains the rule."[114] It is also important to point out that China, another permanent member of the Security Council, opposed the use of military force against Iraq as a follow-up to Resolution 1441.

A majority of the members of the UN opposed the war. At a meeting of the Security Council on March 12, 2003, most of the African members of the General Assembly expressed their opposition to the war, unless the use of force was sanctioned by the Security Council. The African states were concerned that the unilateral use of military force not only would constitute a violation of international law and the UN Charter but would have adverse economic consequences for the continent as well. Earlier, on February 3, 2003, the African Union had stressed that "multilateral cooperation was the only option."[115] Furthermore, the United States was urged by the European Union, the Non-Aligned Movement, the Organization of the Islamic Conference, and the Arab League not to rush into war. Earlier in the debate, Arab states such as Lebanon had emphasized what it considered to be the double-standard that was followed by the United States in tolerating Israel's possession of nuclear weapons, while advocating the use of military force to disarm Iraq of its WMD.[116] It should also be pointed out, however, that there were a number of countries, such as Albania, Japan, El Salvador, Georgia, Nicaragua, Bolivia, Thailand, the Philippines, and Latvia, that did support the position of the United States.[117]

Operating under the threat of a French veto, the United States engaged in a frenetic amount of diplomatic activity to gather up the necessary majority of nine votes out of fifteen for a resolution to gain some semblance of legitimacy for military action, by attempting to persuade some of the nonpermanent members of the Security Council to vote for it. Spain and Bulgaria were aligned with the United States on this issue, but other nonpermanent members, such as Mexico, Angola, and Cameroon, aligned themselves with the French position and would not vote for the adoption of a resolution calling for the use of force against Iraq.

Not being able to secure the adoption of the resolution authorizing the use of force, the United States and the United Kingdom launched the war against Iraq in March 2003 without any authorization from the Security Council. At a Security Council meeting on March 26, 2003, Secretary-General Kofi Annan expressed his "profound . . . sadness" and sympathy for the Iraqi people. In the postwar stage of the crisis, attention was focused on the restoration of the unity of the Security Council, which had been fractured by the divisions over the Iraqi war, and in a broader sense to restore the central role of the Security Council as a major actor in the international system in the maintenance of international peace and security. Before the war had been launched, Kofi Annan had warned the United States that it might need the UN later, a prediction that turned out to be quite true. But Annan had stated on August 22, 2003, that UN blue helmets "would not take over from the coalition, since it did not have the resources to do so, but broached the idea of a Security Council mandated force," a multinational force. The coalition occupying Iraq, which consisted of the United States, the United Kingdom, and some allied states, would need a UN "umbrella" or mandate to persuade states such as France (already somewhat overextended in other UN peacekeeping ventures in 2003), Germany, and Russia to participate in a "post-conflict" stabilization force. This task was complicated by the failure of the Bush administration to initially secure collective legitimization from the UN for going to war.

As resistance to the coalition occupation force in Iraq mounted, the United States found that France, Germany, Russia, India, and Pakistan were not willing to internationalize an occupation force without Security Council authorization, a timetable to restore Iraqi sovereignty, and a greater role in the administration of postwar Iraq.[118] There were some countries that indicated that they would be willing to help the United States in Iraq, including the "new" Europeans, such as the former communist states of Albania, Bulgaria, the Czech Republic, Poland, and Romania, as well as Spain, among others. But obviously, these countries did not have the military capacity that such larger powers as the "old" Europeans, including France and Germany, could bring to bear.[119] In sum, the effects of the second Gulf war on the concept of UN peacekeeping might best be summed up by a statement made by Germany at the 4,818th meeting of the Security Council on August 23, 2003, that "peacekeeping by its very nature must remain compatible with the universal role of the UN and the principle of international solidarity."

Conclusion: The Reform of UN Peacekeeping

The dark memories of Rwanda and Srebrenica have also propelled the United Nations in the direction of finding ways to improve its capacity to engage in peacekeeping.[120] Also, the second Gulf war has again raised the issue of creating a permanent standing force for the UN, as called for in the UN Charter, and as discussed in the introduction to Part 4. But the members of the UN still would be reluctant to surrender their sovereignty over their military forces to such an international organization. Moreover, there is no desire, either, to create an international force of mercenaries that could be quickly dispatched to a conflict, a sort of international French Foreign Legion that owed its allegiance to no state but to the United Nations.[121]

Since peacekeeping represents an ad hoc invention, the UN will have to continue to improvise. The best that the UN can do is to deal with more recent reform proposals that have emphasized the need for a greater degree of transparency in making peacekeeping and sanctions decisions (some developing countries believe that the imposition of sanctions against Third World states represent a form of discrimination), more input from the General Assembly that developing countries consider a much more democratic institution than the Security Council, and more focus on clear entrance and exit strategies when a peacekeeping operation is originally mandated. Furthermore, a blue-ribbon Panel of Experts on Peacekeeping submitted a report in August 2000 (the Brahimi Report) that recommended a number of steps, including strengthening the UN's Department of Peacekeeping Operations, which has been greatly underfinanced and understaffed.

After the second Gulf war, Secretary-General Annan urged that the time had arrived for major institutional reforms in the structure of the world organization. An increase in the number of permanent and nonpermanent members of the Security Council, which has been discussed at the UN for years, would certainly democratize and make the Security Council more representative, perhaps generating enhanced legitimacy for its peacekeeping operations. In connection with an expansion of the Security Council, it has been suggested that the Military Staff Committee, which has been mostly moribund since its creation, could be expanded to include more representatives of the Third World and could then function in an advisory capacity on peacekeeping and peace-enforcement issues. In an effort to improve its capacity to function as a more effective instrument of peace-keeping, the Security Council has undertaken more fact-finding field missions within the past few years to conflict-ridden areas and has engaged in open discussions on various facets of improving peacekeeping (such as the need to consult more with troop-contributing countries about questions dealing with the renewal of a mandate or the termination of an operation).

The UN has also put more emphasis on the need to prevent conflicts and potential conflicts from developing, before they escalate out of control. It has also been suggested that the Secretary-General should make greater use of his prerogatives under Article 99 of the charter (to bring to the Security Council an issue that threatens the maintenance of international peace and security), although this does carry with it the risk of a confrontation with a permanent member of the Security Council, as Dag Hammarskjold discovered during the Congo crisis.[122] As the Secretary-General stressed in a recent report on conflict prevention, the responsibility of preventing conflicts rests with the national governments themselves.[123] The preventive deployment of troops based on the model of the UN Preventive Deployment Force in Macedonia—which may have helped to contain the turmoil in Serbia from spilling over into the Former Yugoslav Republic of Macedonia before it was withdrawn—is another possible model for conflict prevention in war-ridden regions of the world.[124] Even though the UN has now realized that it cannot bring peace to an area unless the parties to a dispute want it themselves, it has been suggested that the UN should enhance its capacity to use early-warning systems to alert the international community to a crisis escalating out of control. The Department of Political Affairs in the Secretariat has the responsibility of monitoring crises and potential crises and should be able to indicate when a situation is going to escalate into a serious conflict, so that the UN can avoid finding itself caught by surprise as it was in the case of East Timor in 1999 (although the Department of Political Affairs can also be overwhelmed with the amount of information that it has to process).

The Brahimi Report also stresses that the mandates of peacekeeping operations must be clear and not ambiguous (often peacekeeping mandates may be the result of diplomatic bargaining that represents the lowest common denominator that is acceptable to the members of the Security Council). Furthermore, the Brahimi Report, as well as other proposals, have stressed that the Security Council should not authorize mandates that cannot be implemented just to create the impression that something is being done in response to international public opinion.

One of the main problems with peacekeeping is that it takes too long to deploy a force. The United Nations has created a rapid reaction force, the Stand-By High-Readiness Brigades, which ideally should move quickly into a conflict situation. But states that have promised to supply troops should be willing to actually allow them to be used for such a force, so that they can be rapidly deployed in a conflict without delay. Furthermore, the agreements called for in Article 43 of the charter, whereby states agree to provide military forces to the Security Council, should finally be negotiated, although the United States would probably not participate in the creation of any UN standby force.[125] Other member states of the UN also are not yet ready to surrender their sovereignty over the troops that they contribute to UN peacekeeping operations, which would be entailed in the creation of a UN standing or more permanent type of force. Additionally, more civilian police officers should be on call and available to the UN for service in a peacekeeping operation as suggested by the Brahimi Report. Certainly there are practical changes that can be made in the machinery and infrastructure of peacekeeping, although as always in international relations, the critical element in the establishment of sustainable peace is the willingness of the Great Powers to act and to try to go beyond, as Kofi Annan has said, a narrow conception of their national interest and be impelled by a broader, more collective sense that their national interest lies with world society as a whole.[126]

NOTES

1. For the classic statement of the realist approach to international relations, see Hans Morgenthau, *Politics among Nations* (New York: Alfred A. Knopf, 1985); also see Robert Keohane, *Neorealism and Its Critics* (New York: Columbia University Press, 1986).

2. As G. John Ikenberry notes, "Skepticism within the British government remained over the workings of the League of Nations, but most officials saw it as a way to tie the United States into more active involvement in Europe." See G. John Ikenberry, *After Victory* (Princeton, N.J.: Princeton University Press, 2001), 143.

3. See William R. Keylor, *The Twentieth-Century World: An International History* (New York: Oxford University Press, 2001), 85.

4. See Anne-Marie Slaughter, "The Liberal Agenda for Peace: International Relations Theory and the Future of the United Nations," in *Preferred Futures for the United Nations,* ed. Saul H. Mendlovitz and Burns H. Weston (New York: Irvington-on-Hudson, 1995), 96.

5. For an excellent discussion and critique of the principles of collective security, see Inis Claude Jr., *Power and International Relations* (New York: Random House, 1962), 94–204.

6. See Robert C. Johansen, "Enhancing United Nations Peacekeeping," in *The Future of the United Nations System,* ed. Chadwick F. Alger (Tokyo: United Nations University Press, 1998), 123.

7. Dennis C. Jett, *Why Peacekeeping Fails* (New York: St. Martin's Press, 2000), 169; also see A. B. Fetherston, *Towards a Theory of United Nations Peacekeeping* (London: St. Martin's, 1994), 20; also see *Supplement to an Agenda for Peace: Position Paper of the Secretary-General on the Occasion of the Fiftieth Anniversary of the United Nations,* U.N. doc., A/50/60-S/1990/1, January 3, 1995, 3.

8. Article 2, Section 7 reads: "Nothing contained in the present Charter shall authorize the United Nations to intervene in matters which are essentially within the domestic jurisdiction of any state or shall require the members to submit such matters to settlement under the present Charter; but this principle shall not prejudice the application of enforcement measures under Chapter VII"; see A. Leroy Bennett, *International Organizations: Principles and Issues* (Englewood Cliffs, N.J.: Prentice-Hall, 1984), 458.

9. For example, speaking at the 55th session of the UN General Assembly in fall 2000, President Bill Clinton said: "These conflicts present us with a stark challenge. Are they part of the scourge the United Nations was established to prevent? If so, we must respect sovereignty and territorial integrity, but still find a way to protect people as well as borders." http://www.un.int/usa/00_122.htm.

10. Michael Walzer, *Just and Unjust Wars: A Moral Argument with Historical Illustrations* (New York: Basic Books, 1977), 107.

11. See *Boston Globe,* September 21, 1999, A8.

12. Fetherston, *Towards a Theory,* 11.

13. Raimo Vayrynen, "Enforcement and Humanitarian Intervention: Two Forms of Collective Action by the United Nations," in Alger, *Future of the United Nations System,* 56.

14. See, for example, John G. Stoessinger, *Why Nations Go to War* (Boston: Bedford/St. Martin's, 2001).

15. As Susan Woodward writes concerning U.S. policy toward the former Yugoslavia, "Policymakers were unwilling to commit substantial U.S. resources or any troops to an area no longer of vital strategic interest." See Susan L. Woodward, *Balkan Tragedy: Chaos and Dissolution after the Cold War* (Washington, D.C.: Brookings Institution Press, 1995), 158.

16. Unfortunately, in the case of the League of Nations, the application of economic sanctions was almost diluted immediately after its creation by the adoption of a resolution by the League Assembly in 1921, which left it up to each member of the League to decide whether or not to participate in a sanctions regime. See Bennett, *International Organizations,* 37.

17. Joshua S. Goldstein, *International Relations* (New York: Addison Wesley Longman, 2001), 199.

18. As quoted in Arnold J. Toynbee, *War and Civilization* (New York: Oxford University Press, 1950), 16.

19. For a further discussion of this idea, see Max Singer and Aaron Wildavsky, *The Real World Order: Zones of Peace/Zones of Turmoil* (Chatham: Chatham House, 1996).

20. Also see Zeev Maoz, "The Controversy Over the Democratic Peace: Rearguard Action or Cracks in the Wall? *International Security* 22, no.1 (Summer 1997): 162–98.

21. See James Lee Ray, *Democracy and International Conflict* (Colombia: University of South Carolina Press, 1998), 16, 30.

22. See Christopher Layne, "Kant or Cant: The Myth of the Democratic Peace," in *The Perils of Anarchy: Contemporary Realism and International Security,* ed. Michael E. Brown, Sean M. Lynn-Jones, and Steven E. Miller (Cambridge: MIT Press, 1995), 326.

23. See Fetherston, *Towards a Theory,* 8; also see Clark M. Eichelberger, *Organizing for Peace: A Personal History of the Founding of the United Nations* (New York: Harper and Row, 1977); also see Robert A. Divine, *Second Chance* (New York: Atheneum, 1967).

24. For some discussion at the San Francisco Conference of the decision to have members of the UN enter into agreements to provide national contingents to an international force that would be placed under the aegis of the Security Council, see *Documents of the United Nations Conference on International Organization, San Francisco,* 12 (New York: United Nations Information Organization, 1945), 279.

25. Kumar Rupesinghe, "Coping with Internal Conflicts: Teaching the Elephants to Dance," in Alger, *Future of the United Nations System,* 157.

26. See Paul F. Diehl, *International Peacekeeping* (Baltimore: Johns Hopkins University Press, 1994), 5.

27. See Dan Lindley, "Collective Security Organizations and Internal Conflict," in *The International Dimensions of Internal Conflict,* ed. Michael E. Brown (Cambridge: MIT Press, 1996), 551.

28. For a very critical study of the UN role in Somalia, see John L. Hirsch and Robert B. Oakley, *Somalia and Operation Restore Hope* (Washington, D.C.: United States Institute for Peace Press, 1995).

29. Johansen, "Enhancing United Nations Peacekeeping," 92.

30. See Meredith Reid Sarkees, Frank Whelon Way, and J. David Singer, "Inter-State, Intra State, and Extra-State Wars: A Comprehensive Look at their Distribution Over Time, 1816–1997," *International Studies Quarterly* 47 (2003): 47, 49–70.

31. Thomas G. Weiss, "The United Nations and Civil Wars at the Dawn of the Twenty-First Century," in *The United Nations and Civil Wars,* ed. Thomas G. Weiss (Boulder, Colo.: Lynne Rienner, 1995), 193.

32. For works about UN operations in the Congo in the early 1960s, see Conor Cruise O'Brien, *To Katanga and Back* (New York: Simon and Schuster, 1962); Ernest W. Lefever, *Uncertain Mandate* (Baltimore: Johns Hopkins University Press, 1967); Ernest W. Lefever, *Crisis in the Congo: A UN Force in Action* (Washington, D.C.: Brookings Institution, 1965); Linda B. Miller, *World Order and Local Disorder: The United Nations and Internal Conflicts* (Princeton, N.J.: Princeton University Press, 1967).

33. For the concept of different generations of peacekeeping, see Karen A. Mingst and Margaret P. Karns, *The United Nations in the Post-Cold War Era* (Boulder, Colo.: Westview Press, 2000).

34. Also see James N. Rosenau, *The United Nations in a Turbulent World* (Boulder, Colo.: Lynne Rienner, 1992).

35. For an excellent study of the genocide that was committed in Rwanda, see Philip Gourevitch, *We Wish to Inform You That Tomorrow We Will Be Killed with Our Families* (New York: Farrar, Straus and Giroux, 1998).

36. *The United Nations and Rwanda 1995–1996.* The United Nations Blue Book Series, 10 (New York: Department of Political Information United Nations, 1966), 3; for a general discussion of genconn.ocide, also see Winston E. Langley, *Encyclopedia of Human Rights Issues since 1945* (Westport, : Greenwood Press, 1999), 133–34.

37. *Report of the Independent Inquiry into the Actions of the United Nations during the 1994 Genocide in Rwanda.* Available at http://www.un.org/News/dh/latest/rwanda.htm.

38. Alain O. Destexhe, *Rwanda and Genocide in the Twentieth Century* (New York: New York University Press, 1995), 29.

39. Gourevitch, *We Wish to Inform You,* 179; also see Matthew Vaccaro, "The Politics of Genocide: Peacekeeping and Disaster Relief in Rwanda," in *UN Peacekeeping: American Politics and the Uncivil Wars of the 1990s,* ed. William J. Durch (London: Macmillan, 1997), 369.

40. L. R. Melvern, *A People Betrayed: The Role of the West in Rwanda's Genocide* (London: Zed Books, 2000), 24.

41. See Samantha Power, *A Problem from Hell: America and the Age of Genocide* (New York: Basic Books, 2003), 332.

42. Ivo H. Daalder, "Knowing When to Say No: The Development of US Policy for Peacekeeping," in Durch, *UN Peacekeeping,* 54; also see William Shawcross, *Deliver Us from Evil: Peacekeepers, Warlords, and a World of Endless Conflict* (New York: Simon and Schuster, 2000), 25.

43. Hirsch and Oakley, *Somalia and Operation Restore Hope,* 159; also see Edward C. Luck, *Mixed Messages: American Politics and International Organization 1919–1999* (Washington, D.C.: Brookings Institution Press, 1999), 190–91. The United States had also failed to pay its peacekeeping dues to the UN for a number of reasons including demands that the organization engage in wide-ranging management and budgetary reforms . On December 26, 2000, because of the extraordinary efforts of USUN Ambassador Richard Holbrook, the U.S. and other members of the United Nations finally reached a compromise agreement in which Washington would pay what it owed in return for a reduction in its assessments to the world organization. This replaced the formula for calculating peacekeeping assessments that had existed since 1973 when UNEF II (the second United Nations Emergency Force) had been set up. See Steven A. Dimoff, "General Assembly Reduces U.S. Financing of UN," *Interdependent* 20, no. 4 (2001): 10.The financial veto wielded by the United States was similar to Soviet behavior in refusing to pay for the financial upkeep of UNEF and ONUC in the 1960s, with the Soviets arguing that these peacekeeping operations were illegal and were designed to advance the hegemony of the United States and NATO. See King Gordon, *The United Nations in the Congo* (Washington, D.C.: Carnegie Endowment for International Peace, 1962), 158; also see John G. Stoessinger, *The United Nations and the Superpowers* (New York: Random House, 1965), 90–113.

44. Gourevitch, *We Wish to Inform You,* 153; also see Andrea Kathryn Talentino, "Rwanda," in *The Costs of Conflict Prevention and Care in the Global Arena,* ed. Michael E. Brown and Richard N. Rosecrance (London: Rowman and Littlefield, 1999), 159.

45. Gourevitch, *We Wish to Inform You,* 103; also see Michael Barnett, *Eyewitness to Genocide: The United Nations and Rwanda* (Ithaca: Cornell University Press, 2002), 77–78.

46. Melvern, *A People Betrayed,* 230; Gourevitch, *We Wish to Inform You,* 150; Talentino, "Rwanda," 55.

47. Benjamin A. Valentino, "Still Standing By: Why America and the International Community Fail to Prevent Genocide and Mass Killing," *Perspectives on Politics* 1, no.3 (September 2003): 573.

48. William J. Durch, "Keeping the Peace: Politics and Lessons of the 1990s," in Durch, *UN Peacekeeping,* 14; Gourevitch, *We Wish to Inform You,* 150.

49. Vaccaro, "Politics of Genocide," 40.

50. Daalder, "Knowing When to Say No," 51.

51. Gourevitch, *We Wish to Inform You,* 158; Vaccaro, "The Politics of Genocide," 38.

52. For an excellent analysis of the collapse of Yugoslavia, and the role of the international community there, see Woodward, *Balkan Tragedy.*

53. *Report of the Secretary-General Pursuant to General Assembly Resolution 53/35: The Fall of Srebrenica* (November 15, 1999), 6. Available at http:www.un.org/peace/srebrenica.pdf.

54. Ibid., 83.

55. Ibid., 61,

56. Boutros Boutros-Ghali, *Unvanquished: A U.S.–U.N. Saga* (New York: Random House, 1999), 238; also see Jan Willem Honig and Norbert Both, *Srebrenica: Record of a War Crime* (New York: Penguin Books, 1997), 135; also see *Fall of Srebrenica,* 60.

57. See Robert Weiner, *Change in Eastern Europe* (Westport, Conn.: Praeger, 1994), 141.

58. For the notion that Srebrenica was sacrificed by the Bosnians as part of a deal for the exchange of territory with the Serbs, see David Rhode, *End Game: The Betrayal and Fall of Srebrenica* (Boulder, Colo.: Westview, 1997), 401.

59. See Boutros-Ghali, *Unvanquished,* 239; also see Oliver Ramsbotham and Tom Woodhouse, *Humanitarian Intervention in Contemporary Conflict* (Cambridge, Mass.: Polity Press, 1996), 184.

60. *Fall of Srebrenica,* 108.

61. Boutros-Ghali, *Unvanquished,* 239.

62. *Fall of Srebrenica,* 55.

63. For example, on December 19, 2000, the Security Council failed to adopt a resolution calling for the deployment of an observer force in the Occupied Territories of Palestine by a vote eight in favor and seven abstentions. The governments voting in favor were Bangladesh, China, Jamaica, Malaysia, Mali, Namibia, Tunisia, and Ukraine. See *UN News,* December 19, 2000.

64. For more information about Kosovo, see *Report of the Secretary-General on the United Nations Interim Administration in Kosovo, S/2001/565,* June 7, 2001.

65. China called the NATO intervention in Kosovo an "ominous precedent" and a "violation of the UN Charter." For the Chinese position on Kosovo, see http://www.fmprc.gov.cn/eng/wjdt/zyjh/t24953.htm. Also see Bates Gill and James Reilly, "Sovereignty, Intervention and Peacekeeping: The View from Beijing," *Survival* 42, no. 3 (Autumn 2000): 46.

66. Diana Ayton-Shenker and John Tessitore, eds., *A Global Agenda: Issues before the 56th General Assembly of the United Nations* (Lanham: Rowman and Littlefield, 2002), 56.

67. See Margaret P. Karns and Karen A. Mingst, "Peacekeeping and the Changing Role of the United Nations: Four Dilemmas," in *United Nations Peacekeeping Operations,* ed. Ramesh Thakur and Albrecht Schnabel, 215–37 (Tokyo: United Nations Press, 2001).

68. See Kofi Annan, "Two Concepts of Sovereignty," *The Economist,* September 18, 1999.

69. *New York Times,* April 24, 2001, A4; also see Ayton-Shenker and Tessitore, *Global Agenda,* 20.

70. See David A. Lake, "Regional Security Complexes: A Systems Approach," in *Regional Orders: Building Security in a New World,* ed. David A. Lake and Patrick M. Morgan (University Park: Pennsylvania State University Press, 1997), 43.

71. See Alan S. Henrikson, "The Growth of Regional Organizations and the Role of the United Nations," in *Regionalism in World Politics,* ed. Louise Fawcett and Andrew Hurrell (Oxford: Oxford University Press, 1995), 125.

72. Ibid., 128.

73. A multinational force, approved by Security Council Resolution 1264 on October 25, 1999, and led by Australia, was deployed in East Timor with the permission of Indonesia. This action was followed by the deployment of a multidimensional peacekeeping force consisting of over eight thousand troops under the aegis of UNTAET (the United Nations Transitional Administration in East Timor) authorized by UN Security Council Resolution 1272. UNTAET has been engaged in a process of "Timorization" of East Timor by preparing it for independence since 1991, a goal that was accomplished.

74. Louise Fawcett, "Regionalism in Historical Perspective," in Fawcett, *Regionalism in World Politics,* 32; For an argument that favors relying on regional hegemons to maintain order via the creation of "benign spheres of influence" see Weiss, *United Nations and Civil Wars,* 195.

75. See Inis Claude Jr., "Collective Security as an Approach to Peace," in *Classic Readings of International Relations,* ed. Phil Williams, Donald M. Goldstein, and Jay M. Shafritz (Fort Worth, Tex.: Harcourt Brace College Publishers, 1997), 47.

76. In the case of the application of sanctions by the UN against the Taliban, see Juan Emilio Ane and Edward Thomas, "New Afghan Sanctions Stir UN Debate," *Interdependent* 26, no. 4 (Winter 2001): 11.

77. See "Speech to CNN," June 1, 2001, www.globalpolicy.org/secgen/cnn.htm.

78. Iraq has earned about $40 billion since the "oil-for-food" program began in 1996. Retrieved from www.fas.org/news/iraq/2001/03/iraq-010313.htm; also see Ayton-Shenker and Tessitore, *A Global Agenda,* 44.

79. *New York Times,* June 4, 2001, A7.

80. "Report of the Policy Working Group on the United Nations and Terrorism," http://www.un.org/terrorism/a57273.htm.

81. About thirty states had contributed to it by summer 2003. For example, Romania, an aspiring NATO member, had made its own "niche" contribution in the form of mountain troops, which it had flown into Afghanistan.

82. *New York Times,* August 28, 2003, A5.

83. See Ayton-Shenker and Tessitore, *Global Agenda,* 99. It is interesting to note that the German foreign minister, Joschka Fischer, made a point of stressing the participation of his country in the war in Afghanistan, when presenting the position of his government in opposition to the use of military force against Iraq in the spring of 2003.

84. This expansion would provide NATO with a presence in Central Asia and meant that yet another multinational force, sanctioned by the UN Security Council, would be controlled by NATO. UN–sanctioned NATO multinational forces have been operating in Bosnia and Kosovo as well. Also see "NATO Considers Limited Deployment of ISAF Troops Beyond Kabul." Available at http:www.rferl.org/newsline/2003/06/6-SWA/swa-200603.asp.

85. See "NATO Takes Command of ISAF." Available at http://www.rferl.org/newsline/2003/08/6-swa/swa-110803.asp.

86. See James P. Rubin, "Stumbling Into War," *Foreign Affairs* 82, no.5 (September–October 2003): 48.

87. United Nations, Security Council, Press Release SC/7536, "In Security Council Debate, United States, France, Russian Federation, Others Outline Positions on Possible Resolution Concerning Iraq,", October 17, 2002, http://www.un.org/News/Press/docs/2002/sc7536.doc.htm.

88. For more on the concept of the just war, see Walzer, *Just and Unjust War.*

89. Also see Bob Woodward, *Bush at War* (New York: Simon and Schuster, 2002), 335–36.

90. See ibid., 346. On September 30, 2001, Secretary of Defense Donald Rumsfeld said, "Preemption was going to be necessary and probably sooner rather than later." See ibid., 176.

91. Concern was expressed about "the future of world order, relations between North and South, relations with the Arab world." See Security Council Press Release SC/7536, October 17, 2002.

92. Probably, much to the consternation of the United States, an entente of sorts was formed between Mexico and France, which clearly worked together as a team during this process.

93. See the statement by France at the meeting of the Security Council on October 17, 2002 in ibid.

94. See "Secretary-General's Statement at the Adoption of Security Council Resolution 1441 on Iraq," New York, November 8, 2002, http://www.un.org/apps/sg/sgstats.asp?nid=146.

95. Ibid.

96. See United Nations, Security Council, Press Release SC/7644, "Security Council Briefed by Chief UN Weapons Experts on First 60 Days of Inspection," January 27, 2003, http://www.un.org/News/Press/docs/2003/sc7644.doc.htm.

97. See ibid.

98. Ibid.

99. Ibid.

100. Ibid.

101. United Nations, Security Council, Press Release SC/7658, "Briefing Security Council, Secretary of State Powell Presents Evidence of Iraq's Failure to Disarm," February 5, 2003, http://www.un.org/News/Press/docs/2003/sc7658.doc.htm.

102. Ibid.

103. Ibid.

104. See Anne-Marie Slaughter, "The Will to Make It Work," *Washington Post,* March 2, 2003, B01; also see Clyde Eagleton, *International Government* (New York: Ronald Press, 1957), 610.

105. Article 51 opens with the following sentence: "Nothing in the present Charter shall impair the inherent right of individual or collective self-defense."

106. For example, the notion of anticipatory self-defense as presented by the Bush administration did not fit the test of immediacy of an imminent attack as elaborated by Secretary of State Daniel Webster in the *Caroline* case in 1837. When the British attacked the *Caroline* on U.S. territory because it was anticipated that it would aid Canadian revolutionaries, an attack from the ship was not imminent, and therefore the British preemptive strike was not justifiable. See Frederick L. Kirgis, "Pre-emptive Action to Forestall Terrorism," *ASIL Insights,* June 2002, http://www.asil.org/insights/insigh88.htm.

107. Some effort had been made to establish that one of the leaders of the hijackers had met with Iraqi intelligence before the attack on 9/11, but this had not been definitely established either.

108. The phrase "material breach" was drawn from Article 60 of the Vienna Convention on the Law of Treaties. However, the Vienna Convention dealt with multilateral treaties, not Security Council resolutions. The question was raised by critics of the U.S. position about whether in this regard a multilateral treaty could be equated with a resolution.

109. Although Germany was a nonpermanent member of the Security Council, it carried considerable weight in the international community because of its position in the international structure of power, especially when aligned with other permanent members of the Security Council. Furthermore, German Chancellor Gerhard Schroeder, the leader of the Social Democratic Party, had campaigned for reelection on a platform that opposed the war, which created a highly visible strain in German–U.S. relations. Also, German foreign minister Joschka Fischer was a member of the pacifist oriented Green Party.

110. UN Doc., S/PV.4721, March 19, 2003, 4.

111. Ibid.

112. Ibid., 5.

113. Ibid., 7.

114. Ibid., 5.

115. United Nations, Security Council, Press Release SC/7687, "Security Council Hears from 53 Speakers in Two Days on Iraq's Disarmament," March 12, 2003, http://www.un.org/News/Press/docs/2003/sc7687.doc.htm.

116. For example, see the Lebanese statement on October 17, 2002. Security Council Press Release SC/7536, October 17, 2002.

117. See Security Council Press Release SC/7687, March 12, 2003.

118. For the French position, which left open the option of participating in a multinational force at some point in the future, see "News Analysis: French Pave Way for Role in Iraq," *International Herald Tribune,* July 29, 2003. The Americans had also hoped for a division of about 17,000 Indian troops. See *New York Times,* July 19, 2003, A1.

119. On July 9, 2003, U.S. Secretary of Defense Donald Rumsfeld testified before the U.S. Senate Armed Services Committee, where he said that eighty to ninety countries (with supposedly positive responses from about thirty), had been asked to send troops to help. http://www.au.af.mil/au/awc/awcgate/congress/rumsfeld_09july03.pdf.

120. The most recent efforts at reform of UN peacekeeping and enforcement represent the latest in a long history of such attempts; see, for example, Arthur M. Cox, *Prospects for Peacekeeping* (Washington, D.C.: Brookings Institution, 1967).

121. For the suggestion that a kind of UN Foreign Legion should be created, see Carl Kaysen and George Rathjens, "The Case for a Volunteer UN Military Force," *Daedalus,* Winter 2003, 91–103.

122. See Robert Weiner, "The USSR and UN Peacekeeping," *Orbis* 12, no.3 (Fall 1969): 915–30.

123. See United Nations, General Assembly, 55th sess., Security Council, A/55/985–S/2001/574, Report of the Secretary-General, "Prevention of Armed Conflict," http://www.un.org/Docs/sc/reports/2001/574e.pdf.

124. For an excellent analysis of preventive deployment in the Former Yugoslav Republic of Macedonia, see Alice Ackermann, *Making Peace Prevail: Preventing Violent Conflict in Macedonia* (Syracuse, N.Y.: Syracuse University Press, 1999).

125. For an earlier proposal for a creation of a UN stand-by force, see Lincoln P. Bloomfield, *International Military Forces* (Boston: Little, Brown, 1969), 80.

126. See Alton Frye, *Humanitarian Intervention: Crafting a Workable Doctrine* (New York: Council on Foreign Relations, 2000), 90.

The Role of the United Nations in a Unipolar World

BRIAN URQUHART   To call something irrelevant is, I suppose, the most biting insult you can possibly give to anything, a person or an institution, and the word has been used quite a bit about the UN. But I think that its demise is somewhat unlikely, certainly in the near future.

The last time this insult was thrown at the UN was by none other than the president of the United States. It was over the failure of the Security Council to reach unanimity on the occupation of Iraq and the regime change. Here we are a year later [February 2004] and, God help them, the Secretary-General Kofi Annan and his remarkable assistant Lakhdar Brahimi, who has been holding things down in Afghanistan for the past few years, are now the ones who have to devise some way of gradually transferring power that is acceptable to all Iraqis. This is not an easy job. The Romans tried it in the second and third centuries A.D. and it killed the Emperor Trajan.

This is a poison chalice if ever there was one, because it is extremely difficult to get everybody to agree in Iraq. If they are not successful, we shall hear again about how hopeless the UN is. But never mind, they are going to do it. I must say that it just shows what a difference a year makes and how the word *irrelevant* may seem applicable in some people's minds one year but then not at all the next year.

The UN was founded, as you know, in 1945. The charter was signed in San Francisco in April of that year, before the war was over. It is important to remember that the UN Charter and the whole concept of the UN was the brainchild of Franklin Roosevelt and something that he seems to have paid more attention to and minded more about than almost anything else, including conducting the whole of World War II. Unfortunately, because it was before the war ended, the charter was founded on a false assumption, which was that the alliance that had won the war would continue to observe the peace and if necessary enforce it. This was the basis of the UN's peace and security function and the base, of course, of the five permanent members of the Security Council who have a veto. We need to list here the names again: the United States, the Soviet Union, France, the United Kingdom, and China. Well, within two or three years the relations between the five permanent members had become the main threat to world peace and remained so for forty years. So the UN was to some extent founded on a kind of geopolitical fault from which, in a way, it has never recovered.

From the EPIIC Symposium at Tufts University, "Dilemmas of Empire and Nationbuilding," February 2004

In the Cold War a new function was found for the UN—it just sort of happened like penicillin—and that was what we now call peacekeeping. Peacekeeping was not just a lot of neutral soldiers in blue hats running around the world, it was an extremely important strategic device, which is why the United States very, very substantially supported it though it did not take part in it, and why the Soviet Union never really tried to veto it. They needed it. The importance of peacekeeping was to contain regional conflicts and try to prevent them from igniting the main East-West nuclear conflict; places like the Middle East, Kashmir, Cyprus, later on the Congo, and so on. And if it had never done anything else, I think the UN would have proved its relevance during the Cold War.

Then the Cold War unexpectedly ended, taking everybody by surprise. There was no post–Cold War planning like there had been after World War II. There was a year or two of very unwise euphoria, everybody saying the UN at last was going to work as had been written in San Francisco forty years before. And it did do one thing absolutely according to the charter, which was to authorize the operation against Saddam Hussein to get him out of Kuwait. There was a lot of very over-euphoric talk.

Then the UN plunged into all sorts of problems, mostly in the debris of the Cold War, countries that had been proxy battlefields in the Cold War: Angola, Mozambique, Somalia, Cambodia, and others. It sent in operations to try to pacify what were variations of civil war and failed statehood. Some of these operations were successful so one heard about them; for example, Mozambique. Others were deeply flawed or, indeed, total failures: Somalia, Bosnia, and particularly Rwanda.

What the UN was doing there without thinking about it was trying to apply the old peacekeeping technique, which was designed to keep the peace between countries and provide a pretext for them not to fight each other. But it was no longer dealing with nations, it was dealing with warlords, thugs, lunatics, and all sorts of people who did not give a damn about the UN, could not have cared less about the charter or the Security Council, and really, therefore, could be dealt with only by brute force. But peacekeeping operations are not allowed to use force.

So we had a big confusion, culminating in the disaster with the Rangers in Mogadishu in Somalia, which turned the United States completely against UN peacekeeping, and then, very shortly thereafter, the disaster in Rwanda where nobody comes out well and where the United States was instrumental in not reinforcing the UN force in Rwanda, in fact, withdrawing it and trying to ignore the problem. This was, I think, a direct result of the disaster four months previously in Somalia.

And now we have an interesting period, the period of the presidency of George W. Bush, when the United States obviously does not approve of the whole idea of internationalism or the UN or multilateralism or any of this stuff. But every now and then it is compelled to use it. Maybe the necessity of the UN in Iraq is possibly going to change the minds of Washington. I doubt it. But I do think there is another side to this whole problem. The UN itself is a very staid organization and it must adjust to the future. Now that is not so easily done because the UN in the peace and security field has two major problems; one, as I mentioned before, is the five permanent members of the Security Council who even now do not always agree. Do they ever agree?

But also I think that there is a resolute refusal of governments to allow the UN the identity and the available resources and the degree of preparedness to actually be of use in big international crises. We see it now, for example, in Kofi Annan's problem over sending people back to Iraq. If there were an international UN force for providing security for a very dangerous mission like that it would be much easier. As it is, they are dependent either on private contractors or on the coalition forces. Every year there has been something; last year it was Liberia and northeastern Congo, where a capacity to deploy immediately would have made a huge difference instead of having to wait five months and then get a not very efficient force in. So we have a problem in improving the performance.

I wonder how many more disasters it is going to take before governments realize that if they are going to dump problems on the UN and pretend it can solve them, they are going to have to give it the means to do it. If they do not do that the UN will continue to be very inefficient, ineffective, and bureaucratic. That's a pity because it is not necessary.

We hear a great deal now about a unipolar world, a single superpower. There is no question the United States is the most powerful country in history. But where does that leave us? A hundred years ago, less than a hundred years ago, Great Britain controlled 25 percent of the land surface of the world; it controlled the oceans and the seas, the navy, and it also controlled the world's economy. Such an imperial sweep is inconceivable now even for the United States, partly because, of course, the United States does not want it, and also because the world has got past the imperial phase at long last. It is really something that does not work.

No matter how powerful a country is, there is great resistance at all times to one country's taking over another. We see it, of course, all too often, most recently in Afghanistan and Iraq. It seems to me the outcome in both those countries is still very much up for grabs. And we have a vast development now of the traditional weapon of the poor, terrorism. It has now become terrorism linked to high technology and to suicide bombing, which is something that died out in the thirteenth century but has come back. This turns out to be an extremely effective means of opposing powerful countries. We have always known that a low level but effective guerrilla activity is something that very powerful armies cannot really deal with. We learned that in Vietnam, and, unfortunately, we are going to learn it again.

The news is dominated, quite rightly, by 9/11, Afghanistan, and Iraq. But while that is going on there are things that literally are going to determine whether human life can be sustained on this planet in not such a very long time. And it seems to me, it is a disaster if our short-term concerns somehow manage to over-shadow our vital, and I mean vital, long-term concerns; long-term threats to security, stability, even to existence. We all know what they are; they are poverty and despair, economic imbalance, the degradation of the environment, the destruction of natural resources, the problem of overpopulation in some parts of the world, and so on. And that is what is going to determine the future of the human race.

Now that imperialism is dead, I think the notion of preventive war is an extremely limited concept. In the first place it depends on extremely good intelligence, and we have not had very good experiences with that lately. It also is something with great limitations. It is very inadvisable, for example, to unleash preventive war in countries with nuclear weapons; North Korea is a classic case in point, and also countries that can absolutely ruin the country next door before they go down themselves, also North Korea.

I think everyone agrees that the United States is the indispensable international leader. It is not really a matter for argument. But I think it is the form of that leadership that is important, and that is where it does seem to me that we must hope that what we see is leadership within a framework of international cooperation. Part of that framework is the UN and other international organizations. This, incidentally, is what Franklin Roosevelt had in mind. Franklin Roosevelt was a great president and a great patriot and he had no illusions that the United States was the most powerful country in the world; of course it was, but he believed that the United States would be most influential and most powerful and would be able to do best if it functioned in the context of an international system. He believed, also, that that was essential not only for meeting immediate threats but also for looking at long-term problems, most of which did not exist in 1945. We have gone very far in creating long-term global problems.

I think he also believed that with a world as volatile as this one, and it has become more volatile since 1945, you have to have legitimacy. The UN, with its various councils and assemblies, is a useful source of legitimacy. You have to have rules, which are in the charter, and you have to have international law to govern human activities that go way beyond national boundaries, and that covers virtually everything now.

Otherwise, even in 1945, people were convinced that the future would be anarchy, and it might not necessarily be Hitler or Mussolini all over again, it might be something even worse, a kind of erosion of the whole system of society and government. I think what alarms people in the world outside is that the current leadership in Washington appears not to believe this is very important and that

America is an exceptional country that does not necessarily have to go along with the rules and the treaties and the ways of doing things. It has even declared preventive war—a direct contradiction of the charter, which was, incidentally, written by the United States.

The UN is in many ways an antiquated organization and it is an organization that desperately needs to be shaken up. I was there for forty-one years and I want to tell you, it is a nice idea the UN, it is one of the most exasperating, sometimes worse than exasperating, absolutely humiliatingly awful place to work because suddenly it does very stupid things for various national or other reasons, which really do not make any sense at all. The UN Security Council is a sort of museum piece. It represents the situation of power in 1945 and that, of course, has changed.

We all thought the Cold War was terrible, but the nuclear threat was so imperative, so universally terrifying, that there really was a much greater sense of trying to avoid disaster in the Soviet Union, or perhaps particularly in the Soviet Union, than there is now. Now we have new faces of danger. There is nuclear proliferation, all sorts of other proliferation of weapons of mass destruction, which are much easier than nuclear weapons to acquire. There is the related problem of rogue states and failed states, which become breeding grounds for danger and despair and also the homes of organizations like Al Qaeda.

It seems to me that if the UN is not to become a kind of museum piece itself, it is going to have to get around to how it can respond actively and rapidly to a menacing situation. It is going to have to have criteria for intervention and ways of getting to an agreement on intervention quickly. This is a major problem but it is a problem I think the UN has to face and, incidentally, I think if it does not face it you will not get the United States back into the international framework of the UN.

We have to try to do much more to avoid a new era of religious wars. Twenty years ago it would have been inconceivable that we could even think about religious wars. Now on all sides there are all sorts of possibilities of that.

One thing that is quite encouraging about the UN is the development of the Office of the Secretary-General. Unlike the Security Council, this is an office that has evolved. In 1945 the Secretary-General was mostly an administrative official, but now, because of the Cold War and because of the paralysis of the Security Council and because of the quality of some of the Secretary-Generals, it has become an extremely important part of the world mechanisms to try to avoid disasters of all sorts. The UN is very lucky to have Kofi Annan. He is an indefatigable, very, very level-headed and very decent person. Dag Hammarskjöld once described the Secretary-General as a secular pope, and for most of the time, a pope without a church. I think he just about got it right. There may be nowadays more support for the Secretary-General than there was then because both the Soviet

Union and President de Gaulle's France did not believe that the Secretary-General ought to mix in anything important at all; they thought it was an infringement of sovereignty. Well, the day of the Secretary-General is a twenty-four-hour day because of the time difference around the world and he is, I think, a really indispensable person in times of trouble.

Let me finish with a mention of Ralph Bunch. I think he would have been the first to say that the UN needs to be revitalized, and rethought. I think that he would also have thought that a great country like the United States loses nothing by understanding and being courteous to other nations and would be more powerful by far if it worked as the leader in the UN. Bunch was a person who hated ideology and deeply disliked fundamentalism of all kinds. I think he would have been extremely uneasy about all of the evidence that fundamentalism in many forms is on the great increase all over the world now. I think he would have been dismayed that the UN cannot get a peacekeeping force anywhere within five months. Bunch's record was four days. My record was seventeen hours, which was in the 1973 Middle East war where the United States declared a nuclear alert and the Soviet Union moved airborne troops. Now it takes much too long, and I think that he would have, therefore, been very insistent that if the UN is to be given important tasks, it must be able to react effectively and quickly.

Bunch believed that "no problems of human relations should ever be thought to be insoluble," but he also knew that you need endless patience and determination and time to solve the most difficult ones. And you must never, never give up. I think the idea of a quick change to democracy in the Middle East he would have found laughable. When Lakhdar Brahimi, special adviser to the Secretary-General, came back from Iraq, somebody asked him about how soon democracy would come to Iraq and he said, "Well you know, there's a general feeling that it's like instant coffee, you pour hot water on the grains and that's it, but actually it's a matter of at least two generations before you get anywhere near it."

I think that Bunch would have felt very strongly that you must stick with problems. You cannot go away or find they are too difficult and leave them. He represented the essential spirit and the potential of the UN at its best. He was a realistic idealist, and I hope that more people like him will be coming up.

MICHAEL J. GLENNON   It is a rather daunting task to respond to the comments of so distinguished an international civil servant as Sir Brian on the UN charter. It is rather like commenting on the remarks of James Madison on the United States Constitution.

I always advise students that it is important to start one's career in the right way. Sir Brian really started his career, with quite a dramatic entry. In 1942, while on a training mission, he jumped out of an airplane and his parachute failed to open. As I understand it, he landed in a freshly ploughed field and while he didn't exactly walk away, he obviously did recover. I think it is fair to say that his career has been a bit more tranquil since then.

I want to comment on just a couple of aspects of Sir Brian's remarks. First, the whole question of relevance of the UN and, second, the complications posed by American hegemony toward the proper operation of the UN charter.

First relevance: I am not persuaded of the relevance of relevance as a standard for judging the UN. If relevance were the test by which the UN is to be judged, the League of Nations would have passed with flying colors. It was, after all, the League that proved relevant following the Italian invasion of Ethiopia in 1936. Lengthy debates occurred at the headquarters of the League of Nations, and if television had existed in those days I am sure everyone would have been glued to those proceedings.

So it seems to me, the standard is not relevance; the standard rather is the one that the UN sets for itself in the opening words of the UN Charter: The test is whether the UN has in fact saved succeeding generations from the scourge of war. That is the core purpose of the UN. I do not think it requires much evidence to suggest that the UN has failed in that objective, as I do later in my remarks. Well over two hundred times since 1945, force has been used by individual states in flagrant violation of the UN Charter. You can make your own judgment about the lawfulness of the United States' use of force early last year [2003] against Iraq. What does not seem to me to be much questioned is the use of force by nineteen western democracies, comprising the North Atlantic Treaty Organization, against Yugoslavia in 1999. It was flagrantly violative of the UN charter.

So the question that I want to address is why the UN has failed; why, in Sir Brian's words, have states not given the UN the tools to do its job? I would suggest to you that one need look no further than a recent article by Sir Brian for the answer to this question. In the *New York Review of Books* on January 15, 2004, he wrote the following:

> The nations of the world have yet to agree on the best way to handle relatively new threats like large scale terrorism or nuclear proliferation . . . ; there is still no clear consensus about humanitarian intervention or any other form of intervention.

Read that last sentence once more because it summarizes the problem succinctly. "There is still no clear consensus about humanitarian intervention or any other form of intervention."

Now I think that Sir Brian's words are indisputably correct, and I commend him for the forthrightness to say directly what many defenders of the UN will not acknowledge. I want to take a moment to elaborate how serious this lack of consensus really is and how it reflects itself over and over in many different contexts and problems that the UN Security Council has had to confront. And it is not simply the UN Security Council. Those of you who followed the International Criminal Court may be aware that aggression is one of four crimes, listed in the Rome Statute that establishes the International Criminal Court, that the court is authorized to prosecute. There is a curious aspect about the Rome Statute; it defines the other three crimes, yet there is no definition of the crime of aggression. Why is that? For precisely the reason, I suggest to you, that Sir Brian identifies in the *New York Review of Books:* There is no clear consensus about what constitutes aggression.

Now it is sometimes said that Kosovo represents an emerging norm, and that there is a consensus emerging around the principle that sovereignty can no longer shield intrastate genocide. Thus when intrastate genocide occurs, states have a right under international law to intervene to stop it. Let me remind you that what the nineteen NATO parties did in Kosovo was condemned by China, was condemned by Russia, and was condemned by India. It was condemned by the Non-Aligned Movement of 105 African and Asian states. Indeed, when you look at the lineup of states you will find that most of the countries of Africa, most of the countries of Central and South America, many of the countries of Asia condemned what NATO did in Kosovo.

So it is very hard to say that there is an emerging norm coalescing around the principle of humanitarian intervention. Indeed, anybody who doubts that ought to look at the reaction in the General Assembly in 1999 to a very forward-looking speech given by Secretary-General Kofi Annan at the outset of the General Assembly session in September 1999. He proposed that, following the bypassing of the Security Council by NATO in Kosovo earlier that year, we needed to agree on a new principle that intervention would now be seen as permissible to stop the sort of massive human rights violations that NATO intervened to halt in Yugoslavia.

The Secretary-General asked the states of the General Assembly, "Now tell us, what do you think of this idea, the notion that intervention ought to seen as permissible to stop gross human rights violations such as ethnic cleansing?" I had a research assistant go back and pull from the General Assembly debates all of the comments made by all of the members of the General Assembly over the two and one-half months following the Secretary-General's speech. About half the members of the General Assembly responded as he requested. Of that half about one-third spoke out of both sides of their mouths and it is really impossible to tell which side they came down on. Of the remaining two-thirds, one-third were for what the Secretary-General proposed and the remaining third was opposed to it. So of the states in the General Assembly invited to respond to the Secretary-General's idea, one-sixth were on one side, another sixth were on the other side, and all the others were silent or somewhere in the middle.

I will not again rehearse the debate about the legality of preemptive or preventive war with respect to Iraq, but you can assess that for yourself, in reviewing the reaction of the international community not simply to the United States actions in Iraq but also to the claims made by the United States about the permissibility of preemptive use of force in the National Security strategy statement of October of two years ago. If you do that I think you will conclude, as Sir Brian has, that there is no consensus on the permissibility of intervention for purposes of preempting a possible future attack.

Now it is easy, and I think wrong, to believe that the United States created this problem. As I said a moment ago, since 1945 well over two hundred times Article 2, paragraph 4 has been breached by states using armed force not in self defense, not subject to the authorization of the UN Security Council. These are the only two instances in the UN charter in which use of force is permissible. France and our ally Britain, I hate to say, in 1956 made an effort to topple the Egyptian government and secure the Suez Canal without any authorization from the Security Council, without any plausible argument that they were acting in self defense. Africa's "Third World War," as Madeleine Albright called it, concluded just a few months ago, a conflict in which over nine African states were involved in a vast interstate conflict involving the deaths of tens of thousands of people.

A few months ago a poll was taken in six different European countries and the United States. The German-Marshall Fund asked the populations of these countries, "Do you agree or disagree with the following statement: War is necessary to obtain justice?" In the United States 84 percent of people polled agreed with that statement. In Europe 48 percent agreed with that statement. So this is not simply a case of the West versus the rest. This is a case of Americans really being from Mars and Europeans really being from Venus on the question of when use of force is permissible.

Sir Brian is absolutely correct when he says there is still no clear consensus about humanitarian intervention or any other form of intervention. Now why do I go on at this length to elaborate this point? Because it is necessary to carry the analysis to the next step, and the next step is this: Ask yourself how is it possible to have law regulating a subject matter on which this lack of consensus exists concerning the most basic question? When is it permissible to enforce the law to use armed force? What constitutes a violation of the law?

Social scientists have studied this issue at some length. You will find it in the literature on cooperation. It is relevant here because law is, of course, a form of cooperation; it is an effort, at the outset at least, to settle disputes amicably. These social scientists have come up with about sixteen conditions that are necessary to make legal regulation effective. One of them is consensus on fundamental values. So all this evidence, I suggest to you, is useful in explaining why the law has failed. It has failed because the requisite conditions to make law effective do not exist. It is rather like asking how you could regulate the use of fireworks in a village in which half the village wants the use of fireworks permitted during the day and the other half wants the use of fireworks permitted at night. There is simply no way to adopt an ordinance that would effectively regulate the use of fireworks absent consensus on when it is permissible to use fireworks. The law reflects underlying political realities. It has to. If it does not, you will end up with a paper rule rather than a working rule. If it does not, you will end up with a law that consists of weasel words that prohibit the use fireworks "when it is inappropriate." These are words, I regret to say, of the sort that we now have in the UN charter that attempt to paper over the underlying lack of consensus.

This is one reason that the UN has failed in its effort to subject the use of force to the rule of law. The other reason is American hegemony. The harsh reality is that hegemony is in tension with the rule of law. There is very limited incentive for an actor within a system to subject itself to restraints when it believes that it is strong enough to work its will and protect its interests through power without accepting legalistic restraints. And that is, in a nutshell, the explanation for the phenomenon that Sir Brian commented on, the United States' resistance to the notion of multilateralism. It turns out that the United States does not have the same incentive that other states have to accept legal rules because it believes that it can get what it wants without law, and, look, let's be honest with ourselves, who can blame it? Look at how the United States got what it wanted in Afghanistan, or Iraq. It is understandable why decision makers in Washington would think, "We don't need law on our side; we have power on our side."

But let me suggest once again, this is not a uniquely American phenomenon. States act to enhance their power as a means of enhancing their security. That is true not only of the United States but of other states as well including the United States' power competitors such as France. During the run-up to the war in Iraq and for some years before the stated objective of French foreign policy, the central strategic objective of Jacques Chirac was to return the world to a multipolar configuration of power. France, China, and Russia a few years ago entered into a treaty positing that as their goal. Their objective is to knock the United States down a peg; the objective is to end the unipolar configuration of power that exists in the world. If American decision-makers were sitting in Paris or Berlin or Moscow or Beijing, they would have exactly the same objective.

I do not fault Dominique de Villepin for using the UN Security Council to advance this foreign policy objective of France, but by the same token I think our power competitors need to understand that if French or German or Russian or Chinese decision-makers were sitting in Washington, it is not probable that they would voluntarily forego the exercise of hegemonic power. No, that is just not how states operate. And lest anyone be confused about that, look at France's record in recent months. It is not simply the power gap between the United States and France that France wishes to eliminate. Consider France's reaction to the effort by the Poles and the Spanish to exercise power that prior to the outset of the Gulf

War the French thought was a bit uppity. They were "not well brought up," Jacques Chirac told them. Jacques Chirac is very happy with maintaining the gap between France and its power competitors, third-tier powers. It is the gap between the United States and France that Chirac wishes to eliminate.

So again, I suggest this is not a problem unique to the United States.

Let me just conclude by suggesting that all of this counsels caution in the expectation that humanity can any time soon come up with a regime governing the use of force that fulfils the dream of the UN founders. That does not mean that the UN cannot function effectively in a variety of different areas. I have spent some time working for the International Atomic Energy Agency [AEA] in Vienna and I have often said that any department or agency of the United States government would regard the AEA as a model of administrative probity in every way; and that is true of so many entities of the UN. It does not mean that the UN cannot prosecute an effective war against poverty and disease. It does not mean that international law will fail in insuring smooth and regular international communication and transportation.

No, the world of high politics concerning peace, the nerve-center security issues that Sir Brian has been referring to, is very different from the world of low politics in which the conditions for effective regulation are in many cases present. There, however, in the world of high politics, the UN has repeatedly failed and there is, I say it with regret, no reason to believe that in the future success is any more likely. That is useful to know before rather than after the humanity next jumps out of the plane and relies on the UN parachute to open.

Peace Building in an Inseparable World

JONATHAN MOORE

Peace building, the United Nations term and the less cantankerous one for nation building,[1] is not working. Since it takes generations rather than years, a true evaluation is not yet possible. Beauty is in the eye of the beholder, of course, so in order to keep trying and to avoid demoralization, hope lives that success will be achieved. But not yet, and not the way things are going.[2]

A Rich-Poor Microcosm

The countries addressed here are among the sorriest and most afflicted, some regarded as failed or failing.[3] They are radically different from one another, while sharing certain qualities. Each peace-building country has a different configuration of afflictions to be confronted. The problems of Afghanistan, Cambodia, East Timor, Iraq, Kosovo, and Somalia stem from international conflict; Afghanistan, Iraq, Kosovo, and Rwanda live in particularly bad neighborhoods; Afghanistan and Iraq have regional enclaves with strong military and paramilitary forces; Afghanistan, Haiti, and East Timor have pathetically weak institutions; Haiti has a horribly destroyed environment and few natural resources,[4] and Rwanda has a severely damaged psyche and few natural resources; Iraq and Sri Lanka had better-educated human resources and advanced infrastructure than most; Kosovo, Rwanda, and Sri Lanka are split by ethnic conflict; Somalia is dominated by clans and effectively without a central government.

These are countries at the not end of the gap between the haves and the have-nots that are gripped in internal crisis and trying to manage the transition from war to peace. Large portions of their populations struggle for protection, stability, and livelihood; their leaders struggle for power. They are postconflict but remain conflict-prone. Predators sell arms, grab territory, or extract resources, if there are any. It is a mix of a crap-shoot and the Perils of Pauline, in messy, jumbled places, out of control. The "international community"—before, after, or in lieu of military intervention—fusses about what and what not to do, and a mix of policemen, do-gooders, and opportunists arrive from abroad, or don't, to help build peace.

Peace building is a microcosm of the world today. Its countries, both in their inner turmoil and in the impact they have on the world outside, epitomize our moral and material dilemmas. They are havens of resentment and injustice, crucibles of enduring ethnic hatreds; they are the clash points of rich and poor, of traditional and modern; they are the seedbeds of terrorism, disease, drug trafficking, and environmental degradation; they are the beacons of survival and hope. Their numbers are likely to grow; their problems are likely to spread. Waiting for the benefits of globalization, they threaten the harmony of interdependence. Peace building challenges the world to be more connected and less separate.

Challenge and Denial

There are three realities that are important to keep in mind when considering peace building and how to improve it. They tend to be denied or ignored, and to do so constitutes a huge liability.

First, the challenge is prodigious. A poor country in the aftermath of war is afflicted with multiple problems and vulnerabilities that tend to reinforce each other. To turn them around is a massive task. This is especially true when external factors work against progress rather than in favor of it: a highly competitive and discriminatory international economy, a widening gap between the haves and have-nots, technological leaps that exacerbate disparities and resentment, and international pathologies, such as disease, terrorism, narcotics, environmental degradation, and spreading conflicts. In the transition from war to peace, rehabilitation after recent conflict and early development out of poverty—rebuilding and building—are combined. Although priorities must be set, the various needs must be addressed simultaneously because they are mutually interdependent.

Depending on the specific circumstances, peace-building efforts include the following: (1) repairing and upgrading basic infrastructure, such as secondary roads and bridges, wells and irrigation systems, and schools and clinics; (2) restoring basic water, health, and education services; (3) revitalizing agricultural production, livestock, and fisheries; (4) renovating markets, increasing trade, and creating jobs; (5) rebuilding capacity in local authorities and civil society; (6) reintegrating into the society repatriated refugees, displaced populations, and demobilized soldiers; (7) encouraging dialogue and national reconciliation; and (8) building capacity at the national level—in government ministries, the legal and justice system, effective security, elections, political parties and parliaments, and macro-economic policy and the financial and banking system. All this, and more, while attempting to keep politics and security from eating you up, is likely to be overwhelming.

Second, the powerful donor nations, which set the multilateral and bilateral agendas for peace building and provide its financing, do not commit the necessary will and funds. We pretend to do so. But recognizing the need to respond to these human tragedies and political dangers, the "international community" nevertheless tends to lessen the huge size and complexity of this phenomenon to something that matches what it is willing to invest. The true dimensions are distorted, per-

X /281

ception is fuzzed; the Poconos are substituted for the Himalayas. The result is that insufficiency is built into the policies, and their implementation is inherently flawed. Failure results and is followed by recrimination. A different way of describing this is to point out that there is a natural lag between early efforts to deal with a new problem and the greater understanding and strengthened skills that come with experience. Another is simply to say that the situations calling out for peace building, while requiring some attention, do not engage our national interest enough to merit greater investment, so we give some of them a try on the cheap, hoping for the best and trusting to luck. We play catch up, and fall behind.[6] N

The third reality is the disconnect between the root causes of the problems these conflicted states need help coping with and the efforts applied by those outsiders who are offering help. The four principal sectors of effort are security, humanitarian, political, and development. Early effort encompasses rehabilitation and reconstruction programs that well-designed emergency humanitarian relief should have prepared the way for. These efforts lead to longer-term social and economic development, which stretches beyond the postconflict transition period. The terms are inexact and subject to misuse. There is a continuum or spectrum of effort, dynamic rather than static, with discernible phases but also simultaneity, overlapping, and bridging. Development invariably comes in a poor last. Security must be established and sustained for anything else to work. Political/diplomatic efforts proceed throughout. Humanitarian programs come when needed, are generally popular and attract relatively more funding, at least in the short-term, and are run by UN agencies and international nongovernmental organizations (NGOs). Development programs are more complex, controversial, take much, much longer, and must be undertaken in delicate partnership with local authorities and assets.

Secretary-General Kofi Annan's 1997 package of reforms concentrated on humanitarian coordination and peace and security mechanisms; the Brahimi Report in 2000 failed to integrate development programs into UN peace operations; N and the special structures set up under the Special Representative of the Secretary-General (SRSG) to provide overall UN authority in the most critical complex emergencies abroad give short shift to the development agenda. Development efforts tend to be crowded out by more immediate urgencies and pursued almost as an afterthought. Yet socioeconomic development is the most fundamental insurance against future conflict. If it is not made prominent and given sustained priority and strong financing, peace building will end up chasing its tail, costly security-humanitarian-political efforts will be wasted, and the problems will return.

So, from the outset we have three powerful, fundamental obstacles: the enormity of the challenge itself, the insistent underrating of it by those who try to take it on, and the persistent failure to attack the root causes of the crises. Unless

X /282

peace-building efforts are able to recognize and deal resolutely with these broad problems, the specific efforts in individual countries cannot succeed.

Stumbling In

It is hard to say that the United States got into peace building voluntarily, or even consciously. It is more the case that we have stumbled in. Peace building is the by-product of humanitarian emergencies and the interventions to deal with them, and of the associated erosion of sovereignty, of nations committing inhumanitarian acts against their own people.[8] If you have saved lives, then the moral logic that follows is that you should help build livelihoods. A cruder version of the connection is this: "If you destroy it, you own it." But this can lead to lots of trouble: mission creep, intrusiveness in foreign cultures by the humanitarians, political and security factors unwilling to be kept separate, casualties, and getting seriously bogged down.

We have been providing foreign assistance to developing nations for a long time, often motivated by strategic interests and tied to our own pocketbooks. We have nonetheless kept ourselves reasonably immune from local problems, but this is different. Those were "normal development situations" and these are not. These are characterized by severe distress in the midst of grinding poverty, recurrent conflict, and political dysfunction. The setting now is post–Cold War, with a shrinking world offering different threats and opportunities, new kinds of incentives for alleviation and exploitation.[9] Cambodia was followed by Mozambique. Afghanistan staggered along, Zaire was covered up, and Sierra Leone blew up. Thousands of lives were saved in Somalia before the UN and the United States dived into civil war, got whacked, and exited, and soon after, the U.S.S. *Harlan County* was frightened out to sea from Port-au-Prince Harbor. Wars were fought and bombs dropped in Bosnia and Kosovo, together with international regimes devised to run the countries. Rwanda's tragedy was tragically botched. The Aussies provided the punch and the UN follow-on peacekeepers and a civilian administration in East Timor. Then international terrorism struck, the United States retaliated in Afghanistan and presumptively preempted in Iraq, making war on a major scale, followed by prolonged conflict, volatile politics, and limited reconstruction.

The peace-building phenomena resulting from these disparate configurations of provocation and response make the international community look like reeling, staggering Keystone Kops. In extreme cases, we are in danger of creating a witless cycle—making war in order to be able to make peace afterward, making war to get rid of the reasons why war is necessary, not being really serious about the cleanup after war and failing to understand what war is all about. Generally, we have become caught up in peace building without being good at it and without being sure we are really in favor of it. The powers-that-be we have prefer, on the whole, economic and military imperialism to democratic and development imperialism, even with visions of milk and honey, prosperity, and democracy for all. At the same time, significant experience has been gained in acknowledging the importance of afflicted and failing states, in broadly consulting about collective action, in designing multifaceted interventions, and in testing the tolerances of the societies hosting these undertakings.

Among the various aspects that, together, produce the complexity of peace building are three that particularly define it as a microcosm of the world at large. They are the interaction of security and development, the role of the UN, and the delicate relationship between the international and the indigenous players.

Security and Development

The intersection of needs and programs in security and development is fiendishly symbiotic. The two sides do not like each other, they do not understand each other, and they cannot live without each other. If there is violent conflict it must be ended and relative safety and stability established before significant reconstruction can get under way. Even the delivery of humanitarian relief requires some security and protection. In Afghanistan and Iraq, rehabilitation and reconstruction work in the countryside beyond Kabul and Baghdad is severely restricted by lack of security. Personnel dedicated to this work are pinned down and hemmed in at the capitals. The principle has long been established elsewhere: Security comes first. As UN envoy Lakhdar Brahimi ruefully commented, "You can't have peace and justice at the same time and in most cases it's better to have peace first."[10] All sorts of ingenious and noble efforts are attempted to rebuild capacity in the midst of ongoing or recurrent violence, but as the need for security dominates, the military forces and programs to meet that need are so overpowering that they tend to impinge on the other sectors of effort. Yet without socioeconomic progress, insecurity will erupt again.

A major problem occurs when military personnel become involved beyond providing protection for emergency humanitarian relief and engage in rehabilitation projects, such as infrastructure repair, restoring electrical power, temporary provision of human services, rudimentary training, and setting up local governments. Such activity can indeed be valuable, and the military have relevant skills and equipment—for instance, in engineering. But these functions are inherently limited and, taken too far, run into trouble. In Haiti, special forces units sent to the countryside to restore order and demonstrate a show of force did excellent collateral work to help the local populations get on their feet. Yet this was undertaken and justified basically for the purpose of "force protection," that is, it was primarily self-serving, and the mutual benefits extend only so far before conflicts of interest and of culture are encountered. The real expertise and continuing dedication in extended humanitarian and prolonged development assistance lie in the UN agencies and NGOs that have long experience working together with local assets toward sustained growth. To the extent that they are falsely substituted for or preempted from their work, peace building can be set back.

Three specific problems in Afghanistan illustrate the difficulty that the military and development sectors have in working productively together. This is not a matter of fault or blame, particularly; both are trying their best, it is a matter of the radical differences between the two, and of the bubbling cauldron where peace is attempted. First, the civilian rehabilitation and development professionals operate traditionally in a neutral space with regard to the political and military activity taking place around them. The access and cooperation they get and their efficacy depend on not aiding (or being seen to aid) the contending partisans. This is a very difficult and delicate goal in itself, but when military personnel, sometimes in civilian garb, who may be providing protection and support but who are also gathering intelligence and fighting the war mix in, things become confused, and the civilian missions are infected. Second, military units operating in various locations throughout Afghanistan for the purposes of tracking down Al Qaeda and Taliban forces find it necessary to make alliances with regional warlords and local paramilitary commanders who live and exert power in these areas. Such alliances are as nasty as they are necessary, and the U.S. forces find various ways to ingratiate themselves with their local partners, including rehabilitation and local support services, and this can have a threefold negative effect on peace building: (a) the combat mission is emphasized at a cost to the security-establishing mission; (b) professional development personnel and programs tend to be shut out; and (c) the national political strategy jointly pursued by the Afghan leadership in Kabul and its international sponsors to bring the warlords into a coherent national government tends to be undercut. Third, the provincial reconstruction teams combining military and civilian personnel and their missions, which were set up by the United States to contend with the voids of access and safety across Afghanistan's landscape are probably more harmful than helpful. They are oversold, too light and too thin to accomplish the security and reconstruction tasks they pretend to fulfill, and they to substitute for serious area-based regional development programs jointly sponsored by the UN and the Kabul government, which are left struggling with inadequate support.

Militaries cannot substitute for civilian authorities in the political and economic areas of peace building, despite the urgency of the security situation and even if such civilian authorities are not available or prepared. This is not what they do well and they should not be saddled with it. Reports of the 101st Airborne Division's work in Kurdistan recruiting local leaders and building municipal governments were impressive and even reassuring at the time. They provide, however, an example of isolated military units performing resourcefully under pressure but unconnected to national governance strategies pursued by the Provisional Coalition Authority and its international and Iraqi advisers hunkered down in Baghdad and are therefore unlikely to be enduring. At the same time—here is the reciprocating dynamic again—it has also become embarrassingly clear that there must be an adequate number of troops able to supply overall security and that they cannot be withdrawn prematurely in response to local political pressure or pressure from home without causing grave harm to any peace-building commitment that includes sustainable development.

The UN Role

The UN role is at the core of peace building for several reasons, aside from being so mandated by its charter and the global aspirations invested in it. It is likely to play key roles in most if not all of the sectors (security, humanitarian, political, and development) and is the only such organization. It is the best candidate to help coordinate disparate contributions to peace building. It has the programmatic experience and expertise that is crucial to these challenges and with its NGO partners it actually does the work. Many of its agencies are active in the given country before and after as well as during the crisis and, therefore, they have acquaintanceship, memory, and continuity. And the UN provides an international legitimacy and multilateral cover to nations that want to participate but do not want to play too prominent a role.

There are, of course, problems and weaknesses that afflict the UN itself and that circumscribe its peace-building missions, but none that is not attributable to the following: (1) it is assigned hugely daunting and improbable tasks by the often inflated instructions of its major intergovernmental bodies (the Security Council and the General Assembly); (2) it is a notoriously multifarious and loose-jointed collection, not so much decentralized as fragmented, of almost two hundred member nations mixing conflicting interests, ethnicities, and ideologies, producing an imposing bureaucracy; (3) it is totally a creature of the politics of its rulers, its membership, sometimes influenced by the greater numbers of the poorer states but dominated by the wills and wealth of the most powerful ones; (4) it is populated by members of the human species, which has not matched scientific and technological progress with moral and altruistic development. So, what do we expect? Well, enough to keep trying to make it better.

Three characteristics of UN involvement in peacekeeping exemplify the nature of the world at large. The first is that it engages at the convergence of war and peace, which is what these situations are all about, and what our global struggles are all about. The second is that it is an institution deeply committed to fighting the schism between the rich and powerful and the poor and weak, which appears in these instances in the form of both problem and prescription. The third is that

X/286

it represents the major commitment to collaboration and partnership, which is the strategy that an unreconciled but interdependent world badly needs to gain ascendance because of the haphazard bilateral and unilateral practices that will continue.

The in-country structure of the UN presence in peacekeeping operations is a major factor in their effectiveness. Ordinarily, the UN pursues its various humanitarian and development programs in a decentralized manner, which relies on the autonomy of individual agencies, loosely presided over by a UN resident coordinator appointed by the Secretary-General, and supported by the UN Development Program. In situations of "complex emergency" where conflict occurs and security forces are needed, the Security Council authorizes the Secretary-General to appoint his own special representative, SRSG, along with peacekeeping troops and a support staff imported in part from UN headquarters, and to set up a regime on the ground to oversee and to some extent direct the various programs. The military and political elements tend to dominate on-going efforts. Multiple variables come into play, for instance: the quality of international personnel assigned to the field, the setting of priorities and the difficulties of coordination, the policies devised and capacities mobilized by the local government, funding, and the dynamics of the problems themselves. Essentially, this is a very messy situation with inherently limited discipline and cohesiveness, characterized by a lot of dedicated people running around (among a few charlatans), trying to do their best and with progress made despite the obstacles.[11]

A selective review of UN struggles with peace building suggests its difficulty in aligning its various parts and functions with other actors and events swirling about and throughout. In Afghanistan, the comfort that donor nations felt with the ease and familiarity of humanitarian assistance along with their suspicions of the capacity and integrity of the interim government to absorb more complex development efforts delayed for some time the availability and flow of support for the latter. In Cambodia and Kosovo, the structure of the UN enterprise demoted the rehabilitation and development priority.[12] In Iraq, the United States relegated the UN to a secondary role, which, along with the explosive insecurity, prevented reconstruction programs from getting under way and contributed to the buildup of the Iraqi anti-"occupation" psychology. In East Timor, when the UN was facing the end of its mission and realized its overly ambitious development agenda was falling seriously short, it prepared an inventory of unfulfilled and reformulated objectives to alert the unprepared East Timorese to take them over. In Mozambique and Rwanda, efforts by the UN to coordinate programs in-country were frustrated by instructions from headquarters of its operating agencies not to cooperate.[13] In Somalia, critical UN humanitarian efforts for drought-affected populations saved many thousands of lives, and the stumbling into political and security disaster was not due to the undesirability of "mission creep" itself but to horrendous misjudgments. Subsequently, UN headquarters' insistence in supporting a national government which was not there lost the opportunity to invest in a regional "building blocks" strategy in Somalia.

Particularly intensive challenges emerge when UN programs combining security and political and rehabilitation components must be undertaken with the joint participation of both bilateral actors and local authorities. The ambition and complexity of these programs should be recognized prior to setting them in motion and burdening them with premature expectations. Two examples are CIVPOL (international civilian police recruited and deployed by the UN) and DDR (disarmament, demobilization, and reintegration of local soldiers and paramilitary) programs. In the case of CIVPOL, there are invariable delays in scaring up enough cops from a variety of countries with different policing concepts, training, and languages—from the start the UN is placed in a disadvantageous situation, lacking reserve monies or personnel. The military forces become upset because policing is not what they are trained for or expected to do. It complicates their mission and delays their exit. Meanwhile, a local civilian capacity for insuring general security and law and order has to be trained, usually by the same CIVPOL component, but without the system of justice yet available that could provide infrastructure and reinforcement for the indigenous police to operate in.

Concerning DDR, the UN must have the skill to consult and collaborate with a number of powerful actors to design, negotiate, and implement integrated programs of extraordinary political and technical complexity. All sorts of conflicting interests are confronted. Different warrior populations have different political allies, regional warlords and the national government jockey for advantage, weapons owners have economic and cultural reasons for not giving them up, and the weapons trade remains robust enough in many countries to replenish fairly quickly. Finally, "reintegration" for reformed fighters—and to a lesser degree the same is true for returning refugees or displaced persons—depends on there existing an economic and social fabric to absorb them in terms of jobs and livelihoods. Here security, political, and developmental concerns can come into serious discord: Security requires demobilization and disarmament, politics wants this to happen quickly, and development will not be ready to fulfill its role prior to a long period of successful effort. So a crucial area of peace building can be described as discordant and disintegrated, for analytically clear reasons, yet the UN is subject to being held responsible for the shortfall or the screw-up, for not controlling the uncontrollables, often by those who are failing to provide the kinds of support that would help the common cause.

Meanwhile, back at UN headquarters, there is some potentially good news for peace building. This is the adaptability of the world body to work with other international entities in various configurations and timing in collaborative peace operations. The UN's authority to act under Chapters VI and VII of its charter lies

X /288

with the Security Council,[14] but that organ may find it difficult to reach agreement about what action it will authorize and it may refuse to approve or endorse at all, depending on the particular exigencies of the threat to international peace and security and humanitarian principles, as well as on the respective national lenses through which the big powers view the issue. In some cases, the capacity and mandate of traditional UN peacekeeping forces proving too weak for the job are a factor. Hence, regarding the UN role in Kosovo and later in Iraq, there was severe disgruntlement and rousting about for acceptable approaches and alliances, but eventually there was compromise and accommodation. The members of the Security Council and the Secretary-General have proved with passing time and changing events to be flexible enough to negotiate different models that preserve a useful role for the UN and its purposes.

In Cambodia and Mozambique, peace agreements and Security Council resolutions preceded intervention, and the UN mandate covered both peacekeeping and rebuilding. In Somalia, the UN and the United States collaborated in security and political and rehabilitation efforts, with an American SRSG bucking his own government and the U.S. military working apart from the UN peacekeepers—resulting in thousands of lives saved, mission creep, disaster, and egregious exit. In the case of Rwanda, the United States collaborated quite congenially with the UN and others in a series of terrible, cowardly, and tragic indecisions. In Bosnia, following a failed UN peacekeeping mission, NATO took military command and later the Dayton Accords powers set up a civilian administration under a high commissioner, with UN acquiescence. In Kosovo, a NATO bombing campaign without UN approval was eventually followed by Security Council endorsement of national contingents of NATO ground troops dividing the province into five sectors, and a UN SRSG overseeing four civilian "pillars," two of which were headed by the European Union and the Organization for Security and Cooperation in Europe. In Haiti, East Timor and Sierra Leone, the Security Council authorized military interventions in advance by the United States the United Kingdom, and Australia, respectively—"multinational forces under the control of lead nations"[15]—in each case followed by UN peacekeeping forces and a UN–led civilian operation. In Afghanistan, the Security Council authorized military intervention by a United States–led coalition, with backup from UN and NATO peacekeepers; the United States retained control of security operations and the UN ran the civilian administration. In Iraq, the United States/United Kingdom–led coalition attacked Iraq on its own, to be followed later by Security Council resolutions acquiescing in control by the coalition of both the security and civilian operations with the UN playing a support role only. In the cases of Cambodia, Somalia, Bosnia, Kosovo, East Timor, and Iraq, the UN or a modified international authority actually took over and ran the given country for an interim period in lieu of any local government.

These mixed mechanisms have not been forged without serious cost to the United Nations, and some diplomats make strong arguments that in recent cases it has compromised away its integrity, especially in the face of U.S. unilateralism as accompanied by arrogance and bullying. But the new world order is not so orderly that the UN has exclusive rights to peace and security action, and it should not, for it is not the boss but the servant of an international community, which although at odds with itself has not given up trying to find ways that work. Despite appearances and behavior to the contrary, the United States has persistently demonstrated that it believes it is not in its interest to renounce or abandon the UN. And we are in a long chapter. Over the past several years, along with misconceived structures, workable models have been produced suggesting resourceful, viable partnerships in the future. It has been a period of trial and error, and of persistence, for the UN in peace building, and we do not yet know which lessons have been learned and which will be missed.

Outsiders and Insiders

The interaction between the outsiders who come to provide assistance and the insiders who live in the countries receiving it is extremely complex and delicate and seldom achieves its optimal harmony and productivity. By definition, this is where the two worlds interlocked in peace building, the international and the local, really meet. The nature of the relationship is especially critical because it occurs at the delivery end, where the outcome of the enterprise is proven. This is not distant negotiation and policy theory but immediate, on the ground, raw implementation. And it is the individual workers at this field level who are the real heroes of this story, operating face-to-face, in intimate engagement with the realities, and with the best opportunity to employ their best human qualities.

The reasons for the difficulty of this interface are not obscure. There are barriers of culture, language, tradition, and ideology; differences in education, training, experience, motivation, and capacity. It is dangerous to overgeneralize here; one must allow for wide variations, and neither side is homogeneous. But the contrasts between those characteristics inherent in a developing society and those in economically advanced ones are in play. These contrasts between the two sets of partners are profound and can easily produce conflict in the relationship. The real problem is the difference in relative power between the two sets of actors. One side is powerful, strong, rich, in a position to be of help; the other is weaker, poorer, and in a position to have to ask for it. The phenomenon of superiority/inferiority is at the same time not only a potentially destructive psychology but also the very basis of the relationship.

There are several elemental principles to keep in mind when attempting to manage the interaction between the two sets of partners. One is to recognize the

X/290

profound differences, not to smooth them over superficially or pretend that they do not exist, let alone try to erase them. Another is to try jointly to understand them better, rather than to accept isolation and indulge resentment. The key is reciprocated respect, which cannot be assumed but takes serious effort, discipline, and patience. A great deal can be accomplished simply by how competently each actor does his or her assigned job in the context of contributing to the mutual goal—concentrating on the work at hand can help focus energies on building common cause and confidence rather than magnifying countercurrents. So, as obvious as they are often ignored, there are some things each side can usefully keep in mind.

The initial obligation for getting the relationship working right lies with the international side, simply because they are the outsiders and because they are the more privileged. Above all, it must not distort the collaboration by domination, nor arbitrarily impose its interests on the local society. This is difficult, since one of the reasons the outsiders are present is that they hold convictions about solving the problems of deprivation, instability, and conflict. An example of the necessary restraint is not to overload local capacity; not to ask local actors to do things they cannot do yet. But also, the international community must be ready to apply certain conditions and enforce certain standards in the kind of assistance it offers. This is dangerous territory with delicate thresholds; but it is not conditionality itself that is bad, it is when the leverage used is unfair or counterproductive. In Haiti, it was the prolonged failure of the international contributors and the Aristide government to reach agreement on the ongoing obligations of each that contributed to stagnancy, instability, and the eventual failure of the government. Who is to blame? Who knows? The point is that greater accommodation was necessary and possible. In any case, Haiti is now in a much weaker position dealing with an international community even more inclined to ensure that its investments are not wasted.

In the political realm, the influence of the external actors is particularly treacherous. They can too easily design their models and project their timetables based on their own concepts and interests, distorting national capacities and warping the emergence of national leadership. Elections are a prime candidate for this danger; for instance, the first winner-take-all elections can produce polarization and propel extremist elements. While outside help is needed to encourage functional self-governance; a consultative approach in preparing both structure and personnel (as in the case of Lakhdar Brahimi, the UN envoy in Afghanistan) to ensure that the result has a better chance of being organic than a largely imposed approach that tempts local rejection (as in the case of L. Paul Bremer III, U.S. head of the Coalition Provisional Government in Iraq). Likewise, foreign assistance programs cannot be designed in foreign capitals and delivered wholesale overseas but must be negotiated locally to match them with the absorption and production capacity of the recipients. Care must be taken in the case of ongoing governments and systems in place to build on what is there rather than with replacement or too much "reform" too quickly.

Expatriate staff working in-country must recognize from the outset, as Maj. Gen. William L. Nash[16] has warned, speaking of peace-building operations everywhere, that "If you're part of the solution, you're part of the problem." They must be freed up from too much headquarters bureaucracy, static templates, and micromanagement, and be allowed to do the job and be supported in their efforts to get it done. They must be allowed to identify what the special circumstances and priorities are in the given country and, working closely with the local authorities, to figure out the best ways to address them. They must be willing to challenge instructions from above that they believe to be wrong. They must be devoted to transparency and to being careful to send the right message to their local counterparts, which is, first of all, to avoid inflated expectations. By not overpromising, indeed even by explicating areas of lower priority that cannot be funded (not a normal talent of the international community), the imperative that local leadership do its part can be underscored.

Which brings us to the performance of the indigenous peoples, those who have the ultimate obligation to make the relationship work right so that peace building will be successful. Their first requirement is to mobilize their best capabilities and apply them to priority needs. They must be able, without subservience, to abide— to tolerate—the intruders; no easy assignment. Candid and precise communications are especially important, keeping in mind that in order for the whole endeavor to work the insiders will have to generate as much understanding as possible about what is going on locally; they will have to work overtime to educate the outsiders—who will believe they know more than they do—about the realities in their country. This means being willing to bite the hand that feeds them, or at least speak up and explain why a given policy or program will not work or is harmful.

But the overriding challenge will be for the coherent exercise of political will locally. The international actors can act in such a way as to encourage or to frustrate the development of political leadership, but the ultimate responsibility rests at home, and only national leaders and groups—institutions, civil society, political parties, to the extent they exist—can inspire limpid and harness fractious energies for the common good. We should not casually assume that local rulers will choose to serve the best interests of their whole populations and reject the temptation to simply secure and expand the power of those in charge. Here again, is the microcosm of the rich-poor gap in peace building—Are we hypocritical in expecting that national leaders not emulate in their own country what they see internationally? In any event, how and whether "getting their act together" will happen is something of a mystery, or at least is not predictable under current circumstances and will be different in every case. //

Although the ultimate outcomes are unknown, there is plenty of evidence of tough going. In Cambodia when UNTAC, the UN Transitional Authority, pulled out in 1993, shortly after supervising elections, the two major political factions joined in a coalition government, but instead of their finding a way to provide the stability enabling sustainable progress and growth, prolonged political struggle took over and has since resulted in a one-party and one-leader dictatorship, institutions that are not accountable, and the majority population remaining in dire poverty. In Haiti, from 1995 to 1998 competent and courageous Haitian officials in partnership with the international community rebuilt the Haitian National Police—an impressive feat. But subsequently, more powerful Haitian actors, fearing a strong, publicly accountable professional security organization immune from political manipulation and corruption, quickly and effectively denuded it, which led to widespread criminality and insecurity. Since NATO intervened in Kosovo in 1999, the obsession with the idea that the province must become an independent state, along with shortcomings in UN security and human rights efforts, drove the deeply embedded hostility of ethnic Albanian extremists to erode prospects for a multi-ethnic society. In Sri Lanka in 2002, Sinhalese, Tamils, and Muslims were unwilling or too frightened to take advantage of a cease-fire and peace talks to participate in consultation and dialogue at the community level to plan a peaceful and secure future.

As late as June 2004 in Afghanistan and Iraq, warlords and ethno-religious factions were sparring for power with evolving fragile interim governments amid serious ongoing conflict, endangering social, political, and economic progress. At the same time, following the return of the UN to Haiti, Famli Lavalas, the largest political party and closest to the once overwhelmingly pro-Aristide peasantry, was still refusing to participate in an electoral council responsible for setting up national elections, and the interim government was unwilling or unable to entice it to join, forewarning another potentially crippling stalemate. Also, in Sri Lanka the inability of the Sinhalese majority government in Colombo and the rebel Tamil Tigers to compromise enough either to undertake badly needed humanitarian and development assistance in the northeast of the country, or to agree on a model for an interim administration there prior to a final political settlement, created a standoff that resulted in serious schisms threatening resumption of fighting.

These are not happy stories, even though they should not be regarded in isolation and are not over. What happens to peace building if the locals do not do their job, do not mobilize and coalesce? The foreigners may perform better and stay longer, but they cannot produce sustained progress by themselves even if they were so inclined, and the failing state will continue to flounder, at best—unless members of the international community were to revisit outright colonialism or trusteeships.

Prospects and Prescription

The prospects for peace building are poor, generally speaking, assuming: (1) the extended existence of unstable, failing, conflict-prone states; (2) the international community not undergoing radical change in raising its sophistication, resources, and commitment to deal with the problem; (3) the further widening of the rich-poor gap. There are some potential bright spots: (1) an increased willingness by the international community to get engaged in these situations in various ways (preemptive war requiring reconstruction afterward not being one of them); (2) such greater involvement producing familiarity and connectedness encouraging less detachment and isolation; (3) learning from more experience and improved performance (though slow, erratic, and painful) perhaps leading to greater public awareness about interdependence and broader perceptions of national interest. Future possibilities include: (1) increasing interdependence and globalization causing more serious response and more reliance on multilateral strategies; (2) bad mistakes, especially in the application of military force, and bad performance in peace building, leading to the proliferation of Vietnam and Somalia syndromes; (3) triage.

Various prescriptions for better peace building are implicit in earlier passages describing its challenges and complexities. But a few can be summarily enumerated here, both macro and micro suggestions for future effort. Some general propositions require change internationally in values, priorities, and behavior. They can justifiably be characterized as bromides, yet also as ideas honored by enlightened opinion but not by enlightened action.

1. More multilateral effort, consultation, and collaboration across the international community (including the Bretton Woods institutions); and the obverse of this, which is less competition and exploitation for selfish advantage by international actors, both in distant foreign capitals and on the ground.
2. Greater tolerance for complexity, respect for incremental effort that expects difficulty and setbacks and is willing to learn as it progresses, which does not expect too much and accepts uncertainty as it proceeds.
3. Infusion of respect and application of programmatic restraint in the interaction with local actors to maximize their mobilization of their own capacity.
4. An appreciation of the time necessary to peace building, requiring a virtually revolutionary change in farsightedness, in perception of how long it takes, and a corresponding commitment and effort.

5. Openness, candor, and transparency both in the characterization of the undergirding and ongoing realities of peace building and in the interests and positions taken by international actors about it.

6. Serious funding, way beyond the financial peanuts now committed for peace building.[17]

7. Various radical, outlandish reforms even less likely to be adopted by the powerful should not be overlooked here—such as the cessation of international arms-peddling, the elimination of agricultural subsidies that distort international trade, and the establishment of serious governance capable of protecting the global environment.

Other proposals for the international side are more specific, programmatic, and operational. It would be a big mistake to think that the following specific proposals are sufficient without progress on the preceding general propositions.

1. Establishing sufficient security to allow peace building to take place requires not only the external military authority responsible to sustain it beyond "combat operations" and deploy adequate troops to do the job but also to (a) undertake initial urgent local rehabilitation projects, such as getting basic facilities and services up and running; (b) hand over policing functions to international and local police personnel in an organized and coordinated manner so such transitions are handled smoothly; (c) connect with and support civilian (UN, NGO, and bilateral) organizations in physical and other reconstruction efforts; and (d) train indigenous security personnel thoroughly so that they can take over. Despite efforts to strengthen broad "peacekeeping operations," or OOTW ("operations other than war"), largely the responsibility of Civil Affairs Reservists and despite claims out of Afghanistan and Iraq about military support for local governance, the U.S. military still really does not like to be saddled with this stuff. The earlier intellectual and operational leadership of Marine general Anthony Zinni to build this kind of capacity should be revived and made an integral part of U.S. military doctrine and capacity.[18] It cannot just be left up to the Reserves.

2. It is important to get the international police in fast, and the CIVPOL program run by the Department of Peace-keeping Operations in the UN Secretariat, which relies on contributions of civilian police contingents of uneven quality from individual nations (with different experience, training, and languages and taking much too long to get into place) recruited after crises have struck, must be upgraded. It might be possible to set up a system of pledges by individual nations, with prefinancing, for a standby corps of reserve police, designated national cadres that have undergone special training by the UN and that can be deployed quickly.

3. When the UN seeks to provide oversight and structure in peacekeeping situations, it should (a) be employed with a minimum of bureaucratic weight and layering from New York; (b) ensure that the flow and ebb from resident coordinator to SRSG models and back again are integrated and converted to ensure that the development role is not subsumed and operating agencies not inhibited; (c) coordinate across the various functions of international actors and programs without making coordination an end in itself;[19] and (d) not undertake these efforts without high-quality personnel to do the job.

4. The various operating agencies of the international peacekeeping enterprise, however it is configured, must design their programs based on an assessment of the capacity level in the various sectors of the given society, rejecting standard stereotypes that ignore the huge variations in absorption and need among and within receiving countries.

5. More sophisticated strategies must be developed on the relationship between conditionality and the mobilization of political will and action, through intensive consultations among the major international actors, including the Bretton Woods institutions, and with the indigenous authorities, country by individual country, so that pragmatic and consistent messages are conveyed about what is expected nationally and what will not be provided internationally. Regardless of the level of anticipated international investment there is an obligation—while committing to nonabandonment and long-term help—to make it clear that there is no bail-out: Without the requisite strength in domestic response, there will be failure.

6. Let the expatriates on the ground, working closely with each other and with their local counterparts, have as much responsibility as possible to determine programs and implement them, and give them the support from above and outside to their jobs. The amount of hierarchical micromanaging, interference, and outright bad judgment, often encouraged by donor states and substituting for reinforcement, is staggering in this business.

7. Democratization should be carefully calibrated and adjusted to work with the traditions and tolerances of individual countries and in any case pursued gradually and with patience, rather than being forced arbitrarily according to external ideologies and political timetables.

8. The international community, most of whose representatives come from advanced rather than poor societies, should not allow its preference for relatively fancy "governance" programs in support of institution building at the national government level to (a) underprioritize more basic programs addressing needs at the grassroots level in poverty reduction, agricultural reform, basic health, education, and welfare services, and support for civil

x /296

society, or (b) overlook regional "building blocks" strategies in the absence of strong central authority. Not only do "bottom-up" efforts address the needs of the most vulnerable but their value is likely to be more enduring in the event of resumptions of violence and instability destructive to some more fashionable "top-down" investments.

9. The availability of competent personnel to be recruited and deployed for peace-building assignments by the international community must be elevated by cooperative national and multilateral effort. This means not only educating and training people so that they know something about the cultures they will be working in and maybe even speak the language as well as have specific expertise and skills to do their jobs but also providing incentives to attract people of exceptionally high quality. Shortfall in human resource capacity is a perpetual plague for the internationals as well as the local actors.

10. There are some organizational and structural changes that can be made at home within governments active in peace building that could help their policies and programs have better results. Some European donor nations have combined their foreign and development ministries, for instance. Suggestions have been made and models are being studied in the United States for a cabinet department in development cooperation, a reconstruction bureau in the State Department, and a remodeling of the National Security Council, for instance. Aggregating and focusing greater expertise and competence is essential, but undue faith should not be placed in such tinkering, which takes a lot of time, energy, and wrangling and sometimes acts as a stealthy substitute for the kind of real change in perception, values, and national priorities that is necessary for true success in peace building.

11. When William James was asked what he thought were the three most important human qualities, he answered: "Kindness, kindness, kindness." That is not irrelevant for peace building, either, but if the question were phrased a little differently to address our purposes here, the answer might be "Capacity building, capacity building, capacity building."

How We Are Going to Treat Each Other

What will happen as this unique crunch between war and peace remains unresolved, in a world both flailing to sort out and trying to ignore a lot of confusion, hope, fear, collision, ambition? There are bigger challenges that may have more impact on our future than these desperate imbroglios, although not wholly separable from them: trade, terrorism, nuclear proliferation, AIDS, the environment, the Middle East, China, for instance. But peace-building circumstances and undertakings combine many of our issues and reveal a lot about ourselves, the human condition. Peace building reasserts pathologies and strengths, both in our nature and in our behavior, in our better angels and meaner shadows. Simply put, because it is important and floundering, it needs more reflection and action.

In concluding, there are some essential thoughts, distillate, from this examination. The first is that the peace-building microcosm manifests most profoundly the disparity between people who have and people who do not, simultaneously a moral and an existential phenomenon, and our challenge is to be sure that the twain shall meet. The rich/poor gap is the philosophical core here. It produces the need for peace building and complicates its pursuit.

Another central idea is that the antidote to disconnectedness—the apartheid, which characterizes our existence—unsurprisingly is greater connectedness. There is need for a more integrated approach to almost everything we do, and it takes a broader perspective and a bolder imagination to translate this into policy. The relationship between peace building and terrorism, for instance, demonstrates this. The circumstances that require peace building also provide an incitement to terrorism, and joint efforts to effect peace building become the targets of the terrorists. One cannot be fought without combating the other; you have to get at the roots, not just go for the head.[20] Those who argue that the relationship between poverty and terrorism is irrelevant or nonexistent have concocted an elitist pretension. Failing states, states in chaos and violence, are breeding grounds for terrorism. People who are miserable are more likely to resort to violence. People who regard with ugly clarity the disparity between their meager existence and the lives of those who are consuming the most and polluting the most will use the weapons distributed with unending efficiency by the same perps to respond, and the response will be destructive. One of the things that peace building tries to confront is what to do with these arms. But the overall goal it aims for is to help build enough security, political stability, and economic sustainability to reduce that disparity.

It follows that this has to be a joint effort: partnership, collaboration. The "us-versus-them," dog-eat-dog mentality does not work, at least not in peace building. Unilateralism and dominance will not work, either. You cannot fight nationalism with nationalism. Multilateralism is needed; peace building will not work without it and the world will not work without it. Unilateral action must not be sacrificed and should always be available, but its limited and negative values as a strategy need to be recognized, particularly when connected to an overreliance on military force, so that it can be seen as a bad idea and relegated to the category of last resort.

The increasing intensity of interdependence, one aspect of which is "globalization," with positive and negative forces moving across continents and seas and political boundaries, ever faster and with more impact and with little control, may bring us to confront its implications and consequences. For the United States this means defining our national interest much less narrowly, recognizing that geopolitical strategy is geodevelopmental, and perceiving our future as integrally connected to people both distant and different from us. The world should not be viewed as good or bad—it is both, and we are part of it—but as inseparable. Here is where the moral and the operational meet,[21] the idealist and the realist join forces. It comes down to how we are going to treat each other, not only here but there, and what that means for our survival.

For this redefining of our national interest, there must be a commitment to open debate and public education about the true nature of the world—what this implies for us and what our obligations are. Shibboleths and slogans that misrepresent without attempting to generate an understanding of the depths of our dangers and opportunities are to be shunned. And either in response to needed leadership or in its absence, the polity—the sovereign of democracy, which is the people of our nation—must assert itself. Dedicated participation in self-government is the patriotic obligation on which our future happiness, not to say survival, depends.

It may be that the remarkable thing about our present experience with peace building, a cause for hopefulness if not exactly optimism, is that we are still trying. Halting, marginal, even agonized progress is being made somewhere some of the time. People are being helped, not just with lives but with livelihoods, and they are responding. Some connections are dynamically, reciprocally active. For peace building to catch, hold, and prevail will require radical rather than merely incremental or gradual change. How fast could that happen? How long will that take? U.S. Major General David Petraeus, during his exceptional tour in peace building in northern Iraq, asked a reporter, "Tell me how this ends?"[22] It doesn't.

NOTES

1. Excerpts from a briefing on terrorism given by the Joan Shorenstein Center on the Press, Politics, and Public Policy, Kennedy School of Government, Harvard University at the National Press Club, Washington, D.C., on November 28, 2001: "Peace-building is different from peace-making (bringing about the end of a war, including negotiations) and peacekeeping (using troops in an attempt to insure that the peace is kept and war doesn't break out again). . . . A section of the Secretary-General's reform program announced in July 1997 contained the following description: 'The concept of post-conflict peace-building refers to the various concurrent and integrated actions undertaken at the end of a conflict to consolidate peace and prevent an occurrence of armed confrontation. . . . Peace-building does not replace ongoing humanitarian and development activities in countries emerging from crises. Rather it aims to build on them.' "

2. When the UN's Transitional Authority departed Cambodia in 1993, following war, genocide, and invasion, a peace agreement, the expenditure of almost two billion dollars in foreign aid, the holding of elections, and the adoption of a constitution, the authority judged the peace building a "success." But this self-serving label was part of an effort to make the exit felicitous and masked the bad news ahead. Mozambique, having "recovered" following an eleven-year civil war and enduring another major presence and effort of the UN and its colleagues, tends to appear on the plus side of the ledger, but it is simply too early to tell. Namibia, farther in

the past, looks like a winner. In the present, Sierra Leone and East Timor have made progress. Elsewhere, the future looks more questionable or forlorn, especially in Africa—e.g., Angola, Rwanda, Somalia, Congo, Ivory Coast, Liberia, and Zimbabwe.

3. The countries in which postconflict peace building has been undertaken that are given the most attention in this chapter are Afghanistan, Cambodia, East Timor, Haiti, Iraq, Kosovo, Mozambique, Rwanda, Somalia, and Sri Lanka. The author draws on direct, in-country experience in all of them except Iraq.

4. The Haitian town of Mapou and the one thousand people who lived there were destroyed by the May 2004 flood. Fernando Gueren, a farmer whose parents and son were swept away, said: "Most people here work the earth, but the most desperate take the trees [to make charcoal]. When they take the trees, there's nothing left to drink up the water. They work the land to survive. This is one of the problems of Haiti too great to solve with a sack of rice." Tim Weiner, *New York Times,* May 31, 2004.

5. "Almost half the world's six billion people live under the poverty line of two dollars a day: 1.2 billion earn less than one dollar a day and are in the extreme poverty category. By the year 2020 the globe likely will add 2 billion more people, 95 percent who will reside in the developing world." J. Brian Atwood, "The Link between Poverty and Violent Conflict," *New England Journal of Public Policy,* 19, no. 1 (Fall–Winter 2003–4): 159. "The rich-poor divide is growing: in 1960, in the twenty richest countries the per-capita gross national product (GDP) was eighteenfold that in the poorest twenty countries; by 1995 this gap had increased to thirty-seven-fold. Between 1980 and the late 1990s, inequality increased in forty-eight of the seventy-three countries for which there are reliable data. Inequality is not restricted to personal income, but other important areas of life, including health status, access to health care, education and employment opportunities are also involved. Relative deprivation, one of the precursors of war, is increasing exponentially among nations and within nations. . . . Growing socioeconomic and other disparities between the rich and the poor within countries, and between rich and poor nations, also contribute to the likelihood of armed conflict." Barry Levy and Victor Sidel, "War and Public Health in the Twenty-first Century," *New England Journal of Public Policy,* 19, no. 1 (Fall–Winter 2003–4): 169, 172.

6. "In 1994, the cost of U.N. peacekeeping operations was running at roughly 4 billion U.S. dollars per year, and the U.N. was spending about the same on emergency assistance. U.N. grants for development worldwide were estimated at about 5 billion dollars annually. Combined bilateral assistance for development was about 60 billion annually (compared to the total net flow of Organization for Economic Cooperation and Development (OECD) countries to developing countries and multilateral organizations of almost 106 billion in l992). . . . Donor response to consolidated emergency appeals were way under half of what was asked; for instance, such requests for Afghanistan set at l22 million for the period October l993 to September l994 raised roughly 40 per cent of that." Jonathan Moore, *The U.N. and Complex Emergencies: Rehabilitation in Third World Transitions* (Geneva: UN Research Institute for Social Development, 1996): 53. The UN requested $35 million in emergency funds for Haiti in March and was still $26 million short of that goal by the beginning of June. Tim Weiner, *New York Times,* June 1, 2004.

7. "Report of the Secretary General on the Implementation of the Report of the Panel on United Nations Peace Operations," United Nations, 2000, 15, para. 6.

8. "Of 55 peace operations the U.N. has mounted since 1945, 41 began after 1989; fifteen were still underway in 2003." James Dobbins, *America's Role in Nationbuilding: From Germany to Iraq* (Santa Monica, Calif.: Rand Corporation, 2003), xiv–xv.

9. One sign of the unpreparedness of the times was that the World Bank was flabbergasted, first by being a bank, but principally because it spurned helping in trouble spots where a nation was in debt, experiencing significant insecurity, or where it was difficult to identify an actual government.

10. Sultan Aziz, former senior adviser to the SRSG in Afghanistan, at the Kennedy School's Institute of Politics Study Group on Nation-Building, Cambridge, Mass., April 15, 2004.

11. "There are various sets of actors, putative partners, who participate in rehabilitation in the field in different ways: l) the host government, or other authority, in the recipient state which bears the primary responsibility for its own recovery and with which external assistance programmes must be closely connected, as well as other native participants such as parties, factions, religious bodies, local and provincial authorities, private sector traders, entrepreneurs, et al; 2) the donor nations which contribute to the UN programmes, but also conduct separate bilateral aid programmes in diplomatic missions in the given country; 3) private, voluntary, nongovernmental organizations (NGOs) both international and indigenous, which run humanitarian and development activities there; 4) UN operational agencies (technically called Related UN Organs, Funds and Programmes), such as the United Nations Development Programme (UNDP), the United Nations High Commissioner for Refugees (UNHCR), the United Nations Children's Fund (UNICEF), and the World Food Programme (WFP); 5) more autonomous Specialized Agencies of the UN system, such as the Food and Agriculture Organization (FAO), the World Health Organization (WHO), and the International Labor Organization; and, 6) other entities, including the UN Secretary General and Secretariat, the Security Council and the Economic and Social Council, the World

Bank and International Monetary Fund, regional banks and other regional organizations, the International Committee of the Red Cross, and the International Organization on Migration." Jonathan Moore, *The U.N. and Complex Emergencies: Rehabilitation in Third World Transitions* (Geneva: UN Research Institute for Social Development, 1996), 26.

12. In both cases, the coordinating structure of the UN under the SRSG included UNHCR, its leading humanitarian assistance agency, and excluded UNDP, its leading development assistance organization.

13. In Mozambique in 1993, a UNICEF team from New York headquarters carried instructions to dissuade its chief representative in Maputo from responding to coordination requests from the assistant SRSG overseeing humanitarian and development programs there. In Rwanda in 1997, UNHCR headquarters in Geneva instructed its chief representative in Kigali not to cooperate with the UN resident coordinator there.

14. Chapter VI of the UN Charter covers Security Council action regarding the "Pacific Settlement of Disputes," and Chapter VII addresses "Action with Respect to Threats to the Peace, Breaches of the Peace, and Acts of Aggression." Chapter VII includes under Article 42 authorization for "such action by air, sea or land forces as may be necessary to maintain or restore international peace and security."

15. Described by former Secretary of State Madeleine Albright as "peace enforcement missions authorized by the United Nations, in which the Security Council deputizes an appropriate major power to organize a coalition and enforce the world's will." Interview published in *Foreign Policy,* September–October 2003, 20.

16. Former regional administrator for the United Nations in northern Kosovo based in Mitrovica, at Kennedy School's Institute of Politics Study Group on Nation-Building, Cambridge, Mass., March 11, 2004.

17. The Commission on Weak States and U.S. National Security and the Center for Global Development recently reported that the United States was one of the "least generous of all donors in its public spending on development assistance as a proportion of the economy." They also stated that the Bush administration and the U.S. Congress rely too heavily on military force and not enough on development aid to fight terrorism: The administration's request for increases in the current budget include $1 billion for HIV/AIDS and assistance to the poorest nations, and $21 billion for the Defense Department (not including supplemental requests for military operations in Iraq). The report also pointed out that failed states were excluded from receiving aid from the new development account set up by the United States for poor nations with a proven track record for fighting corruption and supporting democracy. Elizabeth Becker, *New York Times,* June 9, 2004.

18. See Gen. Zinni's "Twenty Lessons Learned for Humanitarian Assistance and Peace Operations," Center for Naval Analyses 1995 Annual Conference Proceedings, *Military Support to Complex Humanitarian Emergencies: From Practice to Policy* (Alexandria, Va.: Center for Naval Analysis, 1996), 17–21.

19. See "Independent Study of U.N. Coordination Mechanisms in Crisis or Post-Conflict Situations," report by Jonathan Moore for UNDP/ERD, October 3l, 2000: 9 (III, A1, 2).

20. James D. Wolfensohn, president of the World Bank, said in a recent interview: "There is no doubt that today the priority is being given, and maybe correctly so, to terror, to conflict. . . . I would argue that there is also a need for a parallel and equally urgent attention to the question of development as a way to prevent terror, and to prevent conflict—and I really passionately believe that." Elizabeth Becker, *New York Times,* April 22, 2004.

21. See Jonathan Moore, ed., *Hard Choices: Moral Dilemmas in Humanitarian Intervention* (Boulder, Colo.: Roman and Littlefield, 1998), 7.

22. Now Lt. Gen. Petraeus was commander of the 101st Airborne Division, based in Mosul. (In June 2004 he returned to Iraq to head up the training of Iraqi security forces.) His question was quoted in a book review *(In the Company of Soldiers: A Chronicle of Combat* by Rick Atkinson) written by Christopher Dickey, *New York Times,* April 4, 2004, 13.

ㄨ Contributors

J. BRIAN ATWOOD is dean of the Hubert Humphrey Institute of Public Affairs at the University of Minnesota. He served as administrator of the U.S. Agency for International Development under President Bill Clinton.

SUSAN J. ATWOOD is an instructor in global leadership at the University of Minnesota.

JOHN COOLEY was Middle East correspondent for the *Christian Science Monitor* from 1965 to 1978 and worked for ABC News in the Middle East from 1981 to 1999. His books include *Unholy Wars: Afghanistan, America, and International Terrorism* and *An Alliance against Babylon, the U.S., Israel, and Iraq.*

ROMEO DALLAIRE, Lieutenant-General (ret. Canada), was the Force Commander of the United Nations Assistance Mission for Rwanda (UNAMIR) in 1993–94. He is the author of *Shake Hands with the Devil: The Failure of Humanity in Rwanda.*

RAMU DAMODARAN is chief of the Civil Society Service in the Department of Public Information in the United Nations and editor-in-chief of *UN Chronicle.*

VALERIE EPPS is a professor of law and director of the International Law Concentration at Suffolk University Law School. She has also taught international law at Boston University School of Law and Brandeis University.

MICHAEL J. GLENNON is a professor of international law, Fletcher School of Law and Diplomacy, Tufts University, and author of *Limits of Law, Prerogatives of Power: Interventionism after Kosovo.*

STANLEY HEGINBOTHAM is former chief of Foreign Affairs and National Defense Division and senior specialist in American foreign policy, Congressional Research Service of the Library of Congress, and author of *Conversation with a Patriot: What to Do about Iraq.*

ROBERT JACKSON is a professor of political science at Boston University. He is an author or editor of ten books including *Classical and Modern Thought on International Relations, The Global Covenant, Sovereignty at the Millennium, Quasi-States,* and *Personal Rule in Black Africa.*

WINSTON LANGLEY is a professor of political science and international relations at University of Massachusetts Boston.

ALFRED W. MCCOY is a professor of history at the University of Wisconsin–Madison. He is the author of *The Politics of Heroin,* an examination of the CIA's alliances with drug lords, and *A Question of Torture: CIA Interrogation, from the Cold War to the War on Terror.*

GREG MILLS is director of The Brenthurst Foundation, a South African think tank devoted to the study of African economic growth. He is a former national director of the South African Institute of International Affairs and the author of numerous books, including *From Poverty to Prosperity: Globalisation, Good Governance, and African Recovery* and *The Security Intersection: The Paradox of Power in an Age of Terror.*

JONATHAN MOORE is an associate at the Shorenstein Center at Harvard University. He has served as U.S. coordinator for refugees and as ambassador to the United Nations and is now senior adviser to the U.N. Development Program.

CHRIS PATTEN is chancellor of the University of Oxford and formerly European Union commissioner for external relations.

GWYN PRINS is Alliance Research professor jointly at the London School of Economics and at Columbia University, author of *Understanding Unilateralism in American Foreign Relations* and *The Heart of War,* and adviser on security policy to several governments and to NATO.

JONATHAN SCHELL is Harold Willens Peace Fellow, Fellow of the Center for the Study of Globalization at Yale University, and the author of many books, including *The Unconquerable World: Power, Nonviolence, and the Will of the People* and *The Fate of the Earth.*

JOHN SHATTUCK is CEO of the John F. Kennedy Library Foundation and former ambassador to the Czech Republic. He is the author of *Freedom on Fire: Human Rights Wars and America's Response.*

CORNELIO SOMMARUGA is president of the International Association Initiatives of Change/Moral Rearmament and president of the Council of Foundation at Geneva International Center for Humanitarian Demining. From 1987 to 1999 he was president of the International Committee of the Red Cross.

SIR BRIAN URQUHART is former Under-Secretary-General of the UN with special responsibility for peacekeeping operations. He is the author of *A Life in Peace and War* and *Ralph Bunch, an American Odyssey.*

STEPHEN W. VAN EVERA is a professor of political science at Massachusetts Institute of Technology and the author of *Causes of War: Power and the Roots of Conflict,* and *Guide to Methods for Students of Political Science.* He is former managing editor of *International Security.*

ROBERT WEINER is the faculty chair of the international relations track of the MSPA Program at the John W. McCormack Graduate School of Policy Studies, University of Massachusetts Boston. He is also a center associate at the Davis Center for Russian and Eurasian Studies, Harvard University, and has published extensively on Romanian foreign policy at the UN.

(About the Eds,
        back cover)